MEMPHIS, TENN.

Created and Directed by Hans Höfer

OLD SOUTH

Edited and Produced by Martha Ellen Zenfell
Principal Photography by Lyle Lawson

Editorial Director: Brian Bell

Houghton Mifflin

ABOUT THIS BOOK

Höfer

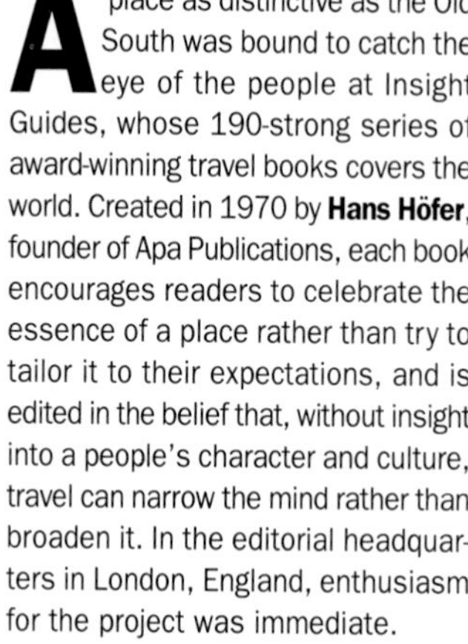

A place as distinctive as the Old South was bound to catch the eye of the people at Insight Guides, whose 190-strong series of award-winning travel books covers the world. Created in 1970 by **Hans Höfer**, founder of Apa Publications, each book encourages readers to celebrate the essence of a place rather than try to tailor it to their expectations, and is edited in the belief that, without insight into a people's character and culture, travel can narrow the mind rather than broaden it. In the editorial headquarters in London, England, enthusiasm for the project was immediate.

Insight's editor-in-chief of North American titles, **Martha Ellen Zenfell**, is a Southerner by birth. With a mother from Virginia and a daddy from Mississippi, she was in a perfect position to distinguish between the Deep (or "Cotton") South and the upper South, the territory that this book covers. In the past she has been the project editor of many Insight Guides; for this book she wrote about the auction of "Mama Lou's house" (her grandmother's) which appears on page 156.

"The South is a fine place to come from," she says, "and in many ways surprisingly similiar to England. Both place great emphasis on good manners, and the green rolling hills in the west of England often remind me of Virginia." It has not escaped her attention, either, that all the great Southern belles, from Scarlett to Blanche to Miss Daisy have been played by British actresses, although she does not know what this signifies.

Lawson

Lyle Lawson, who took most of the pictures and wrote a goodly amount of the text, is another London-based Southerner – a seventh generation Kentuckian – whose energy and enthusiasm for the project never wavered. The photographer of many Insight Guides, this was Lawson's first to a US destination. During the Civil War, one great-grandfather fought on the Confederate side, his brother chose the Union's cause, and afterwards the two never spoke. "Despite frequent trips home to see my family, I returned to explore the state of my birth as a stranger. I had forgotten just how pretty Kentucky is," she says. A highlight of her youth was meeting Elizabeth Taylor during the filming of *Raintree County*, some of which was shot in her great-aunt's old Kentucky home.

Stanfield

Mary Elizabeth Stanfield, who wrote our essay "Southerners," is another woman who knows of what she writes. A Southerner "all her born days" whose ancestors lived in North Carolina and Georgia before the American Revolution, Stanfield is an author, editor and assistant professor at Georgia State University. She also edited her great-great grandmother's social correspondence dating from the years 1861–1864.

Arnow

The other essays were written by a variety of local experts. Another Kentuckian, **Jan Arnow**, was responsible for the words and most of the pictures in our piece on traditional crafts. Her book, *By Southern Hands*, was the result of three years collecting oral histories of Southern craftspeople. "My goal in writing about Southern crafts has been to suggest that contemporary and traditional are not mutually exclusive," she says.

Garvey

Jane Garvey has lived in Georgia for more than 35 years, writing, among other things, a bi-weekly column about food and wine for *The Atlanta Journal and Constitution*. The author of our article on home cooking, she thinks "Southern food validates the notion that food is culture. It is what has kept us together as a people, even as race divided us. We ate the same dishes, drank the same drinks. Food cuts across all race and class lines."

The "Places" chapters are all by locally based writers who put their experience and expertise into practice. **Lynn Seldon** ("Virginia") was born in the Shenandoah Valley and now lives in Richmond. **Carol L. Timblin** grew up in the shadows of Grandfather Mountain in western North Carolina, and moved around for awhile before realizing there was "no place like home." She is the author of *Best Places to Stay in the South*, and a co-author of *Insiders' Guide to Charlotte*.

Timblin

Wick

Our man in Tennessee, **Don Wick**, was responsible, not only for the music essay "Bluegrass and Blue Suede Shoes," but also for two of the three chapters on Tennessee. He has spent most of his adult life traveling around getting to know the people and places of his home state, first based in Knoxville, then in Nashville."Carl Perkins told me the story about *Blue Suede Shoes* in a conversation we had several years ago. I'm sure it's no secret, but I have never seen it in print anywhere," he says. Now he has.

Chase

A graduate of the College of Charleston before moving on to become the associate editor of *Charleston* magazine, **Louise Forrester Chase** recently relocated to Atlanta. She contributed to *IG: Atlanta* as well as wrote our chapters on South Carolina's Holy City and the state's gorgeous coast.

"I'm a history nut and in South Carolina you can stir it with a stick. The Civil War started here, and the American Revoution nearly ended here," says **William Schemmel**, who wrote two of the chapters in this book, including one to South Carolina. In addition to his contribution to *IG: Old South*, Schemmel gave his services to *IG: Atlanta* as a writer and photographer.

Schemmel

"The Black South" is the work of **Joann Biondi**. In addition to having edited six large and small guides for Apa, Biondi is co-author of the book *The Historic Black South*. A Miami-based journalist, she describes the sites she covers as "the heart and soul of the South, areas that have been woefully ignored for far too long, and are crucial to understanding the South's unique personality."

Our history section was penned by **Tim Jacobson**, who holds a doctorate in history from Vanderbilt University in Nashville. He spends summers on a mountaintop in North Carolina, where he wrote *Heritage of The South* (Crescent/Colour Library Books Ltd), from which our chapters are taken.

Toops

Park rangers and other experts were responsible for our pieces on national parks and Civil War sites. Many thanks to **Connie Toops** ("Shenandoah" and "The Outer Banks"); **Rose Houk** ("Great Smoky Mountains"); and **Bill Sharp** and **Elaine Appleton** ("Civil War Sites") for their contributions, adapted from *IG: National Parks East*.

Thanks, too, to **Connie Bruther** of the Kentucky Office of Tourist Development; in Charleston to **Amy Blyth** of the Convention and Visitors Bureau, and to **Susan Davis** and **Manning Williams, Jr**. In the London office, the words were polished, proofread and indexed by **Caroline Radula Scott**, while **James Sumner** helped push the book to completion.

CONTENTS

Kentucky

Tennessee

North Carolina

South Carolina

Maps

TRAVEL TIPS

50
Rawlings

SOUTHERN PERSPECTIVES

The South is a place apart. Most Americans are happy to be identified as Americans, but Southerners are something else as well: Virginians, Kentuckians, Tennesseans, Carolinians. There is a popular bumper sticker in that part of the world, found on beat-up jalopies and even a few Porsches, that sums up what others find hard to understand: "American by birth, Southern by the Grace of God." To anyone who grew up in the South, the implications of this are self-evident.

Just where the South begins, and ends, is a matter of frequent discussion. Is Texas Southern? Is Kentucky? Everyone knows about the Deep South, and this book has chosen to concentrate on what could best be described as the upper South. Strict geographical boundaries are pretty pointless, however, in a region where a clock rarely tells the correct time.

Michael Andrew Grissom, in his book called – appropriately – *Southern by the Grace of God*, explains that when people talk of the east, or the west or the north, they tend to be talking about a direction. When people talk about the South, however, they're talking about a state of mind – a place very different from a mere state in the USA.

"Southerners are, of course, a mythological people," observed writer Jonathan Daniels in 1938, and little has changed in the years since then. Myths flourish in the South like kudzu flourishes in hot, moist heat. Anyone who has seen this leafy vine that can grow, in certain conditions, up to several inches in a single day, will understand the reference. This is, after all, the land of mint juleps, of country music, of Heartbreak Hotel, and, perhaps the most significantly, "the wo-wah."

The war in question needs no name but does, in fact, go by several: the Civil War, to academics; the War Between The States, to most Southerners; but the War of Northern Aggression to the true and faithful. "The old South was ploughed under. But the ashes are still warm," observed Henry Miller.

Warm, it's true, but not bitterly raging. Southerners may be united by a present defined by the past, but you can be sure the future will be of their own making.

Preceding pages: cruising the mighty Mississippi, Memphis; preening peacock, South Carolina; dressed for the Derby, Kentucky; Rebs to the ready, Southern reenactment; Pee-Wee League football team, Tennessee; old Shaker town, Pleasant Hill, Kentucky. Left, suited up for the Civil War.

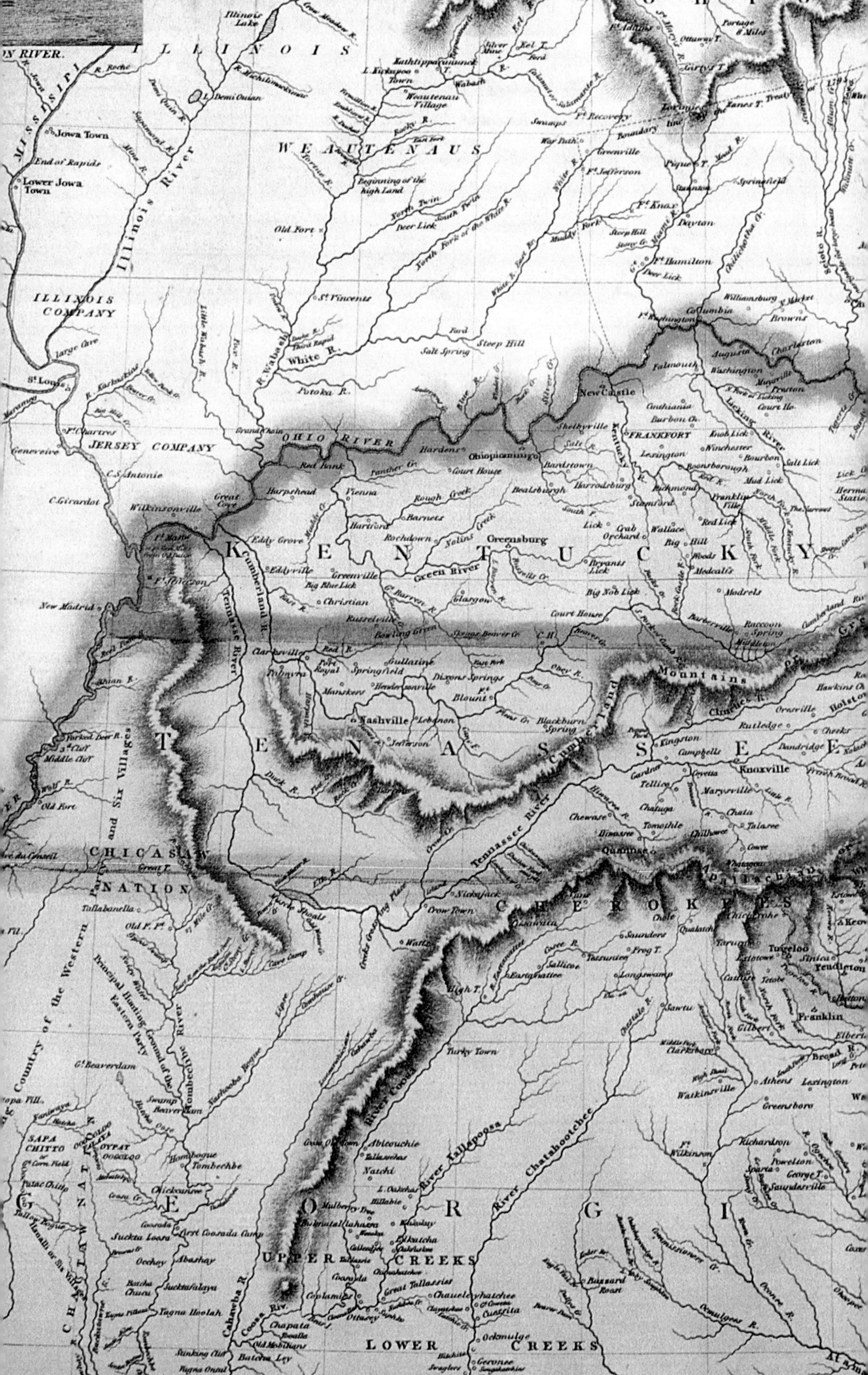

VIRGINIA
NORTH CAROLINA
S. CAROLINA
INDIANA
Pittsburg
Washington
Wheeling
Morgan Town
Clarksburg
Lewistown
Harrisburg
Carlisle
Lancaster
York
Reading
Trenton
PHILADELPHIA
Burlington
Bedford
Somerset
Hagars T.
Baltimore
Frederick Town
WASHINGTON
Alexandria
Annapolis
Chester
Wilmington
Elkton
Dover
Lewis
C. May
C. Henlopen
Salisbury
Fredericksburg
Culpeper
Falmouth
Dumfries
Colchester
Warrenton
Winchester
Woodstock
Staunton
Lexington
Charlottesville
Columbia
Milton
Louisa
Hanover
RICHMOND
Cumberland
Williamsburg
York
Hampton
Norfolk
Portsmouth
Suffolk
Petersburg
Lynchburg
Liberty
New London
Buckingham
Charlotte
Halifax
Mecklenburg
Greenville
Roanoke R.
Dan River
Murfreesboro
Northampton
Hartford
Edenton
Windsor
Halifax
Hilsborough
Salem
Rockford
Wilkes
Salisbury
Morganton
Lincolnton
Statesville
Randolph
Chapel Hill
RALEIGH
Pittsburg
Chatham
Smithfield
Tarburg
Greenville
Washington
Albemarle Sound
Plymouth
PAMLICO SOUND
Cape Hatteras
Ocracoke I.
Portsmouth
NEWBERN
Trenton
Beaufort
C. Lookout
Cape Lookout Shoal
Fayetteville
Rockingham
Lumberton
Wilmington
Brunswick
Cape Fear
Exeter
Kingston
Georgetown
Santee R.
Camden
Charleston
CHARLESTON
Charleston Bar
Dorchester
Jacksonborough
Beaufort
Purisburg
Savannah
Savannah R.
AUGUSTA
Edgefield
COLUMBIA
Statesburg
Winnsborough
Chester
York
Spartanburg
Lancaster
Catawba Town
Newbury
Belfast
Elberton
Allegany Mountains
Blue Ridge
North Mountains
Chesapeake Bay
Delaware Bay
Potomack R.
ATLANTIC

The manner
10
40
PÆSCES

COLONIAL BEGINNINGS

The permanent settlement of what would later become British North America began on the swampy shores of the Chesapeake Bay region in 1607, just four years after the death of England's first Queen Elizabeth and nine before the death of William Shakespeare. After having known of this continent's existence for more than 100 years, northern Europeans, and in particular Englishmen, undertook what became one of the greatest cultural transplants in recorded history. What would become the American South was one of its first and most long-lasting results.

Unlike some of its neighbors to the north, such as Massachusetts and Pennsylvania, the land halfway down the eastern seaboard that would become Virginia was not settled according to some grandiose scheme. Its history witnesses no effort to rule men by the power of a single grand, inspiring, or fearful idea. On the contrary, Virginia and the civilization that developed there and was passed on to the larger South can be understood only if Virginia is seen as a thoroughly earthly effort to transplant the institutions and the general style of living of old England to the soil of a new wilderness world.

Old World virtues: If the Pilgrims and the Puritans clung to the rocky shores of Massachusetts Bay in an heroic effort to flee from the Old World's vices, the Virginia colonists hoped to celebrate and fulfill here the Old World's virtues – an Old World with which the majority of them had no serious religious, ideological, or philosophical complaints. Except in one important respect, these were satisfied men.

What drew them across a wild ocean to the edge of a wilder continent was ambition of a largely economic sort, which could find no adequate outlet in the Old World. For decades, the Spanish had been extracting fortunes in gold and silver from their southern American preserves – perhaps Englishmen could do the same.

In March 1584, Sir Walter Raleigh obtained a charter from Queen Elizabeth to establish an English settlement in Virginia and explore the region. Members of the first team of settlers returned to England disgruntled, but Raleigh remained determined to establish an outpost, and in 1587 he sent 150 settlers to the New World once again. Although their original destination was Chesapeake Bay, these settlers landed first at Roanoke Island, on a narrow strip of land off the coast of what is now North Carolina, and remained there. As the settlers struggled to carve out a niche of civilization, Spain cast its acquisitive eyes toward England, and the British government diverted most of its efforts toward defeating the Armada.

Lost colony: When matters in Europe settled down, Raleigh dispatched another expedition carrying supplies and new settlers to the Roanoke colony. What these settlers found when they arrived in 1590 was not a thriving community. All the original settlers had vanished and the only clue to their demise was the word "Croatan," the name of a tribe of Indians carved in the bark of a tree.

Despite the mysterious and frightening end of the 1587 lost colony, Englishmen continued to devise new methods of financing settlements in the New World. Joint-stock companies, such as the London Company and the Plymouth Company, were formed with an eye toward maximum profits and minimum risks.

To that workaday end, the London Company secured from King James I a royal charter to found a colony in the southern part of "Virginia," as the entire region claimed by England was called. Not quite sure of what they would find, the company bosses sold shares and set about recruiting settlers. They paid each settler's passage and the latter agreed to work for the company for seven years before striking out for himself.

In 1606, 120 men set sail toward Virginia in three ships under the command of Captain Christopher Newport. Their instructions were to establish a fortified post from which they were to trade with the natives and search for a passage to the Pacific Ocean. The ships reached Chesapeake Bay in April 1607, after a four-month voyage that claimed the lives

Preceding pages: map of the Southern states of America, 1817. Left, drawing showing one of the first British settlements in Virginia.

of 16 members of the party. The group sailed 30 miles (48 km) up the James River and selected as their site a densely wooded area bordering a mosquito-ridden swamp. The settlers then split into three groups, each with a specific task: constructing a fort, planting crops, and exploring the region further.

By August, mosquitoes brought an epidemic of malaria, and eight months after their landing, only 38 of the original settlers were still alive. Their salvation was due in part to the efforts of Captain John Smith, who negotiated with the Native Americans and persuaded them to trade with the settlers for maize.

The Native American tribes in the region were loosely bound in a confederacy headed by a chief called Powhatan. A shrewd leader who mistrusted the English objectives, Powhatan resisted efforts by the English to force the native tribes into a tributary status. Peace was achieved between the English and the Native Americans in later years, but it was not just due to the Crown's grand scheme to form a partnership. Instead, it was furthered by a marriage between John Rolphe, an English settler, and Pocahontas, Powhatan's brave and stylish daughter.

As accounts of the hardships encountered by the settlers reached England, many financiers of the enterprise realized that much of the difficulty lay in the form of government being imposed in the wilderness region. The original charter had put control of the colony in the hands of the "Council in Virginia," a group of seven men who were accountable to the English government and to the London Company. In 1609 the charter was revised to provide for a governor answerable only to the company.

That year also brought the first women and children to Virginia. Their arrival, together with that of the first black slaves in 1619, marked its transition from trading post to colony. As settlers got control of their own parcels of land, they turned to a new crop that was to be their salvation: a broad-leaved plant, grown by the Indians and refined with West Indian stock, that the world came to know and both love and revile as tobacco. Thanks to tobacco, Virginia attracted labor and capital and became a viable commercial colony. The labor required for the cultivation of tobacco came at first from indentured servants – men and women willing to sell themselves into personal service in return for the price of a passage to Virginia. The problem was that such laborers were white Englishmen who, after a fixed period of time, would have to be paid and would change overnight from cheap bound labor to expensive free labor.

The importation of black slaves ultimately resolved this difficulty. Yet the purchase price of a good African laborer remained substantially higher than the lease price of a good English servant. The relative price of slaves fell only by the end of the 17th century and because the European slave traders and their African suppliers were growing more efficient at their unsavory business. For now, rising life expectancy in the American colonies made it likely that a planter would in fact get a full lifetime's labor out of a slave who had cost him approximately twice as much up front as an indentured servant.

First legislature: In 1618, the London Company concluded that the most practical way to govern Virginia was to let the colonists govern themselves. Under the leadership of Governor Edwin Sandys, the company allowed the planters to elect representatives to an assembly, which, together with the governor's council, was empowered to legislate for the colony. The first such assembly, which became known as the House of Burgesses, met in Jamestown in August 1619. Free white males over the age of 17 elected two representatives from each of Virginia's 11 towns to the assembly, and it is remembered today as the first colonial legislature to be set up in the New World.

A high degree of social stratification characterized this early Southern world. On the bottom rung labored the black slaves, constituting half the population of Virginia on the eve of the Revolution – the War of American Independence – at about 170,000 people. Although at the bottom, their influence penetrated all levels, from African forms of speech infiltrating the King's English through to harsh legal codes. At the top, in baronial splendor and prestige, resided the great planters, who were probably as close as America ever came to having a European aristocracy.

Yet they were different in one respect: in Virginia and, later, the rest of the South, the top echelon was relatively open-ended. New people were always moving up, either through the acquisition of broad acres and troops of slaves or through marriage. In either case, the single prerequisite was land.

The yeoman farmer formed the backbone of society in the early years of the colony. These men possessed small tracts of land, which they worked themselves, for themselves, with the aid of family members and, occasionally, indentured servants or one or two slaves.

The patterns of settlement and ways of living in the South of the 1600s were as varied as they were elsewhere in North America, and it is wise to remember that "the South" was at no point in its history the great monolith of popular myth. A look at the two Carolinas reveals facts vital to the rest of the story in that there is a common thread running through life in the South which makes it seem more of an entity. However, the South is a very large place indeed and "Southerness" is sometimes in the eye of the beholder. In what would become the state of South Carolina, but which was then usually referred to just as "Carolina," it is possible to see some familiar ideals and aspirations that later generations of Southerners inherited, for better or for worse.

Two themes drown out all others. The first is racism, or more precisely racial fear. For it was in the rice lands of the South Carolina Low Country that the enslaved blacks vastly outnumbered the whites. The second theme is ruralism, which, like racism, shaped the

Left, watercolor of the first inhabitants of Roanoke Island. Right, Pocahontas, daughter of chief Powhatan, married John Rolphe, a white settler. She later went to Europe and was feted by royalty.

character of colonial South Carolina much as it did that of Virginia. But in South Carolina a different context rendered the otherwise quite ordinary into something peculiar, eccentric, curious and even bizarre. For while most of the region was intensely rural, South Carolina spawned, on the little peninsula between the Ashley and Cooper rivers, what was if not the largest then surely the most glittering of cities anywhere in the Americas. Charleston ruled, literally and figuratively, the vast rural back country which provided so much of its wealth.

Settlement in the Carolinas had got its start in 1653 when settlers from Virginia pushed southward into the area around Albemarle Sound. Eager to escape the taxes and all the trappings of civilization taking hold in Virginia, these settlers found that life in the Carolinas was no better when, 10 years later, Charles II granted large tracts of land in the region to eight men who had supported the restoration of the English monarchy.

The eight new proprietors were determined to increase the population of their colony and not to depend alone on refugees from Virginia. They promised prospective settlers from England freedom from customs duties on wine, silk, capers, wax, and other goods shipped from the colony back to England for seven years. Then in 1669, the proprietors each agreed to contribute £500 to a proposed settlement at Port Royal. Three ships had set off from England in August 1660, landing first in Virginia to purchase supplies and then in Barbados to recruit more colonists. That fall, the ships sailed for the Carolinas, but one was wrecked in a gale in the Bahamas. The other two took refuge from the storm in Bermuda and after repairs took to the seas again in February 1670. Led by William Sayle, a Puritan settler in the Bahamas and former governor of Bermuda, the group abandoned their plans to land at Port Royal and selected instead a site on the Ashley River. They named their new home Charles Town in honor of the king.

Glittering city: Shortly after landing, the settlers began constructing another town, which they also called Charles Towne, having renamed their original town Kiawah. By the beginning of the 1680s, the new city was home to around 1,200 people.

Despite the intention of the proprietors to speed growth in both Upper and Lower Carolina, they generally directed most of their attention to the southern region of the colony, and settlers in the north became dissatisfied. Governors were deposed, and direct appeals were made to the Crown. In 1719, the Carolinas' petition to be made a royal colony was granted, and a few years later Parliament divided the region and made North Carolina a separate royal colony.

The differences between the two colonies ran deep. North Carolina had been settled as early as 1653, 10 years before Charles II granted land to the proprietors. Many of the first settlers had completed terms as indentured servants and were eager to grab bits of land for themselves. In addition, ever-increasing numbers of new settlers were attracted by laws that forbade suits over debts incurred earlier, and also by laws that exempted them from taxes for one year.

Tobacco road: Tobacco became the primary crop of North Carolinians, but because of the area's treacherous shoreline, the settlers found it difficult to move their produce to the marketplace. Generally, they were forced to haul their crops overland to Virginia where government agents imposed importation taxes. As a result, for a long time North Carolina remained a region of small farms, where subsistence rather than trade was the main rule.

South Carolina, on the other hand, became a region of great plantations growing easily marketed crops such as rice and indigo. By the 1730s, the commercial possibilities of the rice culture were being realized on a large scale along the length of the tidal and inland swamplands of the Low Country. Indigo, a plant grown for its rich blue dye, thrived on the drier soils unsuitable for rice, ideally complementing it. Neither did indigo require attention in the winter, leaving the slave labor force available for other tasks.

Within a few years of the establishment of the first rice plantations in South Carolina at the end of the 17th century, the black population was greater than the white. Laborers died quickly in the malarial conditions of the swamplands, but planters grew rich and replaced their dead and sick workers with an ever-increasing number of black slaves. Owners of the sprawling plantations often lived in Charleston and left the management of their land and workforce in the hands of overseers. Cruel punishments were inflicted on many South Carolina slaves for minor infractions, and overseers were generally more concerned over the commissions they received for harvests than over the health and welfare of the workforce.

Between 1740 and the Revolution – the golden age of colonial South Carolina – prices rose and planters increased production. Rice exports tripled, those of indigo

Left, Charleston, South Carolina, grew to become one of the most glittering cities in the Americas. Above, tobacco, the colony's first successful crop, was dependent on the slave trade.

quadrupled, and the annual value of these crops soared five times over. Everywhere planters prospered, many to a degree that would never be experienced again in the South. Both of South Carolina's great crops were much better suited to large-scale farming units than tobacco, which meant that, even though South Carolina was a much younger colony than Virginia, its plantation system, totally dependent on slave labor, established roots fast and deep.

The white planters bestowed themselves with all the trappings of aristocracy they could think of, and they gave to their new native land a patina it has hung on to ever since. Not every white lived like a grandee, but many of the wealthy, haughty Low Country planters not only ruled South Carolina but supplied its culture with a mold and a standard of aspiration. History proved their strength when, even after there had grown up in the South in the antebellum era a substantial and genuine middle class – independent people, neither rich nor poor, but ever jealous of their freedoms – observers still remarked about the pervasive influence of the planter class. While the planters never ruled the larger South in years to come as indisputably as they did colonial South Carolina, their presence and way of life undeniably set the tone and defined the goals for much of Southern culture until the Civil War laid that remote, peculiar civilization to waste.

Go west: Interest in western lands began as early as 1650 when Captain Abraham Wood led an expedition through the Blue Ridge Mountains to the falls of the Roanoke River. Over the next 50 years, many Virginians made fortunes in the fur trade in the west, reaching as far as the Tennessee Valley. In 1716, Virginia's governor Alexander Spotswood led a group of explorers into the Valley of Virginia, returned to Williamsburg, and petitioned the Crown for grants of land in the western territory.

Joining the Tidewater émigrés were settlers from Pennsylvania, whose colonial government encouraged individuals who had completed terms as indentured servants to move south. They moved to areas around Martinsburg and Shepherdstown in what is now West Virginia and to the region around Winchester, Virginia, in 1726. Within just eight years, the Virginian colonial government had organized Orange County to impose a governmental system on the new western settlements, and four years after that the districts of Frederick and Augusta were established. Further west, the area that contains the present-day states of West Virginia, Kentucky, Ohio, Indiana, Illinois, Michigan and Wisconsin was named West Augusta.

North Carolina's western region filled up with Scots-Irish and Germans from Virginia, and six counties were formed between 1743 and 1762. South Carolina's western lands were parcelled out to prospective settlers who also received livestock and supplies from the colonial government. The western settlers were of a different temperament than the Tidewater settlers, and their surroundings imposed a contrasting lifestyle. Because of the ongoing difficulty of moving their produce to markets, the western settlers generally operated small farms not dependent on slave labor.

My old Kentucky home: Daniel Boone ("the father of Kentucky") began his famous western explorations and hunting expeditions in 1769. Returning to North Carolina in 1771, he enticed Richard Henderson to finance an expedition and settlement in Kentucky. The Transylvania Land Company, including Henderson, John Sevier, James Robertson, and Isaac Shelby, persuaded the Cherokee Indians to sell all of Kentucky and part of

Tennessee for £10,000 worth of goods. Henderson's far-reaching goal was to make Kentucky the 14th British colony. In order to encourage settlement, he employed Boone and a party of tree-cutters to blaze a trail (which became known as Boone's Trace) from Cumberland Gap to recently founded Boonesborough. Five years later, the Kentucky settlements were incorporated into Kentucky County, Virginia.

Unlike other frontier explorers and settlers, Daniel Boone never earned great financial rewards. His business acumen did not match his hunting and tracking skills, so the land Boone surveyed and should have owned, was lost by his failure to file the correct legal papers. Late 19th-century depictions of Boone as an ignorant woodsman are both unjust and unfair. Despite only a basic education, Boone's courage, tracking skills, and proficiency with Indian languages were unmatched during his lifetime. Without his steps into the unknown, the westward expansion of what was to become the United States would have been setback by many years.

Independence: In 1763, the year generally regarded as the end of the Colonial period and the beginning of the Revolutionary, the South was inhabited by 700,000 people, not counting the Native Americans. Basically of English descent, the white population carried on their cultural traditions in the face of the more recent arrivals of Germans, Roman Catholic Irish, Scots-Irish, and French Huguenots. The population included about 300,000 black slaves – approximately two-fifths of the total.

A large number of slaves were American-born, but the slave trade with Africa continued. Virginia had more slaves than any other colony, about 100,000 in 1763, whereas about 50,000 slaves lived in North Carolina and 70,000 lived in South Carolina. These slaves manned the plantations, raising tobacco, rice and indigo for export.

As an economic institution and as a system of racial control, slavery defined relations between black and white. Racial prejudice came to these shores with the Europeans, and in the 18th century abstract questions about the morality of slavery were, in the face of that institution's indisputable economic utility, kept muffled and largely private. On the eve of the Revolution, slavery was practiced in the Northern colonies as well. However, nowhere north of the Potomac River did blacks constitute anything approaching 40 percent of the population, as they did in Virginia and in most other Southern colonies, to say nothing of the 66 percent living in South Carolina.

The war by which America became one nation was fought between 1775 and 1781 throughout the English colonies, from New England to Georgia. Southerners and Northerners alike shed blood in the attempt to throw off the British yoke. The leader of their armies, George Washington, was a Virginian and a slaveholder.

Left, in the 1770s, Daniel Boone blazed a trail to Kentucky, opening up the western frontier. Right, Thomas Jefferson, Virginian, planter, architect and third US president.

The war began on Northern soil at Lexington and Concord in Massachusetts. It ended on Southern soil, on the Yorktown Peninsula in Virginia, only a few miles from Jamestown and Williamsburg.

In the wake of independence, all the states drew up constitutions, reducing the powers of the Crown-appointed governors, but none granted universal male suffrage. The Church of England was disestablished everywhere, but efforts to create public schools failed. Most Southern states began to abolish the slave trade, but not slavery itself. Many planters felt that the existing order depended on the continuation of a massive black labor force and thus, necessarily, of slavery, and while there was genuine moral aversion to it within the South, it was usually coupled with the conviction that emancipation was unthinkable without "colonization" of the blacks back to Africa.

As the states emerged from war with a great world power, there was much to bind them together despite themselves. They had a common enemy and felt a healthy fear of further British aggression long into the postwar period. The war had enlisted men in a common army, but could the more populous North, progressively turning toward commerce and manufacturing, coexist contentedly with a staunchly agricultural South?

Virginia dynasty: Virginian George Washington was 57 when he was inaugurated the first president of the United States under the new Constitution in 1789, and also one of the richest men in America. Washington was seceded in office by John Adams, but it was the presidency of Thomas Jefferson (1801–1809) that ushered in the palmy days of the "Virginia dynasty."

For the next 25 years Virginian planters occupied the White House and presided over a nation generally enjoying a flush of nationalism and optimism about its prospects. For its part, the South entered into the most nationalistic phase of its history.

Jefferson and his largely Southern-led Republican Party (not to be confused with today's party of the same name) in some ways halted the trend toward centralization of governmental power, but they did not reverse it.

The President showed two sides to his character. Jefferson "the good Republican" simplified the operations of government, repealing the federal excise tax and allowing the Alien Act and the Sedition Act to expire. He halted the expansion of the navy and reduced the standing army; he sped up repayment of the public debt; and he attacked Federalist appointments to the judiciary. Indeed, he would have appointed a strict constructionist, Virginian Spencer Roane, to the Supreme Court, if the departing John Adams had not first named a nationalist, Virginian John Marshall.

Jefferson "the nationalist" bought the vast Louisiana Territory from Napoleon in 1803, although there was nothing in the Constitution that gave the president the right to acquire new lands. He refused to abolish one chief agency of a centralizing program, the Bank of the United States. In 1804, he approved a plan calling for a protective tariff, and he called for an amendment permitting the federal government to subsidize internal improvements, as public works – chiefly harbors, canals, and roads – were then called. In 1805, he asked Congress for money to buy the territory of Florida from Spain.

Southern sectionalism: The difference between North and South was thus one of emphasis, for Jefferson believed the republic was safe in the hands of the Republicans. John Randolph of Roanoke, an aristocratic slaveholder, long-time Jefferson supporter, and leader of the Republicans in the House of Representatives, did not agree and opposed the President on every apparent compromise of principle. Sometimes called the "Father of Southern Sectionalism," Randolph invoked states' rights and agrarian theory throughout both of Jefferson's administrations in order to defend the old republican order.

All men were not created equal in either capacity or ability, he said, and government attempts to make them so led to certain tyranny. "I love liberty; I hate equality," he put it plainly, and on his death, he freed his 400 slaves. John Taylor of Caroline, another Virginian, also broke with Jefferson over policy and emerged as the most consistent philosopher of agrarianism in the country.

Left, slave auction, painted by Erye Crowe. Above, *The Plantation*, artist unknown.

Such opponents within the Republican house (by the end of Jefferson's presidency they called themselved the "Old Republicans") neither split the party nor utterly derailed it. What brought this house if not quite down, then certainly to the point of serious division, was the onset of hard times and the dawning realization that the economic interests and patterns of future development of the North and the South were not only far from identical but were perhaps not even very complementary.

As the price of staple crops tumbled 75 percent and the industrial revolution took hold in the North, old sectional realities, based since colonial times on subtle but profound cultural differences, re-emerged now heightened by economic grievances. When this was combined, from the 1830s onwards, with the emergence of the slavery issue as the most powerful agent of sectionalism, one era in Southern history gave way to another.

The nationalist South, which had won independence in concert with the North, written the Constitution, and forged the federal republic, gave way to the sectional South, which, due to the burden of slavery and its own understandings of the American polity and the good life, finally forsook that republic for a nation of its own imaginings.

DIXIE BLOSSOMS
MARCH-TWO-STEP
BY
PERCY WENRICH
JEROME H. REMICK & CO
DETROIT
5
NEW YORK

ANTEBELLUM ERA

There is something about the history of the South between the Revolution and the Civil War that makes it, in the popular imagination, loom larger and more vividly than any other moment. That period is strewn with durable images of masters and slaves and Southern belles, of plantation houses with white pillars and broad fields of cotton. This is the South immortalized in Margaret Mitchell's *Gone With the Wind* and trivialized in countless subsequent volumes of historical romance. It is a South that seems both content and sure of itself as being a place apart from, and superior to, the rest of America, even as it headed for disaster. It is a picture that only truly characterizes the South of the late antebellum period and then only unevenly, and it is a South that was the product of a gradual evolution.

A place apart: To understand that point of arrival, it helps first to consider the texture of Southern life before the divisiveness of sectionalism took hold and then to observe the political flashpoints that marked the South's increasing self-awareness as a place apart, with a destiny all its own. On the eve of the antebellum era, the South had ample reason to be satisfied with national affairs. The Republican Party – then the only political party worthy of the name, and not to be confused with the antislavery party of Abraham Lincoln, which was not founded until the 1850s – was strongly influenced by Southerners.

James Monroe, a Southerner and the last of the "Virginia dynasty," was still president; William Crawford of Georgia, John C. Calhoun of South Carolina, and William Wirt of Virginia constituted half of Monroe's cabinet. Henry Clay of Kentucky was speaker of the House of Representatives.

The flush of nationalism from the Revolution itself and from the second war with Britain in 1812 still warmed the land. Five signatories of the Declaration of Independence were still alive. Thomas Jefferson, its author, was still master of his magnificent mountaintop house, Monticello, in Virginia,

Left, many consider the pre-Civil War years of the 19th century the Golden Age of the South.

and was also still a reminder of the boldness of the American national experiment and of America's genius for a new kind of politics.

But if the South was politically still at peace with the rest of America, there were palpable differences in its cultural and economic life from which political particularism, aggravated by the debate over slavery and western expansion, would grow. At the time the Constitution was written, and for some years into the early history of the young republic, it appeared that the population of the Southern states would at least equal, and perhaps even exceed, that of the North.

Population change: But the census of 1820 revealed a disturbing fact: the population of the ten states south of Pennsylvania and the Ohio River – Maryland, Virginia, North and South Carolina, and Georgia, plus the younger western states of Kentucky, Tennessee, Alabama, Mississippi, and Louisiana – had declined as a proportion of the national whole to about 4.3 million, which was half a million short of half the national population.

As important, the character of these people was different from the population of the North. A third of them were black, and they were mostly slaves; in the North the figure for blacks was just 2 percent. There were about 116,000 free blacks in the South and about the same number in the North, but there were 1½ million slaves in the South and practically none in the North. There were some 2.6 million white Southerners, but approximately twice that many white people in the North.

Within the South, the white population was remarkably homogeneous, with only 12,000 unnaturalized foreigners, compared with more than 40,000 in the North. The colonial Southern melting pot of English, Irish, Scots and Germans had done its job pretty well. Obviously there was still some variation, but much less than in the North, whose cities would soon swell with new and ever greater waves of European immigration, little of which reached the South.

Black or white, slave or freeman, the South's was a population clearly bound to agriculture and with few signs of movement into other areas of economic activity. All

America was a farming country, with an average of 77 percent of its citizens engaged in agriculture, but in the South that figure was 90 percent. And the quality of Southern agriculture differed from Northern, for in addition to feeding itself on its own corn, wheat, vegetables, cattle and chickens, the South raised vast quantities of the great staple crops for sale on world markets. These crops – tobacco, rice, sugar, hemp, and particularly cotton – constituted the wealth of the region and had no equivalent outside it.

King cotton: In the 18th century, the South's great crops had been those of seaboard Virginia and South Carolina: tobacco and rice. In the 19th century, it was short-staple cotton, which could be grown anywhere, either by gangs of slaves or by white yeomen, on rough land as well as fertile. The Deep South states of Louisiana and Mississippi especially thrived on the new crop's popularity.

The introduction of Eli Whitney's cotton gin in 1793 made possible the rapid combing of the plant and vastly increased the South's cotton output and its profitability. By 1820, it had already surpassed all other Southern produce, and three-quarters of the crop of 353,000 bales went for export. Over the next 30 years, the price declined steadily, but yields increased, almost doubling in every decade up to the Civil War.

For many people, cotton represented their big chance, not just of making a living but of achieving real success, and the legendary path from dog-trot cabin to white-columned splendor was genuinely trodden by countless Southerners who started with little, but who, by the 1850s, took their proud place as grandees of "The Cotton Kingdom."

Before the railroad era, which did not reach much of the South until the 1840s and 1850s, the need to transport bulky 500-lbs (230-kg) bales of cotton to market put a premium on water transportation and briefly sustained the fleets of steamboats that had plied the Mississippi River from 1811.

Slavery, which had attached itself to the South in colonial times, proved well adapted to the cotton trade and helped fuel its expansion. However, much of the enlightened opinion of the age, both in the North and the South, had doubts about the morality of the institution. In the 1770s, Thomas Jefferson, a slaveholder until the day he died, proposed repatriating – "colonizing" as it came to be known – the blacks back to Africa. Slavery was obviously a Southern problem and one that involved both the moral problem of holding other humans in perpetual bondage and the practical problem of what to do with an alien race should it be emancipated. The American Colonization Society was founded in 1816 and was headed by Southerners James Madison, James Monroe, and John Marshall from Virginia and supported by Henry Clay from Kentucky.

In 1826, of the 143 emancipation societies in existence in the country, 103 had been founded in the South, many of them by Quaker Benjamin Lundy, who spread the abolition message through the mountainous regions of Tennessee and North Carolina. In addition, there were several anti-slavery newspapers in the South, including the *Emancipator* in Tennessee and the *Abolition Intelligencer* in Kentucky.

It was not a modern, color-blind morality that moved these men, but an 18th-century rationalist one that was also combined with a profound racism. If the slaves should be freed, then the freedmen must also be removed from the area. Means of controlling masses of blacks, other than slavery, were not then generally considered, and the idea of equality was utterly unthinkable.

Some blacks were in fact "colonized" back

to Africa, and the west African nation of Liberia owes its existence to the movement; its capital city, Monrovia, was named for President James Monroe. But the numbers were simply too daunting – and the economic stakes simply too high – for "colonization" ever to be tried widely.

Besides, there was the pull of cotton, which was so compatible with slavery, and which not only profited the Southern planters but also represented the bulk of United States exports and fueled the entire national economy. For a country trying to establish itself, Southern cotton, whether or not it was grown by slaves, constituted a tremendous economic resource that no one, not even Northerners, were prepared to put at risk.

It was not agricultural patterns alone that distinguished this early antebellum South from other places in America. In 1820, there were in the slave states just seven cities with more than 8,000 people, and Baltimore, which was the biggest at 62,000, sat on the very edge of the region. All of the others – New Orleans at 27,000, Charleston at 24,000, Washington, DC at 13,000, Richmond at 12,000, Norfolk and Alexandria at 8,000 apiece – were cities located on water engaged primarily in trade (or in the case of Washington, a government center) rather than manufacturing.

Southern towns developed almost without exception along coasts or fall lines that separated the interior uplands from the coastal plains. At this time there was no town of more than 2,500 inhabitants that was not on navigable water. Many of these places worked almost as city-states after the manner of colonial Charleston, though not nearly so opulent, with a river as their bond with the agricultural hinterland and the ocean as their corridor to the outside world, where the fruits of that hinterland found their market.

But it was always decentralized, for Southern rivers diverged outward along an extensive coastline, which mitigated against the development of any single great metropolitan entrepôt. The smaller towns scattered across the region were agricultural service centers, some of them becoming county seats and others becoming adorned in time with numerous churches, schools, and colleges. In this, they did not differ all that much from their Northern counterparts as centers of cultural, religious, and political life in an agricultural region, the rural gathering places for a farming people.

Left, Eli Whitney and his cotton gin. The machine speeded up the combing of cotton and vastly increased profits. Above, 90 percent of the South's population was engaged in agriculture.

The South's increasing reliance on staple-crop agriculture had consequences both inside and outside the region that no one could fully foresee. Indeed then, with cotton constituting the lion's share of American exports, that reliance did not seem excessive. But Southerners relied heavily on others to transport their precious staples to faraway markets, as they themselves sailed few ships and built almost none.

Thus, like it or not, they found themselves locked into a sort of triangular trade, in which cotton from the South went to England, manufactured goods from England and Europe came to New York City, and these were then sold to the South. It was a far-flung economic system, which in general relied on the factories of the Old World, the commercial and transportation services of the American Northeast, and the staple agricultural products of the American South.

As a key player in such an international system, Southerners came early and strongly to believe in free trade as a cornerstone for prosperity. Potential for abuse existed, but the pattern usually fitted the region's needs, and Southerners generally felt well served by it. With their exports exceeding $30 million a year, some Southerners enjoyed great credit far and wide, displaying it splendidly.

Insofar as Southerners manufactured things for themselves, they made relatively simple items necessary to service the needs of their agricultural society. They worked with wood, iron, and hides, and they ground grain into meal, grits and flour. In most of the South, the white artisan class, which also had to compete with trained plantation and urban slaves, were too few in number and too dependent on agriculture to become as important as they would be in the North. Such trades were all very small-time, with usually only two or three men to a shop, and they served largely local markets.

By contrast, tobacco and iron were sometimes worked in establishments of considerable size. Virginia, which was the nation's largest coal producer, turned out pig iron, castings, nails, firearms, and farm implements. In both Virginia and Kentucky, tobacco factories transformed half the tobacco crop into plugs and twists for chewing, snuff, pipe tobacco and cigars.

The distribution of even such modest manufacturing resulted in the greatest concentration of factories in Virginia, Maryland, and Kentucky, which contained the larger establishments and two-thirds of all those Southerners who did not make their living from the land. Still, there were probably more field hands in some single counties of the South Carolina Low Country in 1820 than there were factory workers in the whole South.

Many voices: It would be a mistake to regard the South, at this point still 40 years before the Civil War, as a place powerfully united by either character or conviction. Two types of internal tension in particular strained the unity of Southern life, creating political ramifications as the antebellum years wore on. The conflict between Low Country and Up Country reached back to colonial times, when the coastal regions of South Carolina and Virginia had boasted more advanced social institutions, more ample material possessions (including more slaves), and larger towns than the remoter regions.

In Tennessee, it was the fertile central and western regions that corresponded to "Low Country," while the mountainous eastern sections played the role of "the backwoods." Obviously much could depend on which of these groups controlled the state governments, and the unity of the South would depend in part on whether the same type of groups were in power in each of the states.

The second source of internal division was between the upper South and the cotton, or Deep, South. Agriculture in Virginia and Kentucky was more diversified, and much of those states' produce was sold domestically; they boasted more commerce and manufacturing and enjoyed greater proximity to the outside world. In most of the Deep South, cotton was the predominant money crop, with rice and sugar at the edges, and it sold abroad on the world market. The upper South had more free blacks; the Deep South had the heaviest concentration of slaves. Of all the Southern states, South Carolina probably shared the least with anybody else. Virginia still enjoyed the most revered heritage but seemed somehow to be losing its economic and political grip. And the transmontane states such as Tennessee were assuming new vigor and importance every year.

Civil unrest: With "colonization" providing an outlet for moral frustrations about slavery, and with cotton constituting a key to national prosperity, it would seem that the matter of slavery might not necessarily have led, as it did, to the dissolution of the Union and civil war. Indeed, slavery was basically left as something to be regulated by the several states as they themselves saw fit. So it might have remained, at least for a much longer time, had the new American nation been a fixed, static place, as most older nations were by then.

But America in the early 19th century was a land on the verge of both economic growth and geographical expansion the likes of which the world had not seen before, and it is in this context that slavery – localized in the South but linked to the growth of the cotton trade – became the explosive issue of the later antebellum era. It invited the resurgence of sectionalism, which increasingly came to mean the slavery question, and finally provoked the constitutional crisis that nearly ended the American experiment.

Left, James Monroe advocated sending blacks back to Africa. Monrovia, the capital of Liberia, is named after him. Above, Richmond, Virginia, *circa* 1835.

Thomas Jefferson called it forging "an empire for liberty" – the process of statemaking outlined in the Northwest Ordinance of 1787, which became the manual for the orderly growth of the American republic westward across the continent. Slavery ceased to be merely a local Southern matter, and Southern sectionalism, which was increasingly aggravated by both anti- and proslavery arguments, pushed the nation toward disunion. In 1819, there were 22 states, 11 slave and 11 free – the careful result of admitting first one type and then the other so as to maintain equal representation in the Senate. The problem came in the House when the slave states, falling behind their Northern sisters, filled 81 seats compared with the North's 105. At this early stage, it is foolish to dwell too closely on purely sectional divisions in the halls of the national government. The Republican Party was a national organization with major constituents, united by class and interest, on both sides of the Mason Dixon Line – the state boundary between Maryland and Pennsylvania considered to be the dividing line between North and South.

The Missouri Compromise: In 1820, what focused attention so sharply on the matter of Congressional balance was the imminent admission to the Union of the state of Missouri. It was an occasion with precedent-setting potential for, if Missouri went "free," Southerners had reason to fear that so might the whole of the trans-Mississippi West. If that happened, the South, with its "peculiar institution" comprising hordes of black slaves, would find itself in a permanent minority in the national government. Should that government then ever choose to amend the Constitution so as to attack slavery, the South would be at its mercy.

On March 3, 1820, a compromise was reached in which Missouri would be admitted as a slave state but was to be paired with the admission of Maine as a free state. That much seemed fair to everyone and portended no ill for the future admission of other states. What did set off the alarm bells and a new precedent was Congress's extension of the 36/30 latitude straight west across the whole Louisiana Purchase, for the purpose of dividing future free from future slave territory.

On the surface and in retrospect, this would seem a plausible enough thing to have done, but that is not to take into account the expansive spirit of nationalism that was then suffusing American life and whose compelling symbol was the Great West.

Congress, now boldly legislating with regard to slavery in the new territories acquired in the West since the Revolution, banned it from some of that territory not yet even organized into states. The 36/30 line cut across the boundless spirit of the age and left a livid scar that said the West was now split. Thomas Jefferson most memorably captured the long-range meaning of what had happened. The compromise struck him, he said, as a fire bell in the night, and he warned the nation that any such fixed geographical line that divided the North and the South and was identified with political and moral principles could never be erased peacefully. In the compromise, the old Southern nationalist heard a distant death knell for the Union.

The South's marriage to both staple-crop agriculture and the system of slave labor that made this possible continued to set the region apart from the rest of the country, even as cotton became an ever more valuable national asset. Cotton's value was tied to conditions in the world market, and the more the trade expanded and prospered, the more Southern agricultural interests became convinced that everything depended on free trade. So it was that, at the end of the 1820s, the issue of the tariff became as sectionally divisive as the issue of slavery expansion.

The problem for a staple-crop producer such as the South was a classic dilemma of selling cheap, if the world price happened to be low, and buying dear, for the manufactured goods that Southern planters had to buy came at prices that were artificially inflated by tariff protection.

As far as Northern factory owners were concerned, protective duties encouraged growth in the early take-off stages of industrialization; as far as the South was concerned, the extra duty imposed by the tariff was robbing them of valuable profit.

Unhappy with the Union: As the nation expanded to the west and as the North's growth and vigor began to outdistance the South's, support would grow for secession from the Union. Even as the tariff declined as a divisive issue, that of slavery, infinitely more complex and emotional, took its place. To the very large extent that no Northerner was being asked to bear the burden of emancipation, it seemed to many Southerners that the North's allegedly noble convictions about the universal rights of man were actually very cheap convictions to hold.

Like no other issue before it, anti-slavery laid bare the critical rifts inherent in the American nation, even as that nation was striving to reproduce itself in the West. To oppose slavery was, to Southerners, to oppose the way the South lived and prospered.

In a sense, either side could claim that it

was the other side that threatened the Union. Northern anti-slavery voices argued that no nation founded on liberty could live up to those first principles as long as it tolerated slavery anywhere in its midst.

Southern pro-slavery voices argued that when the Union was put together in the 1780s, it was done in the complete knowledge of the existence of slavery in the Southern states, for whose concern alone slavery must remain. To attack it, therefore, was to attack the contract that had been established between the states that constituted the Union, putting something else – a "higher law" – above the Union. This was, of course, exactly what Northerners would accuse Southerners of when the latter spoke of nullification and the right of a state to secede: of putting something else – states' rights – above the Union. It all depended on just where a man stood, and from the 1830s, Southerners stood more and more firmly on defensive ground.

As the anti-slavery movement and the abolitionists shouted about a "higher law," Southerners responded by erecting an elaborate structure of economic, ethnological and Biblical arguments defending it. They warned of abolition's dire consequences which would mean economic ruin for the South and the nation, destitution for the blacks, and extermination of the whites. They argued that the Old and the New Testaments were strewn with references to masters and servants. Paul had commanded obedience, and Christ himself had never spoken against the institution, which was all around him. Slavery had obviously worked well for the Greeks and Romans, whose civilizations 19th-century Americans professed to admire.

Immutable laws of nature, pro-slavery apologists argued, ordained a "mudsill class," on whose crude labors a higher culture could be built by those of superior knowledge and power. In the South, so the argument went, this meant a cultured and leisured white planter class at the top and, at the bottom, black slaves whose natural burden it was to hew the wood and haul the water, but whose inestimable benefit it also was to have been redeemed from African savagery and converted to Christianity. The slaves suffered no greater physical hardships than did Northern "wage slaves," and they enjoyed a good bit more security.

And so, as the end of the 1850s approached and as the threats to slavery multiplied, even once moderate Southerners again raised radical doubts about the wisdom of union.

<u>Above</u>, the romance of the riverboat. These cargo boats were later supplanted by the railroads.

The American Civil War was a war the likes of which no one had seen before. It was the first real war of the industrial age; it was the first war in which armies were supplied by railway; it was the first war to be conducted by telegraph and so able to be reported quickly to homefront populations. It saw the introduction of the observation balloon, the repeating rifle (an early form of machine gun) and, at sea, the iron-clad, steam-powered warship. When it began in the spring of 1861, there was much talk on both sides of a quick and neat little conflict with the boys being home for a hero's Christmas.

Naive Northerners saw it as a mere police action to curb the recalcitrant South. Naive Southerners boasted that one dashing young Southern cavalier could whip ten cowardly abolitionists. More thoughtful men on both sides, including Abraham Lincoln and Jefferson Davis (*see page 42*), understood that the sectional controversies of four decades had aroused deep passions and that in all likelihood, once the war began, blood would flow until some final settlement was achieved.

Seeds of secession: The intemperate economic arguments over tariffs that strained the Union in the 1850s, and the South's reputation as the "wealth-producing" section of the country, giving reason to believe it could go it alone, went hand in hand with perceived moral and cultural rifts. Demand rose in the South for Southern textbooks and Southern teachers and for the South to emancipate itself from literary dependency on Northern and European writers.

The most tangible cultural bond had already snapped in 1845 when the two largest Protestant denominations in America, the Methodists and the Baptists, had divided over the slavery question into Northern and Southern groupings. In each case, the stigma of immorality was placed on the slaveholding South. But it was the publication of one particular book in 1852 – *Uncle Tom's Cabin or Life Among the Lowly* – that contributed to the course of disunion more than any other single cultural event. Author Harriet Beecher Stowe's experience of the South's peculiar institution was limited, to say the least, but the impact of her novel was not. Stowe, a member of a Northern anti-slavery family, drew heavily on the highly negative reports of conditions in the South to be found in Theodore Dwight Weld's propagandistic *Slavery As It Is*, and she reflected all its simplicities: overseers (Simon Legree) were universally sadistic; slaves (Uncle Tom) were angels in ebony. Slavery was worse in the Deep South.

Explosive literature: While Stowe shared all the white racist attitudes of her time, slavery and not racial equality was her point, and she made it brilliantly. In the South, reaction to Stowe's book was vehement. Attacking the author and the book equally, newspaper editors claimed that Stowe had no knowledge whatsoever of the conditions of slaves in the South, possessed no "moral sense," and had plagiarized Charles Dickens. The book achieved a permanent place in American literary history, but at that particular time it also added the explosive element of moral self-righteousness to the slavery debate by strengthening the stereotype of slavery as a malevolent institution that stood, literally and morally, in the path of national progress. Thousands of Northerners, having previously held themselves aloof from the moral question, were swayed by the book to join the abolition cause.

Self-righteousness settled on both sides, as the South counterattacked the libel on its character with no less than 15 novels of its own and with sweeping arguments that Northern wage earners were actually worse off than slaves. For in the late 1850s, as troubled as the political landscape had become, the South's actual landscape of plantations and farms enjoyed enormous prosperity. For this reason, the myth that cotton was indeed king grew strong.

This myth lent acceptability to the momentous decision to leave the Union by many Southerners who reasoned that a cotton-hungry Great Britain would have to give support to the South if she herself were to survive. But places other than the South

Left, Fort Sumter, 1863. The first shot of the Civil War had been fired from here two years earlier.

grew cotton, and the only calculation that went into Britain's decisions about whom to support in the American Civil War was the cool calculation of which side it was that was most likely to win.

Each of the remaining three years of the decade had brought grim omens. In 1857, the Supreme Court, five of whose nine justices were Southerners, waded into the slavery controversy with the Dred Scott Decision. The case involved the migrations of a black slave, Dred Scott, who during the 1830s had been carried by his master, John Emerson, an army surgeon, from the slave state of Missouri to Illinois, where the Northwest Ordinance of 1787 forbade slavery, and then to

Wisconsin Territory, where the Missouri Compromise also forbade slavery. Scott finally returned to Missouri and sued for his freedom on the grounds that his stay in free territory made him a free man.

In a broad decision, the court seemed determined to vindicate the South and inflame the anti-slavery North. As a black and as a slave, the court decided, Dred Scott – and therefore all other black slaves and their descendants – was not a citizen and could not sue for his freedom.

John Brown's raid on the federal arsenal at Harpers Ferry, Virginia, in October 1859, also had an irrational impact on the course of events. John Brown, destined to become a mythical figure in American history, may well have been a madman. Certainly his scheme to liberate a number of slaves, whom he would then turn into guerrilla bands in the Virginia mountains, had a bizarre quality about it, while his tactics in trying to carry it off suggest greater theatrical than military genius. His band of 21 included his own sons and several blacks, and no local slaves came to their aid, as had been anticipated they might. When a passing train alerted the outside world to their attack, Brown's raiders proved no match for the contingent of Marines, commanded by Robert E. Lee, who were sent to quell them.

Most Northerners, while disapproving the raid's methods, lauded its aims. Moderate Southerners, responded slowly at first, but hardened their attitudes when it was revealed that Brown had been financed by a secret cadre of wealthy Northern abolitionists. As extreme reactions set in on both sides, the raid became a turning point in the fast-developing secession crisis. Southerners who came to identify John Brown with the North – an oversimplification certainly, but a compelling one – concluded that they must secede to be safe, and the fear that moved them, thanks to John Brown, was both real and immediate.

South Carolina, predictably, responded first and, in December 1860, set in motion the train of secession. By February 6, 1861, all five of the other Deep South states – Mississippi, Florida, Alabama, Georgia, Louisiana, and Texas – had followed. The states of the Upper South – Virginia, North Carolina, Tennessee, and Arkansas – hesitated, but warned that they would resist any attempt by the federal government to coerce any state that left the Union. President Abraham Lincoln, in his inaugural address on March 4, attempted to walk a fine line aiming to preserve what was left of the Union and to reassure the South: "I have no purpose directly or indirectly to interfere with the institution of slavery in the states where it exists." He also asserted that secession was legally not possible: "No state upon its own mere action, can lawfully get out of the Union." Both sides hesitated to make a move toward violence, and while the famous "first shot" was fired by the South, it was said to be in response to overt Northern aggression.

Coercion, or at least the appearance of it in

the South's eyes, came in April 1861 when Lincoln, after much delay, attempted to resupply Fort Sumter in Charleston harbor, one of the few federal military installations in the Deep South that had not surrendered to state authority. The garrison commander, Major Robert Anderson, refused South Carolina's ultimatum, and at 4.30am on April 12 South Carolina forces commenced a bloodless bombardment of the island fortress. The national colors came down 34 hours later.

A Southern nation: The confrontation instantly galvanized the North in defense of the Union, and Lincoln issued a call for 75,000 three-month volunteers to put down the, as he put it, "insurrection." Lincoln's call for troops at last forced the hand of the states of the moderate border South: Virginia seceded on April 17, Arkansas on May 6, Tennessee on May 7, and North Carolina on May 20. Slaveholding Kentucky, Maryland, and Missouri did not leave the Union but with their Southern sisters, they joined to declare the independence of a new southern nation, the Confederate States of America.

While neither side ever lacked the resolution to see the fight through to the bitter end, the North had the clear advantage in numbers and economic strength. The 23 Northern states contained a population of 22 million, which was augmented by heavy foreign immigration. The North could, even in a long conflict, replace its losses. Though heavily agricultural like the South, it had a more balanced economy with an advanced industrial establishment, strong financial institutions, an excellent railroad grid, a navy, and a merchant marine. The 11 states of the Confederacy had a population of some 9 million, a third of whom were slaves. Its manufacturing was undeveloped and tied to agriculture; it had no substantial iron industry, and it made no heavy armaments. Its railroad network was still rudimentary and utterly unready for the massive load soon to be placed upon it.

Yet the discrepancy in resources, which Southerners recognized, was not initially compelling, for the South was taking a calculated risk on several counts. These were that the North would not actually fight to save the Union; that Great Britain and France, hungry for Southern cotton, would intervene on the South's behalf; and that the South's control of the Mississippi River would weaken Western support for the Northern war effort. In each case, the South guessed wrong.

The government of the new Confederacy comprising representatives of the six states which had seceded, met at a convention on February 4, 1861. The representatives adopted a provisional constitution, modelled faithfully after the Constitution but specifically clarifying issues of states' rights that had become muddled over the past 70 years. They elected Jefferson Davis to President and Alexander H. Stephens of Georgia to Vice-President. In military preparations, the Confederacy had some genuine advantages. Davis issued a call for a 100,000 volunteers, and most who answered were well armed and clothed.

Left, Robert E. Lee had been offered command of the Northern armies, but turned it down. Right, teenage cadets from the Virginia Military Institute fought and helped win the Battle of New Market.

In its officer corps, the Confederacy had Robert E. Lee, who had served as the superintendent of the crack military academy West Point and was attached to a Western command at the time of secession. Lee had been offered command of the Northern armies but had turned it down, resigned from the US Army, and returned to his home state of Virginia where he was named major-general

JEFFERSON DAVIS

One of many disparaging remarks the "Sphinx of the Confederacy" endured during, and after, the Civil War was "overmatched and outplayed." Some scholars have even suggested that if their roles had been reversed, and Lincoln had been president of the Confederacy, the Union might well have lost the war. Jefferson Davis, the only President of the Confederacy, was a complicated and enigmatic personality who never sought, and didn't want, the job.

Davis was born 10 miles west of Hopkinsville, Kentucky on June 3, 1808, the youngest of ten children. His family had moved there in 1793, but during Jefferson's infancy, moved several more times, eventually settling in Mississippi. In 1816, Davis was enrolled in St Thomas of Aquin school near Springfield, Kentucky. He was supposed to stay for eight years, but left after only two.

Davis returned again to Kentucky in 1822, spending two years at Transylvania College in Lexington. From there he transferred to the United States Military Academy at West Point, graduating in 1828, 23rd out of a class of 33. During his army career, he was stationed primarily in Wisconsin, taking part in the Black Hawk Indian War. Abraham Lincoln was a civilian volunteer in the same conflict, but history doesn't record the two ever meeting.

Love for Sara Knox Taylor, daughter of his commanding officer, Colonel Zachary Taylor (later President of the United States), caused Davis to resign from the army in 1835 because the Colonel opposed the match. They married anyway and moved to Mississippi where Davis bought a plantation called "Brierfield." Tragically, Sara died from malaria within three months. Davis spent the ensuing 10 years working his plantation, and by all accounts his manner toward his slaves was patriarchal rather than brutal. He was a well-regarded local figure.

Davis married Varina Howard in 1845, the same year he was elected to the US Congress as a Representative from Mississippi. When war against Mexico was declared the next year, he resigned to lead the 1st Mississippi Rifles. Davis returned a hero, and a seat in the US Senate soon followed.

Henry Clay's 1850 Compromise Slave Act was anathema to Davis who, as a strong supporter of states' rights, felt Clay's bill violated the terms of the US Constitution. Rather than stay in the Senate and fight for his beliefs, Davis resigned and went home to Mississippi where, in 1851, he was defeated in a race for the governorship. Two years later, Washington once again beckoned and President Franklin Pierce made Davis Secretary of War. He served with distinction until he was re-elected to the Senate in 1857.

The election of Abraham Lincoln in 1860, and his declaration that there would be no additional slave-owning states admitted to the Union, broadened the schism between North and South. In January 1861, Mississippi seceded. Davis resigned his Senate seat and was appointed Major-General of the state's troops. The following month, the deadlocked Confederate Congress, meeting in Montgomery, Alabama, found in Davis a compromise presidential candidate upon whom all could agree, and elected him to the Confederacy's highest office. Davis received the news with something less than joy: "I thought myself better adapted to command in the field."

In the beginning, he was a popular choice; "honest, pure and patriotic" were some of the adjectives showered upon him. His cabinet included men of ability, and he listened to the advice of his generals.

But 1863 saw a turn in Davis's fortunes. Becoming autocratic, he meddled in army matters, countermanding orders and promoting favorite officers. Many felt he had usurped powers not granted by the electorate and called him a despot. Until the war's last days, Davis insisted it would be won by the Confederacy, refusing to consider any peace proposals except those which left the South independent.

When Lee surrendered at Appomattox in April 1865, Davis attempted to flee with his family to Mexico, but was caught and imprisoned, first in the shackles of a common criminal, at Virginia's Fort Monroe, where he was confined until 1867. After his release, Davis eventually settled on a plantation near Biloxi, Mississippi, where he wrote his version of the Confederacy's history, *The Rise and Fall of the Confederate Government*. Mississippians wanted to return Davis to the US Senate, but, proud to the end, he refused to ask for the necessary Federal pardon.

Jefferson Davis died peacefully on December 6, 1889, in New Orleans, Louisiana. His body now rests in Richmond, Virginia. ■

of the Virginia Confederate troops. More than 380 other officers resigned their commissions and took new positions in the Confederate forces.

While Davis was engaged in fielding his new armies, dissension grew in the Southern Allegheny region of western Virginia and East Tennessee. The western counties of Virginia had not been represented at the convention that had approved the state's secession. On June 11, 1861, Western delegates met to denounce secession and form a new government. The delegates elected Francis H. Pierpont governor, selected senators, and adopted a new state constitution for West Virginia, which was admitted to the Union in April 1863. In East Tennessee, only the establishment of martial law kept Unionists from following West Virginia's lead.

Fighting began in earnest in July 1861, as the Northern troops pushed from Washington, DC toward Richmond. The Confederate troops under General Joseph E. Johnston and General P. G. T. Beauregard met at Manassas where Union General Irvin McDowell began an attack. The Confederates drew up along the small creek called Bull Run, forming a wall of resistance for which one of their commanders, General Thomas J. "Stonewall" Jackson, received his nickname. The advantage swung back and forth until at last the Confederates pushed the Union troops back into full retreat. Jackson pressed for permission to pursue the enemy, but the Confederate policy of defensive rather than offensive operations was maintained.

This early victory for the Confederates (whose sympathizers came to label the Civil War "The War Between the States, or even "The War of Northern Aggression") was followed by disaster in the West. The Union forces had wrested control of Kentucky – a state which had proclaimed neutrality in the war – Fort Donelson and Nashville on the Cumberland River in Tennessee, and Corinth, Mississippi. Along the east coast, Southern cities were blockaded by the Union navy to prevent the Confederacy from carrying on vital trade with Europe. By early 1862, the Atlantic Coast was completely under the Union's control, and blockades along the shore of the Gulf of Mexico were then begun in earnest. New Orleans fell on May 1, followed by Baton Rouge and Natchez, Mississippi. New Orleans, however, proved difficult to control. General Benjamin F. Butler was faced with a citizenry openly hostile to its Union captors.

The women of New Orleans, having made a habit of insulting Union soldiers on the streets, were the target of Butler's "woman order," which proclaimed that any woman who insulted a Union soldier was to be arrested as a prostitute. Butler also seemed to disregard his soldiers' penchant for looting the heirlooms of New Orleans's families.

Right, the Confederate flags, top to bottom: the Bonnie Blue Flag of Texas (not official); the Stars and Bars; the Battle Flag; 1863 National Flag (left); 1865 National Flag.

Southerners calculated that most of the city's silverware was carted off by Butler's army, earning the general his nickname "Spoon."

While the Confederate army suffered dismal losses in the West and along the seacoasts, it realized some success in the East. General Robert E. Lee's troops, entrenched around the Confederate capital of Richmond, Virginia, faced Union forces under General George B. McClellan in the early summer of 1862. During the "Seven Days' Battles" at Mechanicsville, Gaines' Mill, Savage's Station, and Malvern Hill, Lee lost 20,000 men and McClellan lost 16,000. Richmond was saved, however. Lincoln remained determined to capture the Confederate capital and sent 50,000 troops into Virginia. Lee's troops routed the new Union army at the second battle of Manassas, and Lee began preparations for an invasion of the North.

The Confederate's push was successful at Harpers Ferry, but at Sharpsburg, Lee lost 8,000 of his 40,000 troops. With no hope of reinforcements, he withdrew across the Potomac River and maintained his position at Fredericksburg. On December 13, Union troops under General Ambrose Burnside attacked. Over the next two days, the Union lost 12,000 men and was forced to withdraw.

The Union army's humiliating performance in the East that summer, combined with increased pressures from abolitionists, influenced President Lincoln to change the purpose of the war to the preservation of the Union. In September 1862, he issued the Emancipation Proclamation, which freed all slaves in states in rebellion after January 1, 1863. In effect the law freed no slaves at all. It did not apply to the states that had fallen to Union control, and in those states still actively fighting, the US government had no jurisdiction. In the South, the proclamation increased support for the Confederate government, and even those people who had opposed secession now rallied to the cause.

The year the proclamation went into effect brought sweeping losses to the Confederate army. Vicksburg, Mississippi, fell to the Union after a prolonged siege in the summer of 1863, and when Port Hudson fell shortly after, the entire Mississippi River was in Union hands. After a victory at Chancellorsville, Virginia – one made less bright by the death of Stonewall Jackson – the Confederates entered Northern territory. At Gettysburg in July, the troops showed stunning gallantry but had to retreat after sustaining heavy losses. In North Carolina, the Confederates were at first successful at the Battle of Chickamauga, and they surrounded the Union army in Chattanooga. The arrival of General Ulysses S. Grant, who created a plan to break the Union army out of the city, kept the Confederates from claiming victory.

The following year, some brief moments of victory came to the Confederacy. In the region called the "Wilderness," General Lee's army outmaneuvered General Grant's forces time and again, but unlike the Union generals who had faced Lee earlier in the war, Grant did not withdraw from his push toward Richmond. He pressed on, losing 55,000 men to Lee's 19,000 along the way. But the Confederacy's elation over the saving of Richmond was darkened by the prolonged siege of Atlanta, which finally fell to General William T. Sherman on September 3.

Sherman then began his march across Georgia toward Savannah, plundering the countryside along the way. When Savannah fell on December 20, the Confederacy was cut in two. The government in Richmond could maintain communications only with troops in Virginia and North and South Carolina. Sherman then pushed north through the Carolinas toward Raleigh. Grant and Sheridan pushed toward Richmond and gained control of the city on April 3, 1865. Lee's army was surrounded. On April 9, he and Grant met one last time, at the home of Wilmer McLean in Appomattox.

Gallant surrender: Lee surrendered his 28,000 troops after receiving terms from Grant that would allow his men to return to their homes. President Davis fled from Richmond in hopes of meeting up with Johnston's troops. The cause was hopeless, however, and Johnston surrendered in North Carolina later in April. The armies in the Deep South and west of the Mississippi followed suit in May. The Confederate president continued his flight, now toward Mexico, but was captured on May 10 in southern Georgia and was taken on to Fort Monroe.

The physical costs of the Civil War were huge on both sides. The war killed between 600,000 and 700,000 young men in a nation totaling only 33 million: a fatality rate around double that suffered by American forces in both world wars. The nation, North and South, lost not only these men, however, but the children and the grandchildren who never were, a cultural loss that is beyond calculation. The South suffered the most physically, for its cities, towns, and plantations were devastated and its economy ruined. During its brief and turbulent existence, the Confederacy, which had failed to stay the run and establish Southern nationhood, had yet crystallized Southern distinctiveness.

Left, the burning of Richmond, the capital of the Confederacy. Above, Lee surrendered to Grant only a few days later, on April 9, 1865.

It left Southerners with a heritage as peculiar as the one slavery had first given them. In their epic bid to secure their independence and preserve slavery, they exceeded their strength – and perhaps the strength of any people trying to defend such an anachronism, even in the staunchly race-conscious 19th century. For their presumption, history judges that they deserved to lose. For their defense of liberty against the centralizing power of the national state – a moral and political stance originating in the 17th and 18th centuries and one which tragically fell into some disuse in the 20th – the Confederate Southerners merit a kinder judgment.

As the Confederacy crumbled and the Union took control of region after region in the South, President Lincoln was determined not to direct malice toward the conquered people. Despite heavy opposition in his party, the President devised a "Proclamation on Amnesty and Reconstruction." This plan called for the restoration of civil rights to all Southerners, except highly ranked civil and military officials, after they took an oath of allegiance to the Constitution. The plan also specified that when ten percent of the state's voters had taken the oath, the state could then re-establish a government. The President's plan had not been signed when, on April 14, 1865, John Wilkes Booth assassinated Lincoln at Ford's Theatre. With Lincoln's death the reconstruction debate fell to President Andrew Johnson.

Johnson, a former tailor from North Carolina and then Tennessee, was a self-educated man who had slowly risen through the ranks of political office from alderman to US Senator. He had retained his seat in the Senate after Tennessee seceded – the only Southern senator to do so – and after the fall of Nashville, President Lincoln had appointed him military governor of Tennessee. Johnson's plan for Reconstruction was announced on May 29. It included all the provisions of Lincoln's plan but added that individuals with property valued at $20,000 or more were excepted from amnesty.

Carpetbaggers: In this way, Johnson attempted to alter Southern society. No lover of the wealthy, white, planter class, Johnson wanted to make room for small farmers and poor whites in the Southern political scene. There were also wide-reaching reforms for blacks. But these same reforms opened up the doors to scalawags (unscrupulous white Southerners who supported Republican policy) and carpetbaggers (Northerners who came South to take advantage of the conditions for personal gain).

For years afterward, most white Southerners couldn't say enough bad things about these times, and it became a sacred part of Southern myth that Reconstruction constituted the "blackout of honest government" and the unforgivable insult to the white race. Others – literate blacks and Radical partisans – recalled it as a noble and well-intentioned experiment in which the native virtue and sterling performance of the blacks was matched only by the unadulterated malice of their Southern white adversaries.

Black vote: For all their ineptitude, the Republican governments in the South did more than take bribes and swindle the taxpayers. Even though the presence of blacks in public office would soon pass away, these regimes made marks that would last longer than they did themselves. The state constitutions on which they rested were superior to, or at least more modern than, their antebellum predecessors. Participation in politics was broadened to universal white manhood suffrage. Even blacks, now guaranteed the vote by the Fifteenth Amendment, usually favored the vote for all whites regardless of the latters' past association with the Confederacy and the defense of slavery.

The new constitutions asserted the right of children to schooling and the new state governments backed this up with appropriations that at least began to support such institutions. These administrations also began to give some tentative legal protection to women, who in much of the region had until this time to rely pretty much on their wits and their sex to get along in a man's world. The government also did what it could to promote the economic rebuilding of the South, though in this it was severely limited by powerful prevailing notions about the limited role the state should play in the economy. The constitutions established both agencies to promote immigration into the South and, especially important, programs to promote industrialization. And of course these were the governments that for the first time gave blacks a real, though limited, chance to show what they could do in positions of power, trust, and responsibility.

But Reconstruction is only part of the story, for better or worse, of the Republican regimes in the state capitals. The South was not just a place being acted upon, but was a

Left, after the war, plantations were divided up into small farms worked by sharecroppers.

place filled with people acting on their own behalf to maintain their values and assert their influence on the nation.

Sabotage: From today's perspective, in the wake of the civil rights movements of the 1950s and 1960s, it is easy to look back on the white Southerners of the Reconstruction era with contempt for a people so morally dulled as to sabotage such a noble experiment in racial justice. But viewed by the standards of that age, it was they and not their reformist antagonists who represented the American mainstream. These were men convinced of the absolute impossibility of the black and white races coexisting in one place, except in a relationship of complete white control and complete black submission.

Their commitment to white supremacy sprang from tradition, and in the 1870s and 1880s, it was also bolstered by the best scientific opinion. Herbert Spencer and William Graham Sumner pioneered a fierce brand of social Darwinism that dovetailed nicely with the practice of white supremacy at home and abroad. White Southerners were not alone; they were not an isolated, embattled minority of evil people who never outgrew nasty habits of whipping their slaves and keeping millions of blacks in their place.

Nevertheless, the first Ku Klux Klan was born at Pulaski, Tennessee, in 1865. It began as an organization of unemployed Confederates and, by the late 1860s, had become an extralegal paramilitary brotherhood, wrapped in legendary bedsheets and shrouded in exotic ceremonies and rituals.

Large themes such as "racial adjustment" always take up prominent places in the history books, but there is a danger in this. For thousands of Southerners, the years after the Civil War were not judged by some far-off national reference points. They were a time neither of the perceived disaster of black alien rule, nor of the sparkling dawn of brotherhood and racial equality. Rather, they were years without any extraordinary moral dimension at all, when Southerners were not as preoccupied as we are commonly led to believe with either momentous political choices or intractable racial dilemmas.

They were years spent trying to make a dollar, and trying to solve the immediate, local, concrete problems that come with trying to stay alive in changed and changing circumstances. The South then was a world of harvest yields, of the weather, of freight rates to market, of prices in that market, of technological change, of social resistance to change. The 1870s were hard times in the South, as elsewhere, and it was the limits of the Southern economy as much as anything else that determined that the radical reforms of Reconstruction would not succeed. In a poor region, concern for prosperity far outweighed concern for civil rights and would continue to do so until that far distant day when the South finally got to its feet.

Sharecroppers: Slavery had been replaced by sharecropping, and all of those alleged new farms were not in fact worked by happy Jeffersonian yeomen but by dour tenants, poor as ever and far from independent. Sharecropping was a simple arrangement whereby the landowner decided what crops were grown and then arranged for their marketing. The proceeds were split into thirds: one for the labor, one for the land, one for the seeds and implements. Or put another way: one-third for the cropper, two-thirds for the owner. The plantations once worked by slaves were divided into plots worked by tenant families – and it was each of these new units that was counted in the census as a "farm." Thus the general structure of the Old South plantation – land held in parcels and worked by cheap labor with no other options – persisted.

Thousands of Northerners had come to realize that the underdeveloped South presented vast opportunities. It offered ingredients of early-stage industrial development in abundance: land, timber, coal, water power, and cheap labor. "How to get rich in the South" propaganda streamed out of the North, and countless after-dinner speeches to eager groups of Northern businessmen and investors began with ringing admonitions to "Go South, young man ..."

Many Southerners, eager to put away the rancor of the war and Reconstruction, seemed keen to embrace their share of the nation's new industrial destiny. In a spirit of sectional reconciliation undergirded by a common desire for profits and prosperity, they welcomed the Yankee investors and industrialists and not just with words.

Beginning in the middle and late 1880s, the South's oldest cash crop, tobacco, proved that it too offered new market opportunities. In antebellum times, the processing of tobacco, once the crop left the field, had been largely a handicraft-type operation. By the turn of the century the production of chewing and smoking tobacco products had been thoroughly mechanized, the demand spurred on by new fashions in smoking that favored a Carolina-grown, bright leaf suitable for that genteel new smoke, the cigarette. At the same time, the number of Southern cotton mills rose from 161 to some 400, which far outstripped the rest of the country.

Viewed on the surface, the South's industrial progress seemed impressive, and yet it was still tarnished not far below. The region had induced capital and manufacturing to come to it by offering everything at its command more cheaply – taxes, power, land, raw materials, and especially labor. But once the initial processing had been done in the South, the final, more valuable (and infinitely more lucrative) work was done somewhere else.

The centerpiece and most lasting symbol of that first new South – the cotton mill crusade – bespoke a determined effort to transform and uplift the material conditions of life in the South, but behind it and related reforms was a stronger drive to alter the South's spirit as well. Much of Southern history in the 20th century – a war of the mind and spirit between the contending forces of tradition and change – springs from these early skirmishes. When, in New York City, on December 21, 1886, Atlanta newspaperman Henry W. Grady delivered an address entitled "The New South," he fathered a movement that long outlived him and that future generations each in their turn and in their own way would call "new."

The New South: Grady had in mind the economic rejuvenation of his native region. To achieve it, he seemed willing to sell his soul to the industrialists and entrepreneurs in his audience. The time had come to put away sectional animosity and to forget the rancor of war and its aftermath. Only if the old suspicions and fears were allayed could the North be persuaded to give of its talents and resources to resuscitate the South's economy. The South must, he said, have Northern know-how, Northern money, and Northern ideas if it were ever to break out of the poverty and powerlessness that had oppressed it since 1865.

All those New York industrialists whom Grady invited down to Dixie, enthusiastic as they plainly were, did not dispense their favors free of charge. The economic price they exacted, and that Southerners such as Grady agreed to pay, has been much remarked upon as imprisoning the South in a

By the new century, the South had started an economic recovery. Above, wedding, *circa* 1900.

self-defeating "colonial economy" of Southern enterprises controlled from Northern boardrooms and Southern factories feeding the profits of Northern shareholders.

The New South, as it was first conceived and ever after elaborated, fitted comfortably within this mainstream. The South had to start from a lower point than the rest of America, and it seemed that Southerners always had to run harder just to keep up. But about the worthiness of the race itself, prophets of the New South had no doubts. So spacious was their faith that there was even room in it for the South's most forgotten man, the black.

It was room of a qualified sort that would in fact later embarrass more modern "new"

Southerners, but that by the standards of an earlier age was neither malicious in design nor completely ill-advised in result. By accommodating black Southerners, however modestly, within their planned new South, the advocates of change hoped fervently, and in sincere good faith, that they could settle the race question at least for their lifetimes. By and large, they did. In this, they were helped by an astounding black man whose fate at the hands of later generations of black and white men, sadly, has not been a particularly happy one.

Booker T. Washington, born a slave, became the greatest black spokesman that the New South produced. He concluded that no sane white man, who truly hoped for the progress of his section, could profit by keeping millions of blacks in a condition of perpetual serfdom. It went against the grain of New South practicality not to allow everyone on to the bandwagon, even though it went without saying that black Southerners would only ride at the rear.

But riding at the rear was better than not at all, and it was, Washington understood, about the best that could be expected. It was more essential for a black to be able to earn a dollar at a good job than to be able to spend a dollar in the same opera house as a white man. So he put forward his famous program for the vocational education of blacks both in skills, to enable them to support themselves and their families in modest comfort, and in trades, to give them some claim to the prosperity brought about by wider economic changes. Washington's enduring monument was Tuskegee Institute in Alabama, an industrial training center where he hoped to educate blacks in the most practical ways of being useful to their own community.

Jim Crow: Today, Washington's measures seem mild, halfhearted, and to some even "Uncle Tomish." Then, however, they appeared prudent and not without a genuine vision for the black race. But the United States Supreme Court effectively scotched any notions of black social equality with its famous doctrine of "separate but equal." Racial segregation in public accommodation and education, the court said, could not be construed as "unequal" or as "discriminatory" so long as the facilities available to both races were comparable in quality.

Even though things in the South were, in fact, almost always separate but unequal, "separate but equal" remained the law of the land for race relations in all of America until the 1950s. And in the South, which was where the vast majority of blacks still lived, a rigorous pattern of social segregation – the era of Jim Crow – clamped down on the black with unrelenting discipline. (The name Jim Crow comes from a song in a black minstrel show.)

With the outbreak of hostilities in Europe in 1914, key cotton exchanges did not open, and prices initially tumbled. But due both to its congressional influence and its felicitous climate, making year-round training possible, military camps and bases proliferated in the South, and many continued on in peacetime. Southern ports – Norfolk, Hampton and Newport News, Virginia – became important embarkation points and home to an ever more immense American fleet.

The wartime boom – once the initial cotton panic had passed – gave fresh substance to the New South's not so new boasts that industrialization was the path to a prosperous future. Munitions factories in Tennessee and Virginia, chemical plants in Alabama, and textile mills all over the region pulled Southerners out of the fields and, in what was a new experience for many, gave them a taste of earning real money.

rettes and an increasing number of female smokers gave new life to the South's oldest source of wealth, tobacco, and it was at this time that names such as "Camel" and "Lucky Strike" entered the American vernacular. But none of these could match the Southern beverage that had first been brewed by an Atlanta druggist in 1886 and then made famous – and fabulously profitable – by Atlantan Robert Woodruff in the 1920s: Coca-Cola.

Everywhere there were new roads, new automobiles, movie palaces, radio stores, real estate subdivisions, and tourist camp grounds. In 1929, when the Great Crash finally put an end to much of the growth, Virginia Governor Harry F. Byrd perhaps

When World War I ended, the whole nation dashed toward the 1920s with pent-up energy. The industrial boom triggered by the war expanded and, in the water-power rich South, this boom was increasingly driven by the magic of a new age: electricity. The chemical and textile industries especially profited from electrification, and the region of the Carolina Piedmont overtook New England as the nation's primary consumer of the South's raw cotton. The fashion for ciga-

Left, Booker T. Washington, black spokesman for the New South. Above, World War I nurses in Roanoke, Virginia.

captured the spirit best, when he likened the South's current experience to the exhilaration that attended the exploitation of other, older American frontiers: "The South is being pointed to today – as the West was in a former period – as the land of promise."

The "promise," however, was better kept in some respects than in others. As clearly as the change seemed to be written into the triumphant New South of the 1920s, there were still many Southerners who were reluctant or unable to read the message. Change could frighten as well as entice, and if one checked the balance at the end of the decade, continuity still counted for much down there.

The Ku Klux Klan, which was reborn on Stone Mountain in Georgia on Thanksgiving night, 1915, still skulks about the South today, representing the anachronistic voice of white supremacy. Then, it was the authentic voice not only of the South's unrelenting race prejudice but also of the more general fear among a rural people that change was making a mess of old moral certainties. In this respect, the Klan did not mirror only Southern anxiety, and indeed some of its greatest "successes" came from far afield such as Indiana where it actually operated a successful political machine.

But the Klan's general lack of a well-articulated program bespoke its truer nature – that of the defense mechanism, and death rattle, of a dying America and a more slowly dying South. For such ill-educated people, whose daily lives were an endless (and for many hopeless) routine of planting cotton and waiting for it to grow, the rituals and mystique of the exotic hooded order fostered a sense of camaraderie and belonging amid the distress of an otherwise grim agricultural existence. The price of admission was $10, and it bought a knighthood in the Invisible Empire of the Ku Klux Klan, where there were wizards and cyclopses – and always someone else to blame. Although the Klan became an influence in state politics, it never had a platform and could never boast the powerful political leadership needed for long-term success. Most of the major urban newspapers of the day vociferously opposed it, and it ultimately fell victim to its own excesses.

Writers: Regionalism pervaded in literature as well as in social and political practises. This marked the beginning of the Southern Renascence, a literary period paralleled in America only by the New England Renaissance of the mid-19th century. Among the many Southern writers were Robert Penn Warren, Katherine Anne Porter, Eudora Welty and Carson McCullers.

In 1935 John Crowe Ransom advanced his theory on why Southern writers had suddenly sprung to such articulate life. The South had fallen victim to decay, Ransom said, but rather than rush to espouse new ideals and new methods to effect recovery, the region's inhabitants and writers clung to the old ideals. The aftermath of the Old South's destruction in the Civil War brought out the most prolific self-appraisal.

Other Southern writers during the Renascence used their masterful eyes for detail and ears for dialect in countless novels whose actions takes place in the South. In his four great novels, Thomas Wolfe, a native of Asheville, North Carolina, explored the themes of loneliness, isolation, and hatred and how they are overcome through sensuous experiences, love and art. William Faulkner wrote of independence and individualism in Mississippi. More Southern writers would soon make their mark, including James Agee, Tennessee Williams, Truman Capote, William Styron, Flannery O'Connor and Walker Percy.

Prolific though the writers were, however, it was not they but President Franklin Roosevelt who had the greater impact on Southerners' lives during the 1930s. Roosevelt, a New York blue blood with a house in Warm Springs, Georgia, always claimed to know the South well – indeed to love it and understand its problems. He was instrumental in furthering the Tennessee Valley Authority (TVA) project, one of the largest public works projects ever attempted.

TVA's genesis reached back to 1916 to the federal authorization, for reasons of national defense, of power and nitrate plants on the Tennessee River at Muscle Shoals in Alabama and to a belief that there should be a public yardstick for measuring the cost of private utilities. At stake was water power, the generation of electricity, the production of fertilizer, flood control, navigation, conservation and other facets of regional planning. The project encompassed an area touching on parts of seven states and nearly as large as England.

TVA became a powerful ally of the New South once recovery came, adding immensely to the region's attractiveness for industrial development. The orchestration of resources by the TVA helped attract Northern capital anew. Along with the continued growth of textile and garment manufacturing, paper milling and furniture manufacturing, and increasingly chemical and petroleum industries, it proved that, despite the drawbacks of outside investment – and thus of outside control – if there were enough of it, there would also be sufficient profits for the South.

World War II was shorter and less traumatic for the United States than for most of the other participating nations, but for a country that still clung tenaciously to old notions of innocence and isolation, it brought the cares – and the challenges – of the world crashing down on American shoulders with resounding finality. Both the goal and the means employed to achieve victory were loaded with important implications for the South, whose people once again eagerly flocked to their country's colors. Those implications meant change.

Left, although started, and active, in the South, the Ku Klux Klan was most successful in the North. Above, sharecropper in rural Tennessee.

PROM
QUEEN

The changes of the past 100 years had been profound ones for the South. From a profitable, self-sufficient land of plantations and Old World values, it had been transformed into a place of small farms and light industry, dominated by Yankee know-how and dependent on Northern investment. This vast sweep of change is also the context for considering the history of the South in recent times. Is there, as the 21st century dawns, a "South" worthy of the name left at all? To answer that question, it helps to view changes in key areas of Southern life in relation to the rest of the country, especially the social and economic determinants that helped shape Southerners' lives and behavior.

New South Triumphant: The framework for this is a familiar one and might well be described as the "New South Triumphant." The gospel of economic and social change, that Henry Grady and his fellow travelers had crusaded for in the 1870s and 1880s, seemed to take hold with a vengeance. But the difference now was that for the first time in the South's troubled pursuit of progress, the New South actually produced much of what it promised. The years after 1945 saw the development of the much vaunted "affluent society" in America, and Southerners made it known once and for all that they intended to be full partners in it.

Southern boosters proclaimed afresh all the region's advantages: abundant natural resources and sources of energy, congenial state legislatures at the ready with favorable tax laws and additional incentives, a cheap and plentiful supply of labor, and long-deprived markets for durable and consumer goods. The conversion of wartime plants helped start the boom, which soon became self-sustaining as factories multiplied, producing air conditioners, washing machines, farm implements and in time even automobiles, in addition to the old standbys such as textiles and chemicals.

Exhibiting a zeal that matched the bonanza-sized opportunities, Southern leaders in both public and private life ceaselessly put the South's case as the undoubted site of America's next industrial revolution.

Southerners thus kept alive the old scalawag tradition of enticing Northern investment, using the lures of relatively low expenses and high prospective profits. Large Northern-based corporations did enter the South to build plants and factories and hired Southern workers to staff them. Management, while commonly non-Southern at first, was eventually recruited from the native work force.

Left, modern times at a high-school prom. Above, praisin' the Lord down in the Bible Belt.

Industrialization wrought very visible changes in the South's economic life. These ranged from the complete domination of the economies of small towns such as Camden, South Carolina, and Waynesboro, Virginia, by Northern-based corporate giants such as Du Pont and General Electric, to the complete remaking of regional landscapes. This is what happened in the Tennessee Valley where, by the early 1970s, the dams and power plants of the Roosevelt-era Tennessee Valley Authority were turning out 10 percent of the nation's electricity.

Along the Mississippi River, oil refineries and petrochemical plants lined the shore all the way from Baton Rouge to New Orleans. Defense contracts provided an artificial, though highly tangible, boost to industrial growth, and as Cold War military budgets swelled, the South's share of them grew disproportionately. America's space race was run from Southern headquarters whose names became world famous in the 1960s and 1970s: Cape Canaveral in Florida, the Marshall Space Center in Alabama, and the Mission Control Center in Houston, Texas.

Change also came to the land itself, which remained for many Southerners, however they made their living, at the core of their identity. Once the "land of cotton" whose "kingdom" stretched from the Tidewater to Texas, Southern agriculture of the post World War II years turned decisively to other more profitable commodities, and at long last it lived up to the New South's original admonition to farmers to diversify, diversify, diversify. By the 1960s, tree farms were as common as cotton fields and produced approximately a third of the nation's lumber. Southern pastures, which likewise profited from the region's generous growing season, fed beef cattle that produced an income for Southern farmers three times that earned by "the great white staple" of yore.

Commercial poultry production soared, and from the long, low-roofed sheds that became a fixture on thousands of Southern farms there came millions of chickens and turkeys and 40 percent of the nation's eggs. Almost all of America's tobacco continued to be grown in Virginia, Kentucky, and North Carolina, and the South still produced the lion's share of America's cotton, though most of it came from regions west of the Mississippi.

Whatever the ancestral and economic pull of the land, however, the demographics of the post-1945 South told a different story. It was a story of the seemingly ineluctable migration of Southerners from the countryside and small towns to the cities. Industrialization speeded urbanization and breathed fresh, new life into old-fashioned settlements such as Nashville, Richmond, and Charlotte in North Carolina. The South's premier city, Atlanta, Georgia, which had always made much of rising from the ashes left by Sherman's Union army in 1864, set the pace, establishing itself as the commercial and transportation hub (first in the era of the railroad and later in the airline age) of the entire Southeast. This, coupled with the enduring lure of a mild climate and a generally lower cost of living, gave birth to the Sun Belt phenomenon.

Southern cities grew out, not up, and they grew in a hurry. There was no time for, and little interest in, the agglomeration of dense

inner-city neighborhoods; the Sun Belt cities sprouted in the middle-class, white-collar era, and because of an ethnic homogeneity utterly unlike the older industrial cities of the North, their residents tended to sort themselves along simple lines of income and, even after *de jure* segregation was made unlawful, of race. In this sense, the cities' growth conformed to old Southern characteristics. But in their renewed promise of an utterly transformed physical and social landscape, the cities clashed sharply with the region's fundamental conservatism.

Atlanta boasted the first Hyatt House Hotel in America with a revolving rooftop restaurant, and, as in many other matters of urban style, this established a model that commercialized and homogenized Southern downtowns into a bland uniformity. It was as if the only alternative to the backwardness of the region's past lay with ever more modern and ever less critical versions of Atlantan Henry Grady's first New South of a century before. That there would be costs of both a physical and cultural nature had been apparent from that first New South, and the Southerners of the post-World War II generations shared their fathers' ambivalent feelings about change even as they voted with their feet and their new careers for progress.

Left, King's civil rights tackled the issue of segregation; right, violent protest, then success as Harvey Garitt goes to a Carolina law school, 1963.

The single change in the South that very few lamented, and that no one would admit to lamenting anyway, involved the issue that most visibly went to the heart of Southern distinctiveness, which was race.

The old "separate but equal" doctrine, which had governed race relations in the 1890s, came under increasing pressure as a result of the fight against the Nazis in World War II, of the fall of the old colonial empires in Asia and Africa, and of a shift in public opinion that said the overt nature of *de jure* segregation in so many public places offended fundamental American values.

In 1954, the landmark Supreme Court decision of *Brown v. Board of Education* set aside "separate but equal" and opened the door on a tense period during which the forces of state and nation faced off as they had not done since the secession crisis of 1860 and 1861. This time no one talked of leaving the Union, but segregationist Southerners did make a series of creative last stands in a not altogether unsuccessful attempt to slow the steamroller of federally mandated racial equality.

Integration: In 1957, Republican President Dwight D. Eisenhower sent federal troops to

Little Rock, Arkansas, to protect black students at the newly integrated Central High School, and the next years witnessed much talk among Southern governors of "state interposition" and "massive resistance" to hold back the tide. They were not alone, and thousands of ordinary white Southerners rallied to their cry. But the times had changed decisively, and there were now thousands of native Northerners who had come to the South in the postwar economic boom and who were at best indifferent to the system of segregation. States' rights held little allure for them, and in the years of the "sit-in" and the "freedom march," the old racial arrangements of the South crumbled because of both outside pressures and internal weariness.

Federal force was used again in the early 1960s against recalcitrant state governors such as Ross Barnett of Mississippi and George Wallace of Alabama, but it was the nonviolence of black leaders in the South, best exemplified by Martin Luther King, Jr, who had come to prominence during the Montgomery Bus Boycott of 1955, that eventually triumphed.

This was reflected in the passage of the Civil Rights Act of 1964 and of the Voting Rights Act of 1965, which finally completed the work begun by the first Reconstruction following the Civil War. That the pattern of racial arrangements changed so quickly, and with so little social disruption, is testimony both to how truly outdated it had become and to the salient fact that white Southerners, who were in a majority in most parts of the region, no longer needed to fear the tyranny of a vengeful black majority.

In the absence of the bogy of race, and despite the persistent populism that boiled to the surface in the third-party presidential bids of Alabama Governor George C. Wallace and, finally, in the election of Georgian Jimmy Carter to the presidency in 1976 on an anti-Washington platform, a sturdy Republicanism was developing among the prosperous citizens of this newest New South. It was helped, of course, by the election of another Southerner, Bill Clinton from Arkansas, to the presidency in the early 1990s.

Bible Belt: It was not in politics but in religion – in the unadulterated orthodox faith of their fathers – that Southerners continued to find the solace of continuity amid rapid social and economic change. Almost half of Southern church members are Southern Baptists, a denomination so all-embracing and so influential that it has fairly been called the folk church of the South. The secular impact of such religious identification, and of the faith it reflects, is notoriously hard to judge, but there can be no doubt that it contributes mightily to the conservative cultural cast of the region. It is often said that a people weaned on adversity cling to faith because they have known nothing else. If so, it is not surprising that Southerners, who until recently knew much about adversity, should have turned their gaze heavenward.

Even as ruralism and race have faded relatively as defining characteristics of Southern culture, the rock-hard militant Protestantism of the Southern Baptists, of the Methodists, of the Churches of Christ, and of the Southern branch of the Presbyterians qualifies as the greatest remaining conservator of Southernism. These churches offered a sentimental and transcendent brand of the faith that did not welcome social reform and did not encourage racial mixing even long after the battle for black Southerners' civil rights had been fought and won. Of all the institutions that could be said generally to serve the public, none have remained more impervious to racial integration than the churches, and not just the white ones.

The black church, which provided so much of the nurturing ground and leadership for the great victories of the civil rights movement, remains today almost totally black. On both sides of the color line, it seems, the church doors are open, but no one chooses to pass through of his own free will. Nor is it something that troubles most Southern Christians, black or white. In a world where, typically, much is desired and much is promised, the skepticism about materialism that springs from Christian orthodoxy may be the modern South's greatest remaining weapon in defense of a unique regional culture.

Small town values: By contrast, another main theme of Southern history seems to have rather less of a future today, at least in the form that most Southerners once knew it. Ruralism is on the wane, and whatever parallels might be drawn between the small farms idealized by the Southern Agrarians who wrote *I'll Take My Stand* in the 1920s, and the "green revolution" of the 1960s and 1970s, the fact remains that, by 1970, 65 percent of Southerners were classified by the census as urban. Yet this was urbanism Southern-style, and in most cases it was on a smaller scale than elsewhere. Only 25 percent lived in cities with populations over 100,000; 40 percent lived in suburbs or in the 4,500 "cities" of less than 100,000 people. It is frequently remarked that most Southern cities, even the big ones, retain the quality of overgrown country towns. Indeed, many urban residents have only recently come from the country and still have ties there. And, in the 1970 census, there was that hefty 35 percent who were still officially "rural."

These were not the rural folk of Jeffersonian myth: four out of five earned a living "in town," commuting by car to an office or factory, while remaining very much country people in outlook. And while the truly rural population was small, it remained divided much as it had been throughout its history into planters, yeomen, and landless laborers, with all the social distinctions to match.

Left, good ole boys are fond of hunting. Above, carrying coal on the Ohio River, Kentucky.

Finally, poverty and a perceived powerlessness will cease to shape the South's future as they once shaped its past. The new prosperity of the Sun Belt boom is not imaginary; this is the New South in the flesh at last, after all those years of blustery talk. It is no coincidence that the world-wide headquarters of the courier company Federal Express are located in Memphis, Tennessee; that Toyota has opened plants in Kentucky; that North Carolina, home of the vastly profitable R. J. Reynolds tobacco company, boasts both the headquarters of the airline US Air and a highly recognized "Silicon Valley" computer corridor; or that the soaring architectural towers of Atlanta, inspired by local son and internationally reknowned architect John Portman, house many corporate headquarters mentioned in the Fortune 100.

There is no reason to suppose that the new prosperity of the South will not grow even greater in the future. It should not be surprising that the region should at last have opted for Grady and his New South. Backwardness, after all, is picturesque only in fiction and old movies. Like Americans in colder climates, Southerners perceive the good life through a lens that is largely materialistic.

They are subject to the same economic pressures and temptations as other people and, in general, they make their choices from the same broad set of options. And yet there remains a difference that is impossible to quantify and that has nothing at all to do with colonial economies, sharecropping, textile mills, high-tech industries or per capita income. Rather, to use the Southern idiom, it is a matter of accent, and to talk about it is necessarily to deal with matters of taste and personal standards. Consider the following: It is a cliché that any real Southerner will remain polite until he gets mad enough to kill. Not that many kill (although deer hunting and the stalking of small animals remain popular outdoor pursuits, and the prevalence of gun stores takes many a foreign visitor by surprise), but it's true most Southerners remain polite even in this age of "candor" and enlightened free expression. In sophisticated New South cities and on urbane university campuses, one can still witness a certain charming deference of man to woman, of youth to age, of student to teacher.

Only the deaf can fail to notice the still pervasive "no, ma'ams" and "yes, sirs" that punctuate ordinary everyday conversation – leftovers for sure of a more class-conscious age but showing few signs of retreat even in these rigorously egalitarian times. Many of the rituals and restraints of etiquette that seem to have fallen out of use elsewhere still thrive in the South, perhaps less in their more outlandish Sir Walter Scott forms than simply as traditions of courtesy and good manners. Church, home, and family still serve as a prime source of social conventions and of cultural and moral values.

Kin: Consciousness of kin – the saints and the sinners alike – remains powerful and, in a much attenuated form, so does consciousness of class. Despite the great movement of people and wealth into the South from outside, a select gentry survives comprising descendants of antebellum planters who owe their existence more to the power of tradition than to money or influence, which have long since passed to others. There is a distinction in the South between "good family" and "good people" that is not often made in Iowa or Pennsylvania. Admittedly, it is only the shade of an aristocratic tradition, but one that, shorn of its less lovely trappings, has been redeemed.

Its heirs can be stuffy and pretentious at their worst – undistinguished in either abilities or assets. But at their best, they can be a happy exception to the boredom and tastelessness of modern mass culture, through which every man is automatically accorded equality with every other man to achieve a uniformity of low regard. Besides this, character traits such as personal integrity, honor, understated graciousness, and the cultivation of "good living" (as distinct from simply making a good living) are praiseworthy wherever they are found. In this case, all over the South.

New ideas and old industries: left, a Toyota plant in Kentucky; right, sorting tobacco.

LITTER

Southerners divide the world into two parts: the South and the rest of the universe. The authority for this view is unassailable. *Dixie*, the South's national anthem, declares that "the world was made in just six days,/ And finished off in various ways/ Look away! Look away! Look away, Dixie Land!/ God made Dixie trim and nice,/ But Adam called it Paradise,/ Look away! Look away! Look away, Dixie Land." To be a non-Southerner, therefore, is to be excluded from Paradise.

Those unfortunate enough to be outsiders generally base much of their knowledge of Southerners on one novel and its movie version: Margaret Mitchell's 1936 bestseller *Gone With the Wind*, immortalized three years later by MGM. What the entire world has imagined – many as they read the novel in translation, and later had confirmed while watching the film on television – was Scarlett O'Hara with skirts billowing as she floated over Tara's sweeping lawns under blossoming magnolias. This was a limited view of the South even in the 1860s. Trying to fit all Southerners into the mold of Mitchell's main characters is to deny the infinite variety of human beings. Yet Southern types as distinct and classifiable as their well-documented Southern accents do exist – as long as you know what to look for.

Past and present: Defying America's defining characteristic of constantly striving towards a better future, the past in the South defines the present. Once you cross the Mason-Dixon line, that imaginary border between North and South, the past ceases to be the past. It just won't lie down. You might easily find, for example, on a summer afternoon, heated discussions taking place on the porches of numerous homes in Rutherford County, Tennessee, about the details of daring cavalry raids under the command of Lt General Nathan Bedford Forrest in 1864. The men who rode with him were known as Forrest's Escort and most came from the immediate vicinity. The discussion is as animated as if the raid had occurred this morning and news of it had just arrived. Who participated. Who did what. The outcome – as if it were still in doubt. As if it still mattered. But it does matter, to them. If it were known that yo' great-grandpappy did *not* ride with Forrest's Escort, you would be permitted no part in the conversation.

The "living in Paradise" attitude dates back even farther in Southern consciousness. Settlers bound for Virginia were assured in an ode by Michael Drayton (1563–1631) that Virginia is "Earth's only Paradise." The Cavalier/planter/Christian gentleman figure appeared hauntingly in the novels of antebellum writers long before he actually trod the soil of Virginia in the person of the ultimate Southern icon, General Robert E. Lee.

Today's descendants may still own the same land or may be two generations away from it, engaged in a profession or business in the city. But there will still be a strong historical recollection, a family group memory. The land, whether still owned or not, confers a strong sense of place on an individual. It's a sense of rootedness rare in other Americans, whose historical continuity is more fragmented.

Contemporaries who have broken with the past, however, point out problems faced by

Preceding pages: belles in their Easter bonnets, Charleston, South Carolina. Left, harvest time in Franklin, Tennessee. Right, board the train to the choo-choos at Chattanooga.

those held in its thrall. "There's nothing wrong with Mr S—," they might say, "except that he's got ancestors." There's an almost Oriental strength to ancestor worship in the South, the Virginia variety being especially intense, with the Carolinas not far behind.

Low Country legends: The semi-tropical landscape of South Carolina's Low Country, with its weirdness and melancholy scenery, was the setting for Edgar Allan Poe's story *The Gold Bug* – specifically, Sullivan Island at the entrance to Charleston Harbor. Today, dank tarns and funereal, coastal woodlands still abound in legends and superstitions.

One of the most celebrated tales of the Low Country started in the back alleys of Charleston and graduated to successful productions in New York and major European cities, including a performance at Milan's La Scala. The odyssey of a work about South Carolina Gullah African-Americans began with the publication in 1925 of DuBose Heyward's novella *Porgy*. The author, an admirer of the poetry and pathos in the lives of those in Charleston's dilapidated quarter, turned his novella into a play two years later. In 1935, George Gershwin's music joined Heyward's libretto to become the folk opera *Porgy and Bess*. The inevitable Hollywood version followed in 1959. Catfish Row is no minstrel world of stereotypes, though. There's Porgy, crippled but a true hero; Bess, a genuinely seductive heroine; Crown, embodiment of erotic primitive brutality; the bootlegger Sporting Life; the matriarch Maria; Clara and Serena and Jake. No clowns, no Uncle Toms, no Mr Interlocutor. It made a refreshing change.

In pinning down the appeal of these characters, the punchline in an apocryphal Southern anecdote may prove as illuminating as critical analysis. As the story goes, a well-meaning white employer suggests that if his employee's conduct over the weekend had not been so improvident, he would be feeling much better and more like working on Monday morning. The employee replies: "Yessir, boss, that's true, but you ain't never been a black man on a Saturday night." Heyward appreciated what he called this "unique characteristic" in the lives of the African-Americans. He saw the person of African descent as the "inheritor of a source of delight" that he would have given much to possess.

Southern belles: A recent best-selling country song advised unwary males that "there's girls, there's women, and there's ladies." The first and last terms are references to Southern belles and Southern ladies, Scarlett O'Hara and Melanie Wilkes being the two best-known in their respective categories. Matriarchs and spinsters are a sub-class of Southern ladies. "Women" includes all other females such as independent "libbers," Appalachian mountain beauties, poor folks and prostitutes.

The code word for Southern belle among those who are and do not have to concern themselves with definitions is "real cute girl." Never refer in public to a young woman as a Southern belle. No one with pretensions to a high social intelligence quotient would prattle in such a manner. Southern belle is a term of convenience applied by outsiders in their attempts to understand an inexplicable life form.

Over time, the persona of the Southern belle has changed. The definitive description was penned in 1959 by Frances Gray Patton for *Holiday* magazine (today called *Travel*). The modern belle, Patton found, sees her "essentially passive" role at odds with a society increasingly based on assertiveness. She must "excite admiration without appearing to demand it, create an illusion of fragility without looking sick and sustain an atmosphere of gentle gaiety without seeming bat-brained." Her physique, shaped by too many vitamins, proteins and work-outs, doesn't help: no fourth-generation belle can slip into her great-great-grandmother's wedding dress, dancing slippers or tiny white kid gloves. As an added burden, her socio-economic position means that she is "thrown early into competition with the opposite sex – a position rife with hazards of coarseness and strident ambitions."

But then did the "gently nurtured Southern girl" ever really exist outside the gothic Southern imagination? She is the girl with cape jasmine (gardenias to others) in her hair. If they are not in bloom, she wears their fragrance. Her personal aura comprises equal parts of purity and passion. And, no matter what she has been doing all day, she can dance all night in high heels to the melodies generated by juke box, band or full orchestra. Her smile makes the old feel young and the poor feel rich. In her presence any male – be he nine, 19, 49 or 90 – feels alternately soothed and energized, gallant, competent, invincible. She does exist, and she confirms his expectations by always doing what is expected of her.

Left, beauty contests are a local tradition. Above, mortar-board marriage; Southern confidence.

Steel magnolias: The Southern female – now typically called a "steel magnolia" – was originally categorized as a Southern lady who, if she survived multiple childbirths, became a matriarch. In Virginia, there's a saying that it takes three generations to make a gentleman, four to make a lady. Ladies had the responsibility of formulating and ritualizing the social conventions that well-bred girls from Richmond, Nashville, Memphis, and all over the South would be taught from their cradles.

The prevailing image of this lady reigning

from her pedestal appears in Anne Goodwyn Jones's *Tomorrow Is Another Day* (1981): she is "physically pure, fragile and beautiful, socially dignified, cultured, and gracious, within the family sacrificial and submissive, yet, if the occasion required, intelligent and brave." Such a lady referred to her husband only by his title and his surname, a custom that has not entirely disappeared. Forced by circumstances to manage and oversee huge plantations and small farms while their husbands and other male relatives were away from 1861 to 1865, the ladies were loath to return to "china doll" status after the Confederacy's collapse.

Rural realities: The contrast between rural past and urban present is fresher in the Southern consciousness than in other regions because the change from one to the other is so recent. It wasn't so long ago that 85 percent of Southerners made their living from the land, and the number remains high. These are ordinary folks, yeoman farmers, lower class and lower middle class, many of German and Scots-Irish descent. In the Carolinas they are textile workers and tenant farmers who raise tobacco; in the mountain South they are coal miners, loggers and hardscrabble farmers – tilling rocky, unforgiving soil called "creek farms" in eastern Tennessee, where "bottom land," rich loamy soil is scarce and precious. These people live a few miles "out from town" in a house trailer on county-maintained roads that were once wagon ruts and loggers' roads.

The Mountain South, especially Tennessee and Kentucky, has long been home to two small groups whose occupations have excited inordinate interest. In the mountain idiom, they are moonshiners and 'sang diggers ('sang is mountain idiom for ginseng). Like farming, moonshining – the illegal distilling of whiskey – was a family business. Producing mountain dew or white lightnin', two other terms for home-distilled whiskey, was a cash crop in a region where a diligent farmer could end the growing season with a lot of corn and not a penny in his overalls. The generations-old family activity was criminalized when a remote federal government decided to collect a tax on the making of such whiskey. The change led to years of violence in the Appalachian hills and, curiously enough, to the development of the South's favorite sport after football. Stock car racing grew out of the ability of the bootleg runner's high-performance car to outrun the cars of government agents.

Ginseng – *panax quinquefolius*, whose forked roots are credited with medicinal and aphrodisiac properties – became an alternative cash crop. Demand for the plant in Asia is high, pushing prices for wild American ginseng, often considered superior to Chinese and Korean varieties, to over $500 a pound.

Bubbas and good ole boys: The three terms used to describe white Southern males are not synonyms – bubba, redneck, and good ole boy. Bubba is a fellow whose reactions are constrained by his limited intelligence. Two of a bubba's three standard reactions involve shooting: (1) shoot it and have it stuffed for a wall trophy; (2) shoot it and cook and eat it; and (3) marry it. Today's bubba can be rural or urban, may even be the over-indulged, spoiled-brat son of a respected small-town lawyer.

A redneck is rural. The term, not originally derogatory, referred to those who labored in the field (today on the construction site) under the South's hot sun. As a result, their neck acquired a red, ridged appearance. The original rednecks were from humble, but honorable, beginnings. Andrew Jackson, seventh President of the United States, came from such folk.

Today's rowdy redneck often has a fairly hefty income, which he spends on camping equipment, fishing, and on weekends at stock car races. Away from the racetrack, the redneck can still be recognized. All drive pickup trucks. All have profoundly conservative politics.

A good ole boy exemplifies all the masculine virtues esteemed by his region. His life is equally devoted to guns, hunting, fishing, drinking, football and women, seasoned with a dash of nostalgia for trains and Kentucky mountain rainy nights. He is affable, amiable, likeable and stubborn beyond belief – "sot [set] in his ways." One of his main activities is swapping anecdotes with his buddies ("stories" would be his word) in some social group variously called a gun, rifle or hunting club. Typically, the group owns a number of acres in an isolated rural area on which members hunt or target practice on a regular basis. For the good ole boy, hunting acquires mythical proportions. Good ole boys can be found at both the high and low ends of the economic scale. The ones whose fathers never got any farther from home than 'coon hunting in the next county or one trip to the state capital will today casually mention just having returned from a month in Kenya or Tanzania. Many a successful lawyer and state politician, who could pose for the cover of *Gentleman's Quarterly*, calls himself a "good ole boy" when interviewed.

Cheerleaders (<u>left</u>) and marching bands (<u>above</u>) epitomize the small-town values of the South.

Southern accents: Given the fact that there are so many different types of Southerners, don't let anyone tell you, in Southern phraseology, that "there's no such of a thing left." They do exist – in all shapes and accents – all over the South. Along with Charleston poet Hervey Allen, visitors might agree to this pleasant petition: "send me a little garden breeze/ to gossip in magnolia trees."

KEENELAND
10
8
7
6
5
4

2
1

WILL PAY
18480
CHURC HILL OWNS

The Business (and Pleasure) of Horses

Steve Cauthen has a hard time remembering when horses did not form a large part of his life: "I always wanted to be on the back of a horse, to ride, and as fast as I could." That passion has taken Kentucky-born Cauthen to heights which other jockeys can only dream of achieving. By the age of 18, astride Affirmed, he had won thoroughbred racing's Triple Crown, flying first across the finish lines of the Kentucky Derby, the Preakness and the Belmont Stakes, the youngest jockey to do so. Cauthen also is the *only* jockey to win both the English and Kentucky Derbies, plus the equivalent races in France, Ireland and Italy. Retired since 1993, the Hall-of-Fame jockey candidly says: "If I didn't have to keep my weight down, I'd probably be racing till I was 60. Now I ride for the pleasure of riding."

Many Southerners have felt the same passion for horses as Cauthen. During the colonial period, wealthier emigrants brought their thoroughbreds with them. The owner of Oaklands plantation in Virginia had emblazoned over its entrance gate: "There is nothing so good for the inside of a man as the outside of a horse." In 1752, Lord Fairfax not only transported his horses to Virginia from England, but his hounds as well, and was a fox-hunting companion of George Washington.

Early days: Virginia lore says that horse racing officially began in the United States in the mid-1600s. Races were usually held on quarter-mile long straightaways where horses would race two at a time, and the one with the most wins at the end of the day was declared the winner. Instead of a cash prize, tobacco, a valuable commodity, was given to the owner.

When pioneers moved westward, their horses went, too. As the late Joe Estes wrote in *Blood-Horse* magazine: "The settlers in Kentucky were in the main from Virginia and the Carolinas, a people of cavalier associations, among whom racing had long been accepted as the sport of kings. When they brought horses with them beyond the Alleghenies, it was as much a matter of course as when they brought their rifles and powder horns."

Preceding pages: Keeneland, Lexington, Kentucky. Left, winners' circle after the Derby. Right, a horse farm near Aiken, South Carolina.

One of the first nine laws enacted by the Boonesborough Assembly in 1775 was aimed toward improving and controlling the breeding of horses. Irish-born William Whitley was so passionate about racing that he built a racecourse before a home. In 1788, he began building a house near Stanford, south of Lexington. That same year, Whitley started, and finished, the first oval race track in the United States (the house was completed in 1794). Fervently anti-British, Whitley ran the races counterclockwise, contrary to the English manner, a practice which is still in use at all US tracks.

Kentucky's Bluegrass region is its horse country, with the highest concentration of horse farms in the world. Culture is one reason, but nature provided another: the rich and well-drained land has always afforded superb grazing pastures and a soft footing to help develop the hard feet and bones needed by racers. Another bonus was limestone: the region is filled with massive deposits of it, and as water filtered through it, the phosphates in the rock not only enriched the soil, but added strength to horses' bones as they drank and nibbled.

What the horses grazed on, and gave Kentucky its sobriquet The Bluegrass State, is, sad to say, neither blue nor indigenous. Healthy bluegrass is a dark green; but, in the spring, the plant produces a very small purple flower and, when viewed from afar, the large sweeps of grass may appear "blue," hence the name.

Selling and buying: Whether it is ponies for youngsters learning to ride or an expensive yearling, more foals are produced in Kentucky than in any other state, and they must be sold in order to make room for the next crop. There are other horse auction centers throughout the US, but Lexington is considered the most important one. Tattersalls, based at Red Mile Race Track, specializes in Saddlebred and Standardbred horses. Fasig-Tipton and the

Lexington Horse Center auction Thoroughbreds and other breeds, but the Keeneland Sales usually attracts the best horses. Auctions didn't exist at Keeneland until World War II when the first sales were held in 1943. Before then, all breeders sent their horses to the Saratoga Sales, held in a small town in upstate New York, where the racing aristocracy spent each August. The war curtailed all but essential traffic, and breeders were forced to find a market closer to home.

Keeneland, often called the nation's prettiest track, opened its dark green gates for the first time in 1936. Its two annual meetings, three weeks each in the spring and in the fall, are timed to occur when the track is at its glorious best, and from the pastels of April to the blazing reds and gold of October, Keeneland's beauty is unsurpassed. If any track can be classified as "laid back," then it is Keeneland. Instead of concrete lots, racegoers usually park their cars under long rows of shade trees. Unusually, loudspeakers are banned, so there's no commentary during any race, and, unlike many tracks, no special passes are needed to visit the stable area which is open to all racegoers. But Kentucky has no lock on a racing tradition or a piece of the industry. In South Carolina, both Camden and Aiken are thriving horse centers, with an equine industry valued at $500 million a year.

Once the summer capital for Charlestonians wishing to escape the city's malaria season, Aiken withered after the Civil War. Only a marriage between a southern heiress and a Yankee gentlemen sportsman in the last decade of the 19th century revitalized the city. Tommy and Louise Hitchcock wanted to spend winters in a temperate climate, and because both had relatives nearby, they built an estate in Aiken. They were a congenial couple,and soon a bevy of Mellons, Vanderbilts, Whitneys, and other wealthy horse lovers came to visit.

Many built mansions complete with stables, training courses and polo fields. During the 1920s and 1930s, private freight trains would descend upon Aiken each November carrying horses, grooms, tack and, in some cases, special food for their four-legged friends. In March, when the "season" ended, the process was reversed. Around town, carriages pulled by matched horses (sometimes with liveried footmen and drivers) were the preferred method of travel, and to make it easier on the horses' hooves, most streets were left unpaved.

Although Aiken no longer has the cachet it once did, the working stables remain. (Several Kentucky Derby winners were trained locally.) The stables work year round (unlike Camden whose season lasts only from October through May), and the Sunday afternoon polo matches draw large crowds.

The official name of the race is the "Camden Cup," but most locals call it the "world's largest outdoor cocktail party." It is held the last Saturday in March, when as many as 75,000 people head for Camden's Springdale racecourse for a day of steeplechasing and flat racing. For women, "Spring Finery" is the order of the day, and tail-gate parties, using china, silver, and crystal utensils with linen napkins, rather than plastic and paper, are part of the ritual. The Cup, first run in 1930, is one of steeplechasing's most prestigious events, and the best in the breed compete for it.

Camden became fashionable in the 1920s when Ernest L. Woodward (who founded the Jello-O company) made Camden his winter home. Steeplechasing was his equestrian love, and he was one of the founders of the Camden Cup race. Upon her death, Mrs Marion du Pont, another enthusiast, donated Springdale racecourse to Camden, thus providing the horse fraternity a permanent place to race.

Billions of dollars: From the $2 gambler to the Queen of England, this Southern industry today derives billions of dollars from its horse flesh. Untold numbers of jobs depend upon the four-legged animals ranging from jockeys to trophy makers. Most, like Larry Fowler, a "silks" man, are unseen by the public.

A former jockey who rode until his height and weight took him over the allowed limit, Fowler spends half the year dividing his time between Keeneland and Churchill Downs. (The rest of the year, he makes custom-designed riding crops for active jockeys.) During the two meets, Fowler logs in each vibrantly colored jacket and cap ("silks") which jockeys wear while racing. He sets up a daily distribution system, and makes sure they're cleaned properly afterward.

"Each owner," says Fowler, "must register the colors and design of his or her silks." Although no two designs can be alike, many are similar, and it's easy to get them mixed-up. To add to the confusion, some owners will enter one horse only during a meet, while others may have a large number of horses running. There also can be over 100 different owners at any meet, but luckily they don't all send their silks at the same time.

Left, Steve Cauthen, jockey and youngest winner of racing's Triple Crown. Above, Larry Fowler and jockeys' silks (*left*); Charlie and Paige Kahn of Le Cheval, bespoke tailors (*right*).

"The silks, with the owner's name printed on each piece, are brought to the track by the horse's trainer. It's my responsibility to make sure that each jockey knows on which peg 'his' silks are hanging, and that the proper set for each race is on the correct peg. With up to 20 horses in one race, it gets hectic; another headache occurs when one owner has a horse in each race, but the trainer has only given us three or four sets of silks. That's when the washer and dryer here are life savers."

Personal pleasures: Southerners take their horseback pleasure in many guises; at the beginner level, ponies are often ridden by those still learning to walk. Some like to keep an old "nag" for quiet rides, whereas others prefer the excitement of polo, horse shows, or four-in-hand carriage driving contests.

Those who like to combine the thrill of steeplechasing with racing join local fox hunts. Most Southern states have active hunts, but none as extensive as the one centered in Middleburg in northern Virginia, which has eight hunt clubs covering five counties. It is no longer a sport for the landed gentry, and most members today hold down a job and ride only on weekends. Foxes are rarely the object of a hunt. Instead, the night before a meet, scented rags are dragged through the countryside. No one seems to care: "It's the chase, the ride, the comraderie," is the phrase most often heard.

Followed by: "and the freedom."

Many foxhunters, and those who compete in horse shows and show jumping, head for (or call) Le Cheval, a Kentucky riding-apparel shop, to order their riding clothes. Charlie and Paige Kahn are continuing the tradition begun by his father, "Whitey" Kahn, making bespoke habits for a mostly amateur clientele. "Most of our clients," says Charlie, "participate in shows where appearance is part of the judging, and they need to look their best. For the serious competitor, a custom-made jacket is a wise investment."

"Like fashion everywhere," says Paige, "styles in the horse world change. It could be the length of the jacket, or the type of pleats, but everyone is aware of new trends, and usually want one. We also have ready-made jackets in stock, but our clients usually buy those for pleasure riding."

Native sons and daughters: Only two horse breeds are Southern-born. The Saddlebred Horse is the breed native to Kentucky. It was created by crossing thoroughbred stallions with easy-gaited mares of Galloway stock which were brought to America from Ireland and England. The result was a horse of endurance, beauty and strength, which took easily to a saddle. During the early 1800s, when most travel was on horseback, these easy-gaited horses were in great demand. By 1824, over 4,000 of them had been sent to eastern US markets.

The Saddlebred today is known for its ability to be trained to perform not only the three normal gaits (walk, trot and canter), but to learn two artificial ones, the slow gait and the rack (all out speed). This last gait is a specialty of those Saddlebreds trained to show in harness, and many a spectator's pulse quickens its beat when the ring announcer roars: "Let 'em rip!" A quick flick of the drivers' whips, and away fly these speedsters, a circle of elegant Pegasuses.

Called the "World's Greatest Show and Pleasure Horse" by its devotees, the Tennessee Walking Horse evolved over a century. The first acknowledged "walker" was foaled in 1837 in central Tennessee. Called Bald Stockings because of his white face and four white feet, the horse was remembered as a high-stepping, stylish animal. Breeders then mated trotters and pacers and, by the beginning of the 20th century, there emerged a horse ranging in size from 15 to 17 hands (a hand equals 5 inches/13 cm), weighing an average of 1,000 lbs (455 kg), with a calm disposition and three gaits. The most common, the flat-foot walk, gave the horse its name; the gait requires no posting, and a horse can easily cover 5 to 7 miles (8 to 11 km) an hour. In 1950, the Tennessee Walking Horse was recognized as a distinct breed by the United States Department of Agriculture. To ensure the breed's purity (and against fraud), all stallions, mares and foals must be blood-typed. Celebrity Walkers include Roy Rogers' Trigger, Jr, and Gene Autry's Champion.

Left, fox hunting in Virginia.

The Kentucky Derby

At 5.30pm on the first Saturday each May, the world's sporting attention is focused on Churchill Downs, a race track in Louisville. That's the starting time for the Kentucky Derby, arguably the most famous race in the world, and the first leg in thoroughbred racing's Triple Crown for three-year old horses. (The other two are The Preakness and The Belmont Stakes.) The Derby is also known as "The Run for the Roses" because of the blanket of roses which is draped over the winning horse.

This is no ordinary garland, by the way. It is created by specially trained staff of the Kroger grocery chain. To watch it being made, inquire in late April at any Louisville-area Kroger store for the address of that year's garland maker. Work commences a few days before the Derby.

It was desperation that created the Derby. In the early 1870s Louisville had no track and breeders threatened to move their stables to Lexington, which did have racing facilities, unless the situation was remedied. Lewis Clark, Jr, a local businessman, was asked to study the possibilities. Knowing little of racing, Clark journeyed to Europe where he studied the more sophisticated English system.

On his return, Clark informed investors that he believed the way to success was to pattern a series of stake races after the great English classics. The centerpiece would be a Kentucky Derby, modeled on the Derby held at Epsom.

Land was leased from the Churchill family, a track quickly built, and in 1875 the first Derby run. Since then, except for a ban on racing during World War II, the 1¼-mile Derby has been a firm fixture on the US racing calendar. Aristides, ridden by Oliver Lewis, a black jockey, was the first winner. (In the 19th century, few jockeys were white.) Eddie Arcaro and Bill Hardtack each have ridden a record five Derby winners. In 1970, Diane Crump became the first female jockey to break into the hitherto all-male fraternity.

Only three fillies have worn the blanket of roses; 11 Derby winners went on to take the Triple Crown, including Virginia-bred *Secretariat* whose 1973 Derby win set a record. The most famous non-entrant was Man O'War, a great racehorse whose owner thought the Derby too strenuous.

A crowd in excess of 125,000 watches a maximum of 20 horses compete for a $1 million guaranteed purse. Box seats are sold out years in advance, and stories abound of heirs wrangling over who gets the deceased's box. *The* place to be is in one of the Sky Terraces (predictably known as "Millionaire's Row"). Here one sits around tables atop carpeted floors while waiters serve drinks and food. For most women, hats are *de rigueur* and, in some cases, the more flamboyant the better.

Above, a wet Derby at Churchill Downs, Louisville.

Those with no reservations, little money and a sense of fun, head to the track infield where (almost) anything goes – from mud wrestling to, in one case, the unexpected birth of a baby. Only the start of the Derby calls a momentary halt to the high jinks.

The Derby wouldn't be the Derby without a Mint Julep. Classically, this bourbon whiskey concoction is served in a sterling silver cup, so cold that the cup is frosted. (At the Derby, juleps come in commemorative glasses and are sold by vendors like popcorn at a baseball game.) For the owner of the winning horse, a special ritual exists: after the race, he (or she) drinks a toast to the horse from a sterling julep cup; the horse's name and the year are engraved on it, and it's added to the collection owned by Churchill Downs.

For casual spectators, the Derby is as much about partying as the race; the Derby Festival is a two-week extravaganza at which Mint Juleps feature strongly.

There are as many recipes for making a Mint Julep as there are bourbon brands, but here is the one which the author inherited from her father (who was famous for his Derby parties): a week before The Day, make a simple syrup by boiling up equal parts sugar and water (figure one-half cup water per expected guest); cool, put in a lidded container, add several sprigs of fresh mint, close, and refrigerate. On Derby Day, remove syrup from refrigerator, discard mint and bring syrup to room temperature.

Rub interiors and rims of sterling silver cups (if not available, use 8-ounce glasses) with fresh mint leaves, then pack with shaved ice and place in freezer for one hour. Just before serving, fill a pitcher with one-quarter syrup and three-quarters Kentucky Bourbon; mix well. Take cups from freezer, pour liquid over the ice, and garnish each drink with a sprig of mint. ■

paco
paris

DOLLS, DULCIMERS AND OTHER CRAFTS

Most crafts have traditions in common: people work with materials they have at hand; they fabricate what they see around them; and they produce things they need. The American South has a particularly rich heritage of craft traditions. This has come about from the blending of diverse cultures – Native American, European and African – and adapting to one environment while borrowing from another. At the same time, all had to look to themselves to provide for their own necessities.

By the end of the 19th century, however, inexpensive factory-made products released people from the often laborious and tedious processes needed to produce items such as crockery, quilts and even toys. As the need for self-sufficiency diminished, so did many of the traditions. However, it is still possible to find a few forms of traditional Southern crafts which have survived and thrived.

Dolls: On almost every toy shelf, amid the jumble of games, crayons and mechanical toys, the face of a doll peeks through. This toy has a long history. In 1585, artist John White sketched a young Native American girl clutching a stylishly fashioned English doll. It had been traded to the Indians by members of his English expedition, which had just landed off the coast of North Carolina.

Her properly dressed English doll, though, was not typical of what most Southern children owned then. More characteristic were the doll forms learned from the Indians, made of materials that were nearby and abundant – apples and nuts, corncobs and corn shucks – and decorated with pokeberry juice for mouths and dots of soot for eyebrows.

Apple-head dolls, made from carved fresh apples left to dry and shrivel, are a traditional doll form still being made today, and long common in the Mountain South. The skills to make apple-head dolls, like other Southern folk crafts, have been passed down from one generation to the next. Whether they are braided from coarse moss grown in coastal areas or carved from tight-grained wood found high in the mountains, handmade dolls have a unique and strange beauty.

Preceding pages: African-American quilt. Left, apple-head dolls. Right, North Carolina dulcimer.

Dulcimers: The mountain dulcimer is one of the oldest instruments in the United States and, like the banjo, is a unique indigenous form. It originated in the Appalachians and, until recently, was made only there. Like many other craft objects, the dulcimer had European origins familiar to the immigrants who settled in the mountain areas of the South. The Swedish *hummel*, the Norwegian *langelaik* and the German *sheitholt* are among its ancestors. While the shapes of the instruments differed from culture to culture, the principle was the

same: strings stretched across an elongated hollow wooden box were plucked, or "swept," with the fingers or a pick to produce sound.

Easily constructed, lightweight and therefore portable, the mountain or Appalachian dulcimer has enjoyed a popularity for generations. As it is played sitting down, it is perfect for quiet, intimate occasions, usually accompanying a single voice. With the introduction of the guitar to America in the early 20th century, however, and the subsequent emergence of amplified music, the quiet sound of the solo dulcimer could not compete. It was saved by the folk music revival of the 1950s.

Today, dulcimermakers in the South are still

producing the narrow-bodied instruments by hand. Although made in several shapes, including teardrop, waspwaist and hourglass, the basic elongated configuration of strings stretched along the top of a narrow hollowed box has not changed for centuries.

Quilts: Few objects in American history have been so treasured as the quilt. As diverse as the people who create them, quilts have been made here since the earliest days of settlement. Although documentation of quiltmaking by colonists is limited, it is believed that the earliest quilts were hurriedly put together, with little decoration, to fend off the cold of wilderness winters. As soon as families became more settled, quiltmaking became more elaborate. Pioneer women used them to beautify their homes, as well as provide warmth.

The patterns these early quiltmakers developed were clear reflections of their lives and stand as historic testaments. Births, deaths, struggles and joys are all reflected in designs that have been passed down, relatively unchanged, for generations. Some of the patterns, such as Straight Furrow, Barn Raising and Wagon Wheel, were named for the obvious elements in their daily lives. Others were modeled after things in nature, such as Harvest Sun, North Carolina Lily and Flying Geese. Patterns were freely exchanged at get togethers such as at quilting bees, barn raisings, agricultural fairs and other gatherings. They were also spread in rural areas by traveling ministers carrying quilt patterns in their saddlebags and by peddlers who, along with pans, knives and sewing notions, brought news of the latest designs.

When quilts became worn, their usefulness did not end. They were draped over the inside of doorways to block the cold, used as padding on tractor seats, or spread over potatoes, apples or other fruits and vegetables that could not be allowed to freeze. Sometimes they became the stuffing for another quilt. Another use was as a cover for harvested tobacco plants in the tobacco barn to prevent the leaves drying out and falling off the stems.

Quilts are also familiar objects in black history. A rich heritage of handicrafts, textile skills among them, accompanied the slaves brought to America from areas that are now Senegal, Ghana, Nigeria and Angola. Quiltmaking was an active part of plantation life for them. Although the techniques of quilting were largely European in origin, the black women incorporated African-derived design elements into their own quilts, and the result was a distinctly African-American patterning tradition that continues to this day.

Contrasting with the tight, symmetrical designs, even and repetitive patterns, and fine, delicate stitching of European-American quilts,

African-American examples are often characterized by random and asymmetrical patterning, bright colors, and a sense of improvisation that can be compared to jazz. Large designs are emphasized and can be seen quite easily from a distance in bright sunlight, a throwback to one of the necessary functions of African clothing. Birds, fish, pigs, human forms and other figurative motifs often appear as appliquéed designs, remnants of the strong communicative function of African textiles.

Today, more people practice quilting than any other craft form in the South. Among them are women who continue as their families have for generations, piecing and working patterns that have become as familiar to them as the images in their family photo albums. Whether their reasons for their diligence is utilitarian or artistic, or both, they are maintaining their connections with the past in remarkable ways.

Baskets: Basketry is one of the oldest known crafts in the world. Some archeologists believe that baskets preceded pottery. Basket specimens uncovered in American digs have been dated as far back as 5000 BC. The early European settlers combined their imported basketry skills with techniques they learned from Native Americans. In contrast, the basketry traditions brought by slaves from Africa remained distinct. Yet each tradition – European, Indian and African – was centered on meeting the everyday needs of rural farm life.

When we think of oak, images of towering, rigid trees come to mind, trees that provide the lumber to build churches and furniture. It is not difficult to understand, then, that the thin, pliable strips peeled from oak trees have produced some of the most durable baskets. Because split oak is pliable as well as strong, it was used to make baskets for a variety of functions, ranging from huge, round hampers for collecting cotton to small "cheek" or "hip" baskets for collecting eggs.

Although baskets made of oak splits or wood peelings are common to almost all traditional communities in the South, the bountiful supplies of white oak in the mountains and valleys of Kentucky, Tennessee and North Carolina have helped maintain the traditions of split-oak basketmaking. There are entire communities, such as those in Cannon County, Tennessee, where almost every family includes either a basketmaker or chairmaker working with white oak and producing the same objects as their forebears did.

Growing densely along the banks and streams of Southern states, common river cane has been the basket material most used by Native Americans in the South. This plant has played

<u>Left</u>, Kentucky quiltmakers Annie Sheroan and Louise Barr. <u>Above</u>, South Carolina basketry.

a vital role in dozens of Native American cultures, including the Cherokees in the Great Smoky Mountains of North Carolina. They fashioned weapons, tools, building materials and even hair ornaments from the plant. But of all the skills at which these native people excelled, the plaiting of river cane into exquisite baskets remains unequaled. The traditions of these tribes are among the most highly developed and active in the South today.

Honeysuckle, a common plant, has only recently been adopted for use by Southern basketmakers. Less than a century ago it was introduced as a material for basketry by immigrants from Japan, where it is commonly used. Although honeysuckle is not strong enough to be used in burden and work baskets, basketmakers have chosen its long, slender stems for making smaller, decorative baskets.

The drive along Highway 17 from Mount Pleasant to Charleston, South Carolina is dotted with dozens of simple wooden stands, each festooned with intricately coiled sweetgrass baskets. The creators of these baskets, descendants of the slaves who worked South Carolina's rice plantations, are the only group of black craftspeople to continue a tradition several hundred years old. They also speak a distinctive patois known as Gullah.

On plantations in the South Carolina Low Country, vital roles were performed by the slaves who brought these basketry skills from their West Africa homelands. Their coiled baskets made from bulrushes and sweetgrass were used everywhere on the plantation, from the rice fields to the Big House. One basket form, the fanner basket used for winnowing rice, was brought directly from Africa. Others, such as the wall-mounted half-baskets, were influenced by European forms that the slaves copied. Derivatives of all these shapes can still be found today along Highway 17 and in Charleston.

Pottery: In the early 19th century, pottery was an important handicraft industry wherever natural clay was present, and especially in central North Carolina and northern Georgia. As the settlers multiplied, so did the need for utilitarian pottery. Staples of their typical diet – salt-cured meats, molasses, milk products, lard, vegetables, whiskey – were processed, stored, preserved and served in churns, jugs, crocks, pitchers and "dirt dishes," named after their earthen origin.

Despite family potting traditions that spanned generations, many Southern potters could not adjust to the variations in the market when inexpensive, factory-made products began to compete. However, some moved their shops to more traveled roads, taking advantage of the growing tourist industry. They expanded their repertoire to accommodate the demand for more decorative ware, which was designed to be more visually appealing as well as useful. Old forms were given new functions – churns became planters, chamber pots casseroles. And face jugs, made by Southern potters since the Civil War, became more popular.

Today's Southern pottery is still linked to the past by form and technique. A few family-operated potteries still produce the traditional shapes – the jugs, the kraut jars, the deep, fluted pie plates. These potters turn their wares by hand, using many of the old methods developed and refined by preceding generations. Many also continue to dig their own clay, and a few still fire their wares with wood in homemade groundhog kilns. Among those who continue to make pots, there remains a regard for their materials. And among those who buy – as with all homemade crafts – there is a respect for the artisan's ability to fashion a beautiful object from a formless mass.

Left, unfinished white oak basket, Tennessee. Right, a face jug created by Burlan Craig.

OLD HATCHET
CORN Planter
COFFEE
COFFEE
COFFEE
COFFEE
Virginia's Finest

SHEEP SHEARER
Foot Adze
Virginia WINES
Wertz's Country Store
Wertz's

The American South, in language, culture and cuisine, strikes many visitors as antiquated. The truth is, the American South is about as close to the country's origins as it is possible to be. A quick glance at its culinary roots clearly shows how much the past can be the present.

Virginia and the Carolina coast, with their strong connections to widely traveled plantation society, always savored a more luxurious, complex cuisine than inland areas. North Carolina, home to the Moravians, who originated in Germany, sees their influence in the cooking (and architecture), around Old Salem, which the Moravians founded in the 18th century.

It is in the American Piedmont where fine cooking first came to these shores, especially to the plantation homes of the wealthy. Early cookbooks such as *Virginia Housewife* (1824), *Kentucky Housewife* (1839) and *Carolina Housewife* (1847) show a cuisine replete with European references. Thomas Jefferson, a Virginian and the third US president, is generally regarded as America's first gourmet. The dishes he served were sophisticated, French and rich, although, when dining alone, he preferred vegetables, viewing meat as "a condiment."

Plantation cooking: If anything distinguishes the cooking of this northern tier of Southern states from the southern tier, it's the geography, points out Scott Peacock, an Alabama native, chef and Southern food historian who is based in Atlanta. Peacock has studied extensively in Virginia, and he points out that the affluent planters, who traveled widely, brought back many culinary concepts. "It's the French influence that you see there, " he says "especially in the desserts." *Langues de chat, blancmange* and similar French desserts are standard fare in Virginia even now, among both black and white cooks.

By the end of the Civil War, the ability of plantation Southerners to sustain this elegant level of cooking had greatly diminished. Young people throughout the Confederacy were reduced to sipping water in wine glasses at social affairs. Yet in 1864, Varena Howell Davis, first lady of the Confederacy, threw a luncheon at the Confederate White House in Richmond, Virginia, at which she served everything imaginable, from duck and gumbo to oysters and champagne. Gossips figured she had bought the provisions on the black market, because a ham then went for $350 and sugar $20.

Today, young chefs across the South are busy rediscovering what Louis Osteen of Louis's Charleston Grill in South Carolina calls the new plantation cooking.

"That's where the finest food in the South was made," he says. Today, his "plantation suppers" menu reflects the culinary traditions of South Carolina's upper echelons. The food rings of tradition – duck and okra gumbo, brown oyster stew with benne (sesame) seeds, pickled shrimp, sweetbreads with field mushrooms and sherry.

For many of the early plantation dwellers, black folks were the keepers of the flame. Like James Hemming, Thomas Jefferson's slave/chef both in France and at Monticello, the role of black chefs in plantation life was

<u>Preceding pages</u>: family-owned deli in Roanoke, Virginia. <u>Left</u>, colonial cooking, Old Salem, North Carolina. <u>Right</u>, Memphis catfish.

critical. The all-important barbecue pit men were usually black, and they not only cooked European dishes, but also brought ingredients and methods of their own to the New World.

Edna Lewis, the grande dame of Southern cooking, grew up in Orange County, Virginia. Her ancestors, freed slaves who were deeded land after Emancipation, carried with them a cuisine that was strictly seasonal, and one that melded English, French and African sources. Her family prepared *boeuf à la mode*, kidney pie in puff pastry and black-eyed peas, all recipes she includes in her autobiographical cookbook *The Taste of Country Cooking* (Knopf, 1985).

Gumbo, perhaps the most quintessential American dish, is an African word referring to okra, and both the pod and the term gumbo came to the New World via the slave trade. Although associated by many with the Creole (French/Spanish/African) and Cajun (French Acadian) cooking of Louisiana, gumbo is enjoyed all around the South from Louisiana to Virginia.

Slaves were also credited with bringing to these shores benne seeds, hidden in their hair and planted in rows near their cabins for good luck, yams (botanically different from sweet potatoes) and black-eyed or cow peas.

"Goobers" is the African-origin name for peanuts, a native New World plant; an old Civil War song tells of a soldier "eating goober peas." Peanut soup is a classic of Virginia cooking, and its composition is similar to versions found in West Africa.

Soul food: So what, then, of "soul food," a term that arose in the mid-20th century as an offshoot of the civil rights movement? The term seems to have arisen in the North among young black people whose forebears left the South generations earlier. Eager to reclaim their lost heritage, these blacks promoted a kind of cooking they thought re-created the dishes of their ancestors.

"Soul food" supposedly denotes dishes only black folks ate, such as chitlins (deep-fried small pig intestines), collard greens, pork neck bone and pigs' feet. But these are the dishes of both races. Saley, South Carolina, holds an annual chitlins festival, and at least as many white people come as blacks.

Pork, for instance, is the ubiquitous meat for all Southerners. "Oh," said a New Yorker recently, "nobody eats pork any more." Don't tell that to a Southerner of either race. Pork is cooked from the ears to the tail. Attend a bash at Tennessee Valley Winery near Loudon, Tennessee, and you'll likely see two of the porcine creatures, each weighing anywhere from 150–250 lbs (70–110 kg), being cooked in huge, black-lidded cookers. They may be stuffed with sauerkraut and apples, or Bermuda onions. The meat is pulled off the frame and presented with assorted barbecue sauces. It is sweet, tender, smoky and divine.

Southerners take the subject of barbecue sauce very seriously, and no two taste alike. In Virginia, the typical sauce is tomato-based, with only a dash of pepper and vinegar. But at Bubba's Barbecue, in Charlotte, North Carolina, it is the sweet, smoky meat, liberally anointed with peppery, vinegar-based sauce that everybody flocks to eat. Traditionally, the meat is topped with coleslaw before being enclosed with the top bun.

South Carolinians have another style of barbecue sauce, not usually found outside the state, based on mustard. "That's for hot dogs," a Georgia gourmet growled disapprovingly. In Kentucky, particularly in the western part of the state, barbecue sauce is based on tomato, vinegar and spice, and mutton is a popular meat to grill. Tennesseans throw another version into the mix called a Memphis dry rub barbecue, in which spices are rubbed dry onto the meat, covering the surface with an aromatic flaky texture.

Beside pork, game is an important aspect of Southern fare. Hunters are probably responsible for two of the region's most popular dishes which are Brunswick Stew, originating most likely in Virginia, and Burgoo, a similar dish from Kentucky. Squirrels, rabbits and sundry birds, shot by a family's male offspring for the evening meal were commonplace in many households, and birds of all kinds – turkey, dove and quail – are still popular today.

Catfish: If not hunting, Southerners often fished for supper. Catfish, peculiar whiskered critters, is served skinned, filleted or whole, rolled in cornmeal and fried. Shad, George Washington's favorite fish, was the spring treat in Virginia, and still is. Trout is a popular fish throughout the region, where it is floured and fried, grilled and smoked. Enterprises in the region are doing brisk business in smoked trout pâté and whole smoked trout. Along the coast, mullet is viewed as poor man's fare, but when smoked, it becomes fit for a king.

Left, Louis Osteen of Louis's Charleston Grill with his delicacy, she-crab soup. Above, catering a ladies' luncheon in Russellville, Kentucky.

Shrimp, oysters, mussels and crab abound along the coast of Virginia and the Carolinas. Besides frying shrimp, Southerners will pound them into a paste, pickle them, and make fritters, pies and soups. Crabs make coastal cooking splendid, whether soft-shell and deep fried or sautéed, or deviled, in crab cakes or in that Low Country delicacy, she-crab soup. For this delicious creation, female crabs are essential, as it is their roe that adds the richness to the soup.

The range of Southern vegetables is enormous and include peas (crowder, field, purple hull, black-eyed or cow peas, sugar snaps); beans (lima, butter, snap, pole); greens (turnip, kale, mustard, collard); salisfy (called vegetable oyster in *Kentucky Housewife*); sweet potato and yams; squash (acorn, butternut, pattypan, crook-neck). Other regions of the country do not have many of these vegetables.

Corn is the chief vegetable of the South, providing that breakfast staple known as grits, an item that causes reactions ranging from bewilderment to anger. Likely arising from Native Americans, the corn is treated with lye which causes it to swell – thus producing hominy. This swollen corn may be cooked as is and served as a side dish, or dried and ground, producing hominy grits – or just plain grits for short. For breakfast, grits are served with butter, pepper and salt as a side dish with a fried egg – never as cereal with milk and sugar.

Grits and grillades: Beyond breakfast, grits appear as the starch in "grits and grillades," grits with beef or veal strips and gravy, and the now-popular cheese grits casserole and garlic grits soufflé. Think of grits as Southern polenta, and you may become comfortable with them, at least after a while. Do not, however, eat them after a night on the town, and if they're lumpy – send them back.

Sweet dreams: Desserts are where Southern cooking really shines. From Virginia's Tyler Pie, with an egg-sugar-vanilla filling, to pecan (pronounced "puh-caan") pie, to sweet potato pie, vinegar pie and buttermilk pie, home-baked goods in the South have a deserved reputation. Fruit cake is essential at holiday time, and coconut, gingerbread, pound and caramel cake are standard fare the rest of the year.

In Tennessee, apple stack cake and jam cake are commonplace. No Southern dessert table would be complete without cobbler – fruit baked under a top crust, and served warm with ice cream or whipped cream. Cookies and candies (especially fudge) are also high on the list of treats.

Fruit preserves, jams, marmalades and jellies make extra sweetening throughout the year. Southerners grow figs, pears, plums, cherries and just about any fruit tree or bush you can imagine, with the fruit finding its way into both sweet and savory preserves.

Despite the region's reputation for being conservative, things do change here. Never much fond of pasta except in macaroni and cheese, today Southerners eat about as much pasta as any other region in the United States. Some of this change is due to the arrival of people from other parts of the country, some due to locals traveling themselves. Young Southerners may take to the starchy stuff with eagerness, but native-born matrons planning at-home affairs still sternly advise caterers not to offer pasta, especially pasta salads. Purists won't touch them.

Other changes in demographics have brought new food to the South, including Chinese, Mexican and Japanese. Popular though all this is, when a Southerner gets really hungry, he thinks about his food roots. There was once a tale, likely false, about authors William Faulkner and Katheryn Anne Porter supposedly dining at La Tour d'Argent in Paris. Having finished a fabulous repast, Faulkner, so the story goes, said to Porter: "The corn is just about coming in now at home." And she, sighing nostalgically, added: "Yes, and the butter beans, too."

Left, country hams from the South are famous throughout the United States.

KENTUCKY BOURBON

Stinginess, or, as a good reverend might have put it, "Waste not, want not," was responsible for the distilled spirit which Kentuckians call their own. In the 18th century, making whiskey was an honorable profession, even for a man of the cloth. He was allowed to drink an occasional dram, too. The practice of preachers having a second occupation began when they could not earn a living solely by the Lord. A Baptist minister, the Rev. Elijah Craig, operated a grist and rolling mill, along with a distillery where he fermented a clear, corn-based whiskey at Royal Spring, on the outskirts of Georgetown.

The year bourbon whiskey came into existence, 1789, is not in question, but history is divided over *how* the drink actually came to be. One story has a fire sweeping through the barn where Rev. Craig kept the barrels he used for storing distilled liquor. Another tells of a hapless slave who accidentally charred the wrong barrels. All sides agree that the Reverend *was* something of a skinflint, and didn't want the expensive barrels thrown away. The clear alcoholic brew was poured into the burnt barrels, and presto, a few months later out came a dark, rich and, in comparison to Craig's previous liquor, very smooth tasting liquid. The new drink was an instant success, and throughout the state, distillers began charring their barrels. (Louisville, Paris, and Bardstown also claim to be the site of the first bourbon whiskey distillery, but history generally credits the Georgetown story.)

In order to distinguish Kentucky whiskey from others produced in the United States, especially from the rye whiskeys made in Pennsylvania, it needed a distinctive name. John Spear named it "Bourbon" after his home county (in turn named in honor of the French royal house in thanks for aiding the American colonies during the American Revolution). It was also in Bourbon County's seat, Paris, at the Duncan Tavern, that the liquor was first sold commercially.

Within two years of its invention, the bourbon industry was the largest in Kentucky. The first known advertisement for the brew appeared in 1821 when an ad in the *Western Citizen*, a Bourbon County newspaper, offered: "Bourbon whiskey by the barrel or keg." Because of the high quality of its limestone water, Kentucky Bourbon was considered better than whiskeys produced elsewhere, and by 1891 the state had 172 distilleries with a capacity of over 35,000 barrels daily, the largest volume in the nation. In 1964, Congress validated bourbon whiskey as a distinctly American product and prohibited the import of any distilled spirits that was labeled "Bourbon Whiskey."

To be classified a bourbon whiskey, the spirit must be made from a fermented mash containing at least 51 percent corn, with lesser amounts of barley, wheat, and rye (each distillery chooses its own combination), along with yeast and distilled limestone water. It must be stored in new, charred oak barrels for at least 24 months. Although public consumption of alcoholic beverages has declined in recent years, bourbon retains its popularity. Kentucky produces 87 percent of the world's supply, plus almost half of the distilled whiskey in the United States.

Bourbon is a favorite additive to many Southern recipes, and a perusal of local cookbooks will find delights such as Bourbon Baked Beans, Bourbon Apple Pie, Bourbon Pecan Bread, and Bourbon-glazed Ham Balls. Southerners use bourbon, rather than rum, when making Christmas fruit cakes. Bourbon Balls, a concoction of chocolate, sugar, pecans and whiskey, are so prevalent many consider them Kentucky's official candy. The most famous bourbon drink is the Mint Julep, which is consumed in great quantities at the Kentucky Derby (*see page 77*).

Above, presenting the indisputable proof.

Although distilleries are scattered throughout central Kentucky, Bardstown, with four, is often called "Bourbonville" because more whiskey is produced there than anywhere else. Three local distilleries offer weekday tours: Heaven Hill, Barton Brands, and James B. Beam. Maker's Mark is farther afield (but worth the trip). Charcoal-gray buildings with red shutters and flowers in neat beds beckon visitors to the site, and connoisseurs call Maker's (only 38 barrels a day are distilled here), one of the best whiskeys in the world. A highlight of the tour is watching the bottle tops being hand-dipped into the red sealing wax which gives Maker's its distinctive look.

Other distilleries to visit include Ancient Age in Frankfort, Wild Turkey in Lawrenceburg, and Brown-Foreman, Louisville (addresses in *Travel Tips*). ■

Billboard
Billboard
Billboard
Billboard

WSM
GRAND OLE OPRY
650

Music is as natural to Tennessee as mountain laurel and Mississippi River mud. It spills from the mountains along the eastern border in the crisp notes of a banjo, as clear and sparkling as the dancing waters of a mountain stream. It settles into big-time sophistication in the recording studios of Nashville, and turns blue or brassy when it reaches the banks of the Mississippi at Memphis.

"We don't actually learn music," many old-time musicians will tell you. "We sort of inherit it."

C Sharp: While Tennessee – especially Nashville – is undeniably famous for its music, it is also undeniably true that the same music can be found in Augusta, Georgia, or Charlotte, North Carolina, or Jackson, Mississippi. So why is it so closely associated with Tennessee? It began with an Englishman, Cecil Sharp, a researcher who came to the remote mountains of northeastern Tennessee in the summer of 1916. He was looking for the English and Scottish folk ballads brought by some of Tennessee's earliest settlers – songs which he discovered had survived in their original 18th and 19th-century forms in the isolation of the mountains. Sharp's interest in the music was scholarly, but he also helped to uncover a popular interest in the old mountain songs.

While early musicians like "Fiddlin'" John Carson and Uncle Dave Macon were making records as early as 1923, the true dawn of country music probably came in the summer of 1925. The place was not Nashville, but the little town of Bristol on the Tennessee/Virginia border. In July of that year, a Victor Records (later to become RCA Victor) talent scout named Ralph Peer showed up in Bristol with his wife, two sound engineers and two cars full of recording equipment. As a means of advertising, he convinced the local paper that his presence in town was newsworthy. The newspaper story brought a flood of telephone calls. Among those responding were two of the most influential early acts in country music – the Carter Family, whose distinctive style is still reflected in much of modern country music, and Jimmy Rodgers, the first true country music superstar.

Perhaps more than anything else, those 1925 recording sessions in Bristol began Tennessee's enduring reputation for music, but radio was the medium that carried the music to the masses through such immensely popular shows as *The WLS Barn Dance* from Chicago, *The Louisiana Hayride* from Shreveport, *The Tennessee Barn Dance* broadcast by WNOX from Knoxville, and *The Grand Ole Opry* from Nashville's WSM Radio.

Only the Opry remains from those glorious days of American radio. Broadcast by WSM Radio every Friday and Saturday night since 1925, the Opry ranks as the world's longest-running live radio program. These days, it originates from an ultra-modern broadcast facility, the Opryhouse at Nashville's Opryland Showpark where nearly 1 million people a year attend the live broadcasts.

Then owned by Nashville's National Life and Accident Insurance Company, WSM (We Shield Millions) originally saw the program as an advertising vehicle to reach potential customers in rural areas. To host the show, WSM hired George D. Hay, a newspaper col-

Preceding pages: Dolly Parton's Dollywood theme park near Pigeon Forge, Tennessee. Left, Nashville's Opryland. Right, as worn by Marty Robbins.

umnist from Memphis who had also been connected with the *WLS Barn Dance* in Chicago. Originally called simply *The WSM Barn Dance*, the show received its colorful name one night in 1927 when it followed a broadcast of operatic music. Hay informally opened the show by announcing, "For the past hour you have been listening to Grand Opera. Now it's time for a little Grand Ole Opry." The name stuck and an American institution was born.

The early Opry programs featured old-time mountain string band music – lively fiddle melodies with odd names like *Soldier's Joy*, *Arkansas Traveler* and *Turkey in the Straw*. Many of the songs had no lyrics at all.

Country music gained more sophistication – and popularity – under the guidance of a troubled young poet, Hank Williams, who carried it to new heights in the 1940s with songs like *Cold, Cold Heart, Jambalaya, Your Cheatin' Heart*, and *I Can't Help It If I'm Still In Love With You*. Williams's country music classics began crossing over into the mainstream of American popular music, and his partnership with publisher Fred Rose helped to establish Nashville as a songwriter's town.

Also in the 1940s and '50s, Bill Monroe and his Blue Grass Boys spearheaded a revival of the old-time string band music with some important new techniques. They also gave that style of music a new name. In tribute to its revivalist, it was called "bluegrass." Among the best places to find authentic bluegrass are at Tennessee's many music and craft festivals. Two of the largest are the Fall Homecoming, which takes place in mid-October at the Museum of Appalachia at Norris just north of Knoxville, and the Old Time Fiddlers' Jamboree on the July Fourth weekend at tiny Smithville east of Nashville.

While Nashville was busy building a legend around WSM and the Grand Ole Opry, Knoxville was doing much the same with WNOX Radio and live programs like *The Tennessee Barn Dance* and *The Mid-Day Merry-Go-Round*, which launched the careers of such entertainers as Roy Acuff, Chet Atkins, Carl and Pearl Butler, Carl Smith, Archie Campbell, and Homer and Jethro.

One of the most influential people in Knoxville country music was not an entertainer, but a groceryman named Cas Walker. While WSM used country music to sell insurance, Walker used it to sell groceries. His live radio programs introduced audiences to many emerging new stars, among them a teenage singer and songwriter from nearby Sevierville named Dolly Parton.

With country music gaining more and more popular appeal, recording studios seemed to be springing up everywhere. At one time Bristol, Chattanooga and Knoxville all had sizeable recording industries, and the trained ear could tell where a record was made by the characteristic sound of the musicians. But it was Nashville that emerged as the major recording center, due in no small part to the presence of the Grand Ole Opry.

The importance of the Opry to Nashville s international reputation as "Music City, USA" cannot be overemphasized. The Opry drew thousands of both well-known and wholly unknown musicians, singers and songwriters to the town, all with the hope of one day performing on the Grand Ole Opry. That is still true today, and it is a very important part of the Nashville music scene.

While records were being made in Nashville as early as 1928, it was not until the 1950s that the city became a major recording center. The two men most responsible for it were a guitar player, Chet Atkins, and a sound engineer, Owen Bradley. It was Atkins who in 1951 convinced RCA to establish the first major label recording studio in Nashville, and it was Bradley who opened a small studio in a Quonset hut on Nashville's Sixteenth Avenue which had such unique acoustics that when Columbia Records bought the place in 1962, it built its entire complex around the little studio, not daring to make any changes which might affect its distinctive sound.

As one hit record after another poured out of Nashville, popular artists like Perry Como began arriving to capitalize on the "Nashville Sound." These artists would usually bring a few key musicians with them. Of course, the first thing these professionals wanted to see was "the chart," or the arrangement for a song. They quickly learned that most of the resident musicians responsible for creating the Nashville Sound didn't bother with charts. Many of them, in fact, couldn't even read music. Most Nashville musicians these days do read music, but the practice of working out an arrangement "by ear" in an unpressured setting is still the hallmark of a Nashville recording session.

Left, Minnie Pearl and supporting acts at the Grand Ole Opry. Above, the B.B. King band on tour.

While Nashville, Knoxville and other assorted cities in the eastern two-thirds of the state were injecting country music into the American mainstream, Memphis was busy creating its own brand of music. In the early part of the 20th century, Memphis – particularly Beale Street in downtown Memphis – was the center of black culture, fashion and music for the entire Mid-South. The music of Beale Street originated on the cotton plantations of the antebellum South. It was a raw, ragged sound born out of both slavery and Reconstruction, and it was called "the blues."

It was an accomplished black musician,

W. C. Handy, who first began writing down the music of the Mississippi Delta country. His compositions, including *The St Louis Blues*, *The Memphis Blues* and *The Beale Street Blues*, were carried by such entertainers as Bessie Smith and Alberta Hunter to wider audiences in the sophisticated clubs and theaters of northern cities like New York and Chicago.

In the early 1950s the blues began evolving into a somewhat different form with stronger, driving rhythms and bass lines replacing some of the plaintive qualities of Handy's day. The new form was called "Rhythm and Blues," or frequently just "R'n'B." It was also sometimes known as "race music," and many white-owned mainstream radio stations refused to play it. Stax Records in Memphis was *the* recording label for rhythm and blues artists like Booker T and the MGs (the initials M.G. standing for Memphis Group). For a musician, Memphis in the 1950s was every bit as exciting a place to be as Nashville.

But Stax was not the only record game in town. Over on Union Avenue a man named Sam Phillips had built his own little recording studio, Sun. To make ends meet, he offered anybody with a few dollars the chance to make a record. Phillips often thought that if he could find a white artist who sounded black, he might have a shot at breaking into the radio market to sell his records.

He got that chance one day in 1954 when a young man walked into his studio to make a record as a present for his mother. Phillips was out of the office at the time, but his secretary had the presence of mind to make a tape of the visitor's recording session. When Phillips heard the tape, he was sure he had found his breakthrough artist. The kid was Elvis Presley, who combined the rhythm and blues sounds of Memphis with a touch of Nashville country and a bit of gospel thrown in for good measure. What emerged from Sun Records in the 1950s was first called "Rock-A-Billy" and then later, the classic: "Rock 'n' Roll."

The most remarkable thing about the Elvis legend in Memphis is how quickly it all happened. In 1954, Presley was working as a truck driver for Crown Electric Company. Only three years later he had bought his famous Graceland mansion.

Sun city: With Elvis Presley, Sun Records became one of the most influential recording studios in American music. In addition to Presley, Sam Phillips's lineup of young stars included Carl Perkins, Roy Orbison, Jerry Lee Lewis, Johnny Cash and Charlie Rich. Perkins, who wrote perhaps the definitive rock 'n' roll anthem in *Blue Suede Shoes*, remembers those days with great fondness. He also recalls how he came to write his classic song.

"We were playing a dance at the National Guard Armory in Jackson, Tennessee," he reminisces. "There was a couple dancing right in front of the bandstand. Suede shoes were a big fad back then. His happened to be blue. I think the girl must have stepped on his toes because I heard him tell her, 'Hey, stay off my suedes!' I couldn't get that line out of my mind. That night I kept waking up with those words running through my head. Finally – about two or three o'clock in the morning – I got up and went down to the kitchen. The only thing I could find to write on was a brown paper bag full of potatoes my wife had bought at the grocery store. I dumped the potatoes out on the counter, sat down at the kitchen table, and wrote *Blue Suede Shoes* on the back of that brown paper sack in about five minutes."

It's just that easy to produce a classic song – *if* you are in the right place at the right time with the right words, and *if* you have both the talent and the means to record them.

Left, rhythm and blues from the Rockola classic. Right, Beale Street blues, Memphis.

B
B
KING'S
BLU
CLU

N6885

PLACES

Mark Twain, writing in *Life on the Mississippi*, remarked that "a Southerner talks music." This may be true, but the types of music talked are as different from one another as country music is to the blues, both of which as it happens, come from the state of Tennessee. A Virginia accent is as distinct from the slow drawl of South Carolina as black-eyed peas are to lima beans. The only thing they have in common is that buttermilk goes down well with all of them.

Regional variations play a large role in the South. For instance, there's Beaufort, North Carolina, and just down the road apiece, Beaufort, South Carolina. The first is pronounced Bo-fort. The second is pronounced Bew-fort. Southern accents indeed. Never, under any circumstances, confuse South Carolinians with North Carolinians, or tried and true Virginians with their namesakes in West Virginia. A war was the contentious issue that resulted in this latter separation of state, and separate the two have been ever since, and in every sense of the word.

To quote Mark Twain again, "In the South the war is what A.D. is elsewhere; they date from it." This is true, but only up to a point. On any given hot summer night, on the front porches of the white houses in the small towns that make up the South, Civil War stories can still be heard. But in the modern Sun Belt cities, like Charlotte and Richmond, a different war is going on – a cultural war. The people in these places may well be from New York or Chicago, not from some honey-voiced Southern town. And therein lies the culture clash.

Southerners are known for their kindness to strangers, but things are different down here (so much so that one Northern company allegedly issued a brochure to its relocated employees on how to live with the natives). Yankees, lured by mild weather, spectacular scenery, wide open spaces and modern technology, are discovering what local people have known all along: this is a mighty fine place to be – if it can be figured out.

Change is happening, but, as with all things down South, a trifle slowly. And some things, of course, never change at all. A Yankee may, in time, become an honorary Southerner, but a Southerner will *never* become a Yankee. Good food. Strong roots. Fine weather. And the living is easy. With so much going on in its favor, why would a Southerner ever want to be anything else?

Welcome to life in the slow lane.

Preceding pages: autumn on the farm; winter in Virginia; spring comes to coastal Carolina. Left, a bird's-eye view of the green, green fields of the Old South.

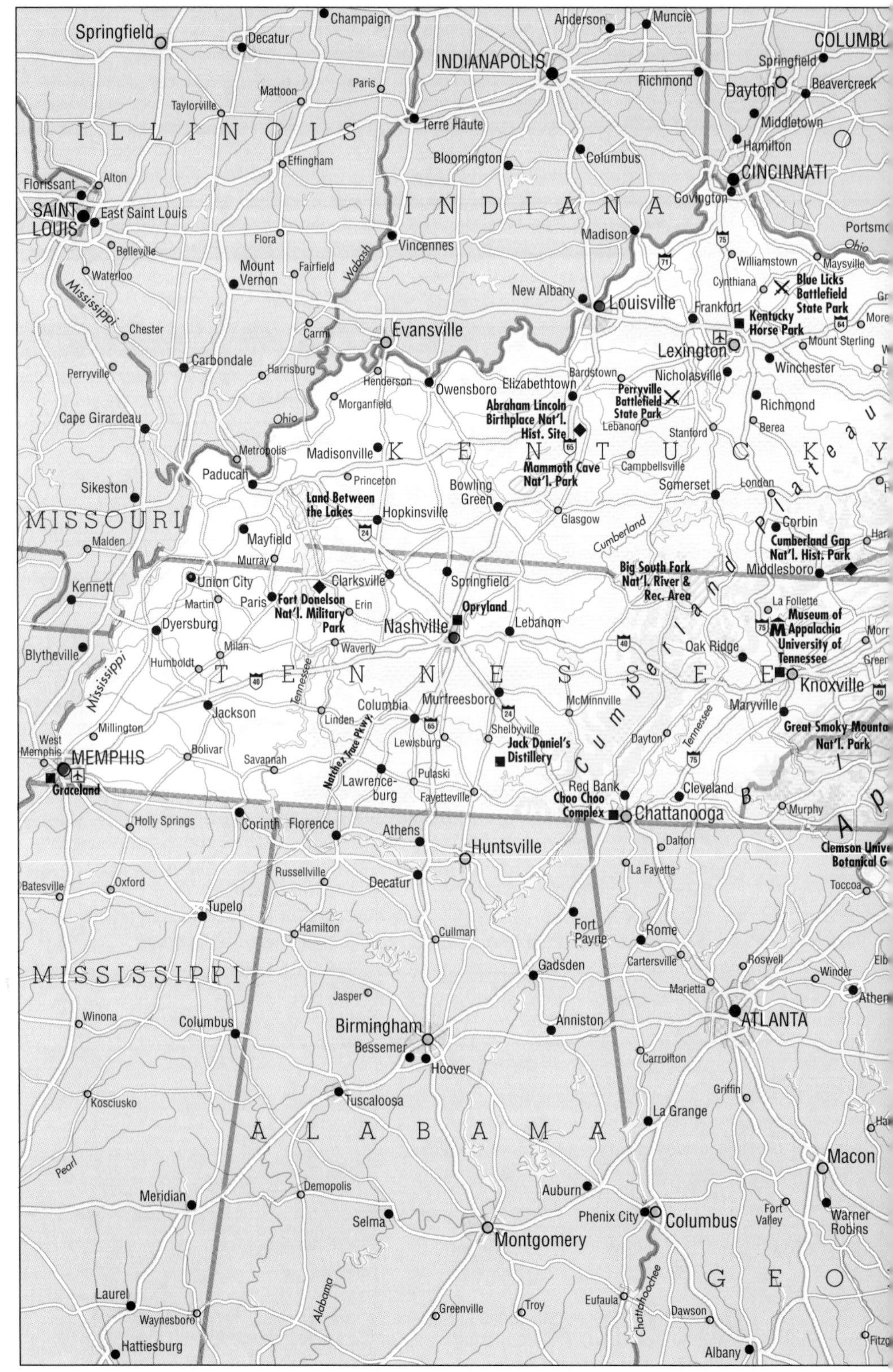
ILLINOIS
INDIANA
KENTUCKY
TENNESSEE
MISSOURI
MISSISSIPPI
ALABAMA
Springfield
Champaign
Decatur
INDIANAPOLIS
Anderson
Muncie
Richmond
Dayton
Springfield
Beavercreek
Middletown
Hamilton
CINCINNATI
Covington
Terre Haute
Bloomington
Columbus
SAINT LOUIS
East Saint Louis
Florissant
Alton
Madison
Vincennes
Louisville
New Albany
Frankfort
Lexington
Evansville
Owensboro
Elizabethtown
Blue Licks Battlefield State Park
Kentucky Horse Park
Perryville Battlefield State Park
Abraham Lincoln Birthplace Nat'l. Hist. Site
Mammoth Cave Nat'l. Park
Land Between the Lakes
Cumberland Gap Nat'l. Hist. Park
Big South Fork Nat'l. River & Rec. Area
Fort Donelson Nat'l. Military Park
Opryland
Nashville
Museum of Appalachia
University of Tennessee
Knoxville
Great Smoky Mountains Nat'l. Park
Jack Daniel's Distillery
MEMPHIS
Graceland
Choo Choo Complex
Chattanooga
Huntsville
Birmingham
ATLANTA
Montgomery
Columbus
Macon
Clemson University Botanical Garden
Paducah
Bowling Green
Clarksville
Jackson
Murfreesboro
Tuscaloosa
Mississippi
Ohio
Wabash
Tennessee
Cumberland
Natchez Trace Pkwy.
Alabama
Chattahoochee
Pearl

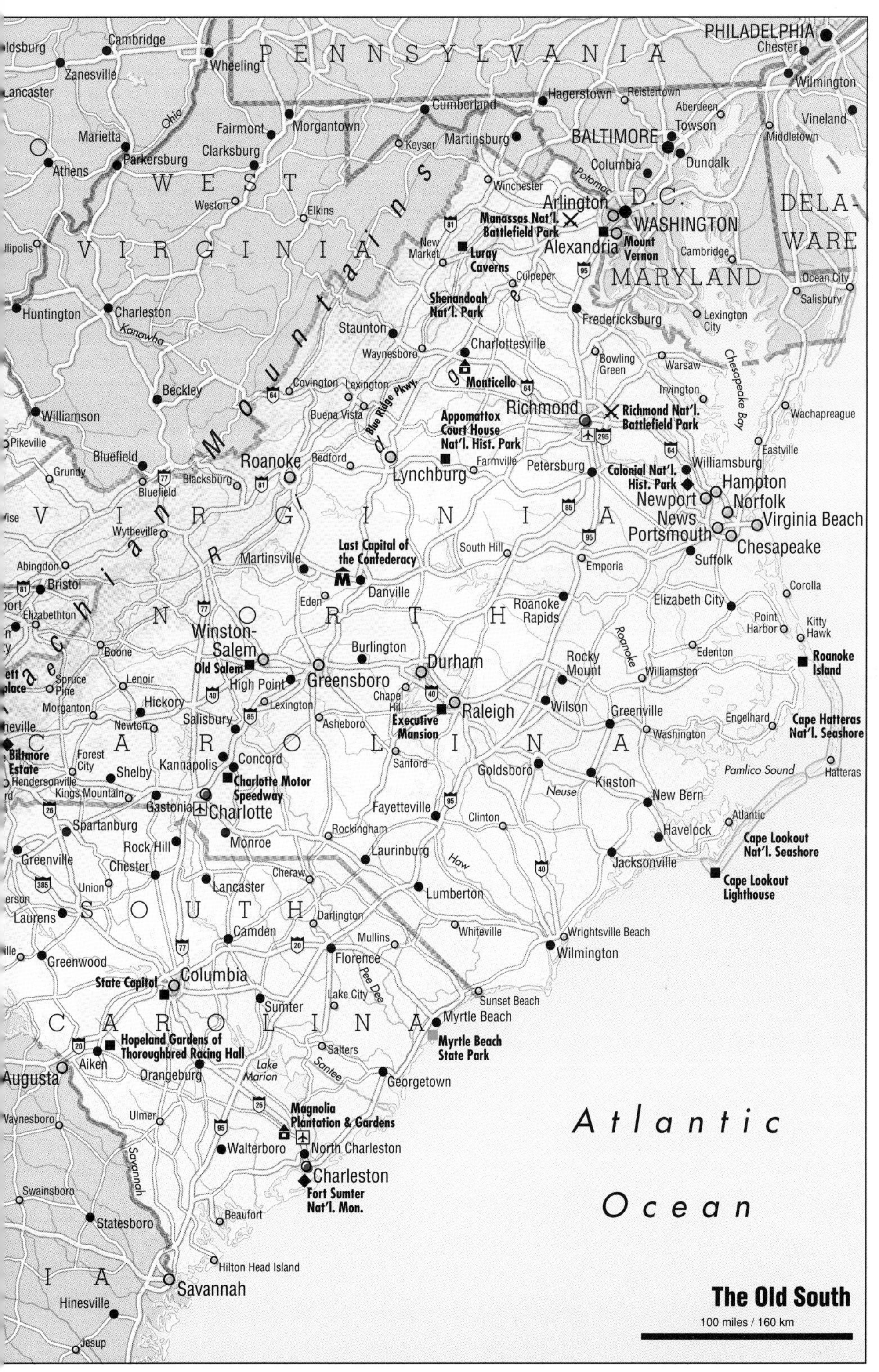

PENNSYLVANIA
PHILADELPHIA
Chester
Wilmington
Vineland
Middletown
Cambridge
Zanesville
Lancaster
Wheeling
Cumberland
Hagerstown
Reisterstown
Aberdeen
Towson
BALTIMORE
Dundalk
Columbia
Ohio
Marietta
Parkersburg
Athens
Fairmont
Morgantown
Clarksburg
Keyser
Martinsburg
WEST VIRGINIA
Weston
Elkins
Winchester
Potomac
Arlington
D.C.
WASHINGTON
DELAWARE
Manassas Nat'l. Battlefield Park
Alexandria
Mount Vernon
New Market
Luray Caverns
Cambridge
MARYLAND
Ocean City
Salisbury
Culpeper
Huntington
Charleston
Kanawha
Shenandoah Nat'l. Park
Fredericksburg
Lexington City
Staunton
Charlottesville
Waynesboro
Bowling Green
Warsaw
Chesapeake Bay
Appalachian Mountains
Beckley
Covington
Lexington
Monticello
Irvington
Blue Ridge Pkwy.
Buena Vista
Richmond
Richmond Nat'l. Battlefield Park
Wachapreague
Williamson
Appomattox Court House Nat'l. Hist. Park
Pikeville
Bluefield
Roanoke
Bedford
Farmville
Petersburg
Eastville
Williamsburg
Grundy
Lynchburg
Colonial Nat'l. Hist. Park
Hampton
Blacksburg
Newport News
Norfolk
VIRGINIA
Virginia Beach
Wytheville
Portsmouth
Chesapeake
Last Capital of the Confederacy
South Hill
Suffolk
Emporia
Abingdon
Martinsville
Bristol
Danville
Corolla
Eden
Elizabeth City
Elizabethton
NORTH CAROLINA
Roanoke Rapids
Point Harbor
Kitty Hawk
Winston-Salem
Roanoke
Boone
Burlington
Edenton
Roanoke Island
Durham
Old Salem
Rocky Mount
Williamston
Spruce Pine
Lenoir
High Point
Greensboro
Chapel Hill
Hickory
Lexington
Raleigh
Wilson
Greenville
Engelhard
Cape Hatteras Nat'l. Seashore
Morganton
Newton
Asheboro
Executive Mansion
Washington
Salisbury
Biltmore Estate
Forest City
Kannapolis
Concord
Sanford
Shelby
Hatteras
Hendersonville
Pamlico Sound
Goldsboro
Kings Mountain
Charlotte Motor Speedway
Kinston
Neuse
Gastonia
Charlotte
Fayetteville
New Bern
Spartanburg
Clinton
Atlantic
Rockingham
Rock Hill
Monroe
Havelock
Cape Lookout Nat'l. Seashore
Greenville
Laurinburg
Chester
Haw
Jacksonville
Cheraw
Cape Lookout Lighthouse
Union
Lancaster
Lumberton
Laurens
SOUTH CAROLINA
Darlington
Whiteville
Camden
Mullins
Wrightsville Beach
Greenwood
Florence
Wilmington
Columbia
State Capitol
Pee Dee
Lake City
Sunset Beach
Sumter
Myrtle Beach
Hopeland Gardens of Thoroughbred Racing Hall
Myrtle Beach State Park
Salters
Aiken
Augusta
Orangeburg
Lake Marion
Santee
Georgetown
Waynesboro
Ulmer
Magnolia Plantation & Gardens
Atlantic Ocean
Savannah
Walterboro
North Charleston
Charleston
Fort Sumter Nat'l. Mon.
Swainsboro
Statesboro
Beaufort
Hilton Head Island
Savannah
Hinesville
Jesup
The Old South
100 miles / 160 km

THE BLACK SOUTH

For generations, the South belittled its African-American heritage. But today, memorials to black history have become popular stops for visitors of all colors, sought out specifically for their vibrant sense of place and rich cultural experiences.

There are well over 500 historic sites of African-American significance scattered throughout the South. Some of them represent the shameful legacy of slavery and the struggle for civil rights; others pay tribute to the black South's rich music and art, and achievements by people such as author Alex Haley and blues great W.C. Handy. While a few sit in shambles, many are perfectly preserved. And, as a collection, they represent the substantial contribution southern blacks have made to their country.

Visit Virginia: Known throughout the US as "the breeder of slaves" during the 1800s, Virginia's many slave auction blocks are haunting reminders of this solemn fact. In **Fredericksburg**, the tourist office on Caroline Street offers free brochures on the city's black history including heritage walking tours of the area. Among the sites are the city's pre-Civil War slave auction house at the corner of Charles and Williams streets, and the **African Baptist Church** which during the 1800s had a mixed congregation of whites, free blacks and slaves. The church's minister, Lawrence A. Davies, was elected the first black mayor of Fredericksburg in 1976.

In Alexandria, the **Alexandria Black History Resource Center** portrays the contributions African-Americans made to the city. And in **Richmond**, the **Black History Museum and Cultural Center of Virginia** does the same for the entire state. Also in Richmond is the **Jackson Ward District**, a 22-block area once called the "Wall Street of Black America." *(For details, see page 136 of the chapter "Around Richmond.")*

Booker T. Washington, the noted African-American author, educator and presidential advisor, was born in **Hardy**, Virginia and raised on the Burroughs Plantation as a slave. The **Booker T. Washington National Monument** now exists on the site and consists of reconstructed slave cabins, a blacksmith shed and tobacco barns. During the summer, costumed dramas of slave life are performed. **Hampton University** in Hampton is where Washington went to school and the university houses one of the oldest and largest collections of black artifacts in the country.

At the **Jamestown Settlement Museum** in Jamestown, visitors can learn about the role blacks played in the colony in the early 1600s. It was in Jamestown that blacks first arrived in America as indentured servants on a Dutch ship in 1619. The museum features replicas of the ships that brought the settlers and the Africans to the colony.

Near Charlottesville, **Monticello**, the home of President Thomas Jefferson, includes historic slave quarters and features a narrated tour of the important role black servants played in running the plantation. Although Jefferson pub-

receding ages: Maceo ural, KY. **eft**, agnolia ardens, SC. **ight**, Mr onnor of the mma Reno onnor allery, KY.

licly opposed slavery, he used slaves to build and maintain his home. And in the small town of **Clarksville** in southern Virginia, the **Prestwood Plantation** contains the oldest standing slave house in the country, along with a slave cemetery, loom house and plantation store.

Uncle Tom's Cabin: Although Kentucky remained neutral during the Civil War, its past was indeed steeped in slavery. It was in **Washington**, Kentucky, that author and abolitionist Harriet Beecher Stowe watched slaves being bought and sold at the auction block on the city's courthouse lawn. The horrific site enraged her, and later inspired her to write *Uncle Tom's Cabin*, a blockbuster morality tale about a Kentucky slave who becomes a martyr, whipped to death by his wicked owner.

Passing through **Maceo**, note the colorful mural painted on the side of the Post Office at the intersection of Rockport Ferry Road. The picture is of Josiah Henson, a local slave, who may have been Stowe's model for Uncle Tom. This stretch of US60 between Hawesville and Owensboro, in fact, is called the **Josiah Henson Trail**.

Blacks in Kentucky were also a major part of the state's renowned horse-racing industry, working as stable hands, trainers and jockeys. At **Lexington's Kentucky Horse Park** is the grave of Isaac Murphy, a black man considered one of the greatest jockeys of all time. Murphy was the first jockey to win three Kentucky Derbies and in his career rode 628 winners in 1,412 races. And the **Louisville's Kentucky Derby Museum** pays tribute to Jockey Oliver Lewis. In the first Kentucky Derby in 1875, all but one of the jockeys were black, and the winning jockey that day was Lewis, who set a world record.

Heading on down I-65 is **Elizabethtown** and the small **Emma Reno Connor Black History Gallery**. The late Emma Reno Connor was a local teacher who collected black memorabilia to help educate her students.

South of Elizabethtown is **Mammoth Cave National Park**. Within the park, Mammoth Cave contains 300 miles (480

MLK, Jr, on the balcony of the Lorraine Motel, Memphis.

km) of underground passages on five levels that were once used as a refuge for slaves escaping the South on the Underground Railroad.

Chicken George's Grave: *Roots*, the celebrated book by the late Pulitzer-Prize winning author Alex Haley, inspired a generation of African-Americans to trace their own roots in the Old South, and his boyhood home in **Henning**, Tennessee, is now the popular **Alex Haley Home and Museum**. A classic example of rural life, the restored house is full of antique furniture and family portraits and feels like a visit to Grandma's. It was here on the front porch that Haley listened to his grandmother and aunts tell stories of their ancestor Kunta Kinte, brought to America as a slave. In the dining room hangs a photo of Chicken George, a relative of Haley's and a colorful character in *Roots* who is buried in a nearby grave. Tours of the home include lessons on lye soap-making, sausage grinding and recipes for poor man's pudding.

Jackson, Tennessee, is home to the **Casey Jones Home and Railroad Museum**. The museum honors the legendary engineer who was immortalized in the song by Wallace Saunders, a black fireman who rode with Jones. It also tells the story of the contribution blacks made to America's railroads, from the laying of tracks to serving as waiters in the dining cars. Housed in Casey's home, the museum is a real delight for train buffs complete with railroad antiques and the actual tender to Casey's Old 382.

In the **Chattanooga Afro-American Museum and Research Center**, displays include the black history of Chattanooga, African-American art, photographs and historical documents. A special collection in the museum is devoted to Tennessee native Bessie Smith, known during the 1930s as the "Queen of the Blues."

For some real blues memorabilia, **Memphis** is the place to go. The **Beale Street Historic District** near the banks of the Mississippi during the early 1900s was the center of nightlife for the Memphis black community. It bustled with saloons, gambling halls and bordellos, and for years whites were not allowed on the streets at night. It was here that the music known as the blues was born. **Beale Street Tours**, located at the Memphis Visitors Center, offers guided tours that focus on the black music and history of the area. *(See the chapters on music and Memphis to learn more about Beale Street.)* Memphis is also where the **National Civil Rights Museum and Lorraine Motel** is located. It was here that Dr Martin Luther King, Jr was murdered in 1968. The former motel is now a museum that offers a comprehensive view of the American civil rights movement.

Carolina sites: During the late 1700s, North Carolina had over 100,000 slaves, approximately one-third of the total population. During and after Reconstruction, the state made significant strides in righting past wrongs and, by the early 1900s, it had more predominantly black colleges and universities than any other state in the country. Among them are **Fayetteville State Uni-**

The Lorraine Motel, where King was killed, is now a national civil rights museum.

versity, **North Carolina Agricultural and Technical State University** in Greensboro, **Shaw University** in Raleigh, and **Livingstone College** in Salisbury. All contain impressive collections on African-American history.

Near **Creswell**, North Carolina, is **Somerset Place**, an 18th-century plantation that was built and maintained by hundreds of slaves. Although many of the slaves who worked here died of exhaustion, historians say that the Somerset Place slaves were better treated than most in the area. When it was a working plantation, it provided medical care, ministry services and relatively comfortable living quarters for its slaves. Although mostly destroyed during the Civil War, portions of the slave buildings, hospital and chapel remain and tours of the property offer a glimpse of what plantation life was like for both the master and the slave.

In **Durham**, the **Stagville Center** was once a several thousand acre plantation with an huge estate at its center. During the late 1800s, it held 900 slaves. Several independent communities existed on the property, and after completing their plantation duties, many of the slaves tended their own gardens, built their own cabins, and conducted their own community affairs. After the Civil War, many of the freed slaves chose to remain on the plantation. Today, Stagville hosts lectures and workshops on historic preservation and black studies.

The town of **Greensboro**, North Carolina, during the 1960s was the site of several civil rights protests, including a pivotal one in 1960 when four black college students refused to move from a Woolworth's department store lunch counter after being denied service. The incident sparked a series of protests across the South, and eventually led to the founding of the Student Nonviolent Coordinating Committee, one of the more radical branches of the civil rights movement.

Gullah dialects and Cabbage Row: One of the most distinct remnants of African culture in the South is found among the Sea Islands of South Carolina, where

Slave quarte[rs] at Boone Hal[l,] South Carolina.

the Gullah dialect – a blend of African, West Indian, Irish and English – is still spoken. Also called "Geeche," this Gullah dialect is the only true form of pidginized English spoken in the US today. Near **Beaufort** on the Carolina coast, an annual **Gullah Festival** is held each May that highlights the arts, customs, dress, language and culture of the Gullah people.

Also in Beaufort is the **Robert Smalls Monument** at the Baptist Tabernacle Church. Smalls was a Civil War hero and member of the Gullah people. Born into slavery in 1839, he worked as a crewman on the *Planter*, a Confederate ship used to haul guns. In 1863 while the white captain and crew were ashore, Smalls and other black crewmen sailed the ship out of Charleston harbor and surrendered it to the Union navy. Smalls was given command of the ship and following the war served as a state legislator and congressman.

In the coastal city of Charleston, the **Avery Research Center for African-American History and Culture** explains the Gullah culture. The **Charleston Museum**, established in 1773, is another fine center noted for its exhibits on black history, arts and crafts. And still standing in the city is the Chalmers Street **Old Slave Mart** where slaves were weighed, examined and sold to the highest bidder. In Charleston, a city ordinance forbade slave trading on the streets.

Also in Charleston is the string of Church Street tenements called **Cabbage Row** that served as the model for Catfish Row in the Broadway play *Porgy and Bess*. Black residents here once hawked cabbages and catfish from their front windows to passersby.

Black sites can be found all around the Charleston area. Many of the surrounding plantations, like **Boone Hall** and **Magnolia Gardens**, have slave quarters that can still be seen. And in the city of **Sheldon**, south of Charleston, is the **Oyotunji African Village**, a Yoruba-style African compound and cultural center set amid the agricultural fields of the Old South.

Gullah woman weaving baskets, South Carolina.

PVT CHARLES G.C ROC
INE B STAN
G.JEF

Civil War Sites

In his famous address at Gettysburg, Abraham Lincoln spoke movingly of hallowed ground. The land which the nation has set aside for preservation bears the peculiar emotional force of these consecrated places. Brutal battles were fought here, pitting kinsmen against kinsmen in an awful conflict that pierced the national psyche. Fighting raged for four years, killing more than 600,000 men and nearly destroying the young republic.

Civil War sites are strung along the Southern states like scars on an open wound, for some locals still feel strongly that the South has never fully recovered from the damage inflicted by "The War of Northern Aggression." The states in the upper South, being closer to the border, saw more action than those in the Deep South. Some historians say that up to 60 percent of all military encounters took place in the green rolling hills of Virginia.

A partial list of sites appears in the back of this book; others, like **Lee's Tomb** at Washington and Lee University in Lexington, Virginia, or **New Market Battlefield**, where teenage cadets from the Virginia Military Institute were called into service, are mentioned in the "Places" chapters that cover each geographical region. Most of the largest, and best preserved sites, are administered by the National Park Service, and these are the ones discussed here. Some parks are clustered together, others require long-distance driving and a serious investment of time. A few lie outside the set borders of the five states covered in this book, but because all can be reached within a couple of hours, they, too, have been included.

The opening volley: It was the fanatical John Brown who touched off the powder keg and turned angry rhetoric into explosive violence. The year was 1859, and the place where he did it is commemorated at **Harpers Ferry National Historical Park**. The park is in West Virginia, where the Shenandoah and Potomac rivers meet, upriver from Washington, DC; George Washington himself had picked it as a strategic site for a national armory. For John Brown, it was the perfect spot to launch the final offensive in his great crusade to end the "peculiar institution" of slavery. On October 16, his 21-man "army of liberation" overran the armory and several outlying buildings. Two days later, his contingent was attacked by US Marines under the command of the then Colonel Robert E. Lee.

A year after the incident at Harpers Ferry, Abraham Lincoln was elected president, and events came in a rush. On December 20, 1860, an angry South Carolina convention voted to secede from the Union, followed quickly by the states in the Deep South. (The Upper South states followed suit in April and May, except for slaveholding Kentucky, which never left the Union.) The Confederate States of America formed in February 1861, electing Jefferson Davis as president. Nearly all Federal forts in the South were seized by Confederate forces.

In South Carolina, Major Robert Anderson realized that Fort Sumter was the only defensible fort of the four Federal installations in Charleston, and he consolidated troops there. When Lincoln took office on March 4, 1861, he made it clear that he would hold the fort. At 4.30 on the morning of April 12, Confederate batteries opened fire on Fort Sumter. The Civil War had begun.

Anderson surrendered late the next day. The Union army laid siege to the fort for 22 months, but never retook it; Confederate troops remained until 1865. Today, boats carry visitors to **Fort Sumter National Monument** from April 1 to Labor Day. One little-known fact about Fort Sumter, told by the park ranger guide, is that Lincoln was scheduled to visit the fort in April 1865, after hostilities had ceased. At the last minute, the president cried off because of a prior engagement – at Washington, DC's **Ford's Theatre**.

Just west of Washington, DC, **Manassas National Battlefield Park** in Virginia was the site of two major clashes. General Irvin McDowell led 35,000 Union troops toward a key railroad junction at Manassas on July 18, 1861, expecting to take Richmond, the Confederate capital, easily and end the war quickly. But waiting there, near the Stone Bridge on

receding ages: tained-glass window to allen VMI adets, New Market, irginia. Left, Manning Williams, Jr n Rebel niform of outh arolina.

Bull Run Creek, was General Pierre G.T. Beauregard and 22,000 Confederate troops. Another 10,000 Confederates arrived later in the day.

Confederate soldiers rallied behind General Thomas J. Jackson's fresh Virginia brigade. Jackson "stood there like a stone wall"–hence his nickname, "Stonewall" Jackson. Union forces fled in disarray, hindered by the carriages of sightseers who had come to watch the fighting; 900 soldiers died on the first day alone.

A self-guided walking tour follows the course of the battle. A second walk covers the area of the Stone Bridge. Union troops who were wounded here received aid and medicine in an effort organized by Clara Barton. At the age of 40 she had quit her US Patent Office job, and would later found the American Red Cross.

The second Battle of Manassas (Bull Run) came more than a year later, this time involving not raw recruits but veteran soldiers. Robert E. Lee, the new commander of the Confederate Army of Northern Virginia, dispatched Stonewall Jackson's force to engage General John Pope's Union troops. After several battles and tactical mistakes by Pope during the engagement, Jackson sent Union forces fleeing once again. The confrontation killed 3,300 men. A 12-mile (19-km) driving tour covers much of the large area of the second battle of Bull Run.

Chickamauga Battlefield, Tennessee.

General George B. McClellan rebuilt the fleeing Federals into the 100,000-man Army of the Potomac and in May 1862 marched on the heavily fortified Confederate capital at **Richmond, Virginia**. On May 15, Confederate fire drove off five Union ironclad ships that had been moving up the James River toward Richmond. June 26 was the start of seven days of fierce battles on Richmond's eastern outskirts. Lee's forces repulsed McClellan's Union troops, with total casualties numbering around 36,000.

Richmond was not safe, however. Battles in regions north of the city continued throughout the coming months. In March 1864, Ulysses S. Grant became commander of the Union field forces, and immediately proclaimed as his chief objective the capture of Richmond.

The battlefield at **Cold Harbor** sits midway between two roadside taverns. When Grant's soldiers attacked on June 3, they suffered 7,000 casualties in 30 minutes, forcing him to change to a siege strategy. Union soldiers, including several regiments of African-American troops, took **Fort Harrison** on September 29. Richmond held on until April 1865, falling only after Lee's forces withdrew. You can trace the progress of the encounter at the 10 units of **Richmond National Battlefield Park**. A complete tour requires an 80-mile (130-km) drive.

Tension in Tennessee: Until 1862, the Union military seemed unable to win an important victory. Confederate defensive lines had few weak points, but Union commanders decided to test the line in western Tennessee, where Fort Henry on the Tennessee River and Fort Donelson on the Cumberland River sat just 12 miles (19 km) apart. Union ironclad gunboats opened fire on Fort Henry on February 6, 1862, while the then virtually unknown Brigadier General Ulysses S. Grant led a ground assault. Grant was slow in reaching the fort, and by the time he arrived, the ironclads had destroyed it, almost the entire garrison fleeing to Fort Donelson. When Union forces attacked on February 14, gunboats could not duplicate their feat against Donelson's heavier guns. Changing tactics, Grant encircled the fort and laid siege; the Confederates surrendered on February 16. These were the Union's first big victories and Grant made a name for himself. Tours of **Fort Donelson National Battlefield**, a mile west of Dover, are available.

After the losses at Fort Henry and Fort Donelson, Confederate forces withdrew. In Mississippi, General A. S. Johnston consolidated a force of 44,000 troops at Corinth, near the Mississippi/Tennessee border, planning to overwhelm Grant. Grant, in turn, moved his own 40,000-man Army of the Tennessee to an encampment around **Shiloh Church**, 22 miles (35 km) northeast of Corinth in Tennessee. Grant drilled his new recruits but set up almost no defenses. Johnston's attack on April 6, 1862, caught Union forces by surprise. Grant's troops spent the entire day in fierce, retreating battles at locations such as **Hornet's Nest**. Confederates used a barrage of 62 cannons – the largest artillery assault of its day – to inflict huge losses on a Union division. Johnston was killed in action and P.G.T. Beauregard assumed command.

By the end of the day, Grant's remaining forces reached **Pittsburgh Landing** and set up a position fortified by gunboats and thousands of men. By the morning of April 7, Grant's forces numbered 55,000, but, not being aware of the reinforcements, Beauregard attacked. By the time he retreated, his troops were low on ammunition, and Confederate casualties swelled to 15,000. **Shiloh National Military Park** includes a Visitor Center and a self-guided driving tour.

As 1862 drew to a close, Major General William Rosecrans took command of the Union Army of the Cumberland, charged with driving Confederate forces under General Braxton Bragg out of Tennessee. Rosecrans found Bragg waiting for him in a grove of cedars near the **Stones River** in **Murfreesboro**, Tennessee, 27 miles (46 km) southeast of Nashville.

Recreating the second Battle of Manassas, Virginia.

Troops on both sides acted out one of the heartbreaking ironies of warfare as they camped within sight of one another on December 30, 1863, singing rousing songs well into the evening. Then, at dawn on December 31, in a day that went badly for the Yankees, the Union forces were driven back a short distance before establishing a new line. There was neither music nor fighting on New Year's Day. On January 2, Bragg's troops drove Union soldiers back to Stones River, where Rosecrans's superior artillery was waiting. Bragg lost 1,800 soldiers at the river, and the battle ended as his forces retreated. The Confederates had lost Tennessee. The casualties after two days of fighting were 13,000 Union and 10,000 Confederate soldiers. **Stones River National Battlefield** includes a driving tour.

War rages on: Halfway between Washington, DC, and Richmond, Virginia, lies the town of **Fredericksburg**. This had been a blessing before the war, but after secession its strategic location became a curse. One hundred thousand men died near Fredericksburg in four major battles. **Fredericksburg and Spotsylvania National Military Park** contains 7,775 acres (3,146 hectares) of land that includes four battlefields and three historic buildings.

Begin at **Fredericksburg Battlefield**, where General Ambrose Burnside's Union troops crossed the Rappahannock River in December 1862 to attack Lee's forces, commanded by Stonewall Jackson. Heavily defended on hills west of Fredericksburg, Jackson handily won the battle, inflicting big losses; more than 15,000 Union soldiers are now buried at **Fredericksburg National Cemetery**. Visit **Chatham**, a Georgian mansion used as a hospital, where Clara Barton and poet Walt Whitman tended to the injured.

Stonewall falls: Next, drive west to the **Chancellorsville Battlefield**, where in May 1863 Jackson's forces again won a victory against Federal troops. Here Jackson was shot by "friendly fire." Following the amputation of his left arm on May 4, General Lee wrote to Jackson: "You are better off than I am, for while you have lost your left, I have lost my right arm." Jackson died six days later at

Appomattox Court House, site of Lee's surrender.

Guinea Station, 15 miles (24 km) south of Fredericksburg, where the **Stonewall Jackson Shrine** now stands.

Lee may have lost his right-hand man in Stonewall Jackson, but not his fighting spirit. To the west is **Wilderness Battlefield**, where Lee and Grant first met in an indecisive battle on May 5–6, 1864. Grant broke away from that battle to march toward the **Spotsylvania Court House**. Lee reached Spotsylvania first, and fended off several small Union attacks. When more Union troops arrived, along with a thick fog, the fighting grew more savage. After 20 hours of hand-to-hand combat and several days of a staunch Confederate defense, Grant called the fight a victory and a key to winning the war.

Struggle for the South: A visit to **Chickamauga and Chattanooga National Military Park** in Georgia, not far outside Chattanooga in Tennessee, stirs the imagination and provides insight into the struggle for the South. As you hike over its fields, hills and hardwood forests, picture two battles – one an empty Confederate victory on September 18–19, 1863, at **Chickamauga Battlefield**; the next, a Union triumph in the Battle of Chattanooga on November 23–25. You can best imagine this battle by hiking up to **Point Park** on **Lookout Mountain**. From here you can see the entire town.

After Grant was named supreme commander on March 9, 1864, the Union army traveled south from Chattanooga toward Atlanta: "Too important a place in the hands of the enemy to be left undisturbed," said General William T. Sherman. The Federal Army wanted to get its hands on the weaponry, the foundries "and especially its railroads, which converged there from the four great cardinal points," he said.

Grant's army was everywhere during the spring of 1864. Even while Sherman waged the Atlanta campaign and smaller forces defended the Nashville–Chattanooga Railroad, Federal troops were focused on Richmond, the capital of the Confederacy. The Union army reached Petersburg, which Grant called "The key to taking Richmond," in mid-June 1864. For 10 months, Grant kept Petersburg under siege. He cut Lee's supply lines, diminishing troop strength through direct attack, hunger and demoralization. Petersburg finally surrendered on April 2, 1865. Richmond soon followed.

One of the most interesting sites at **Petersburg National Battlefield** is the **Crater**. Here, the 48th Pennsylvania Infantry, which included many former coal miners, dug a tunnel toward a Confederate fort at Pegram's Salient. In this tunnel they blew up four tons of gunpowder, planning to send Union troops through the enormous gap it would create, with the intention of shortening the siege. The army went into the crater but were unable to go any farther, sustaining 4,000 deaths when Confederate troops attacked.

From here, visit the 27 historic structures within the restored village of **Appomattox Court House**, east of Lynchburg, where Lee surrendered to Grant only one week after Richmond fell, ending the fight for the Old South. *(See also history and Richmond chapters.)*

A fuller list of Civil War sites appears in the Travel Tips section of this book.

Lee's Tomb in Lexington, Virginia.

VIRGINIA

Thomas Jefferson, third president of the United States, wrote in a letter in 1791: "On the whole, I find nothing anywhere else... which Virginia need envy to any part of the world." He was referring, in this instance, to the weather, but since he was an acknowledged master-builder, ardent gardener and architect of several of his state's most elegant buildings, we hold his truths on Virginia to be self-evident.

The Old Dominion has heritage at its very heart. It was one of the first colonies of the New World, and its governors oversaw territory so vast that it was eventually carved into eight US states: West Virginia, Kentucky, Ohio, Indiana, Illinois, Michigan, Wisconsin and Minnesota. George Washington, the young country's first president, was born here. Jefferson, elected in 1801, ushered in an era commonly known as the Virginia Dynasty: for the next 25 years the leader of the nation would be a Virginia gentleman.

Another leader of a different nation felt so strongly about the land that he gave up a career to follow a cause: Robert E. Lee was offered the command of the Union forces in the War Between The States. He could not bear to take up arms against his Virginia kinsmen, however. History books the world over record the consequences of this decision.

So what is it about Virginia that so moved these men of distinction? The very things that anyone visiting now cannot fail to appreciate: blue hazy mountains with trickling waterfalls and deer so unafraid they wander right up to strangers; small towns where, even today, children use rubber innertubes to float on the water of clear mountain creeks; a sea with fine shell-laden golden sands that stretch mile upon mile along the coast.

Richmond is the capital of Virginia and the capital of the old Confederacy. Although one of the last Southern states to secede from the Union, in many ways it was the worst affected: many historians agree that over half the battles fought in the war took place in the green rolling hills of Virginia.

In this state of great beauty and great men, the final word should belong to yet another. The poet Walt Whitman, only two months before the end of this most tragic of American conflicts, was moved to write in 1865: "Dilapidated, fenceless, and trodden with war as Virginia is, wherever I move across her surface, I find myself roused to surprise and admiration."

Preceding pages: dress parade at Virginia Military Institute, Lexington. Left, Thomas Jefferson spent 40 years designing and refining Monticello. The building appears on the flipside of US nickels.

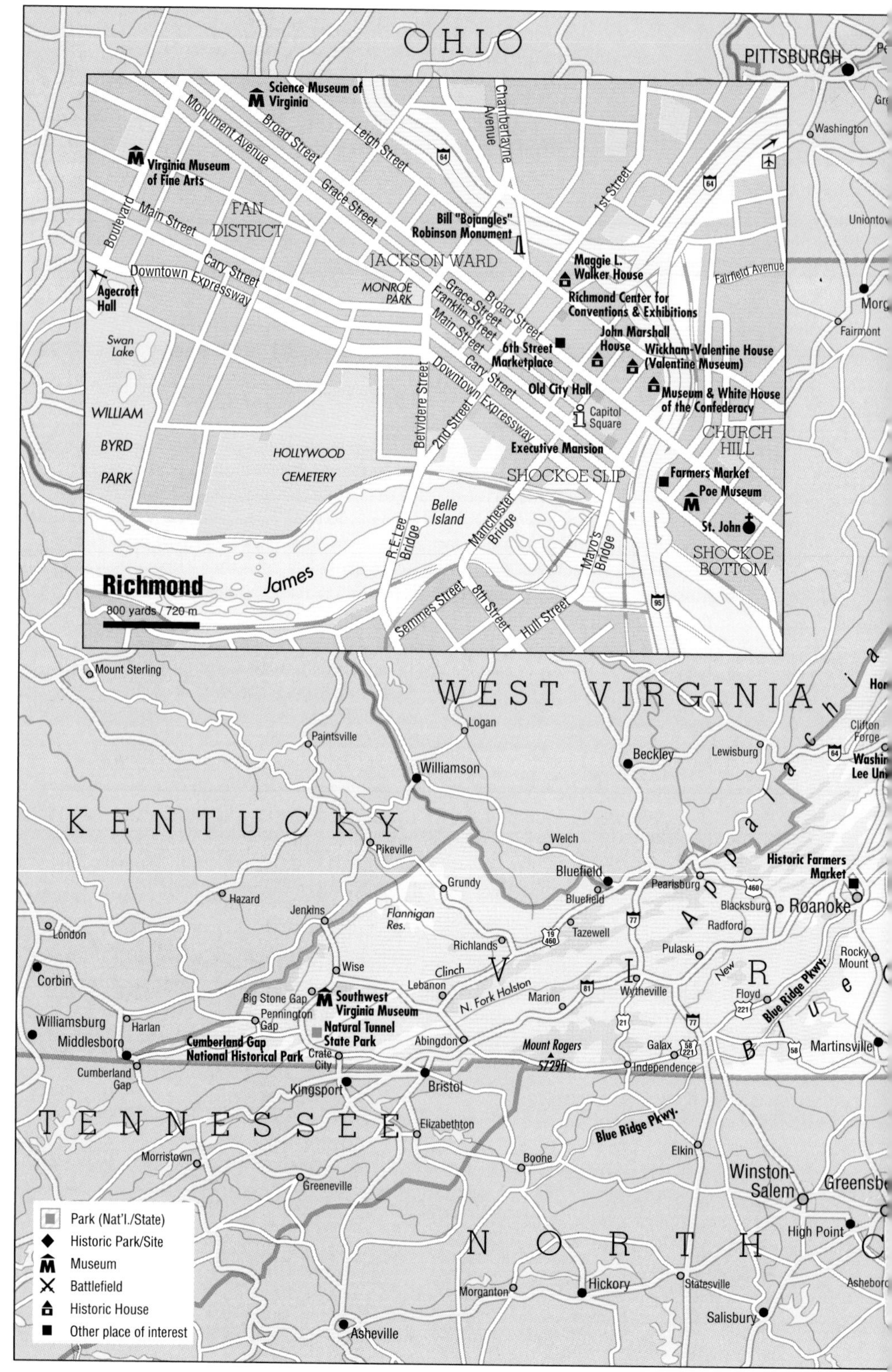

OHIO
PITTSBURGH
Washington
Uniontown
Fairmont
Science Museum of Virginia
Monument Avenue
Broad Street
Leigh Street
Chamberlayne Avenue
Virginia Museum of Fine Arts
Boulevard
Main Street
FAN DISTRICT
Grace Street
Bill "Bojangles" Robinson Monument
1st Street
JACKSON WARD
Fairfield Avenue
Maggie L. Walker House
Richmond Center for Conventions & Exhibitions
Cary Street
Downtown Expressway
Agecroft Hall
MONROE PARK
Franklin Street
John Marshall House
Wickham-Valentine House (Valentine Museum)
6th Street Marketplace
Swan Lake
Belvidere Street
Old City Hall
Museum & White House of the Confederacy
Capitol Square
WILLIAM BYRD PARK
HOLLYWOOD CEMETERY
2nd Street
Executive Mansion
CHURCH HILL
SHOCKOE SLIP
Farmers Market
Poe Museum
Belle Island
Manchester Bridge
St. John
R.E.Lee Bridge
Mayo's Bridge
SHOCKOE BOTTOM
Richmond
James
800 yards / 720 m
Semmes Street
8th Street
Hull Street
Mount Sterling
WEST VIRGINIA
Logan
Paintsville
Beckley
Lewisburg
Clifton Forge
Williamson
KENTUCKY
Appalachia
Welch
Pikeville
Bluefield
Historic Farmers Market
Grundy
Hazard
Pearisburg
Blacksburg
Roanoke
Jenkins
Flannigan Res.
London
Radford
Tazewell
Richlands
Pulaski
Rocky Mount
Corbin
Wise
Clinch
VIRGINIA
New R
Big Stone Gap
Southwest Virginia Museum
Lebanon
N. Fork Holston
Marion
Wytheville
Floyd
Blue Ridge Pkwy.
Blue
Pennington Gap
Williamsburg
Harlan
Natural Tunnel State Park
Middlesboro
Cumberland Gap National Historical Park
Crate City
Abingdon
Mount Rogers 5729ft
Galax
Martinsville
Independence
Cumberland Gap
Kingsport
Bristol
TENNESSEE
Elizabethton
Blue Ridge Pkwy.
Elkin
Morristown
Boone
Winston-Salem
Greensboro
Greeneville
High Point
NORTH CAROLINA
Hickory
Morganton
Statesville
Asheboro
Salisbury
Asheville
Park (Nat'l./State)
Historic Park/Site
Museum
Battlefield
Historic House
Other place of interest

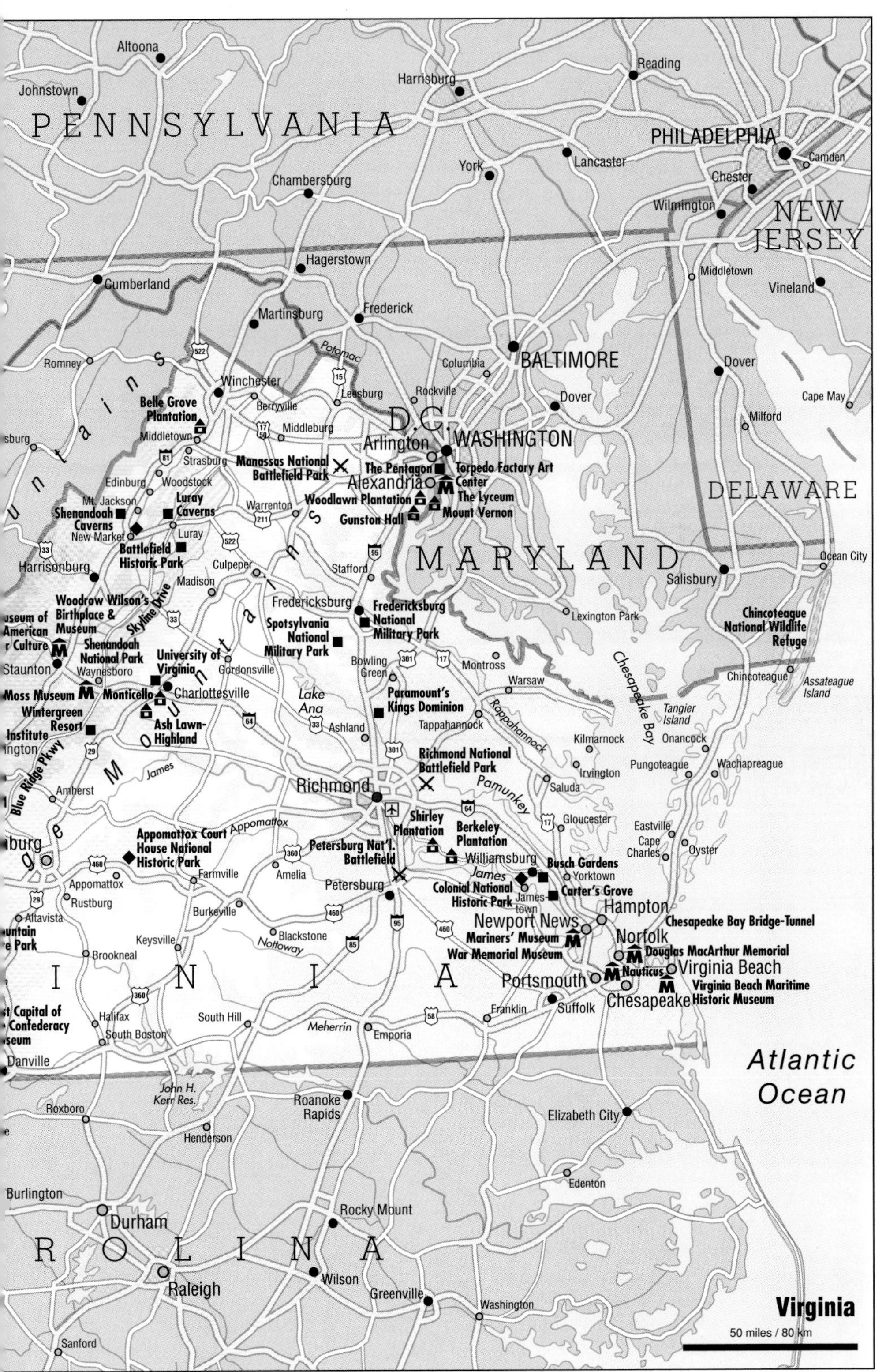

PENNSYLVANIA
Altoona
Johnstown
Harrisburg
Reading
PHILADELPHIA
Camden
Lancaster
York
Chambersburg
Chester
Wilmington
NEW JERSEY
Hagerstown
Cumberland
Middletown
Vineland
Martinsburg
Frederick
Potomac
Romney
Columbia
BALTIMORE
Dover
Winchester
Leesburg
Rockville
Cape May
Belle Grove Plantation
Berryville
Middleburg
Milford
D.C.
Arlington
WASHINGTON
Middletown
Strasburg
Manassas National Battlefield Park
The Pentagon
Torpedo Factory Art Center
Alexandria
The Lyceum
Mount Vernon
Woodlawn Plantation
Gunston Hall
DELAWARE
Edinburg
Woodstock
Mt. Jackson
Shenandoah Caverns
New Market
Luray Caverns
Luray
Warrenton
Battlefield Historic Park
Harrisonburg
Culpeper
Stafford
MARYLAND
Salisbury
Ocean City
Madison
Woodrow Wilson's Birthplace & Museum
Skyline Drive
Fredericksburg
Fredericksburg National Military Park
Spotsylvania National Military Park
Lexington Park
Chincoteague National Wildlife Refuge
Shenandoah National Park
University of Virginia
Staunton
Waynesboro
Gordonsville
Bowling Green
Montross
Chesapeake Bay
Charlottesville
Monticello
Ash Lawn-Highland
Wintergreen Resort
Lake Ana
Ashland
Paramount's Kings Dominion
Warsaw
Tappahannock
Rappahannock
Chincoteague
Assateague Island
Tangier Island
Kilmarnock
Onancock
Irvington
Pungoteague
Wachapreague
Richmond National Battlefield Park
Blue Ridge Pkwy
Amherst
James
Richmond
Pamunkey
Saluda
Gloucester
Eastville
Cape Charles
Oyster
Appomattox Court House National Historic Park
Appomattox
Shirley Plantation
Berkeley Plantation
Petersburg Nat'l. Battlefield
Williamsburg
Busch Gardens
Yorktown
Farmville
Amelia
Petersburg
Colonial National Historic Park
Jamestown
Carter's Grove
Hampton
Rustburg
Burkeville
Altavista
Newport News
Mariners' Museum
Chesapeake Bay Bridge-Tunnel
Norfolk
Douglas MacArthur Memorial
Keysville
Blackstone
Nottoway
War Memorial Museum
Nauticus
Virginia Beach
Brookneal
Portsmouth
Virginia Beach Maritime Historic Museum
Chesapeake
Suffolk
Halifax
South Boston
South Hill
Franklin
Meherrin
Emporia
Danville
Atlantic Ocean
John H. Kerr Res.
Roanoke Rapids
Roxboro
Henderson
Elizabeth City
Edenton
Burlington
Durham
Rocky Mount
ROLINA
Raleigh
Wilson
Greenville
Washington
Sanford
Virginia
50 miles / 80 km

AROUND RICHMOND

Richmond is at the heart of everything good about the Old (and new) Dominion. Over a billion dollars of shiny new buildings grace the downtown skyline, giving a misleading first impression, for on the back streets and leafy neighborhoods are graceful, restored mansions, new museums, and rejuvenated warehouses now being put to use as art galleries and downtown apartments. The city is located on the James River, and although the city has spread south, most of the interesting sites are located on the north side, following the city's colonial layout of 1737.

Situated less than an hour's drive from Williamsburg to the east and Jefferson's Monticello to the west, Richmond makes a perfect base for exploring most of central Virginia. The city's importance cannot be overestimated, for it is both the former capital of the old Confederacy and the new hub of the northern "New South." All of which can be savored at a southern gentleman's (or gentlewoman's) pace.

Historic haven: Indians first settled in the area, taking advantage of the James River for food and transportation. Colonists soon followed, establishing one of the first English settlements in America. Named for Richmond-on-Thames in England, which its founders thought it resembled, the city developed quickly into a political and industrial power.

During the Revolutionary War, patriot Patrick Henry spoke the words immortalized in every American child's history book: "Give me liberty or give me death!" while standing near St John's Episcopal Church on Church Hill.

As the new nation developed, so did Richmond, prospering with industries that included tobacco, coal, flour, furniture, and textiles. But it was the Civil War that changed the face of the city forever. Richmond became the Capital of the Confederacy and the site of many bloody battles. By 1865, it was obvious that the Union forces would take control, so on April 2, the city was set alight by the Confederates, destroying many of its important buildings.

Left, Old City Hall. Right, Easter bunny bonnet, Richmond.

Rebounding from the Civil War, the city has been on the move ever since, and is the home of many famous sons and daughters: Maggie Walker was the first female bank president in the country; Edgar Allan Poe inaugurated a new form of American literature; Arthur Ashe Jr, Willie Lanier, and Lanny Wadkins have graced the sports arena; Bill "Bojangles" Robinson, Shirley MacLaine, and Warren Beatty have entertained America. Plus, it is the present capital of Virginia.

Downtown delights: In many ways, Franklin Street could be called the "Gateway to Downtown Richmond" and all that it holds. Richmond landmarks like The Jefferson Hotel, **The Commonwealth Club**, and many others provide the perfect prelude to how the old blends so well with the new. All along Franklin Street, historic houses saved from the wrecking ball now serve as private residences or as offices for organizations like the Garden Club of Virginia, the

Junior League of Richmond and The Woman's Club. **Main Street** is where Richmond means business, for all along this road are industrial, business, financial, government, and legal offices.

The **Broad Street Old and Historic District** features 19th- and 20th-century commercial buildings that are quickly becoming new stores and apartments. This section has also been dubbed **"President's Row"** because of the presidential streets running across it, names that ring throughout the colonial history of America: Adams, Jefferson, Madison, and Monroe.

Broad Street itself presents a mini-history of architecture, from Romanesque to Art Deco, and leads downtown to **City Square**. This area has seen the arrival of successful ventures like the **Richmond Coliseum** and the **Richmond Center for Conventions and Exhibitions**, as well as **Sixth Street Marketplace**, a shopping, dining, and entertainment complex.

Just a few blocks from the Coliseum is the **Jackson Ward Historical District**, a quintessential urban neighborhood that shouldn't be missed, but should be approached with caution late at night. Jackson Ward had its heyday earlier this century. The area was home to many prominent Richmond blacks, including Maggie Walker and Bill "Bojangles" Robinson. The **Maggie L. Walker House** memorializes the woman who founded the nation's oldest, continuously operated, black-owned bank. Nearby, a statue commemorates "Bojangles," the fast-as-lightening tap dancer who grew up in Jackson Ward before achieving fame with his feet. He is caught in a typical pose, dancing down some steps. Jackson Ward also has more cast-iron architecture than anywhere else in the US.

Court End: Within an eight-block section of the downtown area, Court End contains nine National Historic Landmarks, three museums, and 11 other buildings on the National Register of Historic Places.

The focal point of Court End's past is **the Capitol** at Second and Grace streets,

Aerial view of Richmond.

the second-oldest working capitol in the United States (Maryland is the first). The Capitol was designed by Thomas Jefferson and was modeled after a Roman temple in Nimes, France. It was later used as the model for the Capitol building in Washington, DC. Tours of the Capitol are available from Southern Belle guides, complete with accents and anecdotes. Also situated on the grounds is an old bell tower, which now houses a visitor center.

Other buildings of notable interest surround the Capitol. The **Executive Mansion** is the home of Virginia's governor. Richmond's **Old City Hall**, on **Capitol Square**, is in the Gothic Revival style and houses the courtroom from which the area derives its name. **Morton's Row** along Governor Street provides a look at the Italianate residences that used to surround Capitol Square (these are now state offices). Farther along on the Court End neighborhood tour is the **John Marshall House** at Ninth and Marshall streets. This was Mr Marshall's residence for 45 years during which time he served as Secretary of State, Ambassador to France and Chief Justice of the Supreme Court of the United States.

ːourt End ontains ɪine ɬational ɬistoric .andmarks.

The **Wickham-Valentine House** on Clay Street provides a glimpse into the life of John Wickham, Richmond's wealthiest citizen when he built the house in 1812. The property includes the **Valentine Museum**, which relates Richmond's varied history through excellent exhibits and slides. Nearby on Clay Street, the **White House of the Confederacy** provides further insight into Richmond's role during the Civil War. The home served as the residence of Jefferson Davis, president of the Confederacy from 1861 to 1865. It is the centerpiece of the **Museum of the Confederacy**, which houses the largest Confederate collection in the nation. Most of the exhibits from the war were contributed by local veterans and in the early days of the museum, they, or their descendants, often worked as guides.

South of Capitol Square and down by the riverside is **Shockoe Slip**. Perhaps

no other area best displays the way Richmond can combine the past and present to make for an enjoyable future. In the 19th century, Shockoe Slip was a lively area full of stores and tobacco warehouses, but fell into decay when commerce along the James River slowed. Today, the Slip is active again, but now it's full of diners, shoppers, and strollers taking full advantage of the revitalization. This is also the case in nearby **Shockoe Bottom**, a warehouse district experiencing renewed growth with the completion of a flood wall preventing the reoccurrence of damaging high water.

The area is the perfect Richmond blend of old and new. Trendy restaurants, offices, and residences are housed in renovated redbrick buildings from the earlier commercial boom. For example, the old **Belle Bossieux Building** (now a popular restaurant) on 18th Street, was built as a row of shops, with residences above. It was designed by Edmund Bossieux, a New Orleans native who obviously liked the city's architectural style. The oldest, continuously operating **farmers' market** in the country is situated on 17th and Main. Area farmers have been bringing their produce here for over 200 years.

An eerie contrast to the lively Shockoe Bottom commercial scene is provided by the **Poe Museum** on Main Street. Richmond's oldest structure is now an interesting memorial to one of America's finest writers. It presents the life and career of this strange, but talented, local author.

Metropolitan Richmond: If time allows, there are many attractions that are also worth seeing located away from the city center. If you're fascinated by science or looking for a venue the entire family can appreciate, head for the **Science Museum of Virginia** on Broad Street. Housed in the former Broad Street Railroad Station, there are very few "Do Not Touch" signs here. Instead, visitors are encouraged to observe, interact and experience the impact of science on life. The museum is best known for **UNIVERSE**, one of the world's most advanced planetariums and space theaters.

On statue-laced **Monument Avenue**, there are many tributes to the South, including General Robert E. Lee astride his horse Traveller, erected in 1890. Also along the avenue are some of Richmond's most beautiful metropolitan homes, a testament to the city's former gentle and gracious beauty. Nearby, the **Fan District**, so-called because of the shape of its streets, also has some lovely renovated Victorian homes, plus lots of local restaurants.

The **Virginia Museum of Fine Arts**, on the broad and spacious avenue appropriately called **The Boulevard**, contains one of the finest modern art collections in the nation. The collection of Fabergé jeweled Easter eggs and "objects of fantasy" is the largest such collection in the Western world. One block away on North Boulevard is the **Virginia Historical Society**.

With its rolling hills and bluffs overlooking the James River and downtown, serene and forested **Hollywood Cemetery** is the perfect place for a sobering walk through history. The cemetery con-

Jefferson Davis, Hollywood Cemetery.

tains the resting places of more than 18,000 Confederate soldiers, including Confederate president Jefferson Davis, and US presidents James Monroe and John Tyler.

The Jefferson Hotel is an elegant stop on your way back downtown. Built in 1895, one of the oldest and grandest hotels in the South has now been restored, and greets visitors with genuine southern hospitality.

On the other side of downtown, **St John's Episcopal Church** stands on historic **Church Hill**, overlooking the city skyline. It was here that Patrick Henry made his famous "Give Me Liberty or Give Me Death!" speech. Guided tours present the history of the church and allow visitors to stand where Patrick Henry stood surrounded by the likes of George Washington, Thomas Jefferson, and Benjamin Harrison on that famous day in 1775. The speech is often recreated on Sundays.

Around Richmond: There's more to Richmond a bit further afield. The **West End** takes in both the west side of the city and part of Henrico County. The highlight is **Agecroft Hall**, a restored 15th-century English manor house and gardens. It's perfect for a day excursion out of town, as is a cruise aboard the *Annabel Lee*, a 20th-century paddle-wheeler. The scenic trip along the James River presents many dining and entertainment opportunities. The whole family will enjoy **Paramount's Kings Dominion**, 20 miles (32 km) north of Richmond on I-95, which has more than 100 rides, shows, and attractions.

Monticello: Thomas Jefferson's home, Monticello (Italian for "little mountain") lies about an hour's drive west of Richmond. Designed and built by the architect/statesman between 1768 and 1809, Jefferson saw to it that Monticello was unlike any other American house of his day. It is indisputably one of the nation's architectural masterpieces and is the only American home named on UNESCO's World Heritage List (along with such international treasures as the Taj Mahal, the Pyramids, Versailles, and the Great Wall of China).

Thomas Jefferson's gardens at Monticello contain plants from his era.

The neoclassical style is highlighted by the dramatic dome, which appears on the back of the US nickel. Jefferson hated the architecture of Williamsburg, and said that if the British-inspired houses had not had roofs they would be mistaken for brick kilns. Hence his penchant for domes, which he placed on several important buildings.

The entrance hall was the president's private museum, displaying, among other artifacts, items collected by Lewis and Clark during their expedition to the West. A tour of the house and grounds reveals many unusual facts about the man, his house, his role as an architect of both houses and domestic items, and much about Virginia and US history. Jefferson is buried under an obelisk he designed himself.

Monticello can be seen from James Monroe's home, **Ash Lawn-Highland**, 2 miles (3 km) away. The fifth president was a great friend of Jefferson's, who designed Ash Lawn. The house is open to the public.

Monticello is situated along what has come to be called the **Constitution Route**, established in 1975 to recognize its historic significance for Virginia. Four US presidents (Jefferson, Madison, Monroe, and Zachary Taylor) and 11 Virginia governors were either born or built their estates along this road.

The Constitution Route runs right through the university town of **Charlottesville**, another ideal central Virginia base. The town revolves around the **University of Virginia**, including Jefferson's renowned **Rotunda** (that dome again). Jefferson planned the university as the first secular college in America, and planned at the same time the university's "academical village" around graceful, languid lawns. Charlottesville itself has been discovered by Washington, DC's intelligentsia and media folk, many of whom have country retreats in the surrounding area. As a result, the town's shops and restaurants are fairly sophisticated. The countryside north of Charlottesville features some of Virginia's finest vineyards set into rolling hills.

Jefferson's Rotunda, University of Virginia.

Civil War sites: Four important Civil War sites lie within easy reach of this old Capital of the Confederacy. Northeast of town is **Richmond National Battlefield Park**, the site of one of the Confederates' largest hospitals, and where around 76,000 wounded soldiers were treated. A film, *Richmond Remembered*, gives an excellent overview of the role of the city during the Civil War.

To the south of Richmond, the town of **Petersburg** was also under siege during this bloodiest of wars, a situation poignantly recalled at the **Petersburg National Battlefield**. Once Petersburg was taken, there was no hope for the capital. The **Olde Towne** area features a number of museums, shops, and restaurants.

Robert E. Lee and Ulysses S. Grant would probably recognize the small town of **Appomattox** even today, thanks to preservation and renovation efforts. This former town west of Richmond was left to souvenir hunters and scalawags after the war, but under the auspices of the National Park Service, it was rebuilt to reflect its importance in American history. For it was at what is now called the **Appomattox Court House National Historical Park** that Robert E. Lee surrendered to Ulysses S. Grant in April, 1865. Lee dressed for the meeting in his finest uniform; Grant was disheveled and untidy. Lee signed the paper requiring Confederate "arms, artillery, and public property to be parked, stacked and turned over," thus marking the end of what poet Walt Whitman called "a strange sad war." **Lynchburg**, 20 miles (32 km) east of Appomattox, provides a good base for anyone wanting to stay nearby.

When the Rebels' cause collapsed, Jefferson Davis fled the area, ending up for a short while in the town of **Danville**, situated on the North Carolina border. The **Sutherlin House** on Main Street is known locally as the **Last Capital of the Confederacy**, and it has a small museum. This attractive little settlement displays traces of Victorian elegance, and seasonal tobacco auctions are held there as well.

:harlottesville.

Colonial Virginia

When many Virginia visitors think of the Old Dominion, they think of colonial Williamsburg, which, along with its two stately companions, Jamestown and Yorktown, form Virginia's Historic Triangle, the oldest part of the state and among the oldest places in the US. The three sites, which make up the **Colonial National Historical Park**, are linked by the lovely 23-mile (35-km) **Colonial Parkway**, a road that meanders through forests and fields. Although I-64 makes the Williamsburg area only an hour's drive from Richmond, the most interesting route back to the capital is on the Plantation Road (Route 5), which allows you to linger in the past a little while longer.

Williamsburg was once the capital of a colony that extended, they say, all the way to the present-day state of Minnesota. It now covers around 85 percent of the 220-acre (90-hectare) town laid out by Royal Governor Francis Nicholson. Bisected by mile-long **Duke of Gloucester Street**, the Historical Area contains 88 original structures, 50 major reconstructions, and 40 exhibition buildings. There are also 90 acres (35 hectares) of gardens and greens, several museums, not to mention nearby **Carter's Grove**, which features a 1754 mansion, **Wolstenholme Towne**, with a museum, a slave quarter, and a reception center. In colonial Virginia, there's much to see.

The town may feel a little bit like a stylish, upmarket theme park, but it's a great way to rid yourself of the strains and stresses of 20th-century life and truly lose yourself in the considerably slower and more laid-back ethos of a 200-year-old culture – an established way of life which for most of the modern world has long since disappeared.

You can effortlessly examine the ins and outs of this colonial town by peering curiously in the windows of smitheries, grocers, and newsagents; by engaging in inconsequential chit-chat with the welcoming locals; or, if you don't feel the need for such formalities, then simply by wandering around at your own leisure and soaking up the atmosphere of this unique settlement.

One of America's very first planned cities, Williamsburg was constructed between 1698 and 1707, after the abandonment of Jamestown. It was conceived as a gentle country town, so each house on the main street was surrounded by half an acre of land to allow for the smokehouse, stable, dairy, orchard and slave quarters. It was a prosperous market town, lying between the **College of William and Mary** at one end and **the Capitol** at the other. The crown's representative in the colony of Virginia lived in the grand **Governor's Palace** situated in between.

Any visit should begin at the **Visitor Center** and *Williamsburg – The Story of a Patriot*, a 35-minute film. The best way to see often-crowded Williamsburg is to arrive just before the center closes at night and buy your admission tickets for the next day. Then settle in for the night, either at one of the upscale hotels

Left, Governor's Palace. **Right,** patriots set the pace at Williamsburg.

in the Historic Area itself, or in one of the modest chain motels nearby.

Visitors wandering through the town may think they have been caught in a time warp. The houses, shops and hostelries are peopled by citizens in 18th-century dress, applying themselves quietly to the trades of the time with traditional implements. They will willingly explain what they are doing – in 18th-century English. The taverns all serve excellent food, some offering traditional colonial fare, indoors and out, and the minstrels, waiters and waitresses are all in colonial dress. The experience presents a thoroughly convincing and fun opportunity for anyone to imagine what life would have been like in early colonial Virginia. **Merchants Square** is good for buying historic knick-knacks.

Jamestown: This small township was the original site of the first permanent English settlement in the New World. The ruins of a 1640s church tower, and the excavated site of the old capital, are among the most interesting things to see. At **Jamestown Settlement**, the settlers' story is told through a well-made film, full-size recreations of ships and outdoor settings, where costumed interpreters portray life in Virginia at the beginning of the 17th century.

As well as the blacksmiths and other colonial trades, be sure to leave time for the **Jamestown Glasshouse**, where skilled craftsmen in knee britches and cotton shirts make fine green-glass vases and statues by blowing through tubes and baking the results in fiery kilns.

Yorktown: Lying 14 miles (20 km) along the Colonial Parkway from Williamsburg, **Yorktown** was the site of the last major battle of the Revolutionary War and, in 1781, the surrender of Lord Cornwallis to General George Washington. The Visitor Center includes a film and the start of a **Battlefield Tour**. From the top of the Visitor Center, it's possible to look out over the earthworks that still mark the battlefield, while a museum displays, among other artifacts, Washington's original tent. The Historic Area's **Main Street** has several gracious homes dating to the time

Colonial chit-chat, Williamsburg.

when Yorktown prospered as a tobacco center. The **Nelson Home** was built in 1711, the domicile of a signer of the Declaration of Independence. Not far away, the **Yorktown Victory Center** documents the story of the American Revolution through a film, thematic exhibits, and outdoor living history.

Had enough history? If so, the Williamsburg area also features two popular theme parks. **Busch Gardens** is one of the country's largest entertainment centers, offering visitors a wide array of thrills, rides, and nine recreated, 17th-century, European-themed hamlets. **Water Country USA** features more than 50 water rides based around a 1950s and '60s theme. For bargain hunters, head west of Williamsburg for dozens of stores and malls offering **factory outlet shopping**.

Plantation Road (Route 5): In a drive of less than 60 miles (95 km), the road between Williamsburg and Richmond winds through more than 300 years of Virginian and American history. The drive is somewhat like a trip to visit wealthy friends at their large country estate.

Leaving the outskirts of Williamsburg on Route 5 (and the encroaching development), you will soon see a large number of Virginia historic markers. Drivers will also notice the pretty Virginia Byway signs (including a cardinal, the state bird) denoting the historic and scenic importance of the road, which meanders past most of Virginia's finest plantations. But do not be mislead: these homes, fine as they are, do not resemble Tara of *Gone With The Wind* fame. Built to withstand the harshest winters, they are robust rather than romantic and resemble Williamsburg rather than a movie director's image of the South.

The first plantation after leaving Williamsburg is **Sherwood Forest Plantation**, former home of President John Tyler, and said to be the longest frame house in America. It has been a working plantation for more than 240 years and is still occupied by members of the Tyler family. You can see the family's pet graveyard located nearby.

Artisans at work, Jamestown.

Further along is **Evelynton**. Even if plantation interiors bore you, take the road up to the house to enjoy the outside, the greenhouse and the gift shop. If you go on a tour, you'll learn that the family's patriarch, Edmund Ruffin, fired the first shot of the Civil War at Fort Sumter. He also earned the title, the "Father of American Agronomy," by virtually saving 19th-century Virginia from a bleak agricultural economy.

Back on Route 5 for just a few minutes, look for the turn to **Westover Church** on the left. The original church was built nearby in 1613 and this site and "new" building were adopted in 1730. If you're traveling on a Sunday, try to time a visit for the 11am service at this fine country church.

The short dirt road to **Berkeley** was designed for carriages in 1725. (A sign asks motorists to drive "leisurely.") Berkeley dates from 1726 and has since played host to George Washington, the succeeding nine US presidents, and thousands of tourists. Colonial-clad tour guides point out that the military song *Taps* was composed here in 1862, while Union forces were encamped at the plantation during the Civil War. William Henry Harrison, Governor Benjamin Harrison's third son, was born at Berkeley and grew up to become the famous Indian fighter "Tippecanoe," the ninth president of the US and grandfather of the 23rd president.

If you can't make it for the Virginia First Thanksgiving Festival, try a meal in Berkeley's **Coach House Tavern**, where the first 10 US presidents dined.

By taking the other fork in the road from Berkeley, you'll arrive at **Westover Plantation**. This home, built about 1730 by William Byrd II, is not open to the public but its grounds, on the banks of the James River, are perfect for strolling in. The best view is seen by walking across the lawn instead of following the path. The small structure by the ice house contains passageways leading to the river in case of attack by Indians.

On the other side of the house, look out for the iron fence whose supporting columns are topped by unusual stone

Earthworks mark the battlefield at Yorktown.

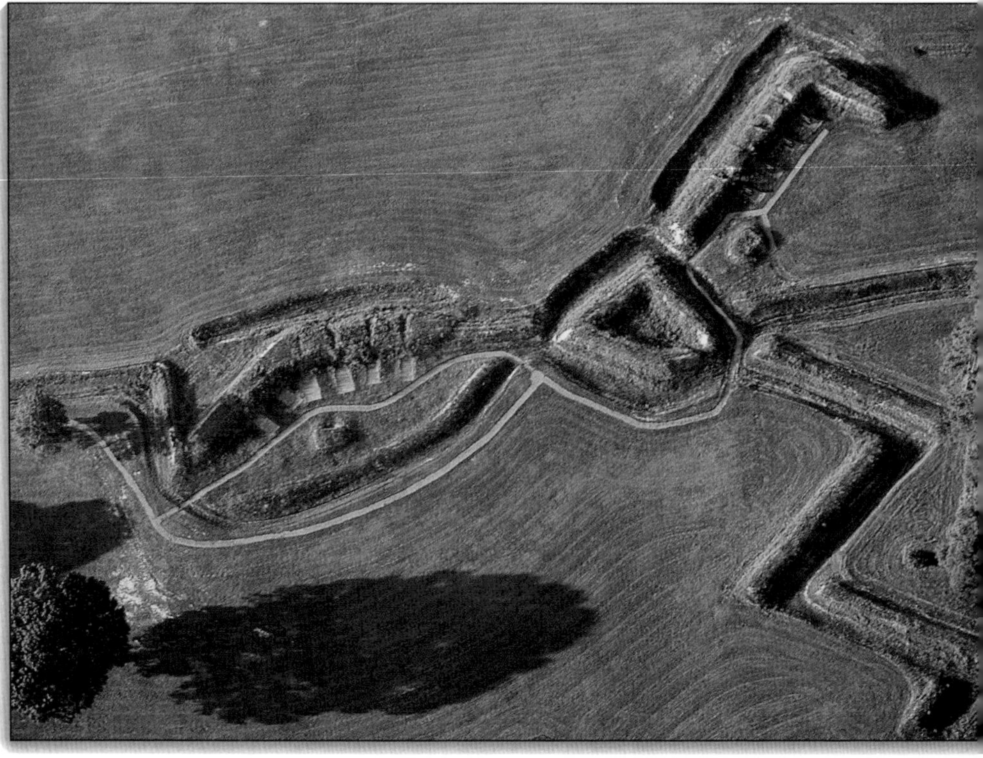

finials cut to resemble an acorn for perseverance (from little acorns great oaks grow); a pineapple for hospitality; a Greek Key to the World for knowledge; a cornucopia or horn of plenty; a beehive for industry and an urn of flowers for beauty.

Leaving Berkeley and Westover, look on the right for one of the best "non-plantation" stops along Route 5, Edgewood Bed-and-Breakfast. Then, only 18 miles (29 km) and hundreds of years away from the soaring skyline of Richmond is the last – and many say the best – of the plantations in the area.

Like many stately mansions, the ride up to **Shirley Plantation** is along a tree-lined road. Shirley was founded in 1613, just six years after the settlers arrived in Jamestown, making it the oldest plantation in Virginia. The brick structure is one of the nation's prime examples of Queen Anne architecture. It has been the home of the Carter family since 1723, and the 800-acre (320-hectare) working plantation is still owned and operated by the ninth and tenth generations of the original family. Anne Hill Carter was the mother of Robert E. Lee.

Many prominent Virginians enjoyed the hospitality of Shirley Plantation, including George Washington and Thomas Jefferson. Look for the plethora of pineapples, a colonial symbol of hospitality, in the hand-carved woodwork of the house and the 3-ft (1-meter) pineapple pinial on the peak of the rooftop. The history- and anecdote-packed tour is good value and a tour of the grounds along the James River is invigorating.

On the outskirts of Richmond, Civil War buffs can head for **Fort Harrison**, one of many large battlefields that comprise the Richmond National Battlefield Park. Fort Harrison was captured by the Union forces led by General Ulysses S. Grant in 1864 with more than 15,000 Yankee troops. The battle was the beginning of the downfall of Richmond, and hence the war, six months later. There's a pretty walking tour or drive through the park that can be accomplished before eventually heading back to Route 5.

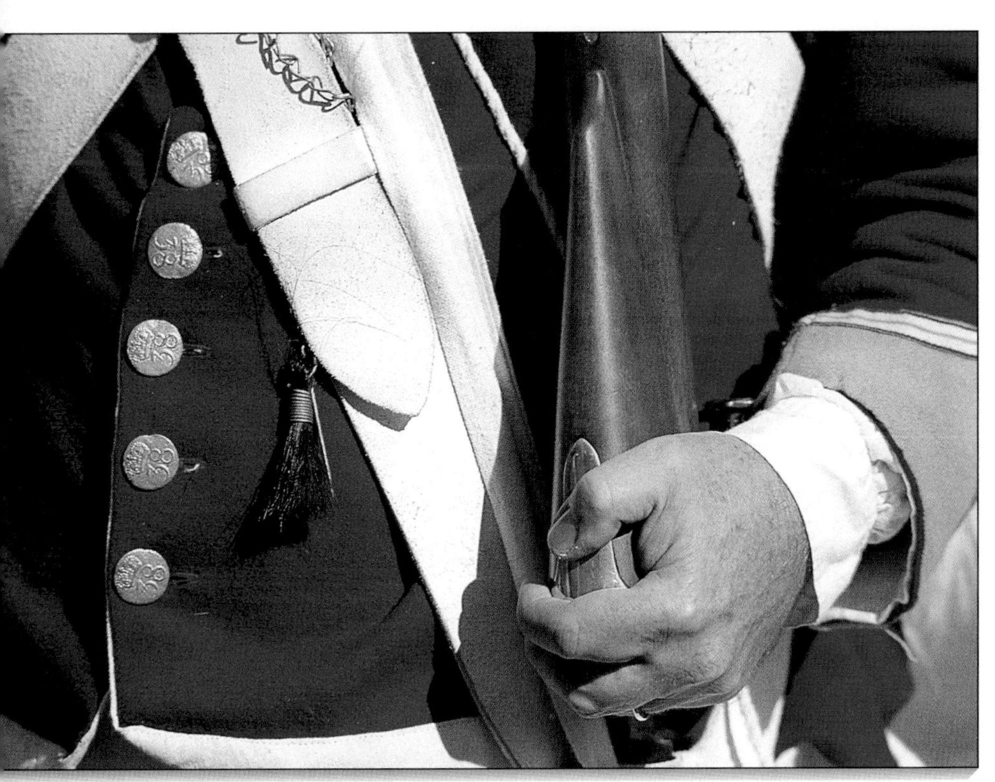

Revolutionary rifles, Yorktown.

Around Virginia

Virginia starts with the ocean and ends at the awesome Blue Ridge Mountains. Its development mirrors its topology. Colonial settlers founded Jamestown and later, Williamsburg, on the far eastern shore as early as the 1600s. Then slowly, as the state grew and prospered, they moved themselves and their families westward. At one point the state's boundaries also encompassed West Virginia, but a dispute over the War Between the States put paid to that. Do not, under any circumstances, confuse the two: Virginians do not take kindly to being compared with their more rural, West Virginia cousins.

In many ways, the Old Dominion has it all: a chic coastline (the Eastern Shore); a popular coastline (Virginia Beach); old money (Northern Virginia) and new business (Richmond's skyscrapers). In amongst all this are rolling hills, misty mountains, subterranean caverns and small towns full of just plain folk. Presided over, and kept safe, by the warships of the United States Navy, what could be better?

Sea breezes: For more than 300 years, the ocean has sustained and romanced the **Tidewater** area, the region in southeastern Virginia along the inlets and river coves to the sea. In the wake of US Navy warships, foreign merchant ships, fishing vessels, and weekend pleasure craft, visitors will find a region in love with the water.

Norfolk is right at the heart of the Tidewater area and serves as a great base for exploring the region. Visitors may find **Waterside** a delightful place to begin and end any visit to Norfolk. This festival marketplace has almost 150 shops stretched along the waterfront, and from the promenade there's a choice of harbor tours on a variety of vessels.

To understand the area more fully, you may also be interested in **Nauticus**. This three-level, 120,000-sq. ft (11,000-sq. meter) maritime museum features one-of-a-kind interactive exhibits, allowing visitors to go on an adventure in marine discovery. The **Douglas MacArthur Memorial** presents an opportunity to reflect on World War II and the role played by this controversial war hero. The memorial houses 11 galleries of memorabilia tracing the life and military career of the general, including surrender documents signed by Japan's Emperor Hirohito. The general's trademark corncob pipe and even his official 1950 limousine are also on display in this museum.

Ships ahoy: The **Norfolk Naval Base** is home port to more than 125 ships, 50 aircraft squadrons, and 65 shore-based military activities. It opened in 1917 on a tiny site and has grown extensively to 5,200 sprawling acres (2,100 hectares), playing a major role in the history of the military and becoming the US Navy's capital base.

Tours on and off the tour buses are conducted by Base personnel, providing an insider's view of military life. Highlights include the massive ships along the waterfront, the huge dry docks, and the historic houses on Dillingham and Willoughby boulevards (built for the Jamestown Exposition in 1907).

The salty tang of the sea is never far away in these parts. Across the river in **Portsmouth**, more military history awaits. The **Portsmouth Naval Shipyard Museum** was established in 1949 in the shipyard itself and later moved to its current waterfront site. This comprehensive museum covers local and naval history, from pre-Civil War times to modern events.

Just around the corner from the shipyards is the bright red **Lightship Museum**. In addition to standard lighthouses, lightships (with lights fixed to their masts) were used to help mariners avoid dangerous shoals or to enter harbors safely at night. This museum (the lightship *Portsmouth*) has been restored to the original condition it was in when commissioned in 1915.

Well-situated on a strategic peninsula, the **Hampton/Newport News** area has been home to many military bases and huge shipbuilding facilities, and has been a port of embarkation and

eft,
irginia's
astern
hore.

debarkation for troops throughout American history. The **War Memorial Museum of Virginia** provides a good look at the state's role in various military conflicts, with around 50,000 artifacts on display, documenting American wars from 1775 to the present. Located on Fort Eustis in Newport News, the **US Army Transportation Museum** examines more than 200 years of army transportation history, from miniature models to huge aircraft, trains, and bulky marine craft.

For anyone interested in the area's military presence, the Hampton/Newport News area includes other sightseeing possibilities. For instance, the **Virginia Air and Space Museum** and the **Hampton Roads History Center** feature 10 air and spacecraft suspended from the 94-ft (30-meter) ceiling, as well as the official Visitor Center for NASA **Langley Research Center**. They also provide a significantly detailed look at the history of the area.

Also in Hampton, the **Air Power Park and Museum** reveals the indispensable role the area has played in early space exploration and aircraft testing. The extensive military presence there has been greatly influenced by the ocean; the **Mariners' Museum** in Newport News has many displays related to military life at sea.

Jutting out into the ocean, **Virginia Beach** is the Atlantic Coast's longest resort beach, stretching a golden 28 miles (45 km). The sand and surf are, of course, Virginia Beach's major attractions, and the hot dog stands, arcade games, razzle-dazzle nightlife and general bonhomie are never far way. But there's lots more to this resort. On a rainy day you might enjoy the Virginia Beach **Maritime Historical Museum**. The building was originally a US Life-Saving/Coast Guard Station and now houses nautical artifacts, scrimshaw, ship models, photographs, marine memorabilia, and a great gift shop for those who want to take a little bit of the Atlantic home with them.

The Northern Neck: The northern portion of the Tidewater area northeast of

Wild pony swim at Chincoteague, Eastern Shore.

Richmond provides a less urban environment, where a trip through the region is rewarded with pretty watery scenery and quiet water-oriented towns. After crossing the Rappahannock River on Route 3, the town of **Irvington** provides a perfect introduction to the Northern Neck, in part due to **The Tides Inn**. This elegant waterfront resort offers lovely rooms, golf, dining, and many water-based amenities.

In **Kilmarnock** due east of Richmond, look for the road to **Christ Church**; it's well worth the detour. Historic Christ Church is the only virtually unchanged colonial church in America and it's a beauty. It was built in a lovely setting by Robert "King" Carter between 1730 and 1734 and has been used continuously for services since 1850. The church has been carefully restored and features fine brickwork, windows, pews and a rare three-decker pulpit.

Further north, **Warsaw** is a quaint Northern Neck town that serves as the Richmond County seat. The **County Courthouse** has been in existence since 1748, as has the **Clerk's Office** nearby, still heated by the original open fireplace. Continuing on Route 3, the road passes through many other attractive Northern Neck towns, including the Westmoreland County seat of **Montross**, with its small museum and Visitor Center.

The Eastern Shore: The Eastern Shore is a distinctive part of Virginia. The people, places and food make this land between Chesapeake Bay and the Atlantic Ocean a very separate place. Well-heeled Washingtonians tend to frequent the Maryland side of the Eastern Shore for weekends away from diplomatic life, while the Virginia side serves as a quiet get-away for people from all over. From the Indians (many towns, like Chincoteague, have Indian names) to centuries-old fishing villages (many towns, like Oyster, have names from the sea), the Eastern Shore is steeped in the past of its people and the water that surrounds it.

Coming from Virginia's Tidewater area, a typical drive starts with the

JS Navy ships, Hampton Roads.

Chesapeake Bay Bridge-Tunnel and heads north. The Bridge-Tunnel is one of the engineering wonders of the world, running 17½ miles (28 km) across the wide-sweeping bay. Once you reach the region, it's best to use US 13 until something takes your fancy and you turn off the main road into another way of life.

The pretty town of **Cape Charles** provides a quick introduction to the Eastern Shore. The railroad and a thriving harbor contributed to an economic boom that lasted until the 1950s, but when these industries stopped the town went into decline. Cape Charles is now experiencing a rebirth, as people renovate the beautiful buildings left over from more prosperous times, and the shops and cafes hurry to cater to their new clientele. Further afield, little fishing towns like **Oyster** and **Cherrystone** are great for a look at Eastern Shore life as it has been lived for decades.

Historic **Eastville** features many beautiful homes, government buildings, and churches. It's all within an easy stroll or drive off the pretty Courthouse Green. Quiet **Pungoteague** ("Place of Fine Sand") is the location of several stately old homes and the oldest church on the Eastern Shore, the very fine **St George's Episcopal Church**, which dates from 1738. Eastville was also the venue for the first drama performed in the New World, *Ye Beare and Ye Cubb*, a smash hit in the year 1665.

The busier **Wachapreague** ("Little City by the Sea") waterfront is popular with both fishermen and tourists. **Onancock** ("Foggy Place") is great for an hour or so of exploration. Market Street, with its attractive shops, leads to the quiet **Wharf**, where you'll find the **Hopkins & Brothers** store, a Virginia landmark that first opened in 1842.

The Wharf is also the embarkation point for boat trips to **Tangier Island**, one of the state's most unusual tourist destinations. The island was first sighted by Captain John Smith in 1608 and has remained relatively unchanged for decades (some say centuries). The local fishermen and their families speak in a pronounced dialect that seems to be left

Virginians with vigor: in the swim (*left*) and getting set to sail (*below*).

over from the days when the island was dominated by fishermen originally from Cornwall, in southwestern England.

Up by the Maryland border, the town of **Chincoteague** is an island community based on the water and, now, tourism. **Main Street** has an old-fashioned feel to it, and many side streets provide good dining, shopping, rooms, and hugely popular annual events. Though any time is good for a visit, one of the biggest draws is the **Chincoteague Volunteer Firemen's Carnival**. This festival takes place in the first two weekends in July and the last two weeks of the month.

In a throwback to bygone times, the carnival grounds feature nightly rides, attractions, games, food and music. But it is the annual **Pony Swim and Pony Auction** late in the month that draws visitors from around the world.

The wild ponies of **Assateague Island** are thought to be the descendants of Spanish ponies, whose owners were shipwrecked on the way to Peru. Some may have bred with runaway horses from the camps of the colonialists. Roaming freely all year round, the animals achieved national fame with the publication of Marguerite Henry's book *Misty of Chincoteague*, and are mostly owned by members of the Chincoteague fire department. On Wednesday in the last week in July, firemen herd the excess foals across the channel to Chincoteague in an event that causes much mirth and even a spot of harmless betting among the sightseeing public, who speculate as to which pony will swim the fastest. On Thursday, the same ponies are driven along Main Street for the annual auction, which raises money for the (volunteer) fire department.

Chincoteague National Wildlife Refuge sits on the southern end of Assateague Island, the perfect place to shed the cares of everyday life. Protected by the National Park Service, this pristine seashore is much like it has been for centuries, a refuge for snow geese, black ducks, terns and sandpipers.

Assateague Island also encompasses Maryland's equally beautiful **Assa-**

Hot-air balloon racing is popular too.

teague State Park, a haven for wild ponies, hikers, bikers, birdwatchers and sun seekers.

Northern Virginia: Thanks to Washington, DC, Northern Virginia is different from the rest of the state. The political machinery and accompanying businesses and people make this region a great deal busier than more outlying areas. However, just under the surface is as much history and as many interesting sites as in the rest of the Old Dominion. Away from the towns, rural Northern Virginia is genteel and civilized. Farms are prosperous and privately owned, and fox hunting is an occasion for weekend house parties.

One of the most important attractions of this region is **Mount Vernon**, George Washington's colonial home near Washington on a bluff overlooking the Potomac River. About 10,000 visitors a day visit Mount Vernon during the peak summer months, so if you're planning a tour of this region, make sure you arrive at this site early *(see page 157)*.

Heading up to Washington, DC from Richmond on busy I-95, visitors will come across the pretty, historic city of **Fredericksburg** along the way. Once considered a part of central Virginia, the suburbs and commuter zeal of the nation's capital has spread so far from its city limits that Fredericksburg, 50 miles (80 km) away, has basically been "annexed" by Northern Virginia. Still, it's easy to understand why upscale Washingtonians would want to live here.

The town was founded in 1728, a small township on the banks of the Rappahannock River. The **Rising Sun Tavern** was the social and political center of early life, built by George Washington's youngest brother, Charles, in 1760. The tavern was host to many of the key colonial patriots, who would come in for a drink and a chat to escape domestic duties back home.The restored building now includes the Tap Room bar (with whalebone checkers) and the gentlemen's chambers, where four men once had to sleep in one bed.

Mercer Apothecary Shop, opened in 1771, is one of the oldest shops of its

Mount Vernon, one of the state's most visited attractions.

kind in the nation and still has shelves filled with Dr Mercer's medicine bottles, pills and prescriptions. The **James Monroe Law Office and Museum** marks the start of a successful private and public career for this Virginia planter and gentleman, the fifth president of the United States.

The **Mary Washington House** was purchased by George for his mother, Mary. Many of Mrs Washington's belongings remain, as well as a beautiful English garden in the back (look for her sundial and the boxwood she planted so long ago). George's only sister, Betty, lived in nearby **Kenmore**, an elegant 18th-century plantation home. The guided tour of this huge house includes Washington family artifacts and much insight into 18th-century plantation life.

The Civil War hit Northern Virginia perhaps harder than any other part of the South – or North, for that matter. Sixty percent of all the military encounters took place in the border state of Virginia, and poignant reminders of these tragic conflicts are everywhere. No fewer than four battlefields make up the **Fredericksburg and Spotsylvania National Military Park**, 17 miles (27 km) from town.

The casualities here, combined with those suffered at **Manassas**, southwest of Washington, were heartwrenching: over 37,000 young men killed or wounded while fighting for their cause. *(See "Civil War Sites," pages 123–7, for more battlefield information.)*

Both Manassas and **Middleburg**, 45 miles (70 km) west of Washington, lie in the region referred to by some as Hunt Country. Anyone interested in horses, horse breeding or fox hunting will feel right at home in the green, rolling hills, pleasant, pasture land and well-heeled, equestrian atmosphere surrounding this pretty town. Middleburg was purchased for $2.50 an acre in 1787 by Revolutionary War Lieutenant Colonel and Virginia statesman Leven Powell. The old-fashioned streets and shops are best explored on foot (if not on horseback) and many of its excellent restaurants serve Virginia wine made from local vineyards. Though larger than Middleburg, **Leesburg** and **Warrenton** are other Northern Virginia towns with small-town appeal.

Big city bustle: The big-city bustle begins as soon as you turn east back towards Washington. In fact, although Manassas is signposted for miles, the highway exits and thundering lanes of traffic are so confusing it is possible to miss the turn-off entirely, ending up back in Washington. Diligent driving and attentive navigating are therefore required. Two areas of Northern Virginia worth seeing are now just suburbs of the capital, and both of these are documented in a companion volume, *Insight Guide: Washington, DC.*

Crossing into **Arlington** on Memorial Bridge from downtown Washington, the first thing to see is **Arlington House**, the home of Robert E. Lee and his wife Mary Anna Randolph Custis, the great-granddaughter of Martha Washington. The couple lived here from 1831 until Lee resigned his commission in the US Army to head the Confederate army. The mansion's former grounds now form a large portion of **Arlington**

Middleburg lies in Virginia's Hunt Country.

This Ole House

On a warm summer's day in Floyd, Virginia (pop. 396), in the heart of the Blue Ridge mountains, nearly 100 years of domestic history went under the auctioneer's hammer. Mrs Ora D. Williams, 94-year-old wife of the late sheriff, was selling up. It was not the sale of the century, but it was the most important the rural community had seen in some time. It was also a glimpse into a way of life that has all but disappeared in most parts of America.

The auction took place under a large tent erected next to the 13-room house on Main Street; in the front row sat four generations of the family. Mrs Williams ("Miz Weyums" to the locals; "Mama Lou" to the family) sat next to her son on a turn-of-the-century loveseat. Sitting in a line alongside were daughters, grandchildren and great-grandchildren.

The event had been publicized, but only up to a point. Had ads been placed in newspapers up North, canny dealers from New England would have gotten the bargains of a lifetime. As it was, most of the 1,000 people in attendance came from the area.

In the days leading up to the sale a steady stream of visitors paid a call on Mrs Williams, and almost everyone brought food: fried chicken, lima beans, homemade bread from the Amish community. The daughters, preparing the rooms for auction, came across items that spanned 60 years in the life of a Virginia family. From the basement came countless jars of canned beans, tomatoes, pears and applesauce made from the produce in the garden.

From the kitchen came some long-forgotten moonshine in a glass bottle ("I asked Mother where it came from. She said Sam had made it, so we knew it was OK to drink"), plus copper pots and pans used for cooking up huge farmhouse breakfasts: homemade sausages, hot buttered biscuits and fresh eggs from the chickenhouse.

On the day of the sale, the temperature was rising fast, and lemonade and soda pop did a rapid trade in a corner of the tent. Men in faded baseball caps discussed farm equipment and guns, while grouped together on the lawn, bedroom suites, rocking chairs and heavy, gilt-framed mirrors presented a surreal domestic picture. Mrs Williams put on her best hat.

The auctioneer's patter was infectious, with one joke after another about straw hats and glass chickens, two items the owner collected by the dozens. Mrs Williams knew the background to each piece on the block, and passed the information on: the dining room suite had been made from trees on Mr Williams' land. The grandfather clock was commissioned from a local craftsman, one clock for each child. Table and chairs, bought from a Sears & Roebuck catalogue in 1919, were fetched from the depot by horse and buggy. While clearing up, a daughter had found the very catalogue; it, too, fetched a price. The living room suite was the only furniture they owned in the beginning, which made the room easy to empty for square dancing. Dancing was the only form of recreation around, as the nearest movie theater was 22 miles away.

During the auction, whenever a member of the family placed a bid, other buyers courteously dropped out, one woman coming up afterwards to apologize for unintentionally driving up the price. After the house contents were sold it was time for the outbuildings: the springhouse, a white, wooden latticework affair much loved by the grandchildren because watermelons were left there to cool; a woodshed filled with logs ready for burning; a barn stuffed to the gills with old sewing machines, washing machines and heavy stone mason jars. The last item to go under the hammer was the white-frame house on Main Street.

The auction lasted far into the evening, over 10 hours in all. Some people, dazed by the heat, went home early, but Mrs Williams, in her navy-blue wide-brimmed hat, stayed till the end. ■

National Cemetery (which includes the Tomb of the Unknowns and John F. Kennedy's gravesite). It is here that the somber and moving **Changing of the Guard** takes place every day and night. At the cemetery's north end is the **Iwo Jima Memorial**, a huge bronze statue commemorating the World War II battle site where more than 5,000 US marines died. South of Arlington Cemetery is the five-sided **Pentagon building**, headquarters of the US Department of Defense. Tours of the huge building are very popular.

South of Arlington is the neighborhood called Alexandria. **Old Town Alexandria** was founded as a seaport in 1749. Known as George Washington's hometown, this is where Washington and fellow patriots attended the theater, church, and political meetings during the formative years of the Revolution.

Among the historic landmarks and museums open to the public are the **Ramsay House Visitor Center**; **The Lyceum** (museum and exhibits); **Gadsby's Tavern Museum**; **Fort Ward Museum and Historic Site** (a large Civil War fort); the **Black History Resource Center**; and the **Torpedo Factory Art Center**. Lovers of history will find much to see here.

George Washington would ride into Alexandria from **Mount Vernon**, his stately plantation, which he shared with his wife Martha. It is now America's most visited historic estate. For almost a century, its custodians have maintained a continuous hunt for the plantation's original furnishings, many of which have been found. The lovely house and 30 acres (12 hectares) of gardens sweeping down to the river provide a provocative image of the colonial era.

It's not surprising that Washington had hoped to retire here, but the call of the presidency meant he was able to visit only once or twice a year, before coming home to rest permanently under the towering trees. Fans of colonial-era architecture will also enjoy **Woodlawn Plantation** (built for Washington's foster daughter, Nelly Custis Lewis) and local politician George Mason's **Gunston Hall** nearby.

The Shendandoah Valley: The country charm and easy convenience of the Shenandoah Valley attracts thousands of visitors annually, especially during the fall, when the colors of the trees turn burnt orange and red, and the Skyline Drive of Shenandoah National Park showcases nature at its finest (*see pages 165–9*). The valley stretches north-to-south, from West Virginia's pretty Eastern Panhandle down through the state towards North Carolina, ending at the town of Roanoke. Made famous by song and history, Shenandoah is flanked by wooded hills and the misty Blue Ridge Mountains, which range in elevation from 3,000 to 5,000 ft (900 to 1,500 meters). The "valley" is about 200 miles (320 km) long and is generally 10 to 20 miles (16 to 32 km) wide.

I-81 runs the entire length of the valley, making it convenient for quick stops at points of interest. But Route 11 is more pleasurable, ambling through small towns, past wineries and subterranean caverns, historic sites and pretty inns that recall a more leisurely time.

Making cider.

For many visitors, the Shenandoah Valley begins in **Winchester**, near the West Virginia border. Vitally important during the Civil War, Winchester changed hands 70 times during the skirmishes and was the scene of six major battles. The Winchester-Frederick County Visitor Center is located just off I-81 in the **Hollingsworth Mill House**. It adjoins one of Winchester's three important museums, **Abrams Delight**, built in 1754 by one of the area's earliest settlers, Abraham Hollingsworth.

George Washington's Office Museum in the downtown area is a small log cabin that Washington used as an office in 1755 and 1756, while he supervised the construction of Fort Loudoun as protection against Indians and the French. Just north on Braddock Street, **Stonewall Jackson's Headquarters Museum** serves as a third draw for museum and history buffs. Winchester visitors may want to time their stop for the first weekend in May, when the entire area turns into a secular version of heaven as the pale blossoms on the hundreds of fruit trees float lazily to the ground or drift languidly in the breeze. This celestial event is celebrated in an annual **Apple Blossom Festival**.

Most visitors to **Middletown**, further down, head straight for the Wayside Inn for a great meal (Southern dishes; try the peanut soup) or for the night. Next door is the **Wayside Theatre**, a popular place for productions. Lying due east of Washington, DC, Middletown in recent years has begun to mirror the preoccupations of its somewhat upscale clientele. Just south of Middletown, **Belle Grove Plantation** is well worth a stop. The stunning house, built in 1794, is architecturally significant because of the involvement Thomas Jefferson had in its design.

Ten minutes down the road from Belle Grove is **Strasburg**, rightfully known as "The Antique Capital of the Blue Ridge." The **Strasburg Emporium** and other small stores give you an opportunity to shop 'til you drop.

South of Strasburg, the Shenandoah Valley continues, with the mountains rising to the skies on both sides. Along the way, friendly towns like **Woodstock**, **Edinburg**, and **Mount Jackson** are perfect places to stop for a look at local Shenandoah Valley life.

Further south, **Shenandoah Caverns** surprises many people with its sheer beauty and stunning lighting. Descend by elevator to Bacon Hall, where the formations here look remarkably like strips of bacon. Other favorite formations include the **Capitol Dome** in Cathedral Hall (it looks like the US Capitol) and **Rainbow Lake** (colorful reflections in a shallow pond).

The New Market area played a key role in the Civil War. The **New Market Battlefield Historical Park** honors the brave charge made by teenage cadets recruited from the Virginia Military Institute to join their older brothers-in-arms on the battlefield. The cadets helped to rally the troops and on May 15, 1864, contributed to a major Confederate victory. There are extensive background exhibits and a walking tour.

Many people are lured to the small town of Luray by the **Luray Caverns**.

Luray Caverns.

This large, spooky cave was discovered by a local entrepreneur in 1878 and has since been the site of several subterranean weddings. Couples are serenaded by a huge "stalacpipe" organ, mentioned in the *Guinness Book of Records*, which plays notes when the stalactites are struck by electronically controlled rubber-tipped plungers. If you plan to visit the caverns, be sure to take a sweater because it's chilly underground, even when it's blazing hot outside.

Luray, a gateway to Shenandoah National Park, is dominated by a beautiful hotel on a hill, **The Mimslyn**. Despite its imposing position, this hostelry with its elegant dining room and indoor roof terrace costs little more to stay in than the nondescript motels nearby.

After passing through the busy college city of **Harrisonburg**, the quieter college town of **Staunton** awaits. This hilly town with its restored train depot is also the site of the **Woodrow Wilson Birthplace and Museum**, which details the life and times of the 28th president of the United States. The most popular exhibit is President Wilson's Pierce-Arrow limousine. Staunton is also the home of the **Museum of American Frontier Culture**. This hugely successful undertaking in the Shenandoah Valley countryside features 18th- and 19th-century working farms from England, Germany, Northern Ireland, and America, providing an insight into Shenandoah Valley frontier life.

A half-hour to the east of Staunton, the town of **Waynesboro** is the home of well-known southern artist P. Buckley Moss. Her stick-figure paintings are collected throughout the world and the **Moss Museum** in Waynesboro displays and sells much of her work. Nearby are several old-fashioned towns, such as **Buena Vista** and **Stuarts Draft**, where life has slowed down to a trickle.

Around Waynesboro, it's easy to pick up I-64, the big interstate that heads east towards Charlottesville and the Jefferson-designed Rotunda at the University of Virginia, then continues east towards Richmond. *(See "Around Richmond," pages 135–41.)*

The General Store, Buena Vista.

History lures travelers to **Lexington**, the prettiest town in the Shenandoah Valley if not in all of Virginia itself. A 19th-century college town, Lexington is home to the **Virginia Military Institute (VMI)** and **Washington and Lee University**. Despite its military heritage, the town is not at all rigid or stuffy. Locals are unfailingly pleasant and helpful, and the plethora of antique shops (including delightful secondhand book shops) makes strolling casually around a great way to pass the hours.

VMI was founded in 1839 and is the oldest state-supported military college in the nation, earning it the sobriquet "The West Point of the South." Stonewall Jackson taught here. Highlights include the cadet barracks, the VMI Chapel and Museum, the George C. Marshall Research Museum, and a dress parade (usually held on Friday or Saturday). Tree-shaded Washington and Lee University was founded in 1749. Tiptoe quietly into **Lee Chapel** to see the final resting place of Robert E. Lee. Popular stops in town (all within walking distance) include the Visitor Center, the **Stonewall Jackson House**, Jackson's pre-Civil War home, and the **Stonewall Jackson Memorial Cemetery**.

Staunton and Lexington are both just an hour from one of the state's (and the nation's) finest resorts. Located west of the Shenandoah Valley amid green rolling mountains, **The Homestead** is a destination in its own right. For more than 225 years, country road drivers have come to The Homestead to restore and refresh themselves in the invigorating mountain air and soothing, healing waters. It was thought that the waters could cure or relieve the symptoms of ailments such as rheumatism, arthritis and hypertension.

Dr. Thomas Walker, an early explorer of the valley wrote in 1750: "We went to Hot Springs... the spring is clear and warmer than new milk and there is a spring of cold water within twenty feet of the warm one." In 1755, George Washington visited Hot Springs while on an inspection tour of forts along the Allegheny frontier. Many travelers fol-

Shenandoah Valley near Front Royal.

lowed and The Homestead grew to accommodate them.

Just 14 miles (22 km) south of Lexington is **Natural Bridge**, which calls itself one of the seven natural wonders of the world. This 215-ft (65-meter) high stone arch was carved by water over countless centuries and stands as one of the Shenandoah Valley's most famous sites. Its popularity owes as much to marketing as to nature, however, for although Natural Bridge is lovely to behold, there are plenty of sites as beautiful – and much less commercialized – up in the mountains of Shenandoah National Park.

Roanoke is the valley's largest city, the southern end of this rolling, pine-scented region. It is known as the "Star City of the South," symbolized by a huge 88-ft (27-meter) neon star on **Mill Mountain** overlooking the city and the valley. Roanoke is known for its historic **Farmers Market**, where growers have been coming by country road to sell their fresh fruits, vegetables, and flowers for nearly 120 years. If you get the opportunity, buy some homemade apple butter for tomorrow's breakfast toast. The little downtown area around the marketplace has been spruced up a treat, as has the 1882 **Hotel Roanoke**, built during the golden era of railroad travel. The **Center in the Square**, a multi-level arts center, throbs with life and live performances. Other attractions include the **Virginia Museum of Transportation** (dozens of big trains and other vehicles) and the **Harrison Museum of African American Culture**. The city provides a fitting end to any Shenandoah Valley visit.

Southwest Virginia: Southwest Virginia often plays second fiddle to the rest of the Old Dominion, but only because of the long drive it typically takes to reach the area from anywhere else in the state. If you do head all this way south, you'll find a pretty and proud region full of music and mountains.

Abingdon, a cultured and dignified little town with several gracious homes, is an ideal base for exploring the area along US 58. Be sure to check the sched-

Roanoke: Star City of the South.

ule of the Barter Theatre for a production of the State Theatre of Virginia, or ask at the antebellum **Martha Washington Inn**, where you may like to stay.

West of Abingdon, up in **Maces Spring**, traditional mountain music fans flock to the Carter Family Memorial Music Center. The original Carter Family (Maybelle, AP, and Sara) was discovered by a talent scout in 1927. The family went on to record 300 songs, including *Keep on the Sunny Side* and *Wildwood Flower*. Traditional and bluegrass music can be heard every Saturday night and at a huge festival held every August.

Natural Tunnel State Park provides a glimpse of Mother Nature's power. Just outside of Duffield, Natural Tunnel is a huge tunnel formed more than one million years ago from the dissolving of limestone and dolomitic bedrock by groundwater bearing carbonic acid. Later, the flow of Stock Creek enlarged the opening, which is now more than 400 ft (120 meters) in height.

Big Stone Gap: Just 15 miles (24 km) north on US 23, **Big Stone Gap** offers an entire day of possibilities. This quiet town is famed for its outdoor drama, *Trail of the Lonesome Pine*. The play tells the love story of a Virginia mountain girl and a handsome young mining engineer from the east. Next door to the small outdoor theatre is the **Jane Tolliver House and Craft Shop**, where the heroine of the drama lived in real life. Other stops in Big Stone Gap include the **Southwest Virginia Museum**, **John Fox, Jr Museum** (author of *Trail of the Lonesome Pine*), the **Harry W. Meador, Jr Coal Museum**, the Victorian homes of **Poplar Hill**, and the memorial at **Miner's Park** (the town is called the "Gateway to the Coalfields").

Daniel Boone came to the area in 1775 and marked out the Wilderness Trail from Cumberland Gap into Kentucky. Mass immigration through the Gap began, with 12,000 people crossing into the new territory by the end of the Revolutionary War and another 100,000 by the time Kentucky was admitted to the Union in 1792. Today, **Cumberland Gap**, situated at the convergence of Virginia, Kentucky, and Tennessee, is worth a look. (*See "Around Kentucky" on page 200 and "East Tennessee" on page 232*).

From music to mountain lakes, there are many other southwest Virginia destinations. Located just 7 miles (11 km) from the Blue Ridge Parkway in southwest Virginia, **Galax** residents call their town the "World Capital of Old-Time Mountain Music." And they mean it. Each winter, the Galax Downtown Association sponsors the **Galax Mountain Music Jamboree**.

The performances feature old-time and bluegrass bands, as well as cloggers and other entertainment. An **Old Fiddler's Convention** and **Fiddlefest** are held the second weekend each August. The Jamboree is held in June, July, and September, making Galax a four-month music mecca. **Mountain Lake** is music to the ears and eyes for those looking for an outdoors getaway, a mountain resort since 1857 featuring thousands of acres of tall trees, stunning mountain scenery, and a clear mountain lake.

Left, the Southwest is known for its fiddle music. Right, rocky mountain view.

SHENANDOAH AND THE BLUE RIDGE PARKWAY

Once upon a time, according to Cherokee legend, everything lived in the sky. When the sky became too crowded, a diving beetle plunged into the ocean and emerged with a ball of mud. The ball of mud grew enormously, but it was too soggy for anything to live on it. So a buzzard volunteered to fly close to the earth and dry it with his wings. The buzzard flapped and flapped but soon tired and fell from the sky. Its outstretched wings form the mountains we know as the southern Appalachians, home of **Shenandoah National Park**.

Unlike most national parks, Shenandoah was pieced together from private land, much of it damaged by logging, farming and erosion. Situated in Virginia's **Blue Ridge Mountains**, an eastern rampart of the Appalachian chain, the park is a long, narrow corridor of ridges and valleys clothed in dense forest and laced with leaping streams and waterfalls. Running along the backbone of the mountains is **Skyline Drive**, a 105-mile (169-km) scenic highway that serves as the park's main thoroughfare.

Twelve thousand years ago, Native Americans made forays up these forested ridges to gather chestnuts, hickory nuts, wild berries and medicinal plants. Hunters stalked deer, woodland elk and bison, often using fire to drive the animals from cover or to lure them into greening meadows recovering from recent burns.

The first European settlers preferred to farm rich bottomlands in the Virginia and North Carolina Piedmont. By the mid-1700s, as settlers proliferated and arable land dwindled, farmers began to clear the lower slopes of the Blue Ridge, named for the ever-present veil of thin blue haze that drifts between the peaks.

At first they "deadened" trees by stripping the bark around the base. After the leaves shriveled, sunlight penetrated to the forest floor. But the thin soil eroded easily, leaving rocky rubble where shortly before corn and beans had flourished. Although the mountains were sparsely populated, families often moved when the fields played out. By the early 1900s, much of the Blue Ridge had been cleared and there were few plots of fertile soil left to exploit.

The effort to create a national park in the Blue Ridge was launched in the 1920s, and construction of Skyline Drive was begun in 1931. Much of the work was done by the Civilian Conservation Corps, created by President Franklin D. Roosevelt to relieve unemployment during the Great Depression. After more than a decade of land acquisition and boundary disputes, the park was dedicated in 1936. More than 2,000 people still lived within the park, however, and relocation was no easy matter. Despite poor economic conditions, many families resisted pressure to move away from their beloved mountain homes.

A second major project – the **Blue Ridge Parkway** – was also started in the 1930s. Described by former Park Service director William Penn Mott, Jr, as "the most graceful road in America," the Blue Ridge Parkway stretches 469 miles (755 km) along the backbone of

_eft, Mabry Mill. Right, entrance to peace and tranquility.

the Appalachian Mountains between Shenandoah and Great Smoky Mountains national parks, crossing the Virginia state border into North Carolina. Along the way are countless overlooks, historic sites, wayside exhibits, hiking trails and museums.

To make finding your way easier, both Skyline Drive and the Blue Ridge Parkway are marked by mileposts starting from their northernmost points. Together, these two scenic drives form the longest and one of the most stunning roads in the National Park System.

Daughter of the stars: The "windshield" views along Skyline Drive are stupendous, but the true essence of Shenandoah lies beyond the pavement. Consider for a moment just how far the park has come in so short a time. Only 60 years ago, these mountains were dominated by bare, eroded ridges and hardscrabble farms. Today, only about 5 percent of Shenandoah is developed; the rest is occupied by a mature and nearly continuous array of pines, oaks, hickories, hemlocks and tulip poplars.

Doe on the Skyline Drive.

The forest is crosshatched with more than 500 miles (800 km) of hiking and horseback-riding trails, including 95 miles (153 km) of the **Appalachian Trail**, which roughly parallels Skyline Drive and then continues south along the Blue Ridge Parkway for about 100 miles (160 km) before veering west.

By early spring, visitors start their annual pilgrimage to the park to see the parade of wild flowers, with a second batch of visitors in October when the foliage flames up into a final burst of color. Gum, sourwood, dogwood, sumac and sugar maple are abundant and especially colorful along southern sections of the Blue Ridge, eliciting "oohs" and "ahhs" of delight from visitors around each new curve.

White-tailed deer graze peacefully along the roadsides, barely raising their heads as cars pass. Does have brought their spotted fawns into the open by mid-summer. Gray squirrels and chipmunks skitter across the leafy forest floor in search of acorns and hickory nuts. Gray foxes prowl from dusk to dawn, as do striped skunks and their rarer spotted cousins. Woodchucks (also called groundhogs) gorge themselves on roadside grasses. Bears forage for nuts, berries and small animals. Combined, the parks shelter more than 200 species of birds throughout the year, including a variety of warblers, woodpeckers, vireos, owls and hawks.

Doing the drive: If you visit Shenandoah from the north in the summer, you will enter a shady green tunnel of hardwoods upon leaving Highway 340 at **Front Royal**. Like a winding staircase, the pavement curves around the hills, then sprawls into a breathtaking overlook above the **Shenandoah Valley**. Nearby **Dickey Ridge Visitor Center** provides an introduction to Shenandoah's natural and human history with exhibits, books, free maps and pamphlets. Just across the road, for approximately 1½ miles (2½ km), **Fox Hollow Trail** loops through old farmsteads reclaimed by pines and hardwoods.

By mile 21, you will be nearing an elevation of 3,400 ft (1,040 meters), and from **Hogback Overlook** on a clear day, you can count the bends in the **Shenandoah River** meandering through the verdant valley. About a mile south, several trails diverge from the **Mathews Arm Area**, including the nearly 4-mile (6-km) round-trip to **Overall Falls**. The double cascade has a drop of 93 ft (28 meters), but it slows to a trickle in dry weather. As with most trails, going downhill is easy. Allow double the time for the more arduous return.

For an easier hike, try the 3½-mile (5.5-km) self-guiding **Traces Nature Trail**, which leads past a few remaining signs of early white settlements now being reclaimed by the forest. Farther south at mile 37, a steep 3-mile (5-km) round-trip leads to **Corbin Cabin**, a log home built in 1909 by George Corbin, whose family scratched a living from the soil in this isolated "holler."

At **Thornton Gap**, Highway 211 crosses Skyline Drive. To rise above the scene, park at **Panorama Restaurant** and hike the Appalachian Trail to **Mary's Rock**, named for the bride of one of the area's first settlers. The nearly 2-mile (3-km) ascent gains 1,210 ft (369 meters), but the 360-degree view is certainly worth the effort. As one continues south, the rocky visage of **Stony Man** appears above the drive as milepost 39 comes into view. The trail up to the 4,011-ft (1,227-meter) summit begins at the **Skyland** resort.

Touch the sky: During the 1890s, George Freeman Pollock, an enthusiastic promoter of the region, built Skyland on a land tract at the head of **Kettle Canyon**. Most original buildings have been replaced, but the resort continues to provide lodging for hikers, horseback riders and those who simply want to relax in the cool mountain air. Across the drive, a 3½-mile (5.5-km) trail follows **Whiteoak Run** as it cascades down a series of six waterfalls.

Hikers can loop back through the **Limberlost**, a superlative grove of hemlocks, some of which are 400 years old. Pollock saved the cathedral-like setting, in which sunbeams are filtered by misty air and sounds are muffled by a carpet of ferns and mosses, by offering

Shenandoah Valley seen from the mountains.

his neighbors $10 for every massive tree they did not cut down.

At 3,680 ft (1,122 meters), Skyland is the highest point on Skyline Drive. A few miles farther south are trailheads for 4,049-ft (1,234-meter) **Hawksbill**, the highest summit in the park, whose cloud-shrouded, windswept peak looms for miles. Three routes give hikers a choice – either short and steep or progressively longer with easier grades.

Continuing south, **Big Meadows** marks the halfway point on Skyline Drive with camping, Visitor Center, nature programs and horseback riding. It is home of the **Big Meadows Lodge**, a model of rustic elegance constructed of local chestnut in 1939. Good Virginia wines are served in the dining room.

It is not unusual to see deer among the waving grasses of the 300-acre (120-hectare) meadow at dawn or dusk. In late spring, brilliant male indigo buntings sing bubbly songs as they flit about in search of mates. Trails radiate east to **Dark Hollow Falls** and west to **Lewis Run Falls**. Dark Hollow, which requires a round-trip of just over a mile, is the waterfall closest to Skyline Drive. The trail to Lewis Run is longer and steeper, but the view of the tiered 90-ft (27-meter) falls is definitely worth the extra bit of effort.

It's a short drive to **Milam Gap**, where you can park the car and begin the 2-mile (3-km) jaunt to **Camp Hoover**, a mountain hideaway built by President Herbert Hoover to escape the pressures of Washington, DC. Getting there can be a little tricky: follow the Appalachian Trail to the **Mill Prong Trail** and then turn onto the access road. A National Historical Landmark, the site is still used by government officials.

Farther along, the **South River** picnic area at mile 62.8 is decked out in white trillium each spring. Lucky hikers may spot yellow lady slipper orchids along the trip to **South River Falls**.

Loft Mountain is the southernmost campground along Skyline Drive. Rangers offer summer nature programs, and the self-guiding, 1⅓-mile (2-km) **Deadening Trail** explores forest succession,

Shenandoah: the valley of the "daughter of the stars."

from the clearing of fields by settlers to the return of locusts, hickories and oaks.

From Loft Mountain, you slowly descend to the terminus of Skyline Drive at Rockfish Gap. For a final streamside hike, try **Doyles River** or **Jones Run**. Both have pretty cascades, accessible from trailheads at mile 81.1 or 84.1. At mile 84.8, a short round-trip to **Blackrock** showcases a stunning vista overlooking the historic villages of **Grottoes** and **Port Republic** in the southern Shenandoah Valley.

Blue Ridge Parkway: To continue your mountain odyssey, cross I-64 at **Rockfish Gap** and head south to **Humpback Rocks Visitor Center** on the Blue Ridge Parkway. Here, a reconstructed farmstead explores the lives of turn-of-the-century mountaineers.

At the **James River** crossing (mile 63.8) are remnants of the **Kanawha Canal**. This antebellum water highway flowed west from Richmond for 200 miles (320 km), with mule-drawn barges bringing salt, cloth, guns and ammunition to mountain communities. The settlers sold cured meats, whiskey and tanned hides, which were transported to willing buyers downriver. A self-guiding trail begins at the Visitor Center.

The Parkway: the most graceful road in America.

The parkway climbs from its lowest point at James River southwest to **Peaks of Otter**. Here a Visitor Center, campground, lodge and restaurant nestle in a forest clearing that offers dramatic views

The parkway skirts the eastern edge of Roanoke, a quiet town that grew into a thriving community with the coming of the railroad in the 1880s. South of Roanoke lies **Mabry Mill**, with a water wheel where corn and buckwheat are ground. Sorghum making, apple-butter cooking and blacksmiths at work are reenacted here. Demonstrations of weaving take place on a century-old, four-poster loom at the **Brinegar Cabin** (mile 238), situated in **Doughton Park**.

Miles of hiking trails radiate from the nearby campground, and deer frequent the meadows at dawn and dusk. Farther south, **Northwest Trading Post** offers mouthwatering country hams, sourwood honey and an array of crafts.

KENTUCKY

Close your eyes, and think the word: *Kentucky*. What comes to mind? First visions might include a horse, racing toward the finish line at the Kentucky Derby or the white-suited, smiling countenance of Colonel Sanders, the founder of Kentucky Fried Chicken. These are accurate images, but merely the most obvious ones, as the traveler who takes the time to explore will discover. For Kentucky is a land of small gems and, from the Appalachian Mountains westward to the Mississippi River, it offers a kaleidoscope of ever-changing, delightful treasures. It is also a region rich in history, and enjoys an abundance of natural resources.

Kentucky is a Commonwealth, one of only four in the country. In 1785, frontier settlers asked that Virginia's western district be recognized as a "free and independent state, known as the Commonwealth of Keentucky." Seven years later it was admitted to the Union, the first state west of the Appalachian Mountains to do so. The Commonwealth has always considered itself "southern," yet during the Civil War it never seceded. Trying, and failing, to remain neutral, Kentucky contributed 100,000 soldiers (including 30,000 freed blacks and runaway slaves) to the Northern cause while 40,000 men fought for the Confederacy. Both Civil War presidents, Abraham Lincoln and Jefferson Davis, were born in Kentucky, within one year and 140 miles (225 km) of each other.

Kentucky is a land of great natural beauty. The 650,000-acre (260,000-hectare) Daniel Boone Forest is one of four national recreational areas. Its rivers, lakes, and streams are blessed with more water than any other state except Alaska. Thanks to an active program by the state fisheries department, fishing throughout the Commonwealth is varied and superb.

A myriad of manmade pleasures awaits, too: Actors Theatre in Louisville is considered one of the finest regional theaters in the country. Recreated forts recall pioneer life; docents bring alive the lifestyles and crafts of early settlers. Antebellum mansions bespeak a population who believed in culture and education. Each October, the Civil War Battle of Perryville is re-enacted. Local festivals celebrate Kentucky's music, flowers, and food; others commemorate the coal mining heritage, or poke fun at its "hillbilly" image. The only Corvette sportscar manufacturing plant in the world is in Bowling Green; nearby is one of Earth's greatest natural wonders, Mammoth Cave.

The legendary Daniel Boone, upon seeing the meadowlands of central Kentucky, wrote: "Nature was here a series of wonders and a fund of delight." It still is.

Preceding pages: the *Belle of Louisville* paddlesteamer cruises the Ohio River. Left, Union and Confederate soldiers reenact the Battle of Perryville. Kentucky contributed soldiers to both sides of the Civil War.

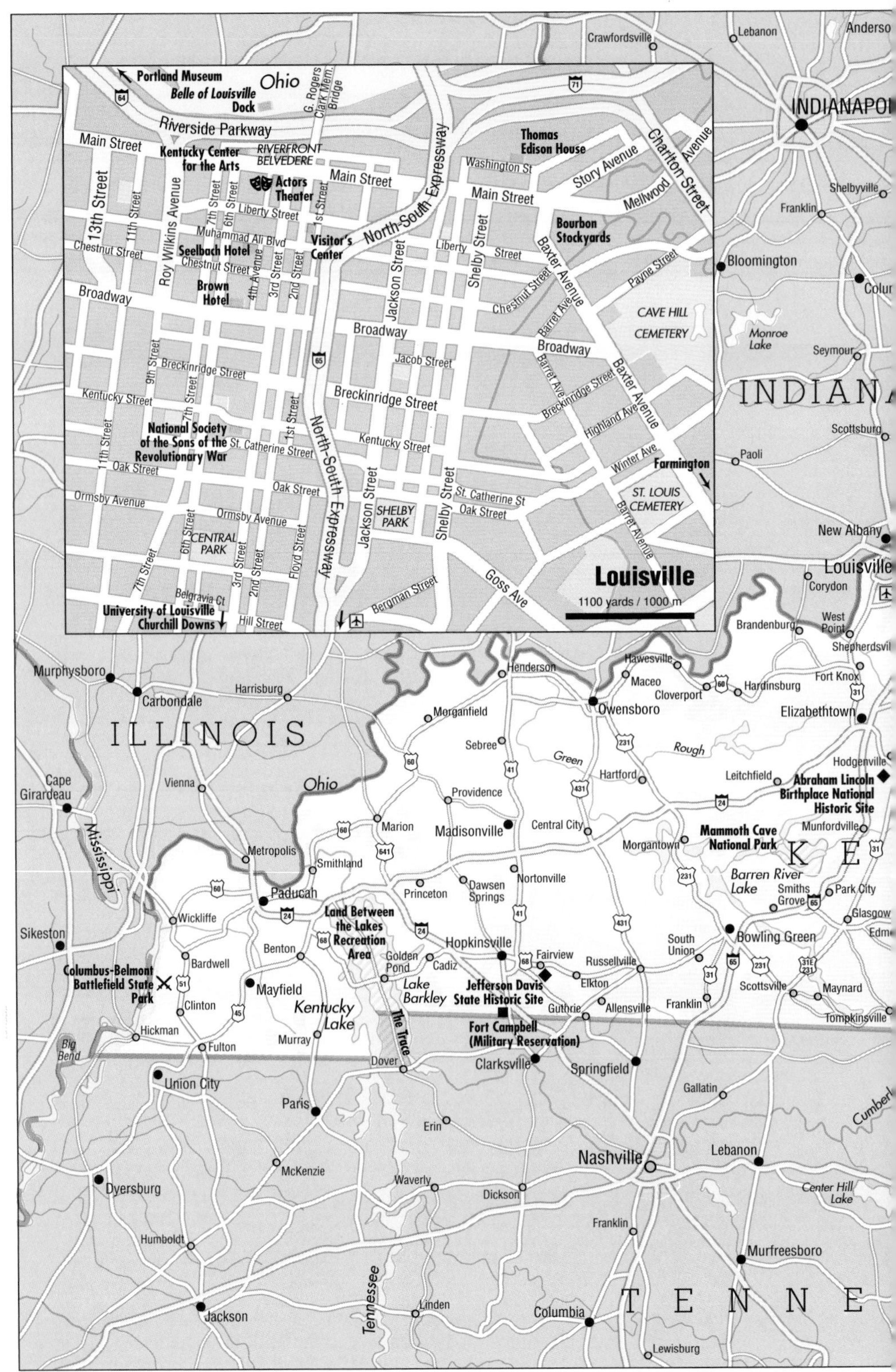
Louisville
1100 yards / 1000 m
Portland Museum
Belle of Louisville Dock
Ohio
Riverside Parkway
Main Street
Kentucky Center for the Arts
RIVERFRONT BELVEDERE
Actors Theater
Visitor's Center
Seelbach Hotel
Brown Hotel
Thomas Edison House
Bourbon Stockyards
CAVE HILL CEMETERY
National Society of the Sons of the Revolutionary War
SHELBY PARK
CENTRAL PARK
ST. LOUIS CEMETERY
Farmington
University of Louisville
Churchill Downs
North-South Expressway
Broadway
ILLINOIS
INDIANA
TENNE
INDIANAPOLIS
Bloomington
New Albany
Louisville
Elizabethtown
Owensboro
Henderson
Paducah
Hopkinsville
Bowling Green
Clarksville
Nashville
Murfreesboro
Jackson
Dyersburg
Union City
Paris
Land Between the Lakes Recreation Area
Kentucky Lake
Lake Barkley
Jefferson Davis State Historic Site
Fort Campbell (Military Reservation)
Mammoth Cave National Park
Abraham Lincoln Birthplace National Historic Site
Columbus-Belmont Battlefield State Park
Barren River Lake
Mississippi
Tennessee
The Trace

OHIO
WEST VIRGINIA
VIRGINIA
COLUMBUS
CINCINNATI
Dayton
Springfield
Reynoldsburg
Zanesville
Cambridge
New Castle
Richmond
Beavercreek
Kettering
Xenia
Lancaster
Caldwell
Circleville
Logan
Middletown
Washington
Marietta
Brookville
Wilmington Court House
Hamilton
Chillicothe
Athens
Parkersburg
Hillsboro
Piketon
Jackson
Pomeroy
Versailles
Covington
Newport
Rabbit Hash
Big Bone Lick State Park
Walton
Peebles
Ripley
Gallipolis
Spencer
Madison
Portsmouth
Kanawha
Ghent
Augusta
South Portsmouth
Carrollton
Falmouth
Maysville
Ohio
Washington
Williamstown
Licking
Vanceburg
Greenup
Ironton
Owenton
Greenbo Lake State Resort Park
Ashland
Catlettsburg
Charleston
Flemingsburg
Cynthiana
Cannonsburg
Huntington
Blue Licks Battlefield State Park
Blue Lick Springs
Goddard
Carter Caves State Resort Park
Grayson
New Castle
Frankfort
Georgetown
Paris
Shelbyville
Morehead
Kentucky Horse Park
Louisa
Midway
Clearfield
Sandy Hook
Big Sandy
Lexington
Mount Sterling
Daniel
Lawrenceburg
Versailles
Frenchburg
Winchester
West Liberty
Logan
Pleasant Hill
Nicholasville
Fort Boonesborough State Park
Clay City
Red River Gorge
Stanton
Inez
Lincoln Homestead State Park
Harrodsburg
Paintsville
White Hall State Historic Site
Salyersville
Van Lear
Jenny Wiley State Resort Park
Williamson
Richmond
Kentucky
Natural Bridge State Resort Park
Perryville Battlefield State Historic Site
Danville
Berea College
Prestonsburg
South Williamson
Perryville
Berea
Boone
Dewey Lake
Majestic
Stanford
Pikeville
Quicksand
Welch
Isaac Shelby State Historic Site
Booneville
McKee
William Whitley House State Historic Site
Renfro Valley
Pippa Passes
Breaks Interstate Park
Campbellsville
Tyner
Grundy
Liberty
National
Hazard
Pittsburg
Jenkins
Manchester
Columbia
London
Hyden
Whitesburg
Somerset
Richlands
Levi Jackson Wilderness Road State Park
Pine Mountain Wildlife Management Area
Jamestown
Cumberland Falls State Resort Park
Lake Cumberland
Cumberland
Corbin
Forest
Monticello
Whitley City
Barbourville
Pineville
Harlan
Stearns
Williamsburg
Abingdon
Gate City
Albany
Big South Fork National River and Recreation Area
Cumberland College
Middlesboro
Cumberland Mtns.
Allegheny Mountains
Cumberland Gap National Historical Park
Jellico
Cumberland Gap
Kingsport
Bristol
Hollow Lake
Oneida
Jamestown
Elizabethtown
Livingston
Johnson City
Elgin
Morristown
Appalachian Mountains
Greeneville
Oak Ridge
Knoxville
Newport
Hot Springs
Maryville
Watts Bar Lake
Tellico Lake
Asheville
Athens
Waynesville
Park (Nat'l./State)
Historic Park/Site
Museum
Battlefield
Historic House
Other place of interest
Kentucky
50 miles / 80 km

AROUND LOUISVILLE

An act of nature helped to create Kentucky's largest city. In 1778, when George Rogers Clark was leading an expedition of soldiers and settlers down the Ohio River, they reached impassable rapids, and were forced to halt. After the soldiers left, the settlers remained, naming their new island home "Corn," after their primary crop. (The island, which was located near the foot of 12th Street, disappeared in the 1800s, a casualty of flood control programs.)

Universally known as the home of the Kentucky Derby, the business and industrial capital of the Commonwealth offers the visitor much more. It is among the South's most progressive cities, a vibrant modern entity comfortably married to the charm of its historic past.

Begin an exploration of Louisville at the **Falls of the Ohio**, which is not a single waterfall, but a series of rapids that dropped 26 ft (8 meters) over a 2-mile (3-km) distance. A trip over the river into Indiana is required to see what remains of them: take the first exit off the Clark Memorial Bridge, and follow signs. At 201 West Riverside is a small museum dedicated to the geology of the falls. While on the Indiana side, make a stop at the **Howard Steamboat Museum** in Jeffersonville (101 East Market) to see a century of riverboat history.

Returning to the Kentucky side, 200 years of river heritage is on display at the **Portland Museum**, 2308 Portland Avenue (I-64, 22nd Street exit). Originally settled by French immigrants in the early 1800s, Portland was born of necessity: boats had to be unloaded and reloaded before and after navigating the falls, and the river bank here offered the safest moorings. After perusing the exhibit, head again for the river to enjoy the views from the **McAlpin Lock and Dam** complex (27th and Canal streets). Looking at the boats as they pass easily through the locks, spare a thought for those intrepid souls who made the journey during more perilous times.

I-64 is the easiest way back to the city center; Exit-4, Downtown, leads to Louisville's **Visitors Center**, located at First and Liberty streets. Among the visual pleasures of the city center are a number of traditional and *avant garde* statues, sculptures, and murals by well-known Kentucky and international artists. To ride, rather than walk, around downtown, the **Toonervile II Trolley** has a set route, but for freedom of choice, rent a **Louisville Horse Tram**.

During the two weeks preceding the Kentucky Derby, Louisville explodes with a range of festivities, including a race between two classic sternwheeler steamboats, the *Delta Queen* and the 1914-built ***Belle of Louisville***. The rest of the summer, and through October, the *Belle* cruises the Ohio from her dock at the foot of Fourth Street and River Road. From here (and most of the riverfront), the **Louisville Falls Fountain**, the world's tallest floating fountain, is visible. One of its more memorable computer-controlled visions is a 350-ft (108-meter) high spray forming a *fleur-de-lis*, Louisville's symbol.

eft, eflecting on he Kentucky enter for the rts. Right, -shirt talk: he many vays to ronounce the ame ouisville.

From the edge of **The Belvedere**, a statue of General George Rogers Clark, the city's founder stands above the river. The 8-acre (3-hectare) expanse at the foot of Fifth Street surrounds the **Kentucky Center for the Arts**, which is home to Louisville's Symphony Orchestra, its ballet and opera companies, and Children's Theatre.

Once the heart of commercial Louisville, **West Main Street**, after years of neglect, is reclaiming its importance. New construction in the form of the spectacular **Humana Building** (guided tours on Saturday mornings), the Kentucky Center for the Arts, and the **First National Tower** (the tallest in the Commonwealth), plus the renovation of the street's 19th-century buildings, have made this one of Louisville's trendiest addresses for restaurants, specialty shops and art galleries. The buildings between Second and Eighth streets are a font of beautifully restored **cast iron facades**, and form the largest single group of their kind outside New York City's SoHo area. To learn more about individual buildings, pick up a walking tour at the **Preservation Alliance**, 716 West Main.

The main lobby building of **Actors Theatre**, 316 West Main Street, was originally a bank constructed in 1837; when the theater recently expanded, the new addition was created from a *circa*-1812 warehouse. The **Kentucky Arts and Craft Gallery**, 609 West Main Street showcases the Commonwealth's rich handicrafts tradition. At the **Louisville Science Center**, 727 West Main Street, children can gawk at the command module of the ill-fated *Apollo XIII* mission (which was featured in the 1995 movie of the same name). Finish with a film in the museum's **IMAX Theater**. The world's largest baseball bat, (120-ft/37-meters tall), marks **Louisville Slugger** (800 West Main). The company has been making baseball bats since 1884. After touring the production facilities, see the sports memorabilia in the museum, including a bat used by Babe Ruth.

Fourth Avenue between Liberty and Broadway was once filled with elegant shops and department stores. Now a pedestrian way, the lobby of the 1905-built **Seelbach Hotel**, at the corner of Muhammud Ali Boulevard, was recently restored to its *belle époque* splendor. Pick up a Kentucky Derby momento at **The Festival Store**, 520 Fourth Avenue. The **Palace Theater**, built in 1928 as a glorious Art Deco movie house, is now a concert hall.

Ever wonder where the Hot Brown was born? That famous sandwich was invented in the 1920s at the **Brown Hotel** (Fourth Avenue and Broadway). The concoction was created by chef Fred Schmidt for after-the-theater suppers. Built in 1923 and decorated in the manner of an English country manor house, the Brown's afternoon tea dances in the 1920s were often the venue for a young lady's first outing with her beau. From here, a car is needed for sightseeing, but in most neighborhoods, find a parking place and walk to specific sites.

All you ever wanted to know about the city's domestic architectural past can probably be discovered in **Old Louisville**. Loosely bound on the north

Elizabeth Kizito, cookie-maker.

by Broadway and the south by Hill Street, its east and west edges are formed by Third and Sixth streets. Within these confines, once the grandest of neighborhoods, is an extraordinary range of homes. For a detailed walking map stop at the **Old Louisville Information Center**, 1340 South Fourth.

For a trove of military information from the Revolutionary War onward, the **National Society of the Sons of the Revolutionary War** at 1000 South Fourth is the place to visit. Local history is the focus of the **Filson Club**, housed in the 1900-built *beaux arts* Ferguson Mansion at 1310 South Third.

Many consider **Central Park** the "heart" of Old Louisville, and **St James** and **Belgravia courts** *the* addresses. Most of the houses are privately owned, but the **Conrad-Caldwell House**, 1402 St James Court, is open to the public. Built in 1895, it is a splendid example of Richardsonian Romanesque architecture. Two free events to note: the park's summer Shakespeare Festival and the October St James Art Fair.

The **University of Louisville** campus is further south on Third Street. Located on its periphery at 2035 South Third is the **J.B. Speed Art Museum**; the largest museum in Kentucky, it has a strong representation in Renaissance and Medieval art and a sculpture garden filled with statues by notables such as Henry Moore. On campus, the **Allen R. Hite Art Institute** features exhibits of local and university artists.

Continuing south on Third (which becomes Southern Parkway), take a right at Central Avenue and a few blocks on, the twin spires of **Churchill Downs** loom up on your left. America's most famous race, the Kentucky Derby, takes place here on the first Saturday of each May. If you can't attend it, or the May and November meets, the **Derby Museum** offers the next best thing: a 360-degree multi-media show which takes the viewer through the exciting event.

East from downtown: The **Butchertown Historic District** was an early suburb of Louisville. German immigrants settled it in the 1830s, naming the area for

Creators of the Derby's Garland of Roses.

the nearby stockyards and meat processing plants. It's hard to imagine the inventor of electricity living in the **Thomas Edison House** at 729 East Washington Street. In the late 1860s, he rented a single room in the small house for almost two years while working for the Western Union Company. Butchertown is fun to explore as many of the Victorian shotgun and camel houses have been renovated, and the neighborhood exudes the flavor of a small village.

Also in Butchertown is **Hadley Pottery** at 1570 Story Avenue. The stoneware company originated in the 1940s when Mary Alice Hadley started giving her distinctive pottery to friends and family. **Joe Ley Antiques, Inc.** does business at 615 East Market in a three-story former schoolhouse, the historic Hiram Roberts School which was founded in 1890. At **Louisville Stoneware**, just outside Butchertown's precincts at 731 Brent Street, watch the famous dinnerware being created.

Since 300-acre (120-hectare) **Cave Hill Cemetery** (701 Baxter Avenue) opened in 1848, it has been nationally recognized as one of the foremost examples of American Rural, a design which takes advantage of the natural contours of the land, instead of making the land conform to the traditional graves-lined-up-in-neat-rows style. Among notables buried here are George Rogers Clark and Colonel Sanders.

From Cave Hill, Baxter Avenue followed by Bardstown Road brings you to one of Louisville's most diverse neighborhoods. Both sides of the street are lined with ethnic restaurants and specialty shops. Typical is **Kizito Cookies**, 1398 Bardstown Road. Shortly after Elizabeth Kizito arrived from Uganda, she tasted her first chocolate chip cookie, "fell in love," and decided the only way she'd ever have enough was to bake her own. Her first "shop" was a basket, balanced proudly atop her head (a Ugandan tradition). The store came later, but Elizabeth and her basket are still a fixture at street fairs.

For a complete break from sightseeing, pick up the makings for a picnic at one of the local shops, and drive to nearby **Cherokee Park**. It's part of an extensive city-wide park system designed by the father of American landscape design, Frederick Law Olmstead, and a wonderful place to relax.

In 1841, Abraham Lincoln walked through the entrance of **Farmington** (3033 Bardstown Road; I-264, Exit 16). The Federal-style house was constructed in 1810 after a design by Thomas Jefferson, and the elegant 14-room home of John and Lucy Speed has been meticulously preserved. Among the striking architectural features are two octagonal rooms, and the almost hidden stairwells (Jefferson was known to hate ostentatious staircases).

The **Zachery Taylor National Cemetery**, 4701 Brownsboro Road (I-264, Exit 22) was the scene of a macabre event in the early 1990s when the 12th President's body was disinterred. Because Taylor died suddenly (in 1850, while still in office), one of his biographers became convinced that Taylor had been poisoned by a political foe; DNA tests revealed no sinister residues and Taylor was relaid to rest.

One mile (1.5 km) from the cemetery, and situated amid 55 acres (22 hectares), **Locust Grove** (561 Blankenbaker Lane), retains the gentle air of another century. Built in the mid-1790s, the 12-room Georgian colonial house was the home of William Croghan and his wife, the former Lucy Clark, a sister to George Rogers Clark (who lived here from 1809 until he died in 1818), and to William Clark, co-leader of the 1803 Lewis and Clark western exploration.

As befits an industrial city, a number of Louisville companies invite visitors to tour their plants and factories, but call for an appointment first. One of the most interesting is the **American Printing House for the Blind**. Alternatively, watch a newspaper being produced at the ***Courier-Journal***. The **Bourbon Stockyards**, founded in 1834, is the sole survivor of a once-thriving industry; the **Ford Kentucky Truck Company** is the largest truck plant in North America, and **Bluegrass Cooperage** makes the barrels in which bourbon whiskey is aged.

Right, high school basketball championship, Freedom Hall.

Coors
THE ROCKY MOUNTAIN LEGEND
HOME
5:41
GUEST
BONUS
56
PERIOD 4
48
BONUS
WELCOME
SWEET
SIXTEEN
FREEDOM HALL
NCAA
1986
CHAMPION
NCAA
FINAL FOUR
1959
1972
1975
1980
1982
1983
1986
Gatorade
LOUISVILLE

ALONG THE OHIO RIVER

Bounded on the north by water, barricaded in the east by mountains, geography offered Kentucky's settlers only two ways of migrating westward: slogging through a mountain pass leading from southwestern Virginia or on a boat floating down the Ohio River. The river, formed in Pittsburgh where the Monongahela and Allegheny rivers meet, offered a 980-mile (1,570-km) direct route to the western frontier.

The start of the Ohio's 665-mile (1,065-km) run along the Commonwealth's shores begins at **Catlettsburg**. Located where the Big Sandy empties into the Ohio, it was an important river port in the early 1800s, but was eclipsed by **Ashland**, some 5 miles (8 km) west. It became a major industrial center where 19th-century industrialists built magnificent homes; some of the best can be found on Bath and Montgomery streets. For a look at the area's diverse history, visit the **Kentucky Highlands Museum**, 1620 Winchester Street. Lovers of Art Deco will want to stop at the **Paramount Art Center**, a former movie theater, also on Winchester. Decorated in the opulent movie-house style of the 1930s, the elegant auditorium has magnificently painted walls depicting 16th-century theatrical characters.

One of Kentucky's best-known authors, Jesse Stuart, lived and worked most of his life near **Greenup**. Stuart's eloquent prose captures the richness and the bleakness of Appalachian life, and to explore many of the sites in his books, stop at the library on Harrison Street for a map. More enjoyment of his work is available in the Jesse Stuart Lodge at **Greenbo Lake State Resort Park** where a reading room is stocked with his books, and filled with memorabilia of his life.

Between Greenup and Maysville, a road runs parallel to the river; it's a pretty drive, with **Vanceberg** the only town of any size along it (and where the Commonwealth's lone Civil War monument honoring Union soldiers stands).

Known originally as Limestone Landing, **Maysville** was formally chartered in 1787. Even before then, it was an important river port; roads from here offered the easiest (and safest) route for settlers heading into the Bluegrass region. During the Civil War, Maysville was a major stopping point on the so-called Underground Railroad which smuggled slaves to freedom across the river in Ohio. (A driving tour of the stops on that perilous journey is available at the **Visitors Center**, 115 East Third Street. There's also a brochure pinpointing the area's **covered bridges**.)

Maysville has an easily walkable historic center containing a rich collection of period architecture. Its centerpiece is the Victorian **Market Square**; around the corner from it on Third Street is **Old Mechanic's Row** (*circa* 1850s) where many of the city's craftsmen once lived; the iron fencing and ornamental grillwork on the townhouses sparkle with the feel of New Orleans. Another era can be seen on Limestone between Third and Fourth streets where **Federal row**

eft, Roebling
ridge,
ovington.
ight, chatting
bout the
ommonwealth,
Vashington.

houses stand in elegant simplicity. A visit to the **Mason County Museum** (Sutton Street) offers an encompassing look at the area's history. The red brick house at the top of **Rosemary Clooney Street** is where the 1950s singer spent her childhood. Maysville also boasts a number of modern craftsmen; one of the most noted is Joseph Byrd Bannon who recreates early American furniture in his workshop on Second Street.

Five miles (3 km) inland sits **Washington**, a village that has capitalized on its historic past with costumed docents giving tours around the town. Architecturally, there are two distinct eras: early pioneer and genteel 19th century. In the former category are **Mefford's Station**, a house constructed in 1787 from the boards of the flatboat on which the family (including 13 children) traversed the Ohio; the **Simon Kenton Store**, restored to its 1790 appearance, and several log cabins. **The Paxton Inn**, built in 1819 belongs to the latter period; one of its owners was a fervent abolitionist, and under the staircase is a hidden cupboard where slaves were secreted until they could be smuggled across the Ohio. Harriet Beecher Stowe visited Washington, staying at the **Marshall Key House** (built 1800). Legend says Stowe witnessed a local slave auction which so horrified her that, years later, she drew upon the vivid experience when writing *Uncle Tom's Cabin.*

Augusta (18 miles/29 km downriver from Maysville) charms. **Riverside Drive** (which allows no cars) is lined with colonial and Federal houses, and as Augusta is one of the few river towns not blighted by an enormous levee, it's possible to stand on the river bank and imagine yourself in the 19th century. It was that lazy atmosphere which persuaded producers to film parts of *Centennial* and *Huckleberry Finn* here.

The town of some 1,400 people offers a plethora of eating places and antique shops. Among them, **The Beehive Tavern** is in a building which withstood a Confederate raid in 1862, as did the present home of the **Piedmont Art Gallery** (built in 1795). Mystery lovers should plan to stay at the **Lamplighter Inn** when its special murder mystery weekends take place.

To take the scenic river route into northern Kentucky, continue on KY 8 which 42 miles (67 km) away leads into Newport. Cross one of the bridges spanning the Licking River and **Covington** arrives. During the 1770s, a small trading settlement called The Point was founded on the western bank of the Licking River where it enters the Ohio. In the 1840s and 1850s ethnic diversity and economic growth were fueled by an influx of Irish and German immigrants.

Start sightseeing at **Covington Landing,** a floating entertainment complex on the riverfront. Boat trips on the Ohio and carriage rides through the historic districts also begin here. The bright blue 1867-built **John Roebling Suspension Bridge** is adjacent to The Landing, making it an easy walk across the Ohio River to Cincinnati. (The designer used this bridge as the prototype for one of his later, better-known spans, the Brooklyn Bridge.)

Fronting **Riverside Drive-Licking**

Joseph Byrd Bannon, furniture maker, Maysville.

River Historic District is **George Rogers Clark Park**, so named because the explorer stopped here to re-supply during his battles against the Shawnee Indians. The park is filled with a series of life-size bronze statues of local historical figures. One of the best is of Little Turtle, a chief of the Miami Indians who died here in 1812. The charming neighborhood is filled with many pre-Civil War homes. Most are private residences, but **Mimosa House** on East Second can be visited.

Covington's Catholic heritage shines most visibly in the Notre Dame-inspired, **Basilica of the Assumption** (Madison and 12th streets). Resplendent with flying buttresses, fearsome gargoyles, and 82 windows created from hand-blown glass, the structure was completed in 1901. The transept's window, measuring 24 ft (7 meters) by 67 ft (20 meters), is the cathedral's pride: it is said to be the largest stained glass church window in the world.

You can't miss **MainStrasse Village**: a 100-ft (31-meter) high 43-bell carillon, the **Carroll Chimes Bell Tower** stands at its center on Main Street, and tolls hourly, accompanied by animated figures depicting the saga of the Pied Piper. Billed as an old German neighborhood, the village is a fun, if somewhat touristy, place to visit and, for those who wish they could attend Munich's Oktoberfest, but can't, MainStrasse's version is the next best thing. The **Railway Exposition Museum** is for children of all ages and climbing on the rolling stock is encouraged.

Further afield is the **Oldenburg Brewery** (Exit 188 off I-71/75). Both the on-site micro brewery and the **American Museum of Brewing History and Arts** are worth visiting.

Six miles (10 km) west of Burlington (Exit 181), the **Dinsmore Homestead** offers a look at turn-of-the-century rural life. Eight miles (13 km) beyond the farm, off KY 338, and perched on the river, **Rabbit Hash** is every tourist's dream of quaint. Pride of place goes to the General Store, in business – and in the same building – since 1831.

Maysville was an important river port in the 1700s.

Kentucky's prehistoric past is on view at **Big Bone Lick State Park** (9 miles/ 14 km west on KY 338). During the Ice Age, this part of Kentucky was marshland filled with salt and mineral deposits; animals were attracted to them, and their bones have been found by archaeologists. Most interesting is the herd of bison which park rangers are trying to re-introduce into the ecology.

From here, US 42 is less than 2 miles (3 km) away; this is the "old" road to Louisville and worth following to Carrollton for its river views. **Ghent** boasts a number of late 18th-century homes; among the finest is the **James Tandy Ellis House**. Like most early river cities, **Carrollton** sits at the confluence of two rivers; here, the Kentucky empties into the Ohio. The historic district covers 350 buildings and the walking (and driving) tour starts at the **Old Stone Jail**, now a museum and information center. The highlight is the **Masterson House**, built in 1770 and reputedly the oldest two-story brick house still standing anywhere on the Ohio. In the **General Butler State Park**, the **Butler Turpin House** is a lodge equipped as an 1859 farmstead and Kentucky's only winter ski center. Louisville is an hour away via I-71.

Westward ho: Leaving Louisville on US 31W/60, the city's urban sprawl lasts until I-265 is passed. The historic buildings in **West Point**, one of Kentucky's oldest settlements, have been transformed into craft and antique shops and B&Bs. **Fort Knox** became the United States' gold depository in 1937 when the first bullion bars were shipped onto the site. Most of the nation's (and much of the world's) gold supply is buried in massive vaults, but only the building where it's stored is visible. One consolation is the **George C. Patton Museum of Cavalry and Armor** whose exhibits trace the history of armed warfare from the Roman Empire to Desert Storm. General Patton's life also is detailed from birth to death.

From Fort Knox, the fastest route to Owensboro, the next major city on the Ohio, is via US 60, but the secondary

Cutting tobacco.

roads near the river offer a journey through delightful rural countryside and add little to the driving time. Backtracking up the main highway, take a left on KY 228 through **Brandenburg** until it becomes, in turn, KY 79 and KY 144. The drive is a lovely one as the road wends through hills, farmsteads and tiny communities.

Cloverport is the first town of consequence; in the early 1800s it was a regular stop for long-distance steamboats, and one story has the Thomas Lincoln (father of Abraham) family crossing the Ohio here in 1816 on their way to Indiana. A few miles before **Hawesville**, a historical marker commemorates the riverboat builder and pilot, John Cannon. His most celebrated boat was the *Robert E. Lee* which defeated the *Natchez* in the 1870 New Orleans to St Louis boat race.

Leaving Hawesville on US 60, look for KY 334 and signs to **Lewisport**. The **Squire Pate House**, a log house built in 1822, was the scene of 18-year-old Abraham Lincoln's first successful trial. (And he was not yet a lawyer.) Charged with illegally operating a ferry service, Lincoln's winning argument was simple: he didn't row the man *across* the river, merely to a boat in the middle of it. Passing through **Maceo**, note the colorful mural painted on the building at the intersection with Rockport Ferry Road. This stretch of US 60 is the **Josiah Henson Trail**, dedicated to the slave who may have been the inspiration for *Uncle Tom's Cabin.*

As early as 1776, westward-bound travelers were stopping at a place called Yellow Banks (after the color of the river mud) which, in 1816, was renamed **Owensboro**. Today, the town calls itself the Bar-B-Que capital of the US, and celebrates each May with a riverfront "pig out." Purists might not expect to find the **Blue Grass Music Museum** this far west of the Appalachian Mountains. However, it's here in the **River Park Center**, and every September, Owensboro hosts a festival which sets the town to strumming and fiddling.

"Hands On!" is the motto of the **Museum of Science and Industry** (South Griffith Street); the **Fine Arts Museum** on Frederica Street is noted for its collection of Kentucky paintings and indigenous Folk Art. For easy sighteeing, take the **Owensboro Trolley**; one ticket allows multiple stops, and its route covers the city's main attractions.

Henderson, 20 miles (30 km) westward, boasts the **John James Audubon Museum**. The internationally renowned naturalist lived here between 1810 and 1819, and many original drawings from his most famous work, *Birds of America*, were created then.

The 100-mile (160-km) drive down US 60 to Paducah ignores the river, but compensates by traversing several charming towns and a region which is home to many of Kentucky's Amish families; during the summer and early fall, look for their produce stands.

Local lore says that **Paducah**, the last major Kentucky city on the Ohio, was named for the legendary Chickasaw leader, Chief Paduke. The Tennessee River empties into the Ohio here, and the city was a major transit port in the

Young farmer on a roll.

19th century. **Whitehaven,** an elegant Greek Revival house, houses Paducah's **Welcome Center**. Like much of the city's recent growth, it is off I-24 (Exit 7), 4 miles (6 km) south of the river. Stop to pick up tours of the area.

Although an ugly, but necessary, floodwall stands along the riverbank, a strip of green between it and the water forms **Riverfront Park**. Two blocks inland is a charming turn-of-the-century historic area. **Market House**, opened in 1905, is at its center; where farmers once gathered to sell their products, the building today serves as museum, theater and art gallery.

Quilt lovers will gaze with delight at the displays in the **Museum of the American Quilter's Society**. Located at the corner of Second and Jefferson, its aim is to preserve and expand the art of quilting. Each April the museum hosts a Quilt Festival, timed to coincide with Paducah's Dogwood Festival. One of Paducah's famous sons is Alben Barkley, known as *The Veep* when he served as Harry S. Truman's vice president between 1949 and 1953; the **Alben Barkley Museum**, at Madison and 6th streets, contains memorabilia of his life and the city's history.

At 19th and Jefferson streets, a statue of **Chief Paduke** stands in solitary splendor. Near the edge of **Noble Park** is the striking wooden sculpture of a Chickasaw Indian. Created in 1985 by the Hungarian-born sculptor, Peter Toth, the carving is called *Wachinton*, or "to have understanding," and honors local Native American tribes.

The Great River Road: Kentucky's western border is formed by the Mississippi River, and this marked road, running from Canada to the Gulf of Mexico, passes through four riverside Kentucky counties (although the scenery from the road seldom includes the river).

Wickliffe stands at the confluence of the Ohio and Mississippi rivers. The nearby **Wickliffe Mounds** mark a Native American village where Mississippian Indians lived between the 800s and the 1300s. Besides three excavation sites, artifacts are displayed in the museum, and a video offers an enlightening history of the tribe.

Ten miles (16 km) southwest of Bardwell on KY 123, the **Columbus-Belmont Battlefield** brings reminders of the Civil War. It was here, in September 1861, that Confederate forces erected an enormous mile-long chain across the river to Belmont, Missouri. That November, General Ulysses S. Grant made several attempts to destroy it, but was unsuccessful. The anchor, links of the chain (which broke of its own accord in early 1862), and several cannons remain in the bluff-top state park.

No less an authority than Mark Twain called **Hickman** "the most beautiful town on the Mississippi," and the small town (2,700 people) still delights. The westernmost town in Kentucky, its business district is anchored near the river, while houses on the upper bluffs have magnificent views of the Mississippi. A walking tour is available at the **Visitors Center**, 109A Clinton Street, and the **Warren Thomas Museum**, 603 Moulton Street, preserves the history of the local African-American community.

Left, Steamboat Gothic architecture. Right, near Hickman on the Mississippi River.

THE BLUEGRASS REGION

As frontier explorers began returning to their Virginia and Carolina homes in the 1770s, they carried stories of a rich and fertile land beyond the mountains, a place the Indians called *Kain-tuck-ee*. There are several meanings to the word, but perhaps the most memorable translation, the one which compelled settlers westward, was the one bestowed by the Wyandot tribe, "land of tomorrow."

And to this land they flocked: early arrivals made their way into Kentucky via riverboat and mountain pass. Their destination was the central heartland, now known as the Bluegrass region due to the grass that produces a purple flower in the spring. It is an area where stockades were first erected, fields plowed under, and a government begun. Kentucky's second largest city, **Lexington**, lies at the center of this historic region. With a superb selection of hotels and restaurants, and a number of sites within just an hour's drive, it makes an excellent sightseeing base.

Much of Lexington can be explored on foot, and the best place to start is **Triangle Park** at the corner of Broadway and Main Street. Immediately behind it are **Lexington Center** (hotel, shops and the **Visitors Center**) and **Rupp Arena**, home of the perennial basketball powerhouse, the University of Kentucky Wildcats. Across Main Street is **Victorian Square**, a commercial center built in the late 1800s; among its restaurants and shops, don't neglect the **Lexington Children's Museum**, filled with "touch and play" exhibits.

Starting in a westerly direction, the **Mary Todd Lincoln House** sits at 578 West Main Street. The wife of Abraham Lincoln was not born here, but moved to the site in 1832 when she was 14. The late Georgian brick residence was home to Mr Todd until his death in 1849. Several of his daughter's possessions are on display, including a pair of silver candelabra and some of the china which were used in the White House.

eft, Henry
:lay's study
ıt Ashland,
exington.

West Short Street forms part of the **Western Suburbs Historic District**, an area dating from the mid-1800s. At 511 West Short, the Italianate-style **Parker Place**, was built in 1871 by a member of Mary Todd Lincoln's family. The **Kentucky Gallery of Fine Crafts and Art** at number 139 sells the wares of members of the Kentucky Guild of Artists and Craftsmen.

East of Broadway, **Gratz Park** is another historic residential area. It was named for Benjamin Gratz, who lived in the house at 321 North Mill Street. The Park's northern boundary is **Transylvania University**, founded in 1780, and the oldest university west of the Allegheny Mountains. The oldest campus building is **Old Morrison**, the pillared structure facing West Third Street. Finished in 1834, it was designed by Gideon Shyrock, and has a portico modeled on the Greek Temple of Theseus.

The **Hunt-Morgan House**, at 201 North Mill Street is an elegant Federal-style house built in 1814 by Kentucky's first millionaire, John Wesley Hunt. But it is his grandson, the Confederate general, John Hunt Morgan, known as the Thunderbolt of the Confederacy, who makes Hopemont a pilgrimage for Civil War devotees.

In 1797, Henry Clay arrived in Lexington, a newly qualified lawyer; a plaque on the building at 178 North Mill Street marks his **Law Offices**. For offbeat dance and art, head for **ArtsPlace**, at 161 North Mill. Its gallery spotlights central Kentucky artists and twice a week at noon, presents dance recitals called Art à la Carte.

The **South Hill Historic District** consists of renovated 19th-century townhouses and cottages. One of the oldest buildings in Lexington is the **Adam Rankin House**, 317 South Mill. **Dudley Square**, now jam-packed with restaurants and specialty shops, began as a school in 1881.

Back on Main Street, follow it eastward to the **Fayette County Courthouse**; the greenery to its left is **Cheapside Park**, where the city's slave auction was located. The statue of **General John Hunt Morgan** in front of the building caused an uproar when it was unveiled in 1911, as the horse on which the general sat was obviously not Old Bess, his favorite mount (as was stated on the statue's base).

Across the street and a block east is **Phoenix Park**. Lexington's **Vietnam Veteran's Memorial** is here, as is the **Nomad and Camel marker**, the zero milestone from which all distances from Lexington were once measured. At 214 East Main, the **Kentucky Theatre** has a dazzling, recently restored Art Deco Roman Adamesque interior. **Thoroughbred Park**, on East Main Street at Midland Avenue (US 60), pays homage to the horse with equine statues sculpted by local artist Gwen Reardon.

Two quite different homes are open to the public: the **Senator John Pope House**, 326 Grosvenor Street, is one of three US homes still extant which were designed by Benjamin Henry Latrobe, one of the finest architects of the late 18th-century. **Loudoun House**, 209 Castlewood Drive, would look more at home in a European setting. The Gothic villa was built in the 1850s and it now houses the Lexington Art League, which showcases avant-garde art.

Ashland was the home of Henry Clay, best remembered for his utterance, "I had rather be right than be President." The house is on Sycamore Road just off Richmond Road (US 25), about a mile from downtown Lexington. Known as The Great Compromiser for his role in simultaneously extending and limiting slavery in the United States, Clay was born in Virginia in 1777, but considered himself a Kentuckian. The house seen today is not the home in which Henry Clay lived between 1806 and 1852. That was torn down to the foundations in the mid-1850s when Clay's son, who inherited the house, decided it was structurally unsound. Ashland was rebuilt, following the original floor plans, but with Italianate embellishments.

Into horse country: Celebrating Kentucky's love affair with the horse is the **Kentucky Horse Park**, a 1,000-plus acre (400-hectare) site located on Ironworks Pike, 8 miles (12 km) north of Lexington (I-75, Exit 120). The legen-

Young at heart.

dary race horse, **Man O'War**, is buried here, and a life-size bronze statue marks his grave. The **International Museum of the Horse** offers insights into the evolution of the horse from work animal into racing machine. To visit the rest of the park, take the walking, self-guided tour, or relax and see everything from a wagon pulled by one of the many types of horses who live in the **Breeds Barn**. At the **working farm**, a farrier and a harness maker ply their trades, and in the **Hall of Champions,** several very famous race horses live out their retirement. The **American Saddle Horse Museum** honors the only breed native to Kentucky.

Driving east on **Ironworks Pike** (pike was an early Kentucky term for road) from the Horse Park, pay particular attention to the fences which line this road, and others, in the Bluegrass region: some are made of native limestone, built by Irish stonemasons in the 1800s, who cleverly constructed them without benefit of mortar. Others are of the traditional rail fencing, some white-painted as seen in movies and advertisements; others in black, rust, and dark green, usually painted to match the trim on the estate's horse barns.

On the south side of the road, about 2 miles (3 km) from the Horse Park look for several examples of the **Kentucky Gate**. Invented in 1865, the long wooden arms allow entry through a closed gate without getting off a horse or out of a (horseless) carriage. A little further, one of the region's most famous stud farms, **Spindthrift Farm**, welcomes visitors, but only after the breeding season. For a tour through the world of horse training, take a right onto US 27/68 to reach the **Kentucky Horse Center** (on the left just beyond Johnson Road).

For more Kentucky history and horse farm viewing, drive north on US 68/27 into Bourbon County, named for the French royal house in recognition for its help during the American Revolutionary War (and *not* for Kentucky's native drink). Its county seat, **Paris** (18 miles/ 29 km from Lexington) is another reminder of French place names in Kentucky. At 225 Park Street is **Duncan Tavern**, built in 1788 by Major Joseph Duncan, and the first place to serve local whiskey. The tavern and the adjoining **Anne Duncan House** are open to visitors. In summer, train buffs can journey to Maysville and back on the steam-driven **Kentucky Central Railway**.

The **Cane Ridge Meetinghouse**, thought to be the largest one-room log structure in the country, is located on KY 537 east of Paris. It was a primary gathering place during the Great Revival, a religious phenomena which swept much of the southern United States in the early 1800s.

Twenty miles (35 km) due west of Paris on US 460 is **Georgetown**, a pretty town awash with antique malls and home to the first Baptist college west of the Allegheny Mountains. A historic marker in the park on West Main Street is the only reminder that bourbon whiskey was invented here in 1789.

The **Toyota Manufacturing Plant**, (I-75, Exit 129) offers tours (call for reservations). The plant is so huge that visitors are shown around in special

Thoroughbred Park, Lexington.

electric powered "trains" which silently scoot along the factory floor.

The Shakers: The larger of the two Kentucky communities founded by this religious sect is at Pleasant Hill, 25 miles (40 km) southwest of Lexington off US 68 (*see page 197*). The Shakers have restored 33 buildings to their original use and 14 of them are open to the public, including the **Centre Family Dwelling** where Shaker furniture is on display. At the **Meeting House**, the haunting strains of Shaker melodies are heard, and the intricate dance steps which accompany the music are demonstrated.

In the **Farm Deacon's Shop**, learn of the many ways Shakers used herbs; in others, watch artisans create a wide variety of Shaker crafts (many are for sale). Meals are served at the **Trustees' Office Inn**, and there are 80 B&B rooms available throughout the village (reservations always a must).

Between April and October, the sternwheeler ***Dixie Belle*** makes short, but highly romantic, trips on the Kentucky River from nearby **Shaker Landing**.

West to Louisville: The dark green gates of **Keeneland Race Course** stand on US 60 opposite Lexington's Bluegrass Airport 6 miles (10 km) from the city center. At the end of the runway, notice the limestone steps; they match a similar set to the left of the track entrance, and were constructed so wealthy patrons could easily walk from their planes to the clubhouse (when the airport was a grass strip and US 60 could be safely crossed on foot). Race meets are held each April and October, training sessions are open to the public. For a "down home" breakfast (good grits), start the day at **The Track Kitchen**.

For the fastest route to Frankfort, go west on US 60; however, for a prettier journey, take a right onto **Rice Road** (KY 1869) which is the first road turning off US 60 after Keeneland. Reaching the T-junction with Van Meter, continue following KY 1869 North until it dead-ends at **Old Frankfort Pike** (KY 1681; turn left). It's known to locals as "Shady Lane" for the trees which used to line its entire length, and was cut in

Vietnam Veteran's Memorial, Frankfort.

the late 1700s to link Lexington and Louisville. Lovers of the decorative arts should stop at the **Hedley-Whitney Museum**; among its treasures is a decorated "shell grotto."

At the junction with US 62, the building on the far left corner is the **Offutt Cole Tavern**; its log section dates to the 1780s. Richard Cole, Jr, who operated the inn between 1812 and 1839, was a great-grandfather of the infamous Frank and Jesse James. **Midway**, 2 miles (3 km) north, was created in 1835, when a rail company wanted a place to service trains. Most of the stores are now antique shops or restaurants, and it's an enjoyable place to lunch. Returning to KY 1681, it continues through a mix of stone-fenced estates, farms, and private homes. Reaching US 60, take a right.

Set on several attractive bends of the Kentucky river, **Frankfort** is often ignored by tourists who speed past it on I-64; from the highway, there's no evidence of the gentle charm of its historic district nor the grandeur of the Capitol building. Settled in the 1770s, its name does not come from any fortification, but from a man, Stephen Frank, who was killed by Indians in 1780. The city became Kentucky's capital in 1792 when several of its wealthier citizens outbid rivals from other towns.

For an overview of Frankfort, and to visit the graves of Daniel and Rebecca Boone, visit **Frankfort Cemetery** (215 East Main). It was opened in 1844, and the Boones were reburied there the next year. The **Kentucky Military History Museum** (100 East Main) is in the Old State Arsenal. The exhibits emphasize the military service of Kentuckians from the Revolutionary War onward.

A more pacific era awaits in Frankfort's historic district. The **Old State Capitol** is a Greek Revival structure designed by Gideon Shyrock. The building, finished in 1831, was the first of its kind west of the Appalachian Mountains. On High Street, the **Lt-Governor's Mansion** can be toured on certain days. The Federal-style house is the nation's oldest official executive residence still in use.

A classic view of Kentucky.

Three charming period homes, on Wilkinson and Wapping streets, are open for visits: **Liberty Hall**, **Orlando Brown House**, and the **Vest-Lindsay House**. Liberty was begun in 1796 by the Commonwealth's first United States Senator, John Brown, who also built the neighboring house in 1836 for his son, Orlando. The Federal-style Vest-Lindsay House was constructed in 1820. Its most famous owner was George Vest, another US Senator who is best remembered for first uttering, in 1870, the words: "Dog is man's best friend."

The **Visitor Center** is in the pretty Victorian-style house at Capitol Avenue and Second Street; the history of **Rebecca-Ruth Candies** is on display in the white frame house at 112 East Second. The local confectioner was the first to produce candy flavored with 100-proof bourbon whiskey.

From the start of Capitol Avenue, the **State Capitol** can be seen as a looming presence at the other end. Called one of the finest and most elegant public buildings ever produced, Frank Mills Andrews was the architect of the *Beaux Arts* building which was dedicated in 1910. The **Executive Mansion**, home to Kentucky's governors since 1914, was modeled after the Petit Trianon at France's Palace of Versailles; it is open for tours certain days.

Behind the Capitol building is the **Floral Clock**, bearing the name "Kentucky." Its statistics astonish: the face measures 34 ft (10 meters); the 20-ft (6-meter) minute hand weighs 530 lbs (240 kg) while the hour hand comes in at 15 ft (4.5 meters) and 420 lbs (190 kg). Each letter in the word "Kentucky" weighs 200 lbs (90 kg) and when, every 60 seconds, the hands move, they do so in leaps of 18 inches (46 cm).

A short distance from the Capitol at 509 Shelby Street sits **Frank Lloyd Wright's Zeigler House,** the only residence in Kentucky which he designed. Built in 1910, it belongs to the architect's "prairie school" period.

In an effort to give a special meaning to the 1,065 Kentuckians who were killed in the Vietnam War, their names were engraved on the **Vietnam Veteran's Memorial** so that the shadow of the gnomon, or sundial pointer, touches each man's name on the actual anniversary of his death. The memorial, on Coffee Tree road, overlooks the Capitol.

Shelbyville, 20 miles (30 km) west on US 60, bills itself the "Antiques Capital of Kentucky." Looking at the number of such establishments on Main Street, it's easy to see how the title was gained. Pride of place, however, must belong to the **Wakefield-Scearce Antique Galleries**, on Washington Street, found in what used to be the Science Hill Female Academy, founded in 1825 as the first institution of higher learning solely for young ladies west of the Allegheny Mountains. After browsing, you can dine in its restaurant (where the students used to eat), or return to Main Street to enjoy a meal.

On farms surrounding the town, Saddlebred Horses graze behind rail fences. The county is one of the sport's leading training centers, and its August horse show is attended by entrants from across the United States.

Shelbyville Horse Show.

THE SHAKERS

Also known as the United Society of Believers, the Shakers religious sect, founded in the mid-1700s, was an offshoot of English Quakerism. Originally named "Shaking Quakers," for the exuberant manner in which adherents worshipped, they were led by Anna Lee, a charismatic Englishwoman who claimed to be in contact with God. Among her revelations was the belief that only through communal living and ownership, perfection in word and deed, and in total celibacy would the individual find a union with God. (Lee herself, however, was married and had borne children.)

But what caused Anna Lee and her disciples to immigrate in 1774 to Mount Lebanon, New York, in order to escape religious persecution was her strongly stated belief that the Millennium had started and that the Holy Spirit was already within her body. Her followers dropped (or had dropped for them) the word "Quaker" and became known as "the Shakers."

Each settlement consisted of several "families" of 100 to 150 people each, men and women sharing the same large home, but living in a sexually segregated environment. Each family was headed by four elders, two male and two female, who acted as spiritual heads. They were assisted by deacons and deaconesses who assigned and oversaw the daily tasks of the other Brothers and Sisters, which were shared according to the ability of the person and the need of the community. In general, the Brothers did the farm and heavy work, the Sisters took care of the house and related chores.

At the community level, a group of trustees saw to economic matters; they sold the goods produced within the community and bought those items that could not be made. Days started at 4am with prayers and ended the same way at dusk; supervision was strict, and vigilant eyes allowed no mixing of the sexes.

The Shakers founded two communities in Kentucky, one at Pleasant Hill, 25 miles (40 km) southwest of Lexington in 1806, and another at South Union 12 miles (19 km) west of Bowling Green the following year. By 1830, Pleasant Hill's population exceeded 500, making it the third largest Shaker community in America.

South Union differed in one respect from all other Shaker villages: blacks lived in their own cabins, and not alongside their fellow Shakers. This flouting of racial equality, a basic Shaker tenet, was probably due to a desire by the Shakers to avoid a schism with their slave-owning neighbors.

Between the 1820s and 1850s, Shaker products were greatly prized and sold for the highest prices. Goods were shipped on Kentucky rivers north to the Ohio River where they were transferred to steamboats and sent to markets throughout America. In the late 1800s, the heavy cloaks worn by the Shakers became desirable items and were worn throughout the nation by fashion-conscious women.

Decline started in the decade before the Civil War as few new members joined to replace those who died or left (if a couple wished to marry, they had to leave the society). Many orphans and homeless children who had been raised by Shakers and grown up began to leave, wishing to marry or to escape the rigid lifestyle.

The Civil War almost ruined the Shakers economically. New Orleans and other Mississippi ports, which were the biggest markets for Shaker products, were blockaded. Trying to maintain their pacifist and neutral stand during the war, the Shakers fed thousands of men from both sides, but their only reward was to have horses, wagons and foodstuffs appropriated.

By the end of the 19th century, there were only 60 Shakers living in Pleasant Hill (and even fewer at South Union); soon there were none at all, and the buildings of both communities gradually fell into a derelict state. In the early 1960s, non-profit trusts were formed and the restoration of Pleasant Hill and South Union commenced (*see page 194*). ■

Woman dressed in Shaker cloak, a fashion item of the late 1800s.

1993
KENTUCKY
KY 64

Around Kentucky

The Commonwealth is a gateway to (or exit from) the Old South. A web of Interstate highway and state parkway systems are punctuated with exit ramps affording easy access to a variety of pleasures for visitors. Some examples:

West to Lexington: I-64 enters northeastern Kentucky from West Virginia; 30 miles (50 km) later take Exit 161 to **Carter Caves**, a state park with three caves, **Saltpetre**, **X**, and **Cascade**, open for (guided) exploration. Each February, amateur spelunkers can participate in the park's *Crawlathon*.

Exit 137 leads to two contrasting sites; 12 miles (20 km) north on KY 32, the **Goddard Covered Bridge**, is the only surviving example of Ithiel Town truss design in the Commonwealth. Photographers will love the way it beautifully frames a white-steepled church in the background. At **Morehead**, the **Folk Art Museum** (119 West Washington) offers an equal mix of traditional and expressive folk art, including the work of an artist whose visions of Hell (and the many ways the Devil can tempt the unwary), both titillate and amuse.

Lexington is 60 miles (100 km) away as I-64 continues through a countryside of rolling, forested hills, punctuated with neat farms.

The Mountain Parkway: After exploring southwestern Virginia, consider one of several routes into Kentucky via the Appalachian Mountains. Eastern Kentucky is beautiful with its acres of forests, and most roads are without a straight line or a level stretch. One of the most spectacular routes is VA/KY 80 which runs through the 4,600-acre (1,840-hectare) **Breaks Interstate Park** on its way to Pikeville. The bi-state park features "The Grand Canyon of the South." A chasm over 1,000 ft (307 meters) deep, it contains The Breaks, a magnificently scenic series of rapids, pools and S-curves. The exhibits at the park's museum concern the early mountain pioneers, coal mining and the locally famous Hatfield and McCoy feud.

Left, a string of Kentucky crappies. Right, gamekeeper, Land Between the Lakes.

Several McCoys are buried in **Dils Cemetery** in **Pikeville**, center of Kentucky's coal mining industry. The old burying ground is located near the top of the hill across the road from the fire station at the junctions of KY 1426 and KY 14. Other grave sites of the two clans are spread in a wide arc from **Toler** in northeastern Pike County to **Majestic** in its south; get a map to them at Pikeville's **Visitor Center** (101 Huffman Avenue). Pikeville pokes fun at itself with a Hillbilly Festival each April when residents dress in outlandish costumes. On a more serious note, nearby South Williamson's Coal Digger Days salutes the people who spend their working lives underground.

A recreational area with historical significance is **Jenny Wiley State Park**, located near Prestonsburg. It honors the woman who, in 1789, survived nine months' captivity by Shawnee Indians. The Park's **Sugar Camp Mountain**, reached by chairlift, affords unlimited vistas. Ambitious backpackers can walk the 180-mile (290-km) **Jenny Wiley**

Trail which traces her journey with the Indians northward to the Ohio River.

Loretta Lynn, one of country music's greatest stars was born in **Butcher Hollow**. To reach it, take US 23 north from Prestonsburg; shortly before Paintsville, look for KY 302, then follow signs to Van Lear. At the end of town, a left leads to **Webb's County Store**, which her brother, Herman Webb, runs. He has the key to the momento-filled cabin where the *Coal Miner's Daughter* spent her childhood.

A short distance off the Parkway's Exit 33 are two sites, both part of the larger confines of the **Daniel Boone National Forest** which covers 21 of Kentucky's 120 counties. North leads to the Red River Gorge while south goes to **Natural Bridge**. From April to October a skylift operates (there's also a half-mile trail leading upward from Hemlock Lodge). Views from the 125-ft (38-meter) long, 25-ft (7.5-meter) wide bridge are terrific; to look *at* the span, follow signs that lead to **Lookout Point** and **Lover's Leap**.

Natural Bridge, Daniel Boone National Forest.

The **Red River Gorge Geological Area** covers over 25,000 acres (10,000 hectares), but the most scenic part is the 25-mile (40-km) stretch bordering the river, an area of towering cliffs, chimney rocks and natural arches. The best-known of the gorge's many geological formations is the 75-ft (23-meter) **Sky Bridge**. Backcountry camping is allowed and there are marked trails of varying lengths; for those who cannot hike, the 35-mile (56-km) **National Recreational Trail** allows drivers to experience much of the region's beauty. An information center, the **Gladie Creek Historical Site**, is in a rebuilt, late 19th-century, logging cabin.

The Wilderness Road: A notice concerning this road appeared in the October 15, 1796, issue of the *Kentucky Gazette*: "The Wilderness Road from Cumberland Gap to the settlements in Kentucky is now completed." That road has become US 25, which enters the Commonwealth from Tennessee at Cumberland Gap (25 miles/40 km) east of I-75. (From Corbin, both roads run parallel to each other.)

Kentucky, Virginia and Tennessee are all clearly visible from **Pinnacle Peak** at **Cumberland Gap National Historical Park**. The first white man to see and survey the gap was Dr Thomas Walker, who, in 1750, found the only natural gap in the forbidding mountains, named it Cumberland, but returned to Virginia without ever going through it. (Native Americans had known of the gap for centuries and it formed part of their *Athiamiowee* or, Warrior's Path, a trail that led to the Ohio River near what is now Ashland.)

At the start of the asphalt road leading to Pinnacle Peak is a **Visitor Center**. Near the peak is **Fort McCook**, built by Confederate troops to guard the gap. The park is a 20,300-acre (8,000-hectare) wilderness area, 80 percent without paved roads, and it has 70 miles (112 km) of hiking trails, the longest being the 21-mile (34-km) **Ridge Trail**. Along its route is **Hensley Settlement**, a restored Appalachian community.

Corbin's fame is linked to Colonel Harland Sanders of Kentucky Fried

Chicken fame. The **Harland Sanders Cafe and Museum** is where the colonel developed his chicken batter recipe. Now, beautifully restored, the restaurant is a great slice of 1940s Americana.

I-75: For a look at coal mining life, or to enjoy the **Big South Fork National River and Recreation Area**, take KY 92 west from Exit 11; at US 27, turn north and follow signs to **Stearns**, which was an archtypical company town. Tennessee Ernie Ford's 1950s hit song *I Owe my Soul to the Company Store* was a true reflection of the plight of many coal miners who struggled to free themselves from unfairly incurred debt. The **Stearns Company Store** is still open (serving tourists) and the **Stearns Museum** chronicles the company's history.

More of mining's harsh realities are visible at **Blue Heron Historical Mining Community**, 7 miles (11 km) by road from Stearns. (A fun way is to travel there via the **Stearns Big South Fork Scenic Railway**.) Blue Heron existed between 1938 and 1962. The National Park Service has built an information center, and erected framework skeletons of the buildings which once made up the town. In each are photographs of, and audio tapes of, former residents relating their experiences. One of the most poignant is heard in the bath-house where a miner describes the difficulties faced in washing coal dust from his body.

Cumberland Falls is less than 25 miles (40 km) from Stearns. The second-largest waterfall in the eastern United States (after Niagara), the Cumberland spans 125 ft (38 meters) and plunges almost 70 ft (23 meters). During the full moon period, the mist from the roaring water creates a unique phenomenon, a "moonbow," which arcs over the falls.

A mile eastward off Exit 62 is **Renfro Valley**, one of the oldest country music centers in the South. Begun in 1939, Renfro Valley has continually entertained Kentucky residents with their "Saturday Night Barn Dance." Taking US 150 northwest from the same exit and driving 12 miles (20 km) leads to the **William Whitely House**. Irish-born Whitely came to Kentucky in 1775, and in 1794 his home became the first brick residence in Kentucky.

The name **Berea** (Exit 76) was taken from a town in the New Testament where people "received the Word with all readiness of mind." Land for a school was given to the Rev. John Fee by Cassius Marcellus Clay, the noted abolitionist. **Berea College** opened in 1855 stating it would be, "Anti-slavery, anti-caste, anti-rum and anti-sin, giving an education to all colors, cheap and thorough."

Today's 1,500-strong student body easily mingles with the town's 10,000 residents. The **Student Craft Industries** is an outgrowth of a program started in the early 1900s to preserve Appalachian crafts; students weave, carve, mold, and shape a variety of items which are sold in the **Log House Sales Room**. One testament to the quality of the collegiate artisans is in **Boone Tavern**, a historic hotel: all its furniture was made by them. The next-door **Appalachian Museum** features exhibits of mountain life from the early 1800s to the present.

Pinnacle Peak, Cumberland Gap.

Among the commercial craft shops, don't miss **Warren May's Dulcimer Workshop** and **Churchill Weavers**.

Exit 95 leads to **Boonesborough**, the second permanent settlement in Kentucky, and to White Hall, the home of Cassius Marcellus Clay. **Fort Boonesborough**, founded in 1775, was named for its founder, Daniel Boone (*see pages 26–27*). It was meant to be the capital of the 14th British colony, but the American Revolution ended those dreams of its financial patron, Richard Henderson. In 1974, the fort was reconstructed; in each of the cabins an artisan creates pioneer crafts using 18th-century tools.

White Hall, an imposing brick house of 44 rooms is located on the opposite side of I-75 from Boonesborough. It was owned by Cassius Marcellus Clay who was Abraham Lincoln's Ambassador to Russia, and many of the decorations and furnishings reflect that posting. (Lexington is 20 miles/36 km north.)

The Blue Grass Parkway: Starting just beyond Lexington's airport on US 60, it runs 75 miles (120 km) southwest to Elizabethtown. Eighteen miles (30 km) south of Exit 59 is Kentucky's oldest pioneer settlement. Founded in June 1774, **Harrodsburg** was named after James Harrod, its first settler. Two years later, when Virginia created Kentucky County (the entire region west of the Allegheny Mountains), Harrodsburg became its first seat of government.

Unlike Boonesborough, Harrodsburg metamorphosed into a full-fledged town. The **Visitor Center** near the entrance to **Fort Harrod** is a good place to start sightseeing and to pick up brochures for self-guided driving and walking tours. In 1934, President Franklin D. Roosevelt dedicated the **George Rogers Clark Monument** (standing to the left of the Fort's entrance). The stockade, rebuilt in 1927, is a replica of the original fort. Inside, costumed docents and craftspeople interpret the history of each cabin while working at the daily chores of pioneer life. In the summer, *The Legend of Daniel Boone* is performed at the outdoor amphitheater.

Morgan's Row, at 220 South Chiles

The McDowell Apothecary Shop, Danville.

Street, is supposedly the first rowhouse built west of the Alleghenies. Marti Williamson, has turned an old cabin into **The Gathering Place**; she and others entertain visitors with performances on hammered dulcimers. Before it became one of central Kentucky's leading country hotels, **Beaumont Inn** was a prestigious girls' school, Beaumont College. Located off US 127 south of Harrodsburg, it is an elegant establishment, known for its antique furnishings and Kentucky cooking.

In 1809, the first successful abdominal surgery to be carried out in the United States was performed in **Danville**, 9 miles (15 km) south of Harrodsburg. The Georgian-style, white-frame **Dr Ephraim McDowell House** sits opposite Constitution Square. His patient for the history-making operation was 47-year- old Jane Todd Crawford, an Indiana resident who was first thought to be pregnant. On Christmas Day, without benefit of anesthetics, the Scottish-trained McDowell removed an ovarian tumor weighing over 20 lbs (9 kg); less than a month later, Mrs Crawford was well enough to go home. The **Apothecary Shop** used by Dr McDowell is next door. Beautifully restored, it gives an accurate picture of early 19th-century medication.

In the center of **Constitution Square** sits a replica of the log **Meetinghouse** which was the seat of Kentucky County's government between 1784 and 1792, and where the State Constitution was written. Other replica structures on the square include the **Courthouse** (where the Kentucky County Supreme Court met) and **Old Jail**. The **Post Office**, opened in November 1792, is original and was the first postal facility west of the Allegheny Mountains.

To view Danville's antebellum architectural splendor, pick up a walking tour at the **Visitor Center** located in the Greek Revival **McClure-Barbee House** (304 South Fourth). A highlight of the walk is the **Rodes House** at 305 North Third where parts of the 1957 Elizabeth Taylor movie *Raintree County* were filmed. The **Great American Brass**

Perryville Ball, Civil War reenactment.

Band Festival is held every June on the campus of **Centre College**.

Penn's Store, near Gravel Switch, is 15 miles (25 km) southwest of Danville on KY 243. Operated in the same location and by the same family since 1850, it has become a local landmark. In honor of the 1990-installed outhouse, the family started the **Great Outhouse Blowout**, an early October festival of games and (very bad) jokes.

Ten miles (16 km) west of Danville on US 150 is **Perryville**, site of Kentucky's bloodiest Civil War battle which was fought on October 8, 1862. (The battle is re-enacted on the weekend closest to this date.) The Confederates were badly outnumbered, but when the day ended, despite overwhelming odds, they had won. As the exhausted men savored their victory, Gen. Bragg, the Confederate commander issued a stunning order to retreat. What he knew, but they did not, was simple mathematics that 40,000 fresh Union troops would shortly be arriving – numbers his beleaguered troops were incapable of withstanding.

Portrait of Stephen Foster in Federal Hill.

Left on the battlefield were 510 Confederate and 845 Union bodies; a further 5,486 were wounded, 2,635 Southerners and 2,851 Northerners.

The **Perryville Battlefield State Historic Site** is on KY 1920, 4 miles (6 km) from the center of Perryville. Unlike many Civil War battlegrounds, commercial development has not intruded, and the peaceful, rolling countryside looks much the way it did in 1862. The small museum covers all facets of the battle, and the self-guided walking tour explains the action between the opposing sides. Reaching Starkweather's Hill, pause and look around at the site of the high-water mark of the western campaign, and the Confederate army's last major thrust into Kentucky.

The marriage between Abraham Lincoln's parents, Nancy Hanks and Thomas Lincoln, took place at **The Lincoln Homestead**. There are three log houses in the park located on KY 528 north of **Springfield**: the **Lincoln Cabin** is a replica of the home where Thomas Lincoln lived; the *circa*-1790 **Berry House** was where Lincoln courted Nancy; he learned his trade at a cabin similar to the reproduction **Blacksmith Shop**. A copy of the Lincolns' marriage certificate is on display at the **Washington County Courthouse** in Springfield.

In the late 1770s, Governor Patrick Henry of Virginia granted 1,000 acres (400 hectares) to David Bard. Entrepreneurially, he and his brother named the land **Bardstown** (Exit 25), divided it into building lots, and sold them to new settlers. Stop first at the **Visitor Center**, 107 East Stephen Foster Avenue, and pick up walking and driving self-guided tours. (Evening **carriage rides** start here. Train buffs can also book seats on ***My Old Kentucky Home* Dinner Train**; dining takes place in restored 1940s cars.)

Pride of Bardstown sightseeing belongs to *My Old Kentucky Home*. According to legend, Stephen Foster was so moved by the beauty of the house he was inspired to write the ballad which became Kentucky's official song. Completed in 1918, Federal Hill (its original name) was named for the Federalist party, not its architectural style. *The Stephen Foster Story* is performed in summer.

Abraham Lincoln, Jesse James and King Louis-Philippe of France have one thing in common: all spent at least one night in **Old Talbot Tavern**. Lincoln was a small boy when his father traveled to Bardstown, bringing his son with him. The exiled French king stopped here in 1797, and is reputed to have painted the murals in one room. Legend says in 1881, Jesse and his gang made the bullet holes in those same walls. Built in the 1780s, Talbot Tavern was Bardstown's first stone structure, and is the oldest stagecoach stop west of the Allegheny Mountains.

Court Square, center of the downtown area is a charming melange of architecture. Near it are the **stocks and pillory** once used for punishment.

Beginning in the 1790s, French Catholics, driven from their country by the excesses of the Revolution and later by Napoleon's edicts, settled in Bardstown. Their numbers became enough to support a see and, in 1816, the cornerstone for **St Joseph Proto-Cathedral** was laid. It was the first Roman Catholic Cathedral west of the Allegheny Mountains, and was known as the Cathedral in the Wilderness.

Spalding Hall on Xavier Drive, a block from the cathedral, houses two museums, the **Bardstown Historical Museum** and the **Oscar Getz Museum of Whiskey History**. From a copy of Abraham Lincoln's liquor license when he ran a tavern in Illinois in 1833 to an authentic "moonshine" still, the museum is a trove of America's whiskey-drinking traditions. *(See Travel Tips for local distilleries which offer tours.)*

Thomas Merton, the philosopher, writer, and monk, lived at the **Abbey of Gethsemeni** (8 miles/13 km south of Bardstown) from 1941 until his death in 1968. The Trappists (or Order of Cistercians of the Strict Observance) are a Roman Catholic order who founded the Abbey in 1848. The fruitcakes and cheeses made by the monks are known nationwide; visitors are welcome to attend vespers and retreats.

ld Talbot avern, ardstown.

South and west: If heading to Kentucky's western border, the **Western Kentucky Parkway** is the most direct way. A more interesting, if longer, route is to follow I-65 south to Bowling Green, then motor west along non-parkway roads. Make the choice at Elizabethtown, where the east/west parkways bisect I-65 on its way north to Louisville or south to Nashville.

In the summer, a walking tour of **Elizabethtown's** historic center has a decidedly different twist: costumed characters from the town's past stand near historic buildings, and narrate their roles in the city's history. Walks start at the **Visitor Center** at 24 Public Square on Thursday evenings.

Emma Reno Connor's Black History Gallery (602 Hawkins Drive) is a focal point for those who want to learn more of the history and cultural heritage of Black Americans. **Schmidt's Museum of Coca Cola Memorabilia**, 1201 North Dixie Highway, takes visitors through a century of Coke's history.

On the banks of Freeman Lake, the **Lincoln Heritage House** has a mantle and staircase reputedly carved by Thomas Lincoln; near it is the **Sara Bush Johnson Lincoln Memorial**, a replica of the house where, in 1819, Sara became Thomas Lincoln's second wife. The **totem pole** standing beside the lake was created by Stanley Schu, a Kentucky sculptor known as the "chain saw artist" for the tool he uses to create his distinctive artwork.

Heading south, **Glendale** (Exit 86) is an old train junction town now becoming an antique shop, B&B and restaurant center. Particularly fun is the **Three Sisters Shop**; hanging on its front is a painting of the owner's three daughters as their brother sees them in old age. Try the **Depot Cafe** for lunch, then visit the **Toy Museum** next door to it.

If Abraham Lincoln returned to the land of his birth, he wouldn't recognize his humble home. Inside an enormous granite monument near **Hodgenville** sits the **Abraham Lincoln Birthplace**, a replicated cabin of the type common when he was born in 1809. Fifty-six steps, one for each year of Lincoln's life, lead to the monument. The grounds include a Visitor Center containing a history of Lincoln's life.

Hodgenville is at the heart of Lincoln country; in its **Town Square** stands the bronze statue of him sculpted in 1909 by Adolph Weinmann, with the **Lincoln Museum** a block away. **Lincoln's Boyhood Home** is reproduced at Knob Creek Farm, 7 miles (11 km) north of town.

One of the natural wonders of the world, **Mammoth Cave National Park**, is reached from Exit 53. ("Mammoth" refers to the opening of the main cavern.) Tourism officially began there in 1838 when a local lawyer, Franklin Gorin, purchased the cave and charged people to see it. By 1850, it was one of the most popular natural attractions in the United States. In 1941, Mammoth Cave became part of the National Park system.

Led by Park Service rangers, the **Historic** and the **Frozen Niagara** tours are operated year round. Seasonal favorites include the **Echo River** and **Lantern** tours. Rangers also lead outdoor walks

Mammoth Cave.

to **Styx River Spring** and **Green River Bluffs**. True devotees of spelunking can reserve a place on the six-hour **Wild Cave Tour** which offers, among other delights, crawling through narrow underground passages.

What makes **Bowling Green** unique? It is the only place in the world where the Chevrolet Corvette sportscar is manufactured. Aficionados can tour the **GM Corvette Plant**, except during model changeover periods. From the plant, drive along Corvette Boulevard to the **National Corvette Museum** where slices of Americana since 1953 (when the first Corvette was introduced) are displayed.

The largest city between Louisville (110 miles/174 km north) and Nashville (60 miles/100 km south), Bowling Green served for a short time as Kentucky's Confederate Capital. Stop at the **Visitor Center**, 352 Three Springs Road (Exit 22), for self-guided walking tours to five separate historic areas.

On the campus of WKU, at Kentucky and 14th streets, the **Kentucky Museum and Library** is a rich collection of material relating to the Commonwealth's history. **Riverview at Hobson Grove** is an elegantly restored and impeccably furnished 1872 Italianate-style house. It is located in the grounds of a municipal park at the western end of Main Street, and December is a delightful time to visit. This is when Riverview is magnificently dressed for a Victorian Christmas.

Heading west from Bowling Green, there are no parkways, only US 68, which rolls through farmland, villages and towns to Paducah. **Shakertown at South Union**, 10 miles (16 km) from Bowling Green, was the second Shaker community in Kentucky. Cornerstone of sightseeing is the 1820s-built **Centre House Museum**, now filled with authentic Shaker furniture and working craftspeople.

A mile away at **Shaker Junction** (where trains serving the community used to stop), the **Shaker Tavern**, built in 1869 to serve as a meeting place between elders of the community and

The Trail of Tears; Hopkinsville Airborne Museum, Fort Campbell.

the "world's people," offers a menu filled with regional specialties.

Russellville delights. Settled in the early 1790s, it was where 116 delegates from 43 Kentucky counties met in November 1861 to form the provisional Confederate Government of Kentucky. Here also Jesse James (who was born in the county) gained national notoriety in 1868, when he robbed the **Nimrod Long Bank** of $9,000 and went from local thug to federal fugitive; the building stands at Sixth and Main streets. Each October, the raid is re-enacted amid much gunfire and many laughs.

Celebrity of a different sort was accomplished by John Bibb who, in the mid-1850s, developed the lettuce which bears his name. Learn about him at the **Bibb House Museum** (Eighth and Winter streets), a Greek Revival house owned by his father, Major Richard Bibb. Filled with antebellum furniture, it sits in the middle of Russellville's historic district. (Pick up a map at the Visitor Center, 116 South Main Street).

Guthrie, the hometown of Robert Penn Warren, is 20 miles (36 km) south on US 79. Warren, the first Poet Laureate of the United States and the only person to have won the Pulitzer Prize for both prose and poetry, lived in the house at Third and Cherry streets.

The region between Guthrie and **Elkton** (on US 68) is Amish and Mennonite country. Some have opened stores and shops to service their community and most welcome tourists. Three of the more congenial are: **Schlabach's Bakery** and **Pecham Tack Store**, both on KY 181, and **Grandma's Cupboard** (KY 79), which sells exquisitely made needlework items. (Watch for the black buggies used by sect members.)

It is impossible to miss the 350-ft (108-meter) tall **Jefferson Davis Monument** in **Fairview**, 9 miles (15 km) before Hopkinsville. The only President of the Confederacy was born near the site in 1808. The monolith, completed in 1924, has an elevator to take you to the top.

Near **Hopkinsville** was a halt on the infamous Trail of Tears, the journey

The first Corvette ever made, Bowling Green.

Cherokee Indians were forced to make in 1838 and 1839 when they were evicted from their ancient lands and moved to Oklahoma. The **Pennyroyal Area Museum**, 217 East Ninth, is a font of information about it, the 1890s' Black Patch Tobacco Wars, and the life of local native, Edgar Cayce, the noted psychic and clairvoyant.

The **Cherokee Trail of Tears Commemorative Park** is on US 41 south of Hopkinsville. Its Heritage Center contains a museum and a shop with authentic Indian crafts. Statues and bronze tablets commemorate those Cherokee who died during the march. Each September, the Trail of Tears Inter-Tribal Pow Wow is held in the grounds.

The Commonwealth's second major military installation, **Fort Campbell**, situated 10 miles (16 km) south of Hopkinsville, sits astride the Kentucky-Tennessee border (Nashville is 70 miles/112 km south).

The **Don Pratt Museum** celebrates the history of the famed 101st Airborne division which is based here. The World War II Normandy invasion is given the most space. The most poignant of its many exhibits is a casual, unposed picture of paratroopers taken just before their D-Day jump. No one in the picture survived.

The Land Between the Lakes: In 1944 the Tennessee River was dammed to create Kentucky Lake; Lake Barkley came in 1965, when the Cumberland River was impounded. The result is a nature preserve 40 miles (65 km) long averaging 7 miles (11 km) wide, covering 170,000 acres (68,000 hectares) of which over 106,000 acres (42,400 hectares) are in Kentucky. Ninety percent of the land is forested and there is over 300 miles (480 km) of shoreline.

The Trace is the north/south roadway through the park; at each end of it are Welcome Centers. The **Golden Pond Visitor Center and Planetarium** is near the junction of The Trace and US 68/KY 80 (the only highway to bisect the park horizontally). The small museum includes pictures of the illegal liquor stills of the region, and relates the history of the 19th-century pig iron industry. At the **Woodlands Wildlife Center** many of the area's wilder denizens are on view.

In 1969, bison were reintroduced into the park in an attempt to repopulate the region with a species whose herds once numbered in the hundred thousands. The herd is kept in the **Buffalo Range and Trail** near the entrance to **Homeplace-1850.** The living museum is comprised of 19th-century buildings brought here from regional farms. Costumed interpreters work at chores, and explain what "their" life is like.

A short drive from Kentucky Lake are two towns that are worth visiting. At **Murray**, 15 miles (24 km) west, the **National Boy Scout Museum** sits on the edge of MSU campus. It's a very modern hands-on museum that features electronic exhibits and over 50 original paintings and drawings by noted American artist Norman Rockwell. In **Mayfield**, (20 miles/36 km from Murray) the **Western Kentucky Museum** chronicles the history of the region and its chief crop, tobacco.

Lake Barkley sunset.

Renee

TENNESSEE

From the mountainous east to the Mississippi River, Tennessee offers the visitor a virtual alphabet of attractions and activities. For instance, the American Museum of Science and Energy; Beale Street; Chickamauga Civil War Battlefield; Dollywood; Elvis; Fort Donelson; Graceland; The Hermitage; Iron Mountain Stoneware; Jack Daniel's Distillery; kayaking on wild rivers; Lookout Mountain; the Museum of Appalachia; the National Civil Rights Museum; Opryland USA; a Parthenon *and* a Pyramid; quiet mountain trails; Rocky Mount; the Sunsphere, Knoxville; Tennessee Walking Horses; the Union Soldiers' monument at Greeneville; Victorian houses; James White's Fort; xylophones in Nashville's Symphony Orchestra; the Sgt. Alvin York Monument; Zoo Choo at the Knoxville Zoo.

Tennessee is very easy to explore, too: in the 520-mile wide and 120-mile deep state, distances are short, and its major cities are no more than a few hours drive from one another. Interstate highways bisect the state, and the Tennessee Scenic Parkway System is 2,300 miles (3,700 km) of well-marked, mostly two-lane roads connecting historic sites with major recreational areas.

Admitted into the Union in 1796, Tennessee was an early destination of frontiersmen whose first settlement was at Rocky Mount. Davy Crockett was born near Jonesborough, and shortly after began a life of exploration. Andrew Johnson, a Greeneville native, never resigned his Senate seat even though Tennessee seceded from the Union; he became president after Lincoln was assassinated. The "rough and ready" reputation of Andrew Jackson is belied by the elegance of his Nashville home, The Hermitage.

Among the many mountains of Tennessee, the Great Smokies shine most brightly. The half-million acre national park offers the ultimate escape from urban life: the terrain is no different today than it was when Native Americans roamed over it; the hills are steep and rugged, the forests dense; sheer cliffs offer magnificent scenery, lush vegetation abounds. The rich variety of wildlife includes an extraordinary number of birds, reptiles and mammals.

But, for those travelers who are not looking for the "great outdoors", other regions of Tennessee entice. Long before it became the capital of country music, Nashville was known as the Athens of the South with a Parthenon, built for the 1896 state centennial, which is an exact replica of the better-known one. Memphis, famous as the home of the blues, also happens to be the birthplace or international headquarters of several industries, notable among them Holiday Inn and Federal Express.

Music. Mountains. Heritage. History. And Elvis Presley, too. With all this going for just one state, how could anyone fail to be impressed by Tennessee?

Preceding pages: the Sunsphere in Knoxville, built for the 1982 World's Fair. Left, Pee-Wee League cheerleaders dressed in the colors of the University of Tennessee.

Memphis
770 yards / 700 m
Hernando Desoto Bridge
The Pyramid
Cook Convention Center
Memphis Belle B-17
Mississippi River Museum
MUD ISLAND PARK
JEFFERSON DAVIS PARK
Amphitheater
Memphis Queen Riverboat Rides
Mud Island
Mississippi
City Hall
Magevney House
Cotton Exchange
Music and Blues Museum
Peabody Hotel
Center for Southern Folklore
Orpheum Theater
A. Schwab's
HANDY PARK
Pink Palace Museum & Planetarium
TOM LEE PARK
ASHBURN PARK
National Civil Rights Museum
Graceland
Calhoun Street
Front Street
Main Street
2nd Street
3rd Street
4th Street
Exchange Avenue
Poplar Avenue
Adams Avenue
Washington Avenue
Jefferson Avenue
Court Avenue
Madison Avenue
Monroe Avenue
Union Avenue
Gayoso Avenue
Beale Street
Linden Avenue
Pontotoc Avenue
Vance Avenue
Danny Thomas Boulevard
Arkansas Riverside Drive
Promenade Street
Center Lane
South Front Street
South Main Street
Hernando Street
MISSOURI
INDIANA
KENTUCKY
TENNESSEE
ARKANSAS
MISSISSIPPI
ALABAMA
Spencer
Bloomington
Vincennes
Loogootee
Paoli
Jasper
Wabash
Evansville
Henderson
Owensboro
Madisonville
Paducah
Sikeston
Poplar Bluff
Mayfield
Hopkinsville
Bowling Green
Russellville
Barren River Lake
Clinton
Kentucky Lake
Malden
Hickman
Fulton
Murray
Lake Barkley
Dover
Fort Donelson National Military Park
Clarksville
Springfield
Union City
Tiptonville
Martin
Paris
Erin
Gallatin
Goodlettsville
Ashland City
Hendersonville
Cumberland
Kennett
Hayti
Greenfield
McKenzie
Tennessee
Lebanon
Nashville
Paragould
Newbern
Dyersburg
Bruceton
Waverly
Dickson
J. Percy Priest Lake
Blytheville
Huntingdon
Milan
Franklin
Murfreesboro
Mississippi
Repley
Nutbusch
Humboldt
Henning
Duck
Lexington
Linden
Jackson
Columbia
Hatchie
Covington
Brownsville
Hohenwald
Lewisburg
Shelbyville
Millington
Henderson
Natchez Trace Parkway
Waynesboro
Tullahoma
Jack Daniel's Distillery
Lynchburg
Bartlett
Somerville
Bolivar
Lawrenceburg
West Memphis
MEMPHIS
Graceland
Germantown
Wolf
Selmer
Savannah
Shiloh National Military Park
Pulaski
Fayetteville
Winchester
Corinth
Pickwick Lake
Holly Springs
Florence
Wilson Lake
Athens
Sheffield
Wheeler Lake
Huntsville
Decatur
Oxford
Batesville
Tupelo
Guntersville Lake

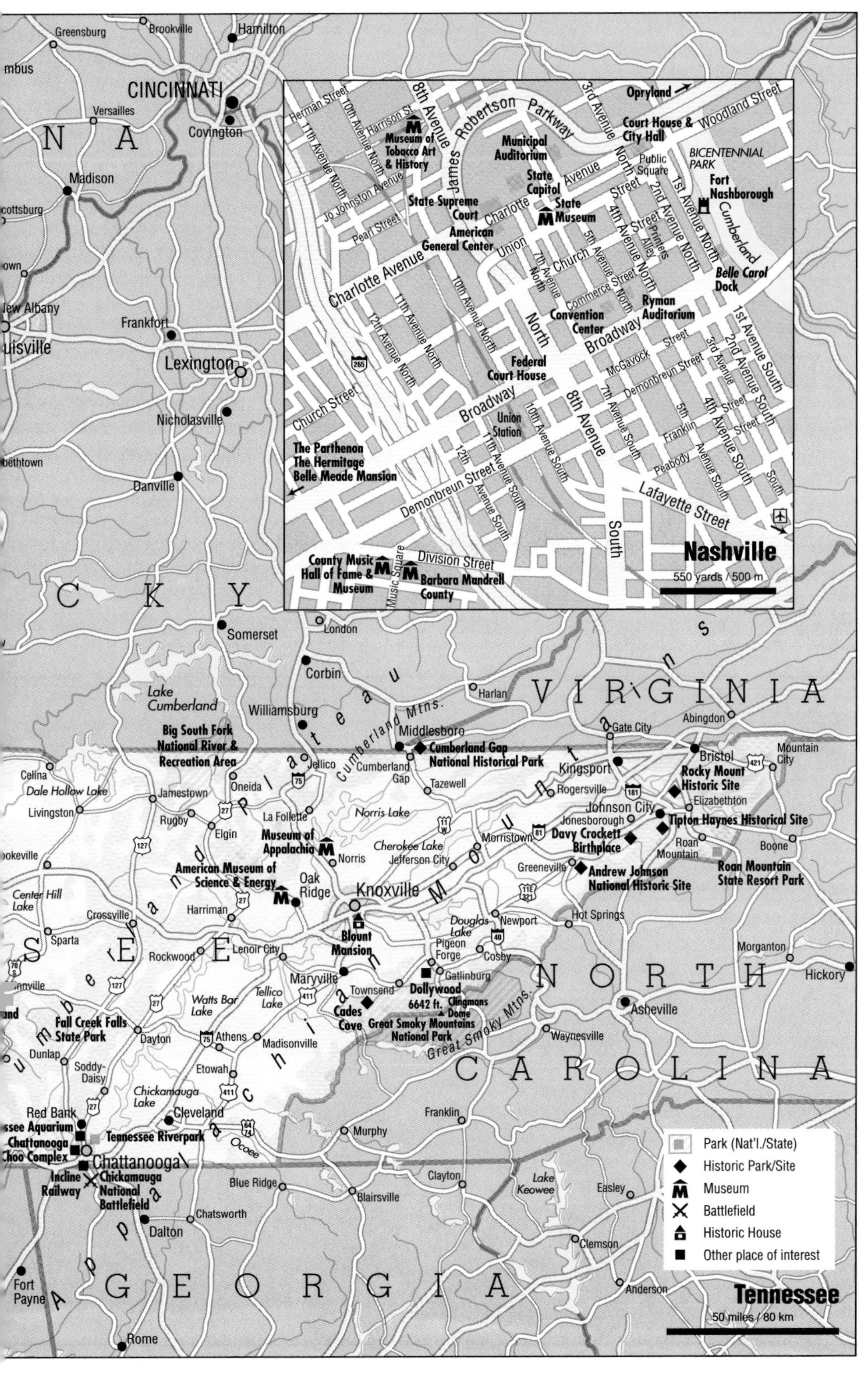
Nashville
550 yards / 500 m
Opryland
Court House & City Hall
Municipal Auditorium
State Capitol
State Museum
Museum of Tobacco Art & History
State Supreme Court
American General Center
Fort Nashborough
BICENTENNIAL PARK
Belle Carol Dock
Ryman Auditorium
Convention Center
Federal Court House
Union Station
The Parthenon
The Hermitage
Belle Meade Mansion
County Music Hall of Fame & Museum
Barbara Mandrell County
Tennessee
50 miles / 80 km
Park (Nat'l./State)
Historic Park/Site
Museum
Battlefield
Historic House
Other place of interest
CINCINNATI
Lexington
Knoxville
Chattanooga
Big South Fork National River & Recreation Area
Cumberland Gap National Historical Park
Rocky Mount Historic Site
Tipton Haynes Historical Site
Davy Crockett Birthplace
Andrew Johnson National Historic Site
Roan Mountain State Resort Park
Museum of Appalachia
American Museum of Science & Energy
Blount Mansion
Dollywood
Great Smoky Mountains National Park
Fall Creek Falls State Park
Tennessee Riverpark
Chickamauga National Battlefield
VIRGINIA
NORTH CAROLINA
GEORGIA

AROUND NASHVILLE

Music is to Nashville what the movies are to Hollywood, or automobiles to Detroit. Tennessee's capital city is internationally known – and with good reason – as "Music City, USA." Approximately half of all the single music recordings made in the United States originate from Nashville's complex of recording studios and songwriting shops. As songwriter Roger Cooke, a transplanted Brit whose credits include the Coca-Cola anthem *I'd Like to Teach the World to Sing* among others, succinctly puts it: "Nashville is the last Tin Pan Alley left on earth. I know. I've looked for it everywhere."

Bibles: Music is not Nashville's largest industry, though. Insurance is much larger, and so is printing, especially the printing of Bibles – this is probably because Nashville happens to be the headquarters of the Gideon Society, the organization which places Bibles in hotel rooms throughout the country.

Music, however, is most definitely Nashville's major attraction for visitors. Many of the more than 100 Nashville recording studios are unassuming little places tucked away on quiet side streets scattered all over the city. For the visitor seeking a sample of the city's most famous commodity, a drive or stroll around the **Music Square** area just south of downtown is worthwhile. This six-block area is home to such giants of the American music industry as RCA, Sony, Warner Bros, United Artists and MCA, and such organizations as BMI and ASCAP which represent the writers of much of America's music. Among the modern buildings on "**Music Row**" are scores of old homes now converted into the offices of songwriting shops, music publishing firms, talent and booking agencies.

Music Square is also the location of two of the city's major music attractions. **The Country Music Hall of Fame and Museum** honors the men and women who have been most influential in the development of country music. The many exhibits include an array of stage costumes and artifacts used by many of the most famous country music stars, a look at country music in the movies, and such oddities as Elvis Presley's "gold" Cadillac automobile.

A few blocks away at **Studio B**, visitors can see how a recording is made, and try their hand at "mixing" the original tape of a popular record. This small studio is one of Nashville's original recording studios, and perhaps its most famous. More hit records were produced in this studio than in any facility in the world, including almost all of Elvis 's recordings. Through videotape, entertainers Dolly Parton, Waylon Jennings and Chet Atkins – all of whom also recorded here – introduce visitors to the magic of this particular studio.

Across the street from the Country Music Hall of Fame is **Barbara Mandrell Country**, one of several museums established by music stars for the thousands of fans visiting the city.

With a little background on Nashville music, most visitors are probably now

eft, Music
ity, USA.
ight, printing
s one of
ashville's
iggest
ndustries.

ready for a sample of the actual product. The city's primary nightlife area is the **Second Avenue Historic District** in the downtown area. Along with an impressive variety of restaurants, shops and micro-breweries, the district offers two major music venues – **The Wildhorse Saloon** and the **Hard Rock Cafe**. Two blocks away is **Printers Alley**, which features a selection of smaller music clubs.

While the majority of visitors to Nashville find their way to the well-advertised attractions of Second Avenue and/or Printers Alley, many of them are not aware of many small clubs where some of Nashville's best music is on display. A listing of these clubs, and the artists featured in them, appears regularly in the Friday editions of the Nashville newspaper. Three of them, however, deserve special mention.

Tootsie's Orchid Lounge on Lower Broadway at Fourth Avenue is, perhaps, the prototype of the "authentic" country music honky-tonk. It is dark and dingy. The walls are covered with posters and autographed photographs of the great, the not-so-great and the never-will-be-great of the country music world. But the beer is cold and the live music genuine Nashville country.

Station Inn on 12th Avenue South is a showcase for the bluegrass variety of country music which traditionally features only acoustic stringed instruments. Station Inn is also dark and dingy, but well worth a visit for anyone who wants to sample the foot-stompin' style of this rural music.

The Bluebird Cafe on Hillsboro Pike is *the* spot for many music fans. It is a place where some of Nashville's best songwriters often appear to try out a new song before a live audience, and a club that well-known country music stars sometimes frequent.

No visit to Nashville would be complete without a trip to **Opryland**, Nashville's musical theme park featuring more than a dozen live shows ranging from full-scale Broadway-style musicals to rock 'n' roll, gospel, country and western shows. The park also offers a

The Opryland Hotel.

variety of rides, but the emphasis is on music – all forms of American music.

The Opryland theme park is just one of the many attractions of **Opryland USA**. There is also the ***General Jackson* Showboat**, a huge stern-wheel riverboat, making daily cruises on the Cumberland River with a full live music show as a part of the cruise. There are **Opryland River Taxis** making regular runs between downtown **Riverfront Park** and the vast Opryland complex north of the city. And do not under any circumstances miss the **Opryland Hotel**. This unique hotel, one of the largest in North America, features – not one, but two – incredible indoor gardens, with a third now under construction.

Another not-to-be-missed experience is a visit to Nashville's famous **Grand Ole Opry**. The Opry is actually a live radio program which has been broadcast to much of the United States over WSM Radio every Friday and Saturday night since 1925. It is the world's longest running live radio show, and it is unique, because no one ever knows more than a day or two in advance who will be appearing on it. The Opry philosophy has always been, "If you can see 20 or 25 of the top acts in country music, does it really matter who they are?"

Strange things also happen at the Grand Ole Opry. There was, for example, the night a teenage yo-yo champion from the Midwest came to Nashville to see veteran star Roy Acuff on the Grand Ole Opry because Acuff often played with a yo-yo on stage. The youngster, however, was unable to get a ticket to the sold-out show, a fact which the Nashville newspaper reported. Acuff happened to read the newspaper story, and since the youngster could not get a ticket to *see* the show, Acuff invited him to *be on* the show. Picture, if you will, the spectacle of an unknown teenager doing a yo-yo act on radio and you have an idea of the Ole Opry philosophy.

While music is certainly Nashville's major attraction, it is by no means the only one. **The Parthenon** in Centennial Park on West End Avenue is an exact-sized replica of the Greek Parthenon.

Andrew Jackson's Hermitage.

Built during Tennessee's Centennial Celebration in the 1890s, the building contains an imposing 40-ft (12-meter) tall statue of Athena and serves as one of several major Nashville art galleries.

The Hermitage, President Andrew Jackson's elegant estate just east of downtown, is the third most popular presidential home in the United States, ranking just behind George Washington's Mount Vernon and Thomas Jefferson's Monticello in the number of visitors it attracts. It is also unusual among presidential homes in that the majority of its furnishings actually belonged to the seventh President of the United States. Jackson, of course, was the first American president from west of the Appalachian Mountains and the first president to come from humble beginnings, a fact illustrated by a pair of ancient, drafty log cabins on The Hermitage property where the future president and his wife lived before and during the construction of their mansion.

The Hermitage is just one of several historic homes open to the public in Nashville. Others include **Travellers' Rest**, the home of Jackson's close friend, adviser and business partner John Overton; and **Belle Meade Mansion**, a *Gone With The Wind*-style mansion which was once one of the most famous thoroughbred horse farms in America. Belle Meade's most renowned horse was Iroquois, the first American winner of the English Derby.

For anyone interested in Tennessee history, a must stop is the **Tennessee State Museum** located in the lower levels of the **Tennessee Performing Arts Center** on Deaderick Street in downtown Nashville. The museum's elaborate exhibits provide a wealth of artifacts and information concerning such famous Tennesseans as Presidents Andrew Jackson, Andrew Johnson and James K. Polk. Polk – by the way – was the last American president to leave office with a balanced federal budget. There is much about the famous Tennessee frontiersman Davy Crockett, and his friend Sam Houston. They served in Congress together before Houston was

Jack Daniel's distillery, Lynchburg.

elected governor of Tennessee, a position he resigned to go west to Texas. World War I hero Sergeant Alvin York is there, along with Cordell Hull, F.D. Roosevelt's Secretary of State who won the Nobel Peace Prize for his work in founding the United Nations. There is also a display of Civil War history.

Tennessee was the major battleground of the western theater of the war, as Virginia was the major battleground of the east. There were more than 400 Civil War engagements fought in Tennessee. Three of the old battlegrounds in the Middle Tennessee area are now preserved as National Military Parks.

Fort Donelson, 90 miles (145 km) northwest of Nashville, was where Union General Ulysses S. Grant first came to national attention with the first major Union victory of the war in February of 1862. **Shiloh**, 135 miles (220 km) southwest of Nashville, followed a few months later (April 1862) and was the first of the unimaginably gory battles of the war. **Stones River**, 30 miles (50 km) southeast of Nashville, contains the oldest of thousands of Civil War monuments. It was erected before the end of the war by survivors of Hazen's Brigade who were involved in the bitter battle for what became known as "The Round Forest."

Other Civil War sites worth visiting include the **Sam Davis Home** at Smyrna, 20 miles (30 km) southeast of Nashville, and the charming, quaint little town of **Franklin** which bills itself as "20 miles south and 150 years from Nashville." While it is not a national military park, Franklin was the scene of one of the bloodiest battles of the last days of the Civil War. Five generals killed in the battle were laid out on the porch of the elegant **Carnton Mansion**, which is now preserved as a historic site, along with the **Carter House** where the Carter family huddled in the basement while the fighting raged around them. Ironically, one of the Confederate casualties of the battle at the Carter House was the oldest Carter son.

Not far from Franklin is a stretch of the beautiful Natchez Trace Parkway (*see page 232*).

Southeast of Nashville, 70 miles (110 km) away, is **Jack Daniel's Distillery** which makes excellent sour-mash whiskey in the tiny town of Lynchburg (pop. 361 according to the label on the bottle). Jack Daniel's calls itself America's oldest registered distillery; charcoal mellowing with hard sugar maple is the reason, apparently, that Tennessee whiskey differs from most Kentucky bourbons. The free daily tours include a stop at Mister Jack's original office which contains "the safe that killed him." Your tour guide will be happy to explain how this event came about.

Plan to spend some time visiting the stores and shops on the town square. The antique **Lynchburg Hardware Store** may be the only place left in the world where a bottled Coke still costs just a dime, and the **Pepper Patch** next door offers such delights as Jack Daniel's Tipsy Cake and a Tipsy Fudge Sauce. For lunch, think about making reservations at Miss Bobo's Boarding House, where the fare traditionally includes three meats, five vegetables, breads, beverage and dessert.

Appalachian music.

AROUND MEMPHIS

Like its namesake on the River Nile in Egypt, Tennessee's Memphis on the Mississippi River is a city dominated by a pyramid. The Memphis **Pyramid**, however, is a much livelier place, a 32-story stainless steel and glass building which serves as a sports and performance venue for Tennessee's largest city.

Memphis is also a city with its own rich musical traditions, but instead of the acoustic guitars, fiddles and banjos of Nashville, Memphis music features saxophones, coronets and the raucous sound of guitars.

It is called "the blues," the raw, sultry, ragged, infectious beat which originated on the cotton plantations of the Old South, and around the turn of the century found its way to Memphis, where Beale Street became its spiritual home. In its heyday in the 1920s and '30s there wasn't a tougher, more swinging street anywhere in America.

Zoot suits: In those days, Beale Street was a center for black commerce, entertainment and fashion. The zoot suit, for example, originated on Beale Street. Its bustling sidewalks were lined with saloons, pawn shops, gambling dens, nightclubs and theaters. It was also a place notorious for its lawlessness. It was a time and place where Machine Gun Kelly peddled bootleg whiskey on the street corner while Bessie Smith sang her heart out at the Old Daisy Theater just down the street.

Beale Street nightclubs and theaters were frequented by such entertainers as Louis Armstrong, Rufus Thomas, Bobby Blue Bland, Gus Cannon, Furry Lewis, Muddy Waters, Johnny Ace and the "Beale Street Blues Boy," better known today simply as B. B. King.

The best-known musician of them all was William Christopher Handy, the legendary "Father of the Blues." It was Handy who first began writing down the music he heard in the cotton fields and honky tonks of the Mississippi River Delta country. He gave it a unique style and his compositions – *The St Louis Blues*, *The Memphis Blues* and *The Beale Street Blues* carried this uniquely American art form from the back alleys of the Delta to modern concert halls and nightclubs all over the world.

The city's reputation was further enhanced by **Sun Studios** (706 Union Avenue), opened by entrepreneur Sam Phillips in 1950. Elvis Presley, Jerry Lee Lewis, B.B. King, Howlin' Wolf, Muddy Waters, Carl Perkins and Roy Orbison all got a boost to their careers here. The studio is still around, open for tours during the day while operating as a studio by night. The **Memphis Music Hall of Fame** (97 South Second Street) and the **Beale Street Blues Museum** in the old Daisy Theater pay tribute to these musical roots.

Music is live and well in the restored **Beale Street Historic District** itself, although the street is a somewhat sanitized version of the original avenue. These days there is a police substation right in the heart of the historic district. It is, however, more for the reassurance of visitors than an actual necessity, al-

eft, detail of painting by onathan ireen. Right, eale Street.

though visitors are advised to keep their wits about them when visiting at night.

One Beale Street business well worth a visit is **Schwab's Dry Goods Store**, founded in 1876. Schwab's slogan proudly proclaims: "If you can't find it here, you're better off without it." The store's amazing variety of merchandise includes a complete line of voodoo supplies, love potions and other exotic items not generally available elsewhere in Memphis – or anywhere else in the South, for that matter.

While the clubs, theaters, restaurants and shops form the heart of modern Beale Street, visitors should also take time to explore the fascinating **Center for Southern Folklore** which has spent a considerable amount of time tracing the cultural history of the street, through old photographs and interviews with some of the remaining natives who remember Beale Street as it was in all its glory. The center is a valuable resource for learning more about the rest of the South, too (although more the Deep than the Upper South), for many years of expertise and some of the best minds in the region have been involved with its development at one time or another.

The restoration and resurgence of Beale Street was closely tied to the restoration of the elegant **Peabody Hotel** on Union Avenue, located only a couple of blocks away.

The Peabody was always a good hotel – an outstanding one, in fact. For more than a century it radiated the warm glow of Southern hospitality over the city of Memphis and the entire Mid-South. The names on the guest register reflect its exalted position. Presidents Andrew Johnson and William McKinley stayed here. So did Confederate generals Robert E. Lee, Nathan Bedford Forrest and Jubal Early. There are scores of celebrity guests on its register, too, such as William Faulkner and Charles Lindbergh.

The Peabody was *the* place to see and be seen, a fact noted by the author-historian David Cohn in 1935 when he had cause to write: "The Mississippi Delta begins in the lobby of The Peabody

Pyramid power: Memphis is named for a town in Egypt.

and ends on Catfish Row in Vicksburg, Mississippi." But it was the ducks that truly elevated the Peabody Hotel to the status of legend.

It all started in the 1930s when the then general manager Frank Schutt went duck hunting. Live decoys were legal in those days, and after returning from a hunting expedition one weekend, Schutt and his friends decided it would be great fun to park their live decoy ducks in the beautiful, but barren, travertine marble fountain in the middle of the hotel lobby. It was the beginning of a tradition that made the Peabody unique among the world's fine hotels. The original ducks are gone, of course, but their descendants still grace the elegant fountain where admiring spectators gather each morning and evening for what has become known as "The Duck Ceremony."

The Peabody Hotel's ducks are famous throughout America.

It begins with the unrolling of a 50-ft (15-meter) red carpet stretching from the fountain to one of the hotel elevators. With ranks of attending bellmen standing at rigid attention along both sides of the carpet and the stirring sounds of *The King Cotton March* filling the lobby, the elevator doors slowly open for the stars of the show, a mallard drake and four hens. Fully aware of their importance in the grand scheme of things, the ducks parade majestically along the carpet, across the lobby and into the fountain where they spend the day entertaining guests. The ceremony is repeated in reverse each afternoon as they return to their nighttime quarters located on the hotel roof – a spot appropriately known as "The Duck Palace."

Memphis is also known for its traditional cuisine, specifically, barbecue ribs. Wet ribs *versus* dry ribs is a constant bone of contention among Memphis natives. While the city is filled with outstanding restaurants specializing in such fare, one of the most famous is **The Rendezvous**, located downstairs in an alley directly across the street from the Peabody Hotel. The Rendezvous has been known to ship its ribs – the dry variety – all the way across the world using one of the city's most famous businesses, Federal Express.

The huge **Federal Express** facility at the Memphis airport, incidentally, offers an intriguing "midnight" tour, when virtually everything sent through Federal Express arrives in Memphis, is sorted, reloaded and shipped out in a remarkably efficient turnaround time.

While Beale Street and The Peabody represent Memphis tradition and are not to be missed, there is no doubt that the city's Number One attraction – and one of the top attractions in all of Tennessee – is **Graceland**, the home of Memphis's best-known citizen, "The King of Rock 'n' Roll," Elvis Presley. Since the singer's death in 1977, hundreds of thousands of fans have flocked to his sumptuous estate. Many spend their time waiting in line to gain admission by carving messages of tribute and devotion on the huge walls that surround the estate. If there isn't time to actually go inside, a quick look at the walls will give an alternative flavor.

"Even before the mansion was opened to the public in 1982, thousands of people were coming just to look at it and walk up the driveway to the Meditation Garden beside the house," marvels Jack Soden, who is the Graceland estate's executive director.

With so many people visiting, Graceland has been forced to set up a staging area across the street to handle parking and tickets for tours of the home. The staging area also offers a look at two of Presley's personal airplanes, one of them a full-scale Convair 880 jet airliner, which was once a part of the Delta Airlines passenger fleet.

Perhaps it is because of all the floral tributes in the Meditation Garden, where the entertainer is buried beside his parents, but the whole experience of seeing Graceland is uncannily similar to visiting a religious shrine. Presley's impact on the entertainment world, however, is clearly displayed in a long hallway inside the house which is lined with his incredible collection of gold and platinum record awards.

Graceland: a King's ransom in gold.

Do not miss the museum across the street from Graceland where some of Presley's automobiles are on display.

The drive-in movie set featuring clips from some of his many movies is worth the admission price. A good time to go to Memphis – or a bad time, depending on your point of view – is during mid-August when the city hosts its annual **Elvis Presley Tribute Week** on the anniversary of the singer's death, an event irreverently known locally as "Death Week."

Also not to be missed is the **National Civil Rights Museum** on Mulberry Street a few blocks from Beale Street. The museum incorporates the balcony of the Lorraine Motel where civil rights leader Dr Martin Luther King, Jr was killed by a sniper's bullet in 1968. The museum, the first of its kind in the United States, conveys in remarkable interpretive exhibits and audiovisual displays much of the sights, sounds and tensions of the sweeping American civil rights movement.

Other worthwhile Memphis attractions include **Mud Island** and the **Mississippi River Museum**. Located on the Memphis waterfront, Mud Island features a 2,000-ft (600-meter) long scale model of the entire Lower Mississippi River from Cairo, Illinois, to New Orleans. Every turn and twist of the real river flowing by only a few feet away is duplicated in the model. Markers tell stories of the people and places along the river, of steamboat accidents and of the river's frequent attempts to change its course.

The adjacent Mississippi River Museum details more of the history, culture and music of "Old Man River." Among the many exhibits is a full-scale model of a 19th-century riverboat where the "conversations" of long-ago passengers can still be overheard in the elegant lounge. There is also a full-scale model of a Union gunboat of the Civil War era, complete with the shouted commands of officers as the boat passes beneath a Confederate shore battery perched on the bluff above.

Outside on Mud Island is a famous World War II Flying Fortress named ***The Memphis Belle***. The huge plane was the first to complete a full comple-

Elvis sat here.

ment of missions over Europe during the war. It came home with its crew to a heroic tour of the United States. A 1990 movie telling the story of *The Memphis Belle* starred Matthew Modine.

For a real ride on the Mississippi River, the ***Memphis Queen* Riverboat** provides daily excursions originating from Mud Island. The tours offer a closer look at some of the rich history of the river and some fascinating stories about the people and events which made the mighty Mississippi America's most famous river.

While you are there, take a close look at the cobblestones lining the waterfront. Most of these stones arrived in Memphis as ballast aboard 19th-century European packet boats, and were deposited on the riverbank as the boats took on loads of cotton to fuel the textile mills of Europe.

Cotton is still a major crop in much of western Tennessee, and much of the entire American cotton crop still passes through the **Memphis Cotton Exchange** on Front Street.

A good place to find out more about the rich cultural and natural history of Memphis is at the award-winning **Pink Palace Museum and Planetarium** on Central Avenue. A portion of the museum includes the distinctly pink mansion home built by Clarence Saunders, the inventor of the modern supermarket which developed into the extensive Piggly Wiggly chain. Piggly Wiggly supermarkets are found all over the South, and are the best places to buy packaged food popular in the region, like Twinkies (little cakes), pimento cheese and Dr Pepper soda pop. There is a replica of the original Piggly Wiggly Market located inside the museum.

The Victorian era is represented in the city's **Victorian Village Historic District** on Adams Avenue where many of the elegant homes from one of the wealthiest periods of Memphis history can be found. **The Woodruff-Fontaine Home** and **The Mallory-Neely House** are both open to the public most days. Be sure to ask, once inside, about the story of Mollie Woodruff, one of the original residents who reportedly still inhabits the house.

The National Ornamental Metal Museum on the riverbank at West California Avenue is both a working artistic metal shop and a museum showcasing the work of artists in jewelry, sculpture and other forms of metalwork. Racing enthusiasts may want to visit the **Southland Greyhound Park** across the river in West Memphis, Arkansas.

Around 50 miles (80 km) north of Memphis on I-51 is **Henning**, Tennessee, and the boyhood home of Pulitzer Prize winning author Alex Haley, whose book *Roots* became an international bestseller and launched a national interest in genealogy. The **Alex Haley House Museum** contains family artifacts, and the author is also buried here. On a less literary note, east of Henning on HY 19 are the city limits of **Nutbush**, Tennessee, birthplace of Anna Mae Bullock. Ms Bullock gained fame and countless new hair-dos when she married Ike Turner and changed her name to Tina. *Nutbush City Limits* was one of Ike and Tina Turner's million-selling hits.

Left, Mud Island River Walk. Right, a scene on the mighty Mississippi.

EAST TENNESSEE

East Tennesee is the Smoky Mountains, the Cumberland Mountains, the Appalachian Mountains, the Blue Ridge Mountains and Lookout Mountain. It's Jonesborough's National Storytelling Festival, the sweet old-fashioned harmonies of banjos and dulcimers, and autumn Saturdays in Knoxville, when the Tennessee "Vols" notch up another victory before 96,000 orange-clad football fanatics in Neyland Stadium. Tennessee is many things, and to just as many people. From high-tech museums to down-home country fiddle sessions, there's a lot to see.

Forking out: In East Tennessee, 10 million people come every year to Great Smoky Mountains National Park. However, less than a tenth of them discover the peace and seclusion on offer in the wilds of the **Big South Fork National River and Recreation Area**.

Big South Fork sprawls across 10,000 acres (4,000 hectares) of rugged grandeur that belongs to the Cumberland Mountains of northern Tennessee and southern Kentucky. Most of its wooded ravines, rocky gorges and whitewater rivers are well away from paved roads, on trails accessible only by foot, horseback and four-wheel drive. The **Bandy Creek Recreation Area**, operated by the US Park Service, has campsites, picnic pavilions, showers and rest rooms. **Charit Creek Hostel** offers the rustic comforts of a log lodge and cabins. Train buffs shouldn't miss the **Big South Fork Scenic Railway**, a two-hour journey through a deep tunnel and beautiful gorge and along the picturesque banks of Roaring Paunch Creek. The **Blue Heron Interpretive Center** recreates an Appalachian coal mining village.

On the edge of Big South Fork, it's possible to go even further back in time to the Victorian English village of **Rugby**. In 1880, Thomas Hughes, a social reformer, established Rugby as a haven for younger sons of English gentry. Under Victorian primogeniture tradition, firstborn sons usually inherited their fathers' estates, compelling siblings to enter "respectable" professions such as medicine or law. Rugby allowed the disinherited to take up farming and other trades without social stigma. Victorian homes, shops, an Anglican church, a 7,000-book library and schoolhouse were built for 450 villagers. For many reasons, the experiment failed, but the village has endured. More than 20 original structures subtly recreate the age of Dickens and Queen Victoria. The colony's rise and fall is chronicled at the **Rugby schoolhouse Visitor Center**. Food and drink remain firmly in character: the **Harrow Road Cafe** serves fish and chips or roast beef with Yorkshire pudding, while accommodation is available in Victorian **Newbury House**.

While roaming the Cumberlands, you may also care to admire the lacy cascades of **Fall Creek Falls**, the eastern USA's second highest waterfall. **Jamestown** offers an unexpected taste of Tennessee at the **Highland Manor Winery**, with good entertainment at the **Cumberland County Playhouse**.

Left, Fall Creek Falls, north of Chattanooga. **Right**, Rugby.

East of the Cumberlands, the Appalachian Mountains jut up to southwestern Virginia and southeastern Kentucky. In the late 1700s and early 1800s, Upper East Tennessee, as the area is known, was the new nation's western frontier. In 1775, Daniel Boone expanded the frontier by opening the Wilderness Road through Cumberland Gap (*see page 27*). Wagon trains followed, then in this century Boone's trail was asphalted to accommodate the heavy traffic on US 25.

In a happy turnabout, in 1996, the Cumberland Gap Tunnel was opened to divert the highway away from the historic trail. The National Park Service plans to remove the asphalt and replant the trail to how it was in Boone's era. Threaded with hiking trails, it will be included in the 21,000-acre (8,500-hectare) **Cumberland Gap National Historical Park**, whose amenities include a Visitors Center and full-service campgrounds. Gift shops, restaurants and an on-the-spot wedding chapel can be found in the little town of Cumberland Gap, which borders the park.

The National Park Service is also responsible for the revival of another historic trail, this one in west Tennessee. The **Natchez Trace Parkway**, southwest of Nashville, was once one of the most heavily traveled – and dangerous – roads in what was then the frontier Southwest. A series of Indian trails, the paths wound their way from the middle of the state towards Natchez, Mississippi, a distance of around 400 miles (640 km). The trail fell into disuse after river travel replaced overland travel as a viable means of transporting goods; the park service took it over in the 1930s. At milepost 385.9, the **Meriwether Lewis Monument** marks the gravesite of the famous explorer who did so much to chart these unexplored frontiers.

Another early American legend – David "Davy" Crockett – was born in 1786 in a log cabin on Limestone Creek, between Greeneville and **Johnson City**. Humorist, explorer and martyr at the Alamo, Crockett once described himself as "Common as bear spoor in a barley patch." His one-room, dirt-floor

Jonesborough.

cabin has been reconstructed in the **Davy Crockett Park and Historic Site**, where there are bounteous picnic spots by the creek and places to camp out.

Crockett's grandparents, massacred by Indians, are buried in the nearby town of **Rogersville**. Founded in 1786, Rogersville's many historic buildings include the **Hale Springs Inn**, which welcomes overnight guests to rooms furnished with 19th-century antiques.

Crockett fans can also follow his trail to **Morristown**, where coonskin caps, buckskins and a likeness of "Ole Betsy," his favorite "shootin' iron," are on the walls of his father's reconstructed tavern, now open as the **Crockett Tavern and Pioneer Museum**.

Crockett and the frontier are very much alive at the **Rocky Mount Historic Site** at Piney Flats, north of Johnson City. The two-story main house was constructed in the 1770s as the first capitol of the Territory of the US south of the Ohio River. Guides wearing colonial dress weave flax into yarn, cook on an open hearth and lead you back in time with engaging we-are-there-dialogue: "My cousin Andy Jackson stays with us right often. Some say he's got political notions, but I doubt he'll amount to much more than a country lawyer."

In **Greeneville**, you'll notice something unusual about the statue on the courthouse lawn. Instead of the Confederate Johnny Reb usually stationed at Southern courthouses, a Union army man stands guard on the pedestal. He symbolizes East Tennessee's strong Union sentiments during the Civil War.

The region's Union loyalties are also personified by Greeneville's most famous son, Andrew Johnson. When the war began, Johnson was the only Southerner to remain in the US Senate. He became Abraham Lincoln's vice president in 1864, and after Lincoln's assassination in 1865, the 17th president. The **Andrew Johnson National Historic Site** includes his log cabin tailor shop, two homes and his tomb.

Cradled in the Blue Ridge Mountain foothills, **Jonesborough**, founded in 1779, is Tennessee's oldest town. After

Guest cabin, Smoky Mountains.

the Revolution, it was briefly capital of the would-be-state of Franklin. For the first weekend of October, its beautifully preserved homes, churches and public buildings are the backdrop for the **National Storytelling Festival**. Raconteurs from the Smokies and Appalachians, the American West, Europe, Canada and Africa delight the thousands who assemble in big tents around town.

The neighboring mountains abound with parks and national forests. In mid-June, the 600 acres (240 hectares) of **Roan Mountain State Resort Park**, 20 miles (30 km) southeast of Elizabethton, are the focus of the annual Rhododendron Festival. If flowers leave you unmoved, there's also swimming, tennis and nature trails. Overnight accommodation is available and there are plenty of watersports on **Watauga Lake**.

Nature lovers of all ages are in for a treat at **Bays Mountain Park**, south of Kingsport. In the 3,000-acre (1,200-hectare) preserve you can join guided nature walks, view exhibits, and gaze at the heavens in the planetarium.

Smoke gets in your eyes: After a hike in the Great Smoky Mountains, why not indulge in **Gatlinburg**'s creature comforts? Bordering the park, the town of 3,500 residents can sleep over 30,000 visitors in its dozens of hotels and motels. Stores on **The Parkway**, its crowded main drag, sell everything from finely made mountain handicrafts and musical instruments to tacky souvenirs, T-shirts, fudge and taffy. Popular restaurants specialize in hearty meals: freshly caught trout or bountiful breakfasts to get you off on a solid footing.

An abundance of museums and attractions – most of them fairly commercial and bordering on the tacky, but nevertheless good, clean family fun – line Gatlinburg's streets. This extends upwards towards heaven, where an aerial tramway transports visitors 2½ miles (4 km) to **Ober Gatlinburg**, a mountaintop amusement complex with a skating rink, craft shopping, cafes, live entertainment and winter skiing.

Some of the best quality mountain crafts are created by members of the

Thrills and spills at Dollywood.

Great Smoky Mountains Arts and Crafts Community. Their studios and shops are on an 8-mile (13-km) loop of Glades and Buckhorn roads, 4 miles (6 km) from downtown Gatlinburg.

There is also plenty of opportunity to purchase handicrafts at **Dolly Parton's Dollywood** theme park at nearby **Pigeon Forge**. Dollywood's several stages set the countryside a-hummin' with live music – country and western, bluegrass, gospel and pop, with special appearances by big-name stars. The park is also brimming with rides and reasonable restaurants.

Townsend bills itself as "The Peaceful Side of the Smokies." The national park's western gateway, on US 321, has plenty of amenities, from log cabins to nature talks. In warm weather, you can rent an inner tube and enjoy a refreshing ride on the mild **Little River Rapids**. Rain or shine, go underground to **Tuckaleechee Caverns** and marvel at stalagmites, stalactites and waterfalls. During summer, the Smoky Mountain Passion Play is performed in an outdoor amphitheater. Before the national park was created in the 1930s, **Cades Cove** (*see pages 242–4*), near Townsend, was a thriving community of farmers, shopkeepers and loggers. Now a National Historic District, the valley is a timewarp seen on an 11-mile (18-km) one-way loop drive that follows the grades and turns created by 19th-century wagons. Lucky travelers in the early morning or late evening frequently see deer, and sometimes even a bear or two.

Knoxville, with a metro population of more than 300,000 people, is the urban gateway to the Smokies. Over 26,000 students on the **University of Tennessee**'s (UT) main campus give the city a lively, youthful flavor. The city especially comes alive on Saturdays in the fall, when 96,000 fans, dressed in bright "UT orange", cheer on the Volunteers football team. Those in search of more intellectual stimulation can take part in the university's numerous film and lecture series or concerts. UT's **Frank H. McClung Museum** is a field day for curious minds of all ages. Its well-displayed collections focus on Tennessee's past through anthropology, archaeology and natural history.

Knoxville has many fine cultural and recreational amenities. **Blount Mansion**, almost hidden among downtown Knoxville's modern buildings, is one of Tennessee's most revered historic shrines. Here in 1796, Territorial Governor William Blount, ably assisted by Andrew Jackson and other prominent minds, drafted the constitution that made Tennessee America's 16th state. One of the first frame houses built west of the Appalachians, the mansion was the social and political center of the territory and new state. Many furnishings in the rooms belonged to the Blounts.

James White's Fort, in musket range of Blount mansion, was the area's first settlement. General James White built the sturdy log stockade in 1786. The fort's seven buildings are filled with pioneer weapons and furnishings.

The city has also revived part of its more recent past. After the Civil War, merchants, wholesalers and industrialists made their fortunes behind ornate

Blount Mansion, Knoxville.

brick facades around Jackson Avenue and Central Street. Forgotten for decades, the **Old City** has come back to life with restaurants, music clubs, artists' lofts, antique stores, art galleries, trendy apparel boutiques and what-not shops that attract fun-seekers day and night.

World's Fair Park is a legacy of the 1982 event that attracted visitors from near and far. It's pretty easy to find – just look for the 26-story **Sunsphere**, crowned by a gleaming, golden glass ball. Stop first at the **Knoxville Convention and Visitors Bureau** at the street-level entrance to the sphere, then ride the elevator to the observation deck for a splendid panoramic view of the city and the lazy, hazy Smoky Mountains on the horizon.

World's Fair Park boasts the **Knoxville Museum of Art**, which has permanent collections of paintings and sculpture by regional, national and internationally renowned artists. The museum also has a sculpture garden, gift shop and cafe. At the nearby **Candy Factory**, you can decide between the sweet temptations created before your eyes by the South's Finest Chocolate Factory or browse through a selection of shops selling arts and crafts. There's more of the same in **Victorian Houses**, a row of brightly painted homes.

1904 Tiffany glass at Knoxville train station.

The **Knoxville Zoo**'s natural habitats are home to more than 1,000 exotic birds and animals. Recent attractions include Gorilla Valley, Chimpanzee Ridge, Cheetah Savannah, African Plains and a river habitat for playful otters. Youngsters will enjoy the Zoo Choo Train and Bird Show, or a once-in-a-lifetime chance to ride an elephant. If the elephants seem too daunting, the camels can offer an alternative.

For a romantic look at Knoxville, lovers of all things nautical can take a sightseeing, lunch, dinner or moonlight cruise on the Tennessee Riverboat Company's 325-passenger sternwheeler.

The **Dogwood Arts Festival** is the city's biggest spring fling, perfect for everyone except hay-fever sufferers. Two weeks in mid-April are filled with parades, bluegrass, rock and jazz concerts, children's activities, sports events and home tours. No fewer than 60 miles (95 km) of dogwood trees and flower gardens are available for touring.

The cultural heritage of the Southern Appalachians is kept alive at the **Museum of Appalachia** in the town of **Norris**, north of Knoxville. Museum founder John Rice Irwin has assembled over 250,000 artifacts including ingenious inventions like a self-resetting mousetrap. Visitors walk through authentically furnished buildings and the Appalachian Hall of Fame to get the best possible feel for a way of life that, someday, will probably vanish. Fiddlers, guitarists and maestros of the dulcimer, harmonica and washtub bass are usually in fine form on the porch of the 1840s Great House.

Also at Norris, a self-guided drive around the Tennessee Valley Authority's 860-acre (350-hectare) **Norris Lake** takes you to the dam and powerhouse, interpretive center and fish hatchery that helped to put the state back on its ecomonic feet during the Roosevelt era.

Oak Ridge, west of Knoxville, was

the birthplace of the Atomic Age. During World War II, this "secret city" was created as part of the Manhattan Project, which developed the first atomic bombs. Now the modern city of 27,000 people welcomes visitors to its energy-related museums and other attractions. You can see everything on the 38-mile (60-km) Oak Ridge Self-Guided Motor Tour. Pick up a map at the **Oak Ridge Convention and Visitors Bureau**, and begin your tour next door at the **American Museum of Science and Energy**.

The museum's 200 exhibits include quizzes, computer games and do-it-yourself experiments relating to everything from fossil fuels to nuclear fission. Nearby, the Oak Ridge National Laboratory's Graphite Reactor was active until the mid-1960s, when it was declared a national historic landmark. Visitors can operate robotic arms that once handled radioactive materials.

Other Oak Ridge attractions include the **Children's Museum**, a hands-on Southern Appalachians heritage center, with 19th-century log cabins and other exhibits; the **Oak Ridge Arts Center**, with permanent and touring collections of paintings, prints and sculpture; and the University of Tennessee fine, sweet-smelling **Arboretum**, 250 acres (100 hectares) of trees and flowering plants from around the world.

Choo-choo: When **Chattanooga** began planning its downtown revival, it looked to an abundant but often neglected resource. Looping scenically through the city, the Tennessee River had few recreational opportunities, but what a difference a few years can make. The **Tennessee Riverpark** is now a 22-mile (35-km) greenbelt that highlights the city's natural beauty, rich history and productive power. Beginning at the Chickamauga Dam and extending through downtown to the scenic Tennessee River Gorge, the Riverpark includes mini-parks, hiking trails, historical sites, playgrounds and fishing piers. Walkways provide access to the Tennessee Aquarium, the Hunter Museum of Art and other attractions.

The **Tennessee Aquarium** is the

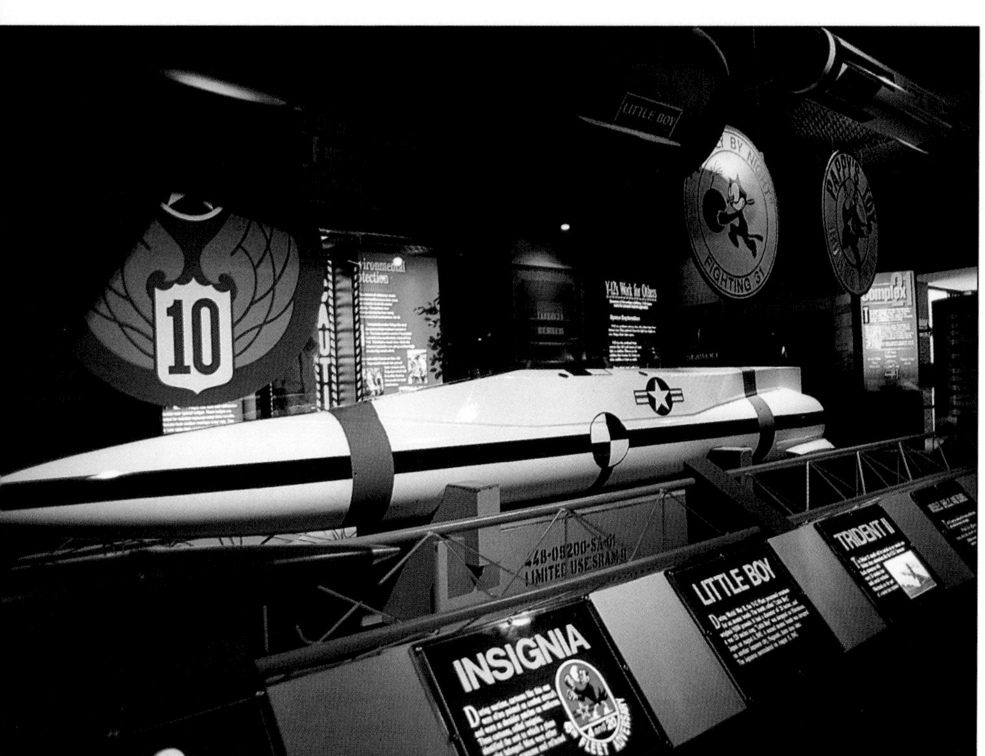

Model of the A-bomb in Oak Ridge museum.

showplace of downtown's revival. The world's first freshwater aquarium is built around a spectacular 60-ft (18-meter) canyon that contains two living forests and 22 tanks. Visitors follow the course of the Tennessee River from its birthplace high in the Appalachian Mountains of northeast Tennessee, to its "marriage" with the Ohio River in southwestern Kentucky. Together the two rivers join the Mississippi and flow into the Gulf of Mexico. At the aquarium, river otters play cheerfully under a waterfall, alligators lurk menacingly, and stingrays, sharks and colorful ocean fish patrol the Gulf of Mexico. The aquarium sits in **Ross's Landing Park and Plaza**, a 4-acre (1.5-hectare) attractive outdoor work of art that traces the city's history through imaginative landscaping, water and artifacts.

Next door, the **Creative Discovery Museum** is hands-on educational fun for kids and adults. This interactive museum includes an Artist's Studio, where budding Picassos can paint and sculpt; Field Scientist's Lab, where they can dig for dinosuar bones; and Musician's Workshop, where would-be Beatles and Beethovens make their own kind of sounds and stage live performances in a recording studio.

The **Hunter Museum of Art** is as renowned for its spectacular setting on a 90-ft (30-meter) limestone bluff above the river as it is for its outstanding collections of American art. The museum is housed in two extremely different buildings – a 1904 classical revival mansion, and a contemporary building with big windows overlooking the river. The two are connected by an interior elliptical staircase and an outdoor rooftop sculpture garden.

The Hunter's treasures include works by artists such as Mary Cassatt, Childe Hassam, Thomas Hart Benton, Ansel Adams and Albert Bierstadt. It hosts many major national and international touring exhibitions. Situated across from the Hunter, the **Houston Antique Museum** displays Anna Safely Houston's 10,000 pieces of antique glass, china and furniture.

Who isn't familiar with the tune *Chattanooga Choo Choo*? Glenn Miller made the song an international hit in the 1941 movie *Sun Valley Serenade*. It celebrated Chattanooga's railroad heritage, which was centered around the grand, Beaux Arts-style **Terminal Station**, built in the early 1900s. Nowadays, the station is the hub of the 30-acre (12-hectare) **Chattanooga Choo Choo** complex that includes a 315-room Holiday Inn hotel, 45 vintage sleeping cars turned into unique accommodation, restaurants, shops, tennis courts, gardens, a model railroad and a 1915 steam locomotive that served the Chattanooga & Southern Railroad.

Train enthusiasts shouldn't miss the **Tennessee Valley Railroad Museum**. The 40-acre (16-hectare) outdoor museum, just outside the city, is a railroader's dream come true. Fans can view an impressive collection of classic locomotives, Pullman sleeping cars, dining cars and cabooses. Best of all, they can take a ride on these old war horses and hear the sweet music of iron wheels and steam engines.

Incline Railway on Lookout Mountain.

Chattanooga's vital role in the outcome of the Civil War is commemorated in the **Chickamauga and Chattanooga National Military Park**. One of the major sites of the war was the **Chickamauga National Battlefield**, across the Georgia state line from downtown Chattanooga. In the fall of 1863, Confederates defeated the Union army in a battle that cost 34,000 casualties. In the subsequent "Battle Above the Clouds," on foggy **Lookout Mountain**, the Union army routed the Confederates and opened the way for their victorious march into Georgia.

At **Point Park Visitor Center**, on Lookout Mountain, three gun batteries mark part of the siege lines. The **New York Peace Memorial** depicts Union and Confederate soliders shaking hands. Exhibits in the **Ochs Museum** tell the story of the battle and its significance to the war's outcome.

At **Rock City Gardens** on Lookout Mountain, it's possible to "see Seven States" from Lover's Leap and work your way through Fat Man's Squeeze and the Swing-Along Bridge over a yawning canyon. At nearby Ruby Falls, an underground passageway leads to a soaring, illuminated waterfall.

A ride on the **Lookout Mountain Incline Railway** is a scenic way to reach the mountaintop. The world's oldest and steepest incline railway – opened in 1895 – scales a steep 72.7 percent grade and affords riders panoramic views of the city through glass-roofed rail cars.

You can make like an Olympian champion on the **Ocoee River**, east of Chattanooga, the site of rafting and kayaking competitions during the 1996 Summer Olympic Games headquartered in nearby Atlanta, Georgia. Several commercial outfitters offer guided trips over high-flowing roller coaster rapids with colorful names like "Diamond Splitter" and "Devil's Slingshot."

You'll also find plenty of uncrowded places for fishing, boating, swimming and watersports on southeast Tennessee's **Hiawassee Scenic River**, **Tellico River** and **Tellico Lake**, created by the Tennessee Valley Authority.

Chattanooga Choo Choo.

Great Smoky Mountains

Everyone who comes to the Great Smoky Mountains, it seems, has a favorite trail, a favorite waterfall, a favorite flower or a special view. These comforting old mountains, which begin in Tennessee and end up in North Carolina, straddling the state boundaries as they go, inspire strong attachments. Maybe it's the history of the place. This national park, one of the East's largest and the most visited in the country, was home to many people not so long ago.

Only about 60 years ago, the 500,000 acres (200,000 hectares) of **Great Smoky Mountains National Park** were carved out of private land. History here is close to the surface and still very much alive. People return to their old homes to reunite with families, fill a jug with clear spring water, lay flowers on the grave of a loved one, sing the old hymns, stitch a quilt or saw on a fiddle.

With the arrival of springtime, they keep their eyes open for ramps. What is a ramp? Well, it's a wild leek, stronger kin of the onion. And when they're ripe, mountain folk offer samples to anyone willing to try them. It's an unforgettable experience. Rising well over 6,000 ft (1,800 meters), the Smoky Mountains also provide much-needed respite from steamy lowland summers.

Visitors are attracted to the flowers that bloom in incredible profusion from spring through summer, and to the mantle of green that softens the mountains' rocky contours. They seek the wild streams and waterfalls, clear impetuous water spilling over rocks with swallowtail butterflies dancing in the mist; the excellent trails, including a 70-mile (112-km) stretch of the **Appalachian Trail**; and the black bears, bobcats, red wolves, white-tailed deer and other wildlife that use the Smokies both as refuge and as nursery ground.

Making the mountains: At the southern end of the Appalachian chain, the Great Smokies are the highest mountains in the East and among the oldest in North America. The basement rock, the crystalline gneisses and schists that underlie everything, were made into their present form about a billion years ago. Even geologists, who measure time quite differently than most mortals, consider this to be very old rock.

On top of this foundation sits a slightly younger group of rocks known as the Ocoee series – mostly lightly metamorphosed sandstones and siltstones. This is the rock exposed along **Newfound Gap Road**, the park's main thoroughfare, which cuts across the mountains between Tennessee and North Carolina. Their nondescript gray color is relieved by splashes of iridescent green moss and grayish-green lichens. Early mountaineers called the house-sized boulders graybacks; other kinds of rock were known in the vernacular as flintrock, dirtrock and slaterock.

Cherokee homeland: When the first white settlers entered the region in the late 1700s, the Smokies were inhabited by the Cherokee Indians, who named the mountains *Shaconage*, "place of the blue smoke." The Cherokees built homes of logs and settled in villages along the **Oconaluftee River** and **Deep Creek**, on the southern edge of the present-day national park. Each of the seven clans chose its own "mother town" and chief. Their famous chief, Sequoyah, invented a written alphabet, and the Cherokees published their own newspaper.

The rocks, rivers and forests furnished the Cherokees with cane for their baskets, stone for their pipes, herbs for their medicines, and food for their stomachs. They held their annual celebrations beside the waters of the Oconaluftee. They believed that Long Man, the river, gathered together his Chattering Children, all the tributary streams. In caves in the mountains lived the Little People. Though mostly benevolent beings, at times the Little People could cause an outsider to lose his way.

The arrival of Europeans, mostly of Scots-Irish heritage, in the 18th century spelled the demise of Cherokee society. Between 1783 and 1819, frontiersmen from Pennsylvania, Virginia and the Carolinas flooded through the gaps in the mountains. Revolutionary War vet-

eft, the mokies and he bears.

erans received land grants in the Smokies, and treaties were signed that left the Cherokee with only a remnant of their ancient homeland.

In 1838–39 most of the Cherokees were marched to Oklahoma on the infamous Trail of Tears. A few hid out in the fastness of the Great Smoky Mountains, in places like Deep Creek, but eventually they were sequestered on the **Qualla Reservation** bordering the park in North Carolina.

A good place to learn more about Cherokee life and history is in **Cherokee**, North Carolina, just outside the park's south entrance. There you can visit **Oconaluftee Indian Village**, a replica of an 18th-century Cherokee settlement; the **Qualla Arts and Crafts Mutual Center**; and just across the street, the **Museum of the Cherokee Indian**. An outdoor drama, *Unto These Hills*, is performed in summer.

The flat valley of the Oconaluftee River was one of the first choices for the homes and farms of the pioneers. Adjacent to the park's **Oconaluftee Visitor Center**, about 2 miles (3 km) from Cherokee, it is possible to get a sense of what life was like on a small, self-sufficient, 19th-century farmstead. The **Mountain Farm Museum** is a collection of historic buildings moved from various locations throughout the park. During the **Mountain Life Festival** (held on the third weekend in September), the museum comes alive with a variety of living-history demonstrations.

A half-mile (1 km) away is **Mingus Mill**, which has a working gristmill and a miller on hand for questioning. In 1886, Dr John Mingus, son of a pioneer Oconaluftee settler, had Sion T. Early build a mill for him on **Mingus Creek**. The long wooden millrace delivers water from the creek to a penstock, then to a turbine beneath the three-story gray building. Inside, corn is fed into the maws of huge granite millstones.

Tennessee's Cades Cove: From the Smokies' windswept crest, Newfound Gap Road winds down the north face of the mountains, following the tumbling water of the West Prong of the **Little Pigeon River** as it flows into **Sugarlands Valley**. Here you can take in the exhibits at **Sugarlands Visitor Center** and then follow **Little River Road** for an excursion to **Cades Cove**, which has one of the country's best collections of pioneer homes and farmsteads in an "open-air museum."

White farmers began settling Cades Cove in the 1820s, clearing trees, planting crops and raising families. By 1850, nearly 685 people lived in the pastoral valley. Settlers built their homes near good "bold" springs that would reliably provide a good supply of pure, sparkling water. Every farm had a springhouse, a small structure which was built over the natural spring to keep out varmints and debris; it also served as a kind of refrigerator. A meat house, corn crib, hog pen, molasses mill, several bee gums, and an outhouse completed the layout of a typical southern Appalachian farm.

To clear the dense forest, pioneers girdled the bark on trees and left them standing in groves called "deadenings." They used fertile, flat land for their

Working with beads, Oconaluftee Indian Village

crops of corn, wheat, oats and rye. But as the ground gave out they were forced to move onto the steep-sided hills.

Corn, a gift from the Indians to white settlers, was the staff of life. "You couldn't live on money; you had to have corn," declared a Smokies farmer. Corn was ground into meal and baked into bread, and it was fed to pigs, chickens and horses. Corn in fermented liquid form – better known as "moonshine" – was also a well-known product.

Most farmers in Cades Cove took their wheat and corn to the **John Cable Mill**, powered by a large wooden water wheel near the **Cades Cove Visitor Center**. John Cable's daughter, known as "Aunt" Becky, lived most of her life in the nearby two-story frame house built in 1879. A big barn of cantilever construction is also located nearby. The tree the pioneers chose to make their cabins out of was the straight-grained yellow poplar, or tulip tree, hewn with a broad axe into logs. Chestnut was favored for split-rail fences. Hard hickory or oak was the best for fuel.

Several other houses either on or near the 11-mile (18-km) Cades Cove loop are open to the public, including the **John Oliver Place**, **Elijah Oliver Place**, **Tipton Place** and **Carter Shields Cabin**. These houses make it easy to imagine just what life was like a century ago. Cabin corners are carefully joined by hand-hewn dovetail notches. Doors swing on wooden hinges, floors bow and creak, slate hearthstones are swept clean. The walls still give back a strong smell of kerosene and a very faint odor of apples.

As soon as a house was finished and the fields were planted, the pioneers set about constructing places where they could worship. Cades Cove was served by the **Primitive Baptist**, **Missionary Baptist** and **Methodist churches**. D.B. Lawson gave a half-acre (quarter-hectare) of land to the Methodist Church and deeded it to "God Almighty." Behind the immaculate white churches are the cemeteries. Gravestones bear the names of many early Cades Cove settlers such as Tipton, Oliver, Gregory

Oconaluftee Indian Village basket weaver.

and Shields. The high number of infant burials bespeak the scarcity of medical care in the mountains in the old days.

Cades Cove is so popular that bumper-to-bumper traffic is a perpetual problem on the loop road. The best solution is to detour onto gravel country roads, like **Sparks Lane**, park the car and take a picnic basket into the green pastures. Early morning is a magical time to see the cove, when the sun burns swirling mist off the surrounding mountains and spider webs sparkle with dew among the grass. Bluebirds perch on fence-posts, and the horses, cattle and deer go on grazing, oblivious to your presence.

Clinging to the borders: The highest peak in the Smokies is **Clingmans Dome**, towering high at 6,642 ft (2,025 meters) and straddling the Tennessee/North Carolina border. If at Newfound Gap, a mile (1.5 km) above sea level, take a 7-mile (11-km) spur road west to the Clingmans Dome parking lot, where a half-mile trail leads to a concrete observation tower.

Be prepared; at these heights, fog is common, and long vistas may be obscured. On a clear day, however, the great ramparts of the Smokies spread before you, blue ridge after blue ridge, separated by deep ravines. Their softness is deceptive; this is rough country.

At Clingmans Dome, the spruce-fir forest reaches its farthest southern limits on the continent. This unique forest fascinates botanists and ecologists because this community is a relict of the ice ages. Once upon a time, glaciers encased a good deal of the southern Appalachians, and the spruce-fir forest enjoyed a wider range. But about 10,000 years ago, the glaciers receded. The boreal forest retreated with them, surviving now only as isolated "islands" in the highest parts of the mountains.

Balds and gaps: Although the Smoky Mountains are not high enough to have a tree line, there are treeless places in these mountains that have drawn people to them for many years. They are called balds, openings covered with grasses or shrubs rather than trees. Pioneers grazed livestock on the balds, and hikers now

Great fall colors in the Great Smokies.

trek to them for their views. **Andrews Bald**, only 2 miles (3 km) from Clingmans Dome, is within closest walking distance. **Gregory Bald** is accessible along trails out of **Cades Cove**. Even though it is a 10-mile (16-km) round-trip hike, it is popular in late June for its world-class wild azaleas.

Wonderful wildflowers: In springtime, the forest is painted with a breathtaking display of wildflowers – serviceberry, redbud, flowering dogwood, bellwort, bloodroot, fringed phacelia, trilliums, trout lilies, violets, miterwort – evidence of a cove hardwood forest, one of the most diverse, productive plant communities in the world.

The **Cove Hardwood Nature Trail** at the **Chimneys Picnic Area** (about 5 miles/8 km from Newfound Gap on Newfound Gap Road) is an excellent introduction. This short walk winds through a cathedral-like cove forest. In spring, the ground is covered in a white cloud of fringed phacelia.

The cove hardwoods were logged heavily during the early part of the century, but some steeper, higher forests were spared because of the difficulty of getting out the logs. It is possible to explore a portion of this virgin, high-country forest along Newfound Gap Road at the **Chimney Tops Trail**, a steep 4-mile (6-km) round-trip scramble to the top of dramatic cliffs with glorious views of the surrounding peaks. About a mile away, the **Alum Cave Trail** makes a strenuous 5½-mile (9-km) climb to the 6,593-ft (2,010-meter) summit of **Mount LeConte**. Along the way are interesting geologic formations such as tunnel-like **Arch Rock** and the towering **Alum Cave Bluffs**. The trail leads to rustic **LeConte Lodge** (no electricity; reservations required), the only overnight accommodation in the park.

There are also no restaurants or gas stations within the park, so be sure to fill up with food and fuel beforehand. Facilities and services are available, however, in all the nearby towns, including several outfitters that specialize in rafting, fishing, cross-country skiing and horseback riding.

Clingmans Dome straddles both Tennessee and North Carolina.

NORTH CAROLINA

North Carolina, one of the 13 original colonies, was once described as a "valley between two mountains of conceit," referring to the border states of Virginia and South Carolina. There's some thread of truth in that, since the state was established primarily by yeoman farmers, not the privileged landed gentry who developed vast plantations using slave labor.

North Carolina is blessed with three distinctive geographic regions – the coast, rolling hills, and the mountains – and a moderate four-season climate. Geography and history have shaped North Carolina's character. With its rugged Atlantic coastline, marked by barrier islands that wrecked thousands of ships, settlement was slow. England made an unsuccessful attempt at colonization in 1587, but it was well over a century before permanent villages and towns were established. In the mid-1700s, Scots-Irish and German settlers followed the Great Wagon Road from Pennsylvania via the Shenandoah Valley in search of fertile farmland. They found the Piedmont region, referring to the land's gently rolling hills, to be ideal for growing the food they needed, as well as cash crops such as tobacco and cotton. Rugged mountains and lack of roads postponed settlement in the western part of the state near the Tennessee border until the mid-1800s.

Three T's – textiles, tobacco, and tourism – are North Carolina's main industries, but high-tech companies have become a larger presence in recent years. Five interstate highways (26, 40, 77, 85, and 95) offer easy access to the state, and five airports (Charlotte, Raleigh-Durham, Greensboro, Asheville, and Wilmington) connect North Carolina to the rest of the world. Stretching westward over 500 miles (800 km) from Manteo to Murphy, the state has plenty of scenic byways, designated by special highway markers, and out-of-the-way places perfect for exploring.

North Carolina's diverse population of 6.6 million is primarily made up of Europeans and Africans, along with Native Americans, Middle Easterners and Asians. Regardless of their ethnic origins, however, these Southerners are a friendly folk. They're likely to greet you with a smile or a nod, willingly give directions (often with an entertaining story or two thrown in for good measure), share their love of good food and welcome you into their homes.

North Carolinians call themselves "Tar Heels" – a nickname given to some soldiers during the Civil War because they stuck in battle like tar sticks to heels. By all means join them in their revelries, their mountain hikes, their coastal cruises and their pleasant daily life, but resist the temptation to use this nickname yourself. A Tar Heel is a Tar Heel, but only if you happen to be one. Southerners are a little bit private, and don't take kindly to folk who overstep the mark. They fought a war over this point, you know.

Preceding pages: Biltmore, near Asheville, was completed in 1895 and is the largest private residence in America. Left, Elizabethan Gardens, near both Manteo and the Fort Raleigh National Historical Site.

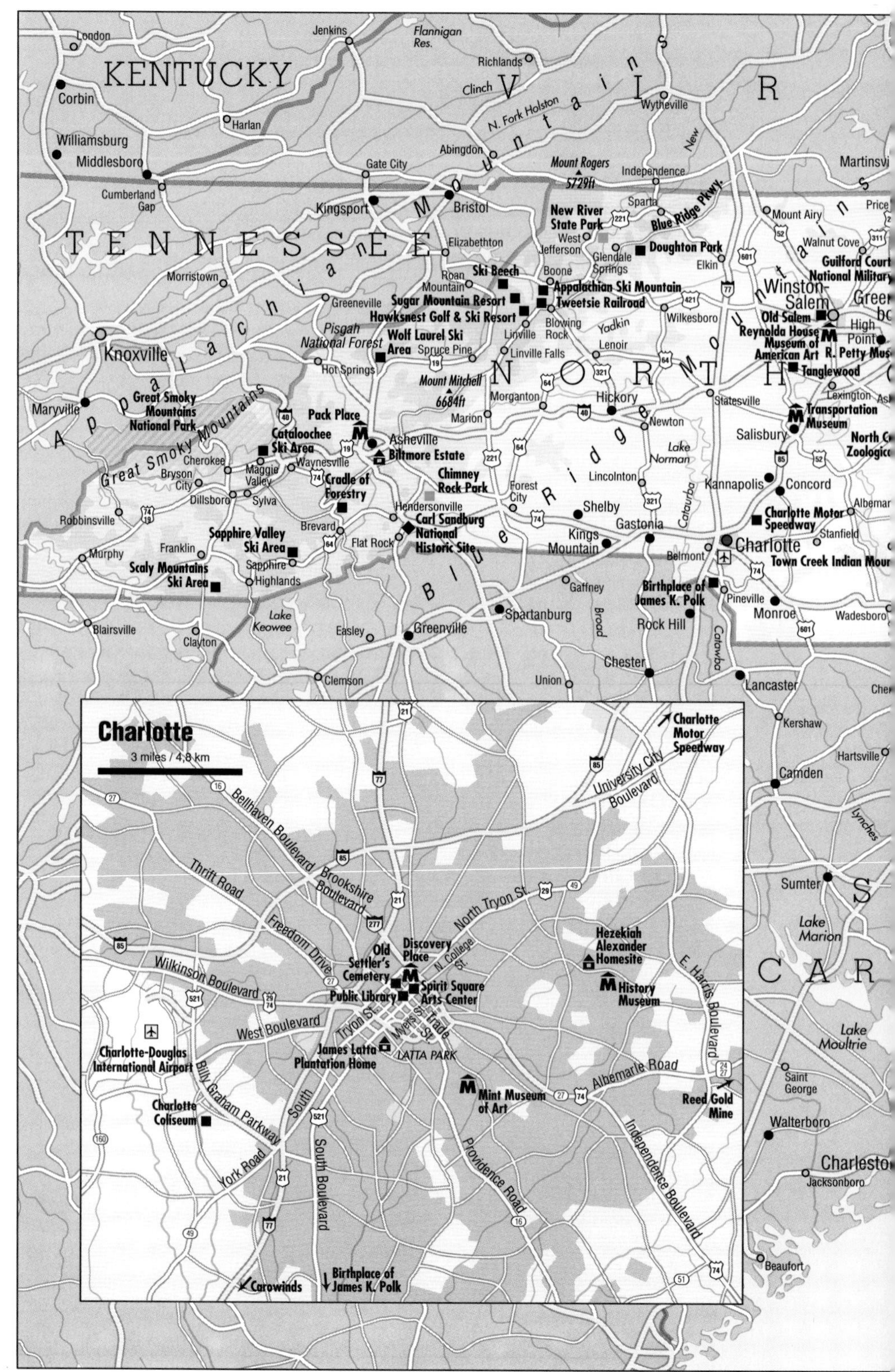
KENTUCKY
TENNESSEE
NORTH
CAR
London
Jenkins
Flannigan Res.
Richlands
Clinch
N. Fork Holston
Wytheville
Corbin
Harlan
Williamsburg
Middlesboro
Abingdon
Gate City
Mount Rogers 5729ft
Independence
Martinsvi
New
Cumberland Gap
Kingsport
Bristol
Sparta
New River State Park
Blue Ridge Pkwy.
Mount Airy
Price
Walnut Cove
West Jefferson
Elizabethton
Glendale Springs
Doughton Park
Elkin
Guilford Court
National Military
Morristown
Roan Mountain
Ski Beech
Boone
Appalachian Ski Mountain
Winston-Salem
Greenbo
Greeneville
Sugar Mountain Resort
Tweetsie Railroad
Hawksnest Golf & Ski Resort
Blowing Rock
Wilkesboro
Old Salem
High Point
Yadkin
Reynolda House Museum of American Art
R. Petty Mus
Pisgah National Forest
Wolf Laurel Ski Area
Linville
Linville Falls
Lenoir
Knoxville
Spruce Pine
Hot Springs
Tanglewood
Mount Mitchell 6684ft
Morganton
Hickory
Lexington
Maryville
Great Smoky Mountains National Park
Statesville
Transportation Museum
Pack Place
Marion
Newton
Cataloochee Ski Area
Asheville
Salisbury
North C Zoologic
Lake Norman
Great Smoky Mountains
Cherokee
Biltmore Estate
Bryson City
Maggie Valley
Waynesville
Cradle of Forestry
Chimney Rock Park
Lincolnton
Kannapolis
Concord
Dillsboro
Sylva
Forest City
Catawba
Albemar
Robbinsville
Hendersonville
Shelby
Charlotte Motor Speedway
Brevard
Carl Sandburg National Historic Site
Gastonia
Stanfield
Sapphire Valley Ski Area
Kings Mountain
Charlotte
Franklin
Flat Rock
Murphy
Sapphire
Belmont
Town Creek Indian Mour
Scaly Mountains Ski Area
Highlands
Gaffney
Birthplace of James K. Polk
Pineville
Monroe
Wadesboro
Spartanburg
Lake Keowee
Broad
Blairsville
Easley
Greenville
Rock Hill
Clayton
Catawba
Chester
Clemson
Union
Lancaster
Che
Appalachian Mountains
Blue Ridge
Blue Ridge Mountains
Kershaw
Hartsville
Camden
Lynches
Sumter
Lake Marion
Lake Moultrie
Saint George
Walterboro
Charlesto
Jacksonboro
Beaufort
Charlotte
3 miles / 4,8 km
Charlotte Motor Speedway
University City Boulevard
Bellhaven Boulevard
Brookshire Boulevard
Thrift Road
Freedom Drive
North Tryon St.
Hezekiah Alexander Homesite
Old Settler's Cemetery
Discovery Place
N. College St.
Wilkinson Boulevard
Spirit Square Arts Center
Public Library
History Museum
E. Harris Boulevard
Tryon St.
Myers St.
Trade St.
West Boulevard
James Latta Plantation Home
LATTA PARK
Charlotte-Douglas International Airport
Billy Graham Parkway
Albemarle Road
Mint Museum of Art
Reed Gold Mine
Charlotte Coliseum
South
York Road
South Boulevard
Providence Road
Independence Boulevard
Carowinds
Birthplace of James K. Polk

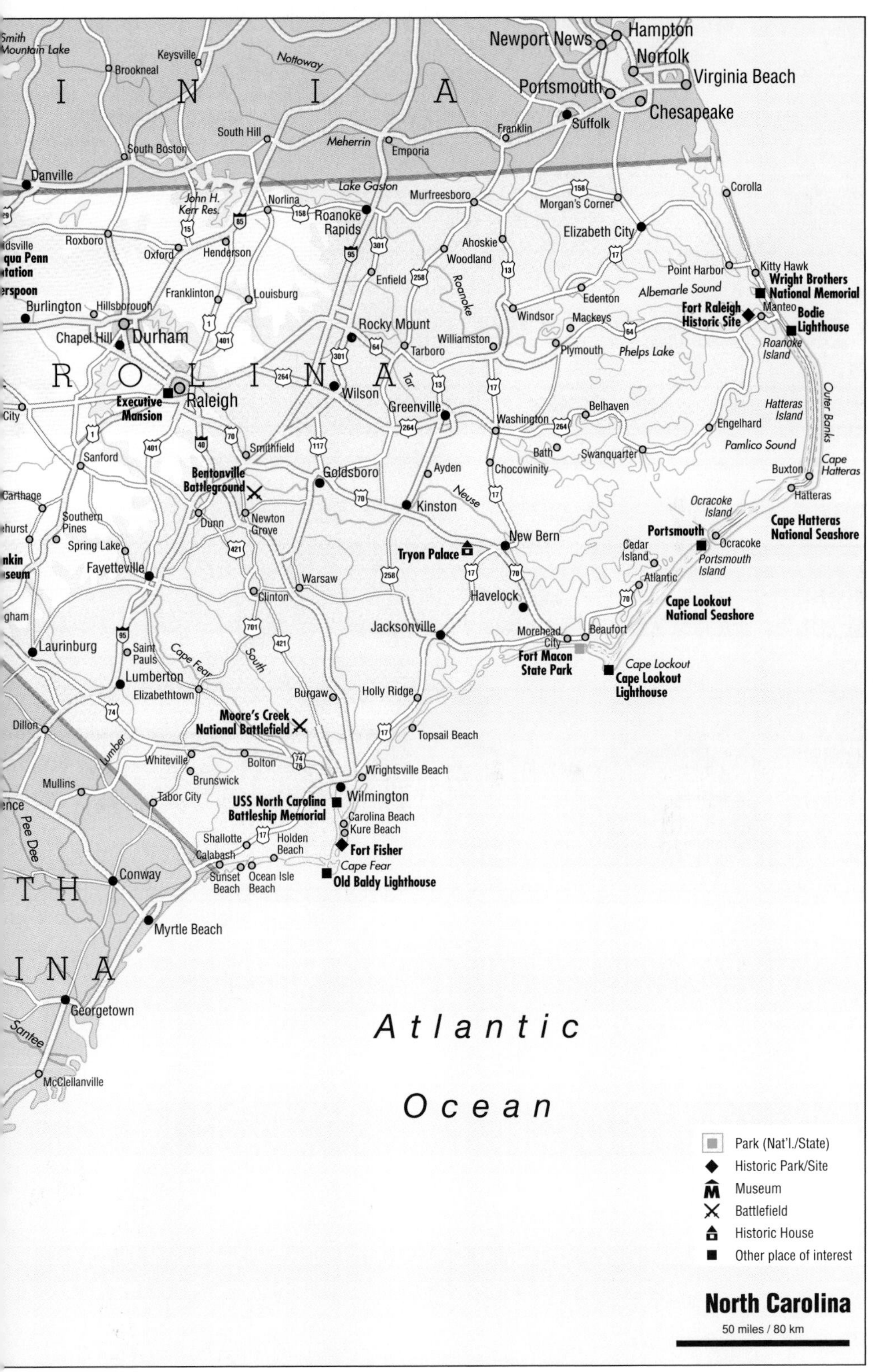
North Carolina
50 miles / 80 km
Park (Nat'l./State)
Historic Park/Site
Museum
Battlefield
Historic House
Other place of interest
Atlantic Ocean
Newport News
Hampton
Norfolk
Virginia Beach
Portsmouth
Chesapeake
Suffolk
Franklin
Emporia
Meherrin
South Hill
South Boston
Keysville
Brookneal
Nottoway
Smith Mountain Lake
Danville
Lake Gaston
John H. Kerr Res.
Norlina
Roanoke Rapids
Murfreesboro
Morgan's Corner
Corolla
Elizabeth City
Ahoskie
Woodland
Roxboro
Oxford
Henderson
Enfield
Point Harbor
Kitty Hawk
Wright Brothers National Memorial
Albemarle Sound
Edenton
Franklinton
Louisburg
Burlington
Hillsborough
Durham
Chapel Hill
Rocky Mount
Windsor
Mackeys
Fort Raleigh Historic Site
Manteo
Bodie Lighthouse
Roanoke Island
Williamston
Tarboro
Plymouth
Phelps Lake
Raleigh
Executive Mansion
Wilson
Greenville
Washington
Belhaven
Hatteras Island
Outer Banks
Engelhard
Pamlico Sound
Sanford
Smithfield
Bath
Swanquarter
Ayden
Chocowinity
Buxton
Cape Hatteras
Hatteras
Bentonville Battleground
Goldsboro
Kinston
Neuse
Carthage
Southern Pines
Dunn
Newton Grove
Ocracoke Island
Cape Hatteras National Seashore
Portsmouth
Ocracoke
Cedar Island
Portsmouth Island
Spring Lake
Fayetteville
New Bern
Tryon Palace
Warsaw
Clinton
Atlantic
Havelock
Cape Lookout National Seashore
Jacksonville
Morehead City
Beaufort
Fort Macon State Park
Cape Lookout
Cape Lookout Lighthouse
Laurinburg
Saint Pauls
Cape Fear
South
Lumberton
Elizabethtown
Burgaw
Holly Ridge
Dillon
Moore's Creek National Battlefield
Topsail Beach
Lumber
Whiteville
Bolton
Brunswick
Wrightsville Beach
Mullins
Tabor City
Wilmington
USS North Carolina Battleship Memorial
Carolina Beach
Kure Beach
Pee Dee
Shallotte
Holden Beach
Calabash
Fort Fisher
Cape Fear
Sunset Beach
Ocean Isle Beach
Old Baldy Lighthouse
Conway
Myrtle Beach
Georgetown
Santee
McClellanville

Around Charlotte

"Charlotte in the forties and fifties was the kind of town she had always been – no nonsense and plenty of grit. She respected character, freedom, money, and trees. She was practical and determined. Almost everybody went to church and wore a hat. There were so many relatives around I had no choice but to behave… The city has changed a great deal and not at all. The land welcomed spirited settlers during the eras of gold, cotton, education, medicine, communication and finance. Now, her people are immigrants again, many of them recognizing what natives know – that Charlotte is a good place. It always has been." – Mary Norton Kratt in *Charlotte: Spirit of the New South.*

Indeed, Charlotte is a good place, and its people have always been immigrants, it seems. Its long and continued prosperity – fostered by gold production, cotton, textiles, transportation, and now high-tech industries – continues to attract people, from both the US and the rest of the world looking for jobs and a better way of life. As the second largest banking center in the country (next to New York) and the largest trading center in the Southeast, even exceeding Atlanta, Charlotte has a great deal going for it. The city is also known for its tree-lined streets, friendly neighborhoods, and soothing climate, yielding blue skies and shirt-sleeve weather most of the year.

Progressive: Charlotteans are characterized as progressive and open-minded with a passion for sports and the arts. They're a gregarious lot, too, and take almost any opportunity to get together, whether for a backyard barbecue, a championship basketball game or a black-tie event celebrating the opening of a new museum. The city's excellent international airport makes it accessible to the world and more than 300 foreign firms have offices here. Like other American metropolises of its size, Charlotte has its fair share of problems. City leaders and concerned citizens continue to combat traffic, crime, poverty and homelessness – with some disappointments, some successes and some rewards; the city became the national model for cross-town busing to achieve racial equality in public schools. Charlotte was recently named America's "most livable city" with a population of more than 100,000 by the US Conference of Mayors, and one of the 10 best US cities in which to live by *Newsweek.* Charlotte's Habitat for Humanity program, aimed at building new homes for low-income families, is the largest in the nation. Former President Jimmy Carter worked on homes alongside residents a few years ago.

Though Charlotte dates to colonial days, its skyline is in continuous flux, and building cranes seem to be part of the landscape. The 60-story **NationsBank**, by architect Cesar Pelli, towers over other buildings in the city, topped by a silver crown, visible for miles. More towers are on the way. The city's growth is not only skyward, however: new shopping malls and neighborhoods now sprawl over what used to be open pastureland.

eft, harlotte: uccessful city f the future. ight, murals dot he downtown rea.

The once sleepy southern city, where at one time the highlight of the year was the arrival of Ringling Brothers Circus in the spring, has obviously awakened. Its New South image is grown-up and sophisticated. Yet Charlotte remains a polite southern city, where roots and age-old traditions still matter, where people still smile and exchange greetings on the street.

Uptown: The center of uptown Charlotte is **The Square** – actually a busy intersection (Trade and Tryon streets) that's filled with buses, cars and pedestrians. Noted for its statues representing the city's past, present and future, the square is also on the crossroads of two ancient Indian trading paths. Office towers on three corners reflect the new Charlotte, and a park on the fourth honors Thomas Polk, a colonial who built the first county courthouse. He is buried in the **Old Settlers' Cemetery** behind the First Presbyterian Church two blocks away.

Most uptown attractions are within easy walking distance of The Square, but the **Gray Line Trolleys** and **Duke Power's Uptown Circuit** provide easy transport.

Two blocks down South Tryon at the corner of Second Street is **Info Charlotte**, offering attention-getting computer screens, graphics, and historical displays, plus souvenirs, brochures, and maps. An orientation video is narrated by Charles Kuralt, who grew up here, with background music by jazz pianist Loonis McGlohon, another local who's made a name for himself in the music world.

Within view of the center is the **First Union Bank Building**, until recently the site of a nine-story mural of NBA Hornets sports heroes. A mural of the mascot, Hugo the Hornet, is scheduled to take its place. The murals are a vivid reminder of Charlotte's fetish for basketball, and sports in general. You can see the players in real life at the **Charlotte Coliseum** west of the city, where the team holds the NBA attendance record for home games.

Three magnificent frescoes by Ben Long, a contemporary North Carolinian who studied under a Florentine master in Italy, decorate the grand lobby of **NationsBank** on the northeast corner of The Square. Based on the Oriental philosophy of "Shingon," the frescoes depict Charlotte's past, present, and future and explore the themes of making/building, chaos/creativity, and planning/knowledge. Long's frescoes can be found all around the city – look out for them.

Adjacent to the NationsBank lobby is **Founders Hall**, with its soaring glass atrium and upscale shops and restaurants and connections to the **Overstreet Mall**, another shopping/restaurant complex. The adjoining **North Carolina Blumenthal Performing Arts Center** offers year-round programs and features performers from around the world.

Three blocks north of The Square via North Tryon Street is **Discovery Place**, an interactive hands-on science museum, that echoes with the voices of school children who've come gaze at the fish in the aquariums, feel the steamy heat of the rain forest that doubles as an aviary, or inspect the rock collection. The museum also houses the **Charlotte Observer OMNIMAX Theater** and the **Kelly Space Voyager Planetarium**. Here on the largest domed screen of its type in North America you may travel to outer space

Artist Ben Long's frescoes can be seen all around town.

with the astronauts or get close-up views of the Big Dipper. Due west of Discovery Place lies **Fourth Ward**, a restored Victorian neighborhood that offers a glimpse of what Charlotte was like years ago when milkmen made deliveries.

Across from the museum is **Spirit Square Arts Center**, formerly a Baptist church that was made into the arts center about 20 years ago. It is a symbol of how Charlotte's private and public sectors have worked together to enrich the community through the arts and arts education, for which Charlotte is now a role model. The **Afro-American Cultural Center**, housed in another renovated church building, east at Myers and East Seventh streets, has black arts as its focus. It, too, is a reminder of Charlotte's cooperative spirit.

A mural by Charlotte's most famous black artist, Romare Bearden, is displayed on the first floor of the **Charlotte Public Library**, at North Tryon and East Sixth streets. Recently named the nation's best library by the *Library Journal*, it hosts the annual NOVELLA festival that draws thousands of people every fall. The event not only features well-known writers but also local authors who've made it into print. A climax to the event is the autograph party, where you can purchase books and get them autographed by the authors.

At the corner of East Sixth and North College streets is **CityFair**, a shopping/ entertainment complex that's making a second go-round after its less-than-successful debut a few years ago. University of North Carolina (UNC)-Charlotte holds classes there. It's also the home of **World Mardi Gras**, a weekend attraction featuring New Orleans food, music and costumes. Here is **Fat Tuesday**, featuring Cajun cuisine and frozen daiquiris. It is one of hundreds of dining options in and around Charlotte, which has attracted several nationally known restaurants.

Except for CityFair's offerings, uptown nightlife is less than thriving, but thousands attend special events such as **First Night Charlotte**, an alcohol-free arts celebration held uptown on New Year's Eve. Charlotteans also like to congregate in coffee houses, restaurants, and pubs in the suburbs. Several new restaurants have opened around the historic **Atherton Mill**, a turn-of-the-century textile mill that's been renovated into shops, a restaurant, and a small brewery in Charlotte's **South End**, about a mile from Uptown. Two restored electric trolleys, kept in the **Trolley Carbarn and Museum** at the mill, will eventually transport visitors between the convention center and South End.

Beyond Uptown: Attractions outside the city center can be reached by car, bus, or sightseeing tour. The **Charlotte History Museum and Hezekiah Alexander Homesite**, the oldest dwelling in Mecklenburg County (1774), lies 3 miles (5 km) east on Shamrock Drive. Life in the early 1800s is portrayed at the plantation home of traveling merchant **James Latta** (also a public park), about 12 miles (19 km) northeast on the Catawba River. **Historic Rosedale** at 3427 North Tryon Street, was built in 1815 by Andrew Frew, a successful merchant. The *faux* finishes in the town home are beautiful, as is the boxwood garden.

The **Mint Museum of Art** on Randolph Road, 3 miles (5 km) east of Uptown, was originally a US Mint, constructed in 1837

The Mint Museum of Art.

to mint the gold ore in heavy production at that time. The building was saved from demolition by a group of foresighted women and made into an art museum a century later. (A network of abandoned mines still lies under Uptown Charlotte, but **Reed Gold Mine**, east of the city off NC 27 near Stanfield, is the only mine from that era that has been preserved.

In addition to hosting internationally acclaimed exhibits, The Mint is known for its permanent collections, which include gold coins minted in Charlotte, Carolina pottery, pre-Columbian art, and American and European paintings. Portraits of King George III and Queen Charlotte of Mecklenburg, honored in the city and county name, are also displayed. (Charlotte is called the Queen City.)

The independent spirit of early Mecklenburgers was paralleled by two US Presidents. The first was President Andrew Jackson, born in the area of the Waxhaw Indians in 1767. The exact spot is unknown, but it was most likely in South Carolina. The second was President James K. Polk, born in 1795 at Pineville, now the fastest-growing area in the Mecklenburg County.

Also across the stateline with South Carolina is the **Radisson Grand Resort**, originally the site of Jim and Tammy Bakker's Heritage USA. The restored home of Evangelist Billy Graham has been moved there from its original location in southeast Charlotte. Straddling the stateline is Paramount's **Carowinds**, an action-packed movie theme park featuring movie characters and hair-raising roller coaster rides.

The glitzy **Charlotte Motor Speedway** at Concord, with its luxurious condominiums over the first turn (northeast of Charlotte via I-85 north), attracts stock car racing fans from all walks of life during May and October. Racing legends such as "King" Richard Petty, Bobby Allison, and David Pearson have claimed fame and fortune here. Aspiring race drivers can get behind the wheel and take lessons from a pro at the **Richard Petty Driving Experience**. (There's a museum to the "king of racing" at **Randleman**, his hometown, near Greensboro.)

A sporting family: the blue hat shows the Hornets basketball symbol.

Stock Car Racing

During the dark years of Prohibition in the 1920s, "moonshine" runners waged a constant battle against "the Feds," government agents who were determined to prevent the illegally brewed whiskey – called "moonshine" because it was usually made and sold only by the light of the moon – from flowing down customers' throats.

The mountain men of the Southeast figured they could hide their whiskey stills from their pursuers in the gullies and crevices of the hills they knew so well, but getting the "white lightning" to their customers was another problem. Blasting pursuers with a shotgun brought more problems than it solved, although according to local feeling, killing a "revenooer" wasn't that heinous a crime. (Stealing a neighbor's pig was further up the list.) But why kill your enemy when you could outrun him? Bending feverishly over the engines of their cars, the moonshine men tinkered and fiddled, finding ways to boost their cars' performance. Soon, the dirt roads were blistered with the noise of roaring engines, and the whirlwinds of dust which followed the racing cars, as lawman chased lawbreaker.

With the end of Prohibition, the speedy transport of whiskey was no longer necessary, but it didn't diminish the desire to speed around dirt roads. However, during the Depression, paying for gasoline for such a pursuit was beyond the means of most people. World War II and gasoline rationing followed, so it wasn't until the late 1940s that this racing became a viable sport.

Throughout the country, crowds filled grandstands, roaring their favorite drivers to victory. The fans of these dirt track extravaganzas were mostly working class individuals. The drivers they supported were men like themselves, and the cars they drove, "stock cars," were automobiles with which the fans were familiar, and, more importantly, were within their purchasing power. Thus was forged a bond between fan and sport. (The term "stock car" refers to the fact that the cars raced are standard automobile models anyone could buy. It was the power of the engine that made the cars different.)

But this loose federation of enthusiasts had no all-encompassing rules; what was allowed at a track in one town was against the rules at another in the same state. In 1947, Bill France, Sr, an amateur racer himself, asked others who were concerned with the future of stock car racing to a meeting in Daytona Beach, Florida. From that, the National Association of Stock Car Auto Racing (NASCAR) was born.

The first NASCAR-sanctioned race was held in February 1948 on Daytona's hard-packed beach. The next year, the NASCAR Winston Cup Series was born. This is the premier stock car racing division, and the circuit to which all stock car drivers aspire. The first race was run on the Charlotte, NC, Fairgrounds' dirt track. As part of a policy of upgrading facilities, the first asphalt NASCAR circuit in the nation was built at Darlington Raceway in South Carolina in 1950. In 1959, the Daytona National Speedway opened, a marvel of aerodynamic engineering. Lee Petty (father of Richard, a stock car racing legend) won the first Daytona 500 over Johnny Beauchamp.

The 1960s saw more growth: the Motor Speedway was built at Charlotte in 1960, and the following year the ABC television network first televised a NASCAR race, the Firecracker 400 from Daytona Beach. Prominent drivers included Richard Petty, Cale Yarborough, Ned Jarrett, David Pearson and Bobby Allison who competed in an average of 60 races a year on tracks across the US, becoming known outside sports circles.

With an average attendance of over 170,000 people per race meeting, Charlotte's Motor Speedway is very popular. Raceway surfaces include a 1½-mile superspeedway, a one-fifth mile clay oval track, and a one-fourth-mile asphalt oval. In 1992, it was the first superspeedway to hold night races. Several motion pictures have been filmed here including *Days of Thunder*, *Stoker Ace* and *Speedway*. ■

Around North Carolina

North Carolina has three regions: the eastern coast, so windswept it was the site chosen by the Wright Brothers for their first efforts in airborne flight; the mountains, specifically Great Smoky Mountains National Park, the largest in the East and the most visited in the country; and the gently undulating hills of the central region, the Piedmont.

Fiercely independent, North Carolina was the last state to secede from the Union; once committed to the South, however, it contributed more than its fair share of soldiers – some put this figure as high as one-sixth of the Confederacy's total troops. Proud and strong, fully functioning and even thriving on its three Ts – tobacco, textiles and tourism – North Carolina looks poised to enter the next millennium with its head held high.

The Piedmont: With its rolling hills and woodlands watered by lakes and streams, the Piedmont region of North Carolina takes up the middle part of the state. It extends roughly from the foothills of the Blue Ridge Mountains in the west to the cities along I-95 in the east. Within the region I-85 runs northeast from Charlotte to Virginia, and I-77 runs due north from Charlotte. Scattered throughout the Piedmont countryside are historic towns and sites, battlefields, museums, and other interesting places to see.

Salisbury, Salem (now Winston-Salem), and Fayetteville were thriving commercial centers in the early days, while other towns sprang up around rivers that provided power to both the textile and furniture industries. Those industries are still going strong today, and shoppers clamber for discounted clothing and household goods at outlet centers at **Kannapolis** and **Burlington**, off I-85, and for furniture in **Hickory**, off I-40, or **High Point**, off I-85. Though manufacturing is still important, the region has become diversified in recent years, with the arrival of blue-chip companies and high-tech industries.

On the edge of the western frontier in colonial times, **Salisbury** welcomed George Washington during his southern tour and many years later was the site of a large Confederate prison. Around the turn of the century, the town turned to railroading. A survivor of those times is the **North Carolina Transportation Museum** at Spencer Shops State Historic Site, a few miles north. Today the **Salisbury National Historic District** is a small treasure of restored homes and shops, best seen on a self-guided walking tour, available at the Spanish mission-style train station on Depot Street. A few miles north of here is **Lexington**, home of more than two dozen barbecue houses and site of an annual festival in October that celebrates this local delicacy.

The Triad: The area encompassing Winston-Salem, High Point, and Greensboro is called "The Triad." **Winston-Salem**, with its brick tobacco buildings – where tobacco baron R. J. Reynolds amassed a fortune producing Camels, Winstons, Salems, and other R.J. Reynolds cigarette brands – still looks like a manufacturing center. However, the wealth produced by tobacco, textiles, and other products, plus the presence of **Wake Forest University**, **North Carolina School of the Arts**, and **Winston-Salem State University**, has made it a cultural center as well.

On the city's west side are **Reynolds House Museum of American Art**, R.J. Reynolds' former home; **Southeastern Center for Contemporary Art (SECCA)**, where hosiery giant James G. Hanes lived; and the **Museum of Anthropology** at Wake Forest University. **Delta Arts Center**, a museum of Afro-American art, is near Winston-Salem State University. The **Stephens Center**, a renovated movie theater, serves as a performance hall, which often stages shows before they go to Broadway.

Winston-Salem is best known, however, for **Old Salem**, a community settled by the Moravians in 1766. From the present-day Czech Republic, the Moravians first put down roots in Bethlehem, Pennsylvania, and later moved to North Carolina at the invitation of a lord pro-

Left, drying tobacco in the hot Southern sunshine.

prietor who wanted industrious people who could make a contribution to the area. Historic buildings in the restored village are open for guided tours, led by docents dressed in Moravian costume, and shops sell merchandise made in the village. At **Winkler's Bakery**, you can buy Moravian sugarcake and wafer-thin gingersnaps. On Christmas Eve and Easter, brass bands play hymns on the street corners prior to services in the village church.

The **Museum of Early Southern Decorative Arts** (**MESDA**) sits on the edge of Old Salem. It features early American furniture, made through 1820. (Nearby High Point's **Furniture Discovery Center**, the only museum of its type in the country, explains the process and history of furniture production in America. If you want to buy furniture, however, you should pick up a brochure listing all the shops that sell to the public. (High Point's International Home Furniture Market, held twice a year, caters to buyers from around the world and is not open to retail shoppers.)

Tanglewood, the former estate of William Reynolds, a few miles west of Winston-Salem at **Clemmons**, offers all types of recreation, including horseback riding. The 1,100-acre (445-hectare) park lights up during the annual **Festival of Lights** in December. Tanglewood also hosts a steeplechase every May and some events associated with the Crosby Golf Tournament every June, initiated by entertainer Bing Crosby in California many years ago. **Wilkes County**, where Tom Dula was hanged for the murder of Laura Foster, lies several miles west. Their tragic love story is the subject of the famous song, the *Ballad of Tom Dooley*.

Situated east of Winston-Salem is **Greensboro**, traditionally a textile city that's home to several colleges and universities and the Greater Greensboro Golf Tournament. At the **Battle of Guilford Courthouse**, now a military park, the British claimed a victory over the Americans in the spring of 1781. The **Greensboro Historical Museum** features the counter where the Woolworth

The town of Old Salem dates from 1766...

civil rights sit-ins of the 1960s were staged. (This event was pivotal in the African-Americans' long struggle to achieve racial equality.) Also here is a replica of the drugstore where American short-story writer William Sydney Porter (O. Henry) worked when he was a boy. Newscaster Edward R. Murrow and First Lady Dolley Madison, wife of President James Madison, who was born near Guilford College, are also honored. The Quaker college hosts the annual **Eastern Music Festival** featuring musicians from around the world every summer. Greensboro has several outstanding art museums which are well worth a visit, including the **Weatherspoon Gallery** at UNC-Greensboro which focuses on contemporary art.

Northeast of Greensboro near Reidsville is **Chinqua-Penn Plantation**, the home of tobacco king Jeff Penn. Open to the public, the 22-acre (9-hectare) plantation is known for its gardens and elaborate holiday decorations.

... and was settled by the Moravians.

Due south of Greensboro at **Asheboro**, which is also a textile town, is **North Carolina Zoological Park**, reputedly the world's largest natural habitat zoo. Nearly 1,400 exotic animals roam freely in African and North American habitats, two of seven continents planned for the complex.

North Carolina's pottery tradition, which dates to colonial times, is also strong here. Today around 70 turn-and-burn potters, including Ben Owen III and Phil Morgan, who produce museum-quality pieces, sell their wares in little shops scattered on and off NC 705.

Early Indian pottery and artifacts are showcased at two nearby sites. The **Rankin Museum of American Heritage** at Ellerbe features Pee Dee Indian pottery, and the **Town Creek Indian Mound** at Mount Gilead portrays the Creek Indians from 1250 to 1450.

A few miles from the simple pottery sheds of Seagrove is **Pinehurst**, a New England-style village designed by Frederick Law Olmsted for developer James W. Tufts a hundred years ago. Best known for its championship golf courses, Pinehurst is also ideal for ten-

nis, bicycling, and equestrian activities. (The Tour de Moore International Bicycle Race is an annual event.) Sam Snead, Ben Hogan, Arnold Palmer, Jack Nicklaus and other golf legends have played the greens here. The oldest courses, including famous Pinehurst No. 2, were designed by Scotsman Donald Ross, who also ran the Pine Crest Inn in the village for years. Irishman Mickey Walsh, who hosted the annual Stoneybook Steeple Chase for nearly half a century, also greatly influenced the Sandhills region.

The Triangle: North of the Sandhills area near I-40 and I-85, is "The Triangle," which includes the cities of Durham, Raleigh, and Chapel Hill. Although these three are separate municipalities, they are so intertwined that people tend to think of them as one. In a recent poll, the area was named the Number One place in America to live by *Money* magazine. The fastest-growing area in the state, next to Charlotte, it has four outstanding universities – Duke, NC State, the **University of North Carolina**, and **North Carolina Central University**. Also here is the 6,800-acre (2,800-hectare) **Research Triangle Park**, known for its high-tech research and Nobel Prize winners. It has one of the highest per capita concentrations of Ph.Ds in the nation. State government has a large presence here, too, with Raleigh, which has been the state capital since 1792.

For many years **Durham**'s claim to fame was Bull Durham tobacco, and its advertising logo became famous. During that same period, while Memphis, Chicago, and the Mississippi Delta were singing the blues, local musicians in Durham were singing the "Bull City Blues." Today the city is the home to the Durham Bulls Class A baseball team, elevated to star status after the hit movie by the same name was released in 1987.

The wealth that gave Durham its first momentum came from the Duke family, who made their fortune in tobacco. The **Duke homestead** where they began their lucrative business just after the Civil War, is open for tours. They also generously endowed **Duke University**, known for its outstanding medical school and research efforts. Today Durham has shed its mere tobacco image and calls itself the "City of Medicine." The focus of the campus is the late Gothic Revival **Duke Chapel**, where you can often hear a free concert on the 5,200-pipe organ. The university hosts the **American Dance Festival** every summer.

Not far from the Duke campus is the **Bennett Place State Historic Site**, where Union General William T. Sherman and Confederate General Joseph E. Johnston hammered out their terms of surrender in the War Between the States. The event is re-enacted here every April. Johnston made nearby **Historic Hillsborough**, a colonial town dating to 1754, his headquarters, and today more than 100 historic structures in the town survive. Prior to the surrender, one of the largest and bloodiest Civil War battles occurred south of here near Newton Grove in Johnston County. The **Bentonville Battleground State Historic Site** on US701 has restored buildings and field exhibits.

Raleigh, North Carolina's capital city,

Executive Mansion, Raleigh.

is named for Sir Walter Raleigh, who headed up England's colonization efforts over four centuries ago. (A statue of him stands on the **Fayetteville Mall** a few paces from the Capitol.) The sprawling city of over 240,000 people is primarily a government center offering museums, art galleries, theaters, shopping centers, restaurants, parks, and eight institutions of higher learning, including **NC State**, the largest university in North Carolina. It is also the home of several state arts organizations, including the North Carolina Symphony, which presents over 200 concerts around the state every year.

You may wish to park near the 1840 Greek Revival **Capitol** on **Capitol Square** and walk to attractions. Or you may catch the **Trolley Through Raleigh**, which runs weekdays during lunch hours. The **Capital Area Visitor Center** at 303 N. Blount Street has maps and brochures.

Within a few paces of the Capitol are the **State Legislative Building**, the **Museum of Science**, the **Museum of History**, the **State Archives**, and the 1891 **Executive Mansion**, where the Governor resides. The state's outstanding collection of European and American paintings is housed in the **North Carolina Museum of Art**, a short drive west of the Capitol. Located in **Mordecei Park**, north of the city center, is the house where US President Andrew Johnson was born in 1808.

You'll find a lot of activity in and around the revived **Moore Square Arts District** and the 1914 Spanish mission-style **City Market**. The area has taken on new life as art galleries, craft shops, restaurants, a small brewery, clubs, and shops have opened in the past few years. Locals go to the **State Farmers Market** on Agriculture Street for fruits, vegetables, crafts, and huge country-style breakfasts. On weekends and holidays you'll find them enjoying the great outdoors at nearby Jordan and Keor lakes.

Chapel Hill is often called the "southern side of heaven," referring to the idyllic life that residents enjoy amid its quiet neighborhoods and tree-lined

Duke Chapel and 5,200-pipe organ.

streets. The town's pulse is best sensed on **Franklin Street**, where students go crazy when they beat a rival sports team. As the oldest state university in the nation (1792), **UNC-Chapel Hill** has produced a long list of outstanding graduates, including the noted writer Thomas Wolfe and movie/television star Andy Griffith, creator of the mythical Mayberry. (Both were affiliated with the Carolina Playmakers while at the university.) Other sights to see are the **Morehead Planetarium** and the **North Carolina Botanical Garden**, offering the largest collection of native plants and herbs in the Southeast.

North Carolina's vast coastal plain lies east of Rocky Mount, Fayetteville, Lumberton, and other cities. Here the rich land produces great quantities of tobacco, soybeans, corn, cotton, poultry, swine, and beef before it totally flattens at sea level. Here tobacco auctions and Eastern-style chopped pork barbecues are part of the entertainment. It was in this area – called "Down East" by the people who live here, but **Smithfield** to be exact – that actress Ava Gardner was born. A museum displays memorabilia relating to her life and explains through a video how the poor but beautiful farm girl became one of Hollywood's hottest starlets in the 1950s. **Greenville**, a tobacco town and home to East Carolina University and the **Greenville Museum of Art**, featuring a fine collection of 20th-century American art, is also worth a visit.

Fayetteville, the home of **Fort Bragg** and **Pope Air Force Base**, has all the trappings of a military town, though it was settled by Highland Scots and was originally called "Cambellton." It was the first city in America to be named for Marquis de Lafayette of France who fought on America's side in the Revolution. (A collection of his letters, books, and artifacts is displayed at **Methodist College**.) Several miles south is the town of **Lumberton**, home of the present-day Lumbee Indians. Their story is told in an outdoor summer drama called *Inherit the Wind*.

The Mountains: The rolling hills of the Piedmont slowly build into foothills in the west before bending and buckling dramatically into towering peaks, some over 6,000 ft (1,800 meters) in height, others over 5,000 ft (1,500 meters). Part of the southern Appalachias, the **Blue Ridge Mountains** extend from the Virginia state line southward into Georgia. On the southwestern side they butt up to the **Great Smoky Mountains**, once inhabited by the ancient Cherokee called Shaconage (*see pages 241–2*).

These lofty summits are connected by the 60-year-old **Blue Ridge Parkway**, which boasts the title of "America's most scenic highway." In North Carolina it begins at the Virginia state line, weaving its way through gaps and gorges, over and around summits, finally ending in Cherokee, the gateway to the **Great Smoky Mountains National Park**. *(See pages 241–5.)* Scattered all along the parkway are parks, historic sites, lakes, nature trails, and scenic overlooks. Among its highlights are Doughton Park, the Moses Cone Estate, Julian Price Park, Grandfather Mountain, Linville Falls (part of the

North Carolina's vast coastal plain is rich agricultural land.

Linville Gorge Wilderness Area), Crabtree Meadows, Mount Mitchell (the highest mountain in the East, with an elevation of 6,684 ft/2,037 meters), the Folk Art Center, Mount Pisgah, and the Balsam Mountains.

Isolation: In pioneer times the isolation of the mountains created an independent and self-reliant cultural enclave that was separate from the rest of the state. That has changed in recent decades, as residents of the Piedmont and surrounding states have built second, often palatial, homes in the mountains. Today mountain and flatland cultures live in harmony, but remain socially separate for the most part.

The mountains have lured visitors since the 1880s, but the area didn't really develop until good roads such as I-26 and I-40 were built, slicing through the high mountains near Asheville. The introduction of snow skiing in the 1960s, first at Cataloochee Ranch near Maggie Valley, catapulted the region into a major recreation area offering golf, tennis, whitewater rafting, hiking, camping, fishing, and other outdoor pursuits. A few ski resorts have come and gone, but the survivors are Cataloochee, Wolf Laurel near Asheville, Sapphire Valley and Ski Scaly in the southwest mountains, and Appalachian Ski Mountain, Ski Beech, Sugar Mountain Resort, and Hawksnest Golf & Ski Resort in the northwest mountains.

Asheville, with a population of 62,000, is the largest city in western North Carolina. It is known for its well-preserved Art Deco buildings (the largest collection in the country next to Miami), arts and crafts, folk music, and indigenous dances, which are celebrated in festivals throughout the year. Many activities occur around **Pack Place Education, Arts and Science Center** in the middle of the city – housing four outstanding museums – **Asheville Art Museum**, the **Colburn Gem and Mineral Museum**, the **Health Adventure**, and **YMI Cultural Center**. Large photographs on display depict three centuries of history revolving around **Pack Place**. Visitors are often surprised to

Shopping near the Blue Ridge Parkway.

find such a vibrant city, complete with nightlife, in the heart of the mountains.

George W. Vanderbilt was so impressed with the beauty of Asheville that he chose this area in which to build his 255-room French Renaissance chateau, called **Biltmore**. Completed in time for Christmas in 1895, the construction took all of five years. Still in the family, it is the largest private home in America, and today thousands of visitors stroll casually through its gardens, taste the wine from its vineyards, share in the annual Christmas celebration, and see how one of America's wealthiest families lived around the turn of the century. Vanderbilt employed architect Richard Morris Hunt and landscape architect Frederick Law Olmsted, plus the world's leading craftsmen, to build this enormous 125,000-acre (50,500-hectare) estate.

In 1913, Dr Edwin Wiley Grove arranged for the **Grove Park Inn Resort** to be constructed of huge boulders on the top of Sunset Mountain, and in less than a year. Patterned after Old Faithful in Yellowstone Park, the resort has entertained US Presidents, America's leading industrialists, and noted entertainers. The great tenor Enrico Caruso sang opera at Grove Park.

Thomas Wolfe put Asheville on the map in a different way with the 1929 publication of *Look Homeward, Angel*, a book that so enraged local citizens, because they recognized themselves depicted in its pages, that the author rarely came home after its release. **My Old Kentucky Home**, his mother's boarding house and the setting for his novel, is open for tours.

Another prominent American author, Carl Sandburg, who wrote the definitive biography on Abraham Lincoln, spent his last years at **Flat Rock**, an old tourist town a few miles south of Asheville. It has been called the "Little Charleston of the Mountains" because Charlestonians have summered here for generations. **Connemara**, the farm where the Sandburg family raised prize-winning goats, is now a National Historic Site.

Blowing Rock, near the Eastern Continental Divide.

East of here is **Chimney Rock Park**, a 1,000-acre (400-hectare) park that's built around a 26-story granite outcropping. It was used as a setting for the 1993 film *The Last of the Mohicans*, based on Daniel Defoe's 1826 classic.

West of the Sandburg farm, you'll find dozens of natural cascades in the "land of waterfalls." The tallest is **Whitewater Falls**, which drops 441 ft (134 meters) near the resort town of **Sapphire**. **Sliding Rock** in **Pisgah National Forest** serves as a natural waterslide for youngsters of all ages.

Near here, Dr Carl Schenck, a German, established one of the first forestry schools in America, the Cradle of Forestry, in 1898. Today it's a perfect place to find rare wildflowers. An added attraction is the **Brevard Music Center**, which stages over 50 different concerts during the summer.

The area between Asheville and the Great Smoky Mountains National Park has much to offer. Every summer Waynesville and surrounding Haywood County, a center for clogging (a native dance involving shuffles and stomps), stage the **North Carolina International Folk Festival** – Folkmoot USA. The two-week event, featuring dancers and music from around the world, culminates in a street festival in **Waynesville**, a hamlet that offers some wonderful craft and souvenir shops. The biggest attraction in nearby Maggie Valley is **Ghost Town In The Sky**, a western theme park featuring gunfights, live shows, and thrilling rides.

In quaint **Dillsboro**, also a center for mountain arts and crafts, you can board the **Great Smoky Mountains Railroad**. The train offers a scenic excursion lasting several hours that goes through the **Nantahala River Gorge**, a popular spot for whitewater rafting. One of the train's engines was used in the making of the movie *The Fugitive*.

South of Dillsboro lies the **Cowee Valley**, "Gem Capital of the South," where you can sink to your elbows in mud looking for rubies and emeralds at the dozen or so mines that are open to the public. The scenic **Cullasaja Gorge**,

View of Ashe County from the Blue Ridge Parkway.

best viewed from US64 between Franklin and Highlands/Cashiers, affords some of the most beautiful scenery in the state, including **Whiteside Mountain**, which has the tallest cliffs in eastern America.

The Eastern band of the Cherokee Indians live on the **Qualla Boundary**, a small portion of what used to be their great nation covering parts of several Southern states. Today they still hunt and fish but also earn income from crafts, local industries, a large bingo operation, and other gaming. Learn more about the tribe at the Oconaluftee Indian Village (*see pages 241–2*). The story of the Cherokee nation, their forced removal to Oklahoma in 1837 along the "Trail of Tears," and their return to North Carolina is portrayed during the summer in the drama *Unto These Hills*.

North of Asheville via the Blue Ridge Parkway is the **North Carolina High Country**, referring to its grand, majestic peaks; lush, narrow valleys; and rushing waterfalls and streams.

The High Country's most celebrated mountain is **Grandfather**, one of the world's oldest and named for the chiseled rock profile that resembles an old man. Located near the resort town of **Linville**, it hosts the annual **Grandfather Mountain Games** and **Gathering of the Scottish Clans**, one of the largest and most prestigious Scottish clan gatherings in North America. **Linn Cove Viaduct**, the final link of the Blue Ridge Parkway which was constructed with little disturbance to the mountain, is considered an engineering marvel. North of Grandfather on the Tennessee state line is **Roan Mountain**, where every June the world's largest gardens of crimson-purple rhododendron dazzle the eye (*see page 234*). An event strictly for lovers of wiggly critters is Banner Elk's **Woolly Worm Festival**.

Blowing Rock, a classic tourist town where flatlanders have summered since the late 1800s, takes its name from a promontory rock situated near the Eastern Continental Divide that overlooks the Johns River Gorge. **Tweetsie Railroad** theme park is based around the narrow-gauge train which ran between Johnson City, Tennessee, and Boone, North Carolina, from the late 1800s through to 1940. Passengers get to ride around 3 miles (5 km) of track and are frequently attacked by pretend Indians and gunfighters.

Early history of the area is portrayed every summer in the outdoor drama *Horn in the West* in the town of **Boone**. It centers around pioneers, including the frontiersman Daniel Boone, who stopped here on his way to Kentucky. The **Appalachian Cultural Museum** at Appalachian State University is also devoted to the local culture, and "Appalachian Spring" features special concerts and programs every summer. Though Boone has a mast store – an old-timey general store that carries everything from brogans to iron skillets – a sidetrip to the original at **Valle Crucis** is well worth the time. Established in 1883, the store remains the hub of the local community.

Northeast of Boone via the Blue Ridge Parkway lies **Ashe County**. It was little known until a few years ago when Ben

Dive shop, Morehead City.

Long asked permission to paint frescoes in two abandoned 19th-century churches. Today visitors from around the world come to see his masterpieces at **Holy Trinity Church** in Glendale Springs and **Saint Mary's Episcopal Church** in West Jefferson. The **New River**, second only to the Nile River in age, runs through Ashe County, and 25 miles (40 km) of it is designated as a National Wild and Scenic River. Canoeists and fishermen love it.

The Coast: North Carolina's coastline has a storied past, filled with the ghosts of Native Americans, marauding pirates, lost seamen, and early colonists. Geography has shaped the history and destiny of this region with its treacherous coastline. Much of the northern coast from the Virginia state line to Cape Lookout is National Seashore. Today commercial activity centers around the state's two ports – Morehead City and Wilmington.

Here on these shores, where the natives still speak with a twinge of an English accent, are some of the state's oldest towns – including Bath (1705), Beaufort (1710), and New Bern (1710), the colonial capital. Here are historic forts, lighthouses, life-saving stations, churches, plantations, and great ecological preserves where endangered species still survive. Here also are small fishing villages, seaside towns, and uncrowded beaches.

Access to the coast has improved greatly, with the completion of I-40 from Raleigh to **Wilmington**, the largest coastal city (population 60,000). People are drawn to this port city's beautiful harbor, historical attractions, museums, cultural opportunities, restaurants and movie production. Among the few places in North Carolina where church spires dominate the skyline, Wilmington boasts one of the largest historic districts on the National Register of Historic Places.

In recent years Wilmington has become such a popular spot for film production that it's commonly referred to as "Hollywood East." Hundreds of movies and television shows, including *King Kong Lives*, *Blue Velvet*, *Crimes of the Heart*, *Matlock*, and other well-known titles, have been made at the **North Carolina Film Studio** (originally Dino DeLaurentis's studio). People have gotten pretty used to seeing city streets blocked off when a shoot is taking place, but don't count on a face-to-face encounter with a movie star, unfortunately, as it's pretty difficult to get beyond all the hefty security guards.

The heart of Wilmington is its waterfront. Here, with great excitement, warehouses once filled with cotton have been converted into shopping and restaurant complexes, and a modern convention center now connects to the extremely interesting **Wilmington Railroad Museum**. Wilmington's stellar attraction is a ship commissioned in 1941 and later made into a memorial to soldiers who served in World War II. Visitors may tour the ***USS North Carolina* Battleship Memorial** and on summer nights watch a sound-and-light show called "The Immortal Showboat." Several sightseeing boats offer tours from the waterfront. One of the most popular is

Diving for wrecks off the coast.

the ***Henrietta II***, an 80-ft (25-meter) replica of an 18th-century steamboat, but with all the modern conveniences you might need, including a lounge and a restaurant.

A few blocks from Wilmington's waterfront are the city's best-known historic sites. The Visitor Center (orientation film, maps, postcards and brochures) is housed in the restored 1892 **New Hanover Courthouse**. The **Cape Fear Museum** focuses on the history of Cape Fear, made famous by the 1962 suspense movie and more famous still by the 1991 Martin Scorsese remake.

Also worth a visit are the **St John's Museum of Art** (1804); the **Burgwin-Wright House** (1770), the **Zebulon Latimer House** (1852), and **Bellamy Mansion Museum of History and Design Arts** (1859). The restored **City Hall/Thalian Hall** (1858) serves as the city's government and cultural center. It once hosted notable vaudeville acts. Wilmington's best-known festivals celebrate spring, jazz and Christmas.

East, north, and south of Wilmington are some truly magnificient **beaches** – Wrightsville (to the east and the closest); Carolina, Kure, Oak Island, Ocean Isle, Sunset, and Bald Head Island Resort to the south; Holden and Topsail Island to the north. Loggerhead turtles nest on Topsail and Bald Head. Bald Head is the site of **"Old Baldy,"** a lighthouse dating from 1817 and the oldest in North Carolina.

Also in this area are **Moore's Creek National Battlefield** to the northwest, where the American patriots won their first victory over the British in 1776; **Brunswick Town** ruins, a colonial seaport that was burned by the British the same year; Fort Fisher, Fort Caswell, and Fort Anderson, all Civil War sites. **Fort Fisher**, with its remaining earthworks and Visitor Center, is the most popular site; one of three aquariums on the North Carolina coast is located here (others are found at Emerald Isle and Manteo).

Calabash, a small fishing village situated on the South Carolina border, is the undisputed culinary capital of the lower coast. Here diners queue up at one of more than two dozen restaurants to eat the lightly fried Calabash seafood, usually served with cole slaw and hush puppies.

North of Wilmington on the confluence of the Trent and Neuse rivers lies **New Bern**, where Pepsi-Cola was invented. Settled in 1710 by Palatine Germans and Swiss immigrants, the city is named for Bern, Switzerland, and noted for its historic structures. The elaborate **Tryon Palace** was built for Royal Governor William Tryon between 1767 and 1770 but lay in ruins for more than a century before it was reconstructed. Costumed guides offer tours of the palace and the gardens, and special programs, including reenactments where you get to meet historical figures such as the governor, are held throughout the year. New Bern also boasts an outstanding **Civil War museum** and the **Fireman's Museum**, featuring rare fire equipment and photographs.

Southeast of New Bern is **Morehead City**, primarily a working port, as well as the surrounding Central Coast. Across

Eco-minded sailors near Beaufort.

Bogue Sound and east of Atlantic Beach is **Fort Macon**, a fort built in 1834 to guard Beaufort Inlet. Today it is a park offering tours, a museum and trails.

East of Morehead City across Beaufort Inlet, is historic **Beaufort** (pronounced *Bo-fort*), which has become a popular stopover on the Intracoastal Waterway. One of the oldest buildings is the **Josiah Bell House** dating to around 1767, but by far the most interesting attraction is the **Old Burying Grounds**. Tombstones, dating to 1731, tell the stories of the occupants, including a soldier buried standing up facing England and a young girl preserved in a keg of rum. Boats and natural history are the subject of the **North Carolina Maritime Museum** in Beaufort. This area is also the place for transportation to the Outer Banks, some of it free.

North of New Bern are several historic towns. **Bath**, the oldest chartered settlement in North Carolina and the first official port of entry, was for a time the home of the infamous pirate Blackbeard. The **Belhaven Memorial Museum** in Belhaven contains the unusual collections of Eva Blout Wray who spent her lifetime saving everything, including 30,000 buttons.

Edenton, a quiet colonial town near the Albemarle Sound, has several historic structures, including **St Paul's Church**, which was organized in 1836 and has three colonial governors buried in the graveyard; the 1767 **Cowan County Courthouse**, the state's oldest courthouse still in use; and the Jacobean-style **Cupola House and Gardens**.

Lost and found: Between the mainland and the Outer Banks was the lost colony of **Roanoke Island**, Sir Walter Raleigh's first, unsuccessful attempt to establish a colony in the New World in 1585. The **Fort Raleigh National Historical Site**, near the town of **Manteo**, includes a reconstruction of Fort Raleigh, while the **Elizabeth II State Historic Site** has a museum devoted to 16th-century life. The **Elizabethan Gardens** are particularly striking, its grounds covered with evocative, antique statues and imported and native plants.

Wilmington's tribute to World War II soldiers.

THE OUTER BANKS

A string of narrow islands and peninsulas along the far eastern shore, the Outer Banks emerge like the head of a whale breaching into the Atlantic. Two National Seashores, Cape Hatteras and Cape Lookout, preserve 120 miles (190 km) of these beaches on **Bodie**, **Hatteras** and **Ocracoke islands** and **Core** and **Shackleford banks**. While most coastal islands lie within 10 miles (16 km) of shore, the Outer Banks belong to the realm of the sea. In places, 30 miles (48 km) of water separate Hatteras Island from the mainland.

The Outer Banks are perfect for anyone who enjoys peace, isolation, national parks, watersports, fishing, hang gliding, and getting away from it all. Lodging and other visitor amenties are available in the areas not designated as National Seashores; for details of these, contact the Outer Banks Chamber of Commerce (*see Travel Tips*).

Bodie Lighthouse.

The National Seashores of the Outer Banks have personalities unique to the rest of the state. The islands have wide, water-thrashed beaches. Scattered patches of sea oats and beach grasses bind low dunes behind them. Clumps of shrubby marsh elder and bayberry dot the swales. Most trees lean away from the sea, a concession to the relentless salt spray that stunts branches on the windward sides.

Two strong navigational currents pass off the Outer Banks. The Gulf Stream flows north from Florida at a speed of about 4 knots. It swings east near Cape Hatteras, providing a perfect send-off for ships bound for Europe. The cooler Virginia Coastal Drift flows closer to shore. It is an efficient southbound marine highway. Near the crook in Hatteras Island, navigational hazards in the form of shifting submerged sandbars reach 8 to 10 miles (13 to 16 km) out to sea. Early ship captains dreaded this passage; the islands are so low that to read natural landmarks, they had to remain close to shore. But they dared not venture too near **Diamond Shoals**, the "graveyard of the Atlantic." Over the centuries, more than 600 ships have ended their journeys here.

Construction of lighthouses to warn ships of hazardous waters was a high priority during colonial times. Cape Hatteras got its first lighthouse, a 90-ft (27-meter) sandstone tower, in 1803. The present one was completed in 1870. Containing 1¼ million bricks, it towers 208 ft (63 meters) above the beach and the seagulls, the tallest lighthouse in the United States.

When completed, the **Cape Hatteras Lighthouse** stood 1,500 ft (450 meters) from shore. Decades of erosion have brought waves within 200 ft (61 meters) of its base. The National Park Service is studying a proposal to move the spiral-striped structure some feet to the southwest, using a rail system similar to the one NASA uses to move the space shuttle to its launching pad.

Lighthouses mark other portions of the Outer Banks. All have distinctive exterior patterns and flash for different time periods at night to help navigators recognize them. The squatty, whitewashed **Ocracoke Lighthouse** was built in 1823, the oldest one operating in North Carolina. Diamond-patterned **Cape Lookout Lighthouse**, completed in 1859, warns sailors of the low-lying Core Banks. Horizontally striped **Bodie Island Lighthouse**, placed in service in 1872, guards Oregon Inlet.

During the late 19th century, the US Life-Saving Service established guard stations at 8-mile (13-km) intervals along the banks. Patrolmen paced the beaches, scouting for ships in distress. When a vessel grounded, they rushed to its aid with a lifeboat and rescue equipment. Two of the original life-saving stations, **Chicamacomico** (at Rodanthe) and **Little Kinnakeet** (near Avon) remain. At Chicamacomico, park interpreters reenact lifesaving drills on Thursday afternoons in summer.

Cape Hatteras's islands are linked by Route 12. The Bodie Island and Hatteras Island sections of the seashore surround **Pea Island National Wildlife Refuge**. Observation platforms and several short trails lead from the highway to excellent viewpoints for watching the Canada and snow geese, whistling swans and migratory ducks that spend the winter at the refuge. Pulloffs along Route 12 offer access to the beach, while long piers at **Rodanthe**, **Avon** and **Frisco** allow anglers to cast for deep-water fish which aren't normally caught in the surf.

Near the northern entrance to Cape Hatteras, on **Kill Devil Hills** – named, some say, for drink that would kill even the devil – is the tall, white **Wright Brothers National Memorial**, which commemorates the first powered airplane flight by brothers Orville and Wilbur Wright on December 17, 1903.

At **Nags Head**, many visitors stop to walk on **Jockeys Ridge**, a towering, unstabilized sand dune that migrates with the prevailing winds. Access to Ocracoke, at the southern end of Cape Hatteras, is via a 2½-hour toll ferry ride from **Swanquarter** or **Cedar Island**.

Ocracoke is also the departure point for a 5-mile (8-km) ferry ride to the historic village of **Portsmouth**, at the north end of Cape Lookout. Early residents of Portsmouth made their living "lightering" (transferring) cargo from oceangoing vessels to boats that served **Core** and **Pamlico sounds**. The town is quiet now. A self-guiding trail winds among remaining structures, providing a glimpse into its former life.

Except for the Visitor Center on **Harkers Island**, Cape Lookout is waterbound. Most visitors ride excursion boats from Harkers Island to the lighthouse on **Core Banks** or from Beaufort to the west end of Shackleford Banks. Ferries that operate from April through November shuttle four-wheel-drive vehicles to the northern section of Core Banks.

Off-road vehicles may be used only on designated sections of beach. Otherwise, Cape Lookout's islands beckon backcountry hikers and campers. Take all necessary supplies and plenty of water with you, and be sure to arrange a return pick-up time with the ferry operator beforehand, since you will be all alone in uninhabited areas where the sun, sea and wind prevail.

ockeys idge.

SOUTH CAROLINA

The visual images that accompany any words about South Carolina run perilously close to cliché, for this is the South of many people's dreams. Here are white-columned mansions with long drives shaded by live oak trees; hot, moist breezes best relieved by tall glasses of lemonade; beautiful townhouses filled with antiques imported by wealthy planters. The accent is a drawl that wraps slowly around the ears very like the cotton that contributed to the state's vast economy in the mid-18th century. South Carolina is truly a place apart. Little wonder, then, that this state, the most southerly in this book, is the most Southern in every other respect, too.

South Carolina was the first state to secede from the Union in 1860, and the first to fire the inaugural shot in the civil war called, in these parts, The War of Northern Aggression. Wealthy South Carolina planters had much to lose by continued association with the north, and its fierce opposition to the way of life personified by the large plantations. Therefore, it isn't surprising to learn that several members of Jefferson Davis's cabinet and staff came from South Carolina.

Founded by the British in 1670, the original settlement of Charles Towne governed territory that included what is now North Carolina, South Carolina, Georgia and upper Florida. Ten years later it moved to its present location, now the city of Charleston. South Carolina saw a great deal of military action during the Revolutionary War, and relics of this time are scattered throughout the state. But it suffered much more during that "other war," and was a particular target for revenge. A soldier under the command of Union general William Tucumseh Sherman wrote of the state: "We will let her know that it isn't so sweet to secede." Reconstruction, too, was a trying time and it was many years before South Carolina recovered, in both financial and family terms.

Traveling around the state, visitors cannot help but notice two evocative, slightly spooky plants commonly associated with the South. Kudzu, a leafy, climbing vine, was brought from Asia in the 1800s as decoration and shade cover. In the 20th century its growth was encouraged by the government to stop soil erosion. But kudzu took to the hot, moist climate so well that it now smothers thousands of acres of land, and, somewhat alarmingly, can grow several inches a day in certain conditions.

Spanish moss is usually found draped over live oak trees like romantic, ethereal canopies. It is not really Spanish, nor is it really moss; it is, in fact, an air plant and a member of the pineapple family. Don't try to pick it up, however: insects find Spanish moss just as attractive as most tourists do.

Many of South Carolina's major highways were once old Indian trails. Route I-26 follows the Cherokee Path, which cuts a diagonal

Preceding pages and left: Boone Hall, near Charleston and the South Carolina coast. Originally a cotton plantation, the driveway is said to have been the inspiration for the road to Tara in *Gone With The Wind*.

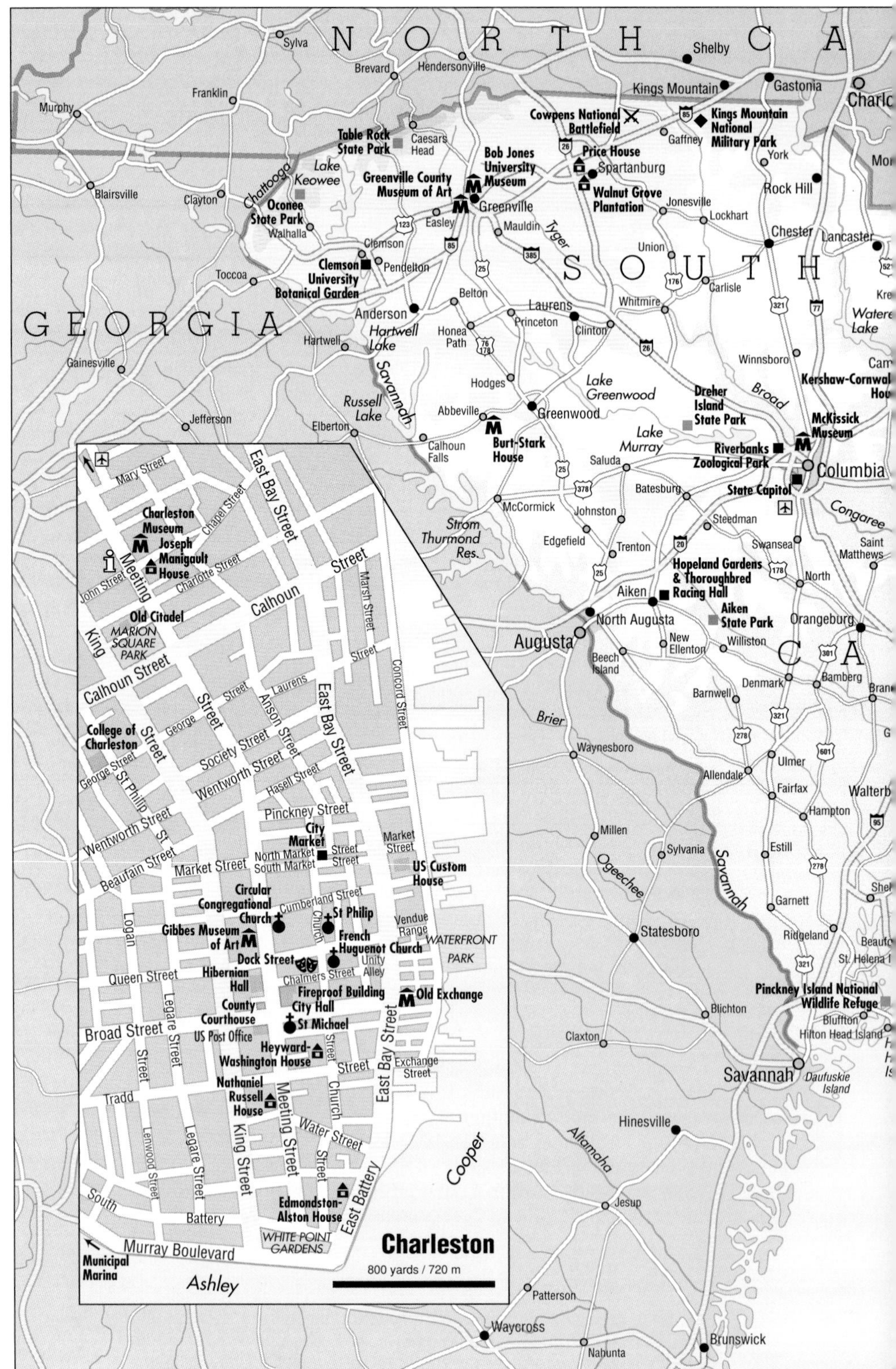
NORTH CAROLINA
SOUTH CAROLINA
GEORGIA
Sylva
Brevard
Hendersonville
Shelby
Kings Mountain
Gastonia
Charlotte
Franklin
Murphy
Cowpens National Battlefield
Kings Mountain National Military Park
Table Rock State Park
Caesars Head
Gaffney
Price House
Spartanburg
Walnut Grove Plantation
York
Bob Jones University Museum
Greenville County Museum of Art
Greenville
Lake Keowee
Oconee State Park
Walhalla
Blairsville
Clayton
Chattooga
Rock Hill
Jonesville
Lockhart
Easley
Mauldin
Tyger
Clemson
Pendleton
Clemson University Botanical Garden
Toccoa
Union
Chester
Lancaster
Carlisle
Whitmire
Belton
Anderson
Hartwell Lake
Hartwell
Honea Path
Laurens
Princeton
Clinton
Gainesville
Winnsboro
Savannah
Hodges
Lake Greenwood
Dreher Island State Park
Broad
Kershaw-Cornwallis House
Russell Lake
Abbeville
Greenwood
Jefferson
Elberton
Burt-Stark House
Calhoun Falls
Lake Murray
Saluda
McKissick Museum
Riverbanks Zoological Park
Columbia
State Capitol
Batesburg
McCormick
Johnston
Steedman
Congaree
Strom Thurmond Res.
Edgefield
Trenton
Swansea
Saint Matthews
Hopeland Gardens & Thoroughbred Racing Hall
North
Aiken
Aiken State Park
North Augusta
Augusta
New Ellenton
Williston
Orangeburg
Beech Island
Denmark
Bamberg
Barnwell
Brier
Waynesboro
Ulmer
Allendale
Fairfax
Hampton
Millen
Sylvania
Estill
Ogeechee
Garnett
Ridgeland
Statesboro
Pinckney Island National Wildlife Refuge
Bluffton
Hilton Head Island
Blichton
Claxton
Savannah
Daufuskie Island
Hinesville
Altamaha
Jesup
Patterson
Waycross
Nabunta
Brunswick
Mary Street
East Bay Street
Charleston Museum
Chapel Street
Joseph Manigault House
Meeting
John Street
Charlotte Street
Calhoun
Marsh Street
Old Citadel
King
MARION SQUARE PARK
Calhoun Street
Laurens
Concord Street
College of Charleston
George
Anson Street
Society Street
Wentworth Street
Hasell Street
George Street
St Philip Street
Pinckney Street
City Market
North Market Street
South Market Street
Market Street
Beaufain Street
US Custom House
Circular Congregational Church
Cumberland Street
St Philip
Church
Gibbes Museum of Art
French Huguenot Church
Vendue Range
WATERFRONT PARK
Dock Street
Chalmers Street
Unity Alley
Logan
Queen Street
Hibernian Hall
Fireproof Building
City Hall
Old Exchange
County Courthouse
St Michael
Broad Street
Legare Street
US Post Office
Heyward-Washington House
Exchange Street
Nathaniel Russell House
Tradd
Lenwood Street
Water Street
Cooper
East Battery
South
Battery
Edmondston-Alston House
WHITE POINT GARDENS
Murray Boulevard
Municipal Marina
Ashley
Charleston
800 yards / 720 m

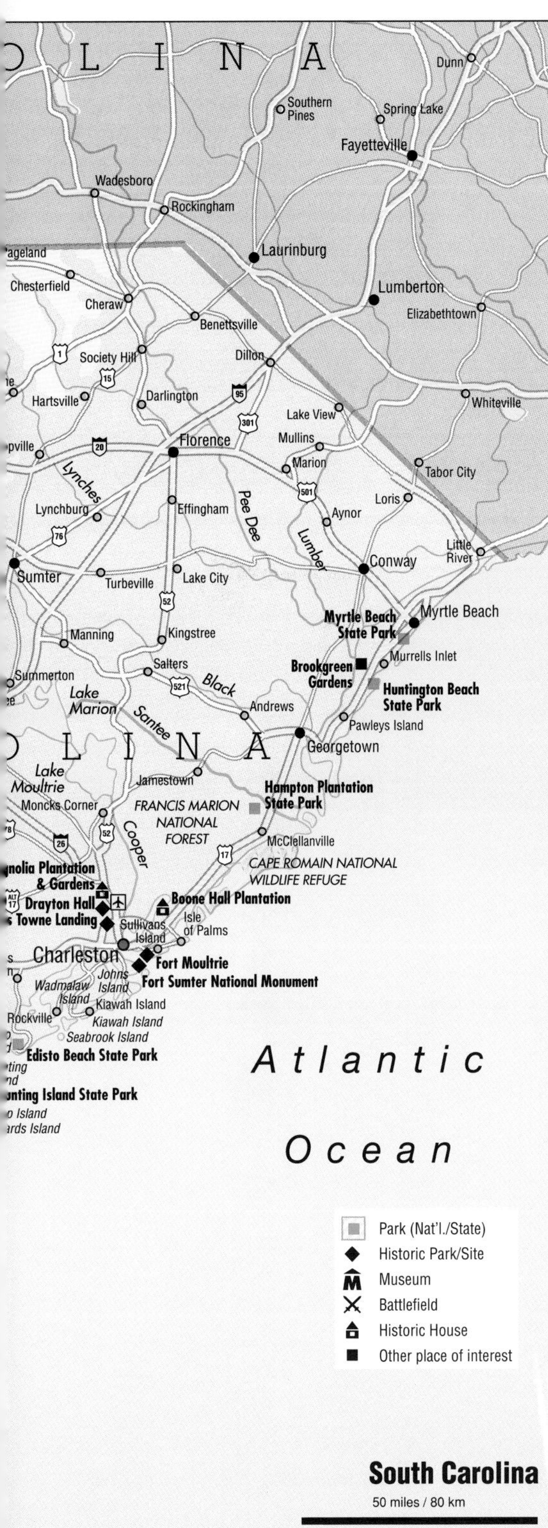

swatch northwest to southeast through the state's three geographical regions. The northwestern tip, with its mountains and lakes, is Upcountry, also familiarly known as the Piedmont. The Midlands includes the central plains and the finest horse-grazing land south of Kentucky.

Hugging the coast is the Low Country, a series of islands and watery highways. The Low Country is home to the Gullah dialect, an Afro-English patois spoken by certain black communities on the island of St Helena and in the town of Charleston. Charleston was the originally capital, not only of the Low Country, but also the entire state. This irritated Upcountry settlers, who felt that not enough attention was being paid to their very different, and very distant, needs. The situation was resolved by creating the town of Columbia and designating it the capital of South Carolina. Unsurprisingly, Columbia lies almost in the bull's-eye center of the state.

The jewel in the crown is, of course, Charleston, destined as early as the 1700s to be the "glittering city" of the young American colony. An architectural gem best appreciated by horse-drawn carriage, it is a town of gracious homes, stately museums and elegant, reasonably priced restaurants. "The manners of the inhabitants of Charleston are as different from those of the other North American cities as are the products of their soil," wrote Johannn David Schoepf in 1783. "There prevails here a finer manner of life, and on the whole there are more evidences of courtesy than in the northern cities."

The Spoleto Festival, a 17-day event held in early summer, has been described by the *Washington Post* as "America's most comprehensive arts festival." Many of the thousands of visitors who attend the festival, as well as countless others, think of Charleston as the finest city in the entire South. The sentiment is mutual. One wealthy old Charlestonian was once asked why she so seldom traveled. Her reply? "My dear, why should I travel when I'm already here?"

AROUND CHARLESTON

Hidden within an intricate system of deep-water creeks and salt marshes lies a city as constant as the tides that have driven its fortune for over 300 years. Charleston boasts a history rich in strife and strength, freedom and diversity, preservation and progress. And its residents remain as dedicated today as the original settlers were when they first set foot on the peninsula in 1680.

Joggling board: Although a steady series of Indian and pirate attacks, wars, fires, earthquakes, tornadoes, and hurricanes have ravaged the city for centuries, Charlestonians have always picked up the pieces. Take a stroll down narrow streets lined with camellia, gardenia, oleander, and azalea. Gaze at the city's vernacular-style **Charleston Single Houses**. One room wide, their narrow ends face the street, with false entrances opening onto a piazza that runs the length of the house – and usually adorned with a joggling board, a long, narrow, 19th-century bouncing bench native to Charleston and used both by courting lovers and rambunctious children. Listen to the clop of horses crossing cobbled streets and the rustling of a summer breeze through palmetto trees.

In 1670, a ship-load of English colonists founded Charles Towne (now open to the public as **Charles Towne Landing**, off Highway 171) on the Ashley River 5 miles (8 km) upstream from Charleston's present location. Named after Charles II, Charles Towne didn't meet with a great deal of success at first. After 10 years of battling malaria, heat, flooding, and the Kiawah Indians – the area's original residents – colonists opted to head for the hills. They packed their bags and moved to the peninsula we now call Charleston.

Flanked on the west side by the **Ashley River** and on the east by the **Cooper River**, the peninsula offered settlers the protection of surrounding barrier islands, an optimal position as a port of entry, and the cool breezes that drifted in off the harbor. It is at the mouth of the Charleston Harbor, the local saying goes, that the Ashley and the Cooper rivers meet to form the Atlantic Ocean. In case you're wondering, Charlestonians tend to be biased toward their city – and particularly exclusive about their citizenship. If you're not from Charleston, you're "from off." And you're not a Charlestonian unless your family has lived here for four generations. Charlestonians even determine guest lists for the annual St Cecelia Society Ball by birth and geography.

But although Charlestonians are exclusive about citizenship they are also some of the friendliest people you'll ever meet. In some polls, their town has been ranked as the most livable and the most mannerly in the nation. You'll always get a hello in return for your greeting to a stranger on the street, and you'll never have to worry about offending the natives – as long as you mind your manners.

The influences of Charleston's original French, Scottish, German, Irish, and Caribbean inhabitants are still evident

eft, church t Dock treet and road Street. **ight**, rchitectural etail.

in the city today from its social clubs to its festivals, functions, and family coats of arms. Nationally it is believed that you have to be a little left of center to live in Charleston, and perhaps a little eccentric. Even the street names express a degree of eccentricity. **Legare Street** is pronounced *Le-gree*, **Huger Street** is *You-gee*, **Hasell Street** is pronounced *Hazel*, and **Vanderhorst Street** is *Vandrost*.

If you are confused, head straight for the **Visitor Reception and Transportation Center** at 375 Meeting Street before you begin a tour of the town. Built in 1856 as a South Carolina Railroad freight depot, the center is one of the oldest railroad structures in the US. You can find the answers to all your questions here, take advantage of the public restroom facilities (rare in the historic district), and enjoy the 20-minute orientation film *Forever Charleston*.

You can also hop on a tour vehicle, join a walking tour, or catch the **Downtown Area Shuttle (DASH)** from outside the center when you're ready to do the town. An all-day DASH pass is cheaper than paying for single rides.

Whatever you do, though, leave your car at the center. Squeezing down narrow streets built before the advent of cars – but later paved, of course – to play "Charleston Chicken" with oncoming vehicles can be harrowing. Turning down a one-way street the wrong way is inevitable, and circling the block repeatedly in hopes of finding a parking place is to be expected (although the city is building more parking garages). And if you happen to be driving when a flash flood hits, you'll need a pair of fisherman's waders because, odds are, you'll shortly be pushing the car out of fairly deep water. Charleston is several feet below the water table; this portion of South Carolina is called the Low Country for very good reason.

Across **Meeting Street** from the Visitor Center, the **Charleston Museum**, the first and oldest museum in the US, features permanent and occasional exhibits focusing on Charleston, the Low Country, and the state. The museum-

Meeting Street.

owned **Joseph Manigault House** next door offers tours of its restored interior and exterior. Built in 1803, the house is considered one of the finest examples of Federal-style architecture in the world and is a National Historic Landmark. Passing through a number of hands and barely escaping destruction several times in its past, the Manigault House today exhibits the grand formal staircase, period furniture, *faux* graining and restored plaster ornamentation and interior woodwork of the original.

Running parallel to Meeting on the other side of the Visitor Center is **King Street**, the city's central business artery. If you travel south on Upper King toward Calhoun Street, you'll notice **Marion Square Park** on your left. The park takes its name from American Revolutionary hero Francis Marion, the "Swamp Fox," known for eluding British officers in the Low Country swamps where he had hunted from an early age.

Facing the park stands the **Old Citadel** – original site of one of the oldest military colleges in the nation, constructed in 1842. Now at its new location farther north on the peninsula, the Citadel battles to "Save the Males," as bumper stickers around town read, and preserve single-gender education in the name of tradition. Located at 171 Moultrie Street by the 65-acre (26-hectare), Victorian-style **Hampton Park** and **College Park baseball stadium**, home of the Charleston RiverDogs, the Citadel has an on-campus museum of its own. It also presents a free **Dress Parade** by the South Carolina Corps of Cadets most Friday afternoons throughout the academic year.

The Charleston **Farmers' Market** is held every Saturday morning from April to October in Marion Square Park, which also plays host to many of the city's festival events. Activities include Southeastern Wildlife Exposition exhibits and food fair in February; Piccolo Spoleto outdoor art and performances for children in May and June; Maritime Festival boat shows in September; and Christmas in Charleston Winter Wonderland in December.

Rainbow Row.

Truly a city of festivals, Charleston's biggest is **Spoleto Festival USA**. During the Spoleto and Piccolo Spoleto arts festivals each year, usually held at the end of May and early June, all the city's a stage, and there's absolutely no telling what you'll see and hear: dance, experimental theater, opera, chamber music, performance art, crafts and visual arts shows. It's certainly the best time to experience Charleston if you don't mind crowds and are willing to book hotels and airplane reservations in advance.

Across from Calhoun Street – named for John C. Calhoun, an important statesman before the Civil War and vice-president of the United States under Andrew Jackson, and whose statue watches from its pedestal in the park – is the entrance to **Middle King Street**. An area heavily populated by College of Charleston (C of C) students, the student-oriented businesses – various record shops, coffee houses, bars and inexpensive restaurants – make it a good spot for casual dining, shopping, or just plain ole creative loafing.

82 Queen Street restaurant.

However, there is more to this area than initially meets the eye. Subway Sandwiches sits next to the elegant French restaurant **Le Midi**, and no more than a block away from the second-hand clothing store are the fine clothes sold at **319 King** and **A J Davis & Co**. The **Garden Theater**, also on King Street, features folk music and theater performances, and a number of nearby bars offer everything from art openings to pool tables, from dancing to all-night drinking. When people say Charleston is diverse, they really do mean it.

From its earliest days, Charleston has been a city known for tolerance and the appreciation of life's little pleasures. By the early- to mid-18th century, Charleston was one of the wealthiest ports in the Southeast. Exporting cotton, rice, and indigo from its "golden coast," Charleston imported in return the riches of Europe and the West Indies. Lured by its lavish lifestyle, grand homes, exquisite taste, and religious freedom not offered by other colonies – hence its nickname the Holy City – artists and immigrants, seamen and merchants, rich and poor flocked here for profit and a good time. Hence its other nickname – the Unholy City.

Taking a right off King into George Street leads past the classical-style **Sottile Memorial Auditorium**. Owned by C of C and opened as the Gloria Theater, one of the many local movie houses operating in Charleston in the 1920s, it's where *Gone With the Wind* had its local premiere.

On the next block, the herring-bone brick pattern of the walkway below reveals that this is the midst of the **College of Charleston** campus. Founded in 1770, it was the first municipal college in the country.

Crossing St Philip Street to the entrance and core of the college, the **Old Main Campus** appears, a National Historic Landmark, on the right. It includes the **Porter's Lodge**, for many years the residence of the college janitor whose goats roamed the College Green behind it until a student riot over the animals put an end to the affair in the 1850s. It now houses faculty offices.

Through its triple arches and Doric columns is the two-story stuccoed brick **Towell Library**; **Randolph Hall**, where the first classes took place; and **The Cistern**, where C of C graduates, clad in white evening dress, receive their diplomas each May.

The large number of students – now up to as many as 10,000 – roaming the streets day and night, on foot and bicycle, is another good reason to be a pedestrian and not a driver. No one yet has quite figured out why, but a number of students believe they are immortal, with absolutely no need to watch where they're going.

Back on King Street, a number of interesting and unusual specialty shops lead down to **Market Street**. Straight ahead, is **Lower King Street**, Charleston's **Antique District**. Situated on the right is the now closed down **Riviera Theater**, which was once a motion picture house. A significant example of Art Deco architecture with its stylized light fixtures, balcony, ticket booth and interior murals, the Riviera remains to this day Charleston's finest historic motion picture theater.

The Shops of Charleston Place are to be found on the left down Market Street. Most people just call this structure **The Omni**, after the hotel it houses, although it also contains a ballroom, meeting halls, and various national retail chains. It's also the location of the well-known **Louis's Charleston Grill** (*see picture on page 90*). A sophisticated late-night dining establishment highly rated by *Esquire* magazine, Louis's features unusual interpretations of Southern food, and, some nights, live jazz in a 1920s atmosphere.

After a block Market Street meets Meeting Street where the 1841 Roman Revival-style **Market Hall** stands, along with the entrance to the **City Market** across the way. In operation as a public market after the Revolutionary War, the market was never used to sell slaves, contrary to popular belief.

The market trails three blocks behind Market Hall. It contains three open-air sheds in which craftsmen, collectors,

Chapter II bookstore; Charleston Market.

artisans and others peddle everything from jewelry and clothes, to sweetgrass baskets, artwork, T-shirts, and 13 Bean Soup mix. (This is a traditional Low Country favorite, along with Hoppin' John, black beans and rice, and shrimp and grits.) They say there's a two-year waiting list to get a spot to sell goods at the market. However, in the 19th century, it was another creature who jockeyed for a position at the market: buzzards who cleaned up scraps of meat around the butcher stalls. While some may consider these ignoble birds, Charlestonians termed the scavengers "Charleston Eagles," and local lawmakers levied a $5 fine on anyone found guilty of killing a buzzard. Truly, anything goes in Charleston.

For a good, affordable meal in a lively, casual atmosphere, Aaron's Deli or Hyman's Seafood can be found if you take a left onto Meeting instead of venturing into the market. In the opposite direction is **The Gibbes Museum of Art**, which houses one of the finest collections of American art in the Southeast, complete with an outdoor sculpture garden. Across the street is the **Circular Congregational Church**, which dates from 1681. The original church, made of white brick, was called White Meeting House, and gave Meeting Street its name. This church features some of the most fascinating tombstones in the city. It may seem odd to be fascinated with cemeteries, but Charleston boasts some of the best, and considering how locals love a bit of ancestor worship, it's not so very odd. Embossed with lounging skeletons atop gray slate, the stones in this cemetery rival those of the adjoining **St Philip Church** on **Church Street**.

In the spring, St Philip also features the Artists Guild's **Sidewalk Art Show** along its wrought iron fence. Arts of all kind are available in this area. Many galleries lie tucked away along these quiet streets, including **The Tradd Street Press** studio of beloved Charlestonian Elizabeth O'Neill Verner, author of *Mellowed By Time* and famous for her etchings of Charleston. She, along with artists and writers such as John Bennett, DuBose Heyward, Josephine Pinckney, Beatrice Smith, Alice Ravenel Huger Smith, Alfred Hutty and various other individuals, were responsible for the Charleston Renaissance of the 1920s.

In addition to Charleston's many galleries, scattered throughout the city are its theater and dance companies, including **Charleston Theaterworks**, **Charleston Repertory Theater**, **The Robert Ivey Ballet** and **The Charleston Ballet Theater**.

The Dock Street Theater, at 135 Church Street, was the first formal theater in the nation and now houses the **Amazing Stage Company**. It, too, has its own gallery inside and a courtyard out back which features the Sundown Poetry Series during the Piccolo Spoleto festival.

Across from the theater, the dominating Gothic Revival **French Huguenot Church**, set up in 1681 by French Protestant refugees, can be seen. It once scheduled its church services according to the tides, so that the plantation owners, who were traveling to the church by

Keeping trim: repairs on Tradd Street.

boat, could make it safely to the service in time for the opening hymn.

Up along **Queen Street** from the Dock Street Theater is the **Footlight Players Theater**, which plays host to the Society for the Preservation of Spirituals each April. Commanding the corner of Queen and Meeting streets is the magnificent **Mills House Hotel**. Its original structure dates from 1853, and it is one of the most elegant hotels downtown. Robert E. Lee stayed here during his visit to Charleston in 1861. From its balcony, he watched as the most devastating fire in the town's history tore out of the Ansonborough neighborhood and swept through the city, wiping out more than 500 buildings.

In addition to the Mills House, a number of elegant inns and historic B&B establishments can be found dotted around Charleston. Although these can be expensive (*see Travel Tips for recommendations*), such accommodation does offer an experience that's uniquely Charleston. Complete with intricately carved English oak woodwork, family antiques, four-poster Charleston rice beds and private courtyards, the B&B inns actually mark a significant point in the city's development. During the period following World War I, Charlestonians noticed the nationwide growth in tourism and took advantage by welcoming visitors into their homes.

Past the Mills House on Queen, between Meeting and King streets, lies **82 Queen Street**. Here is a restaurant which offers a taste of the Low Country in one of its seven dining rooms, its turn-of-the-century courtyard, or its outdoor raw bar. Beside the Mills House on Meeting is the Greek Revival **Hibernian Society Hall**. Built in 1840 and one of the oldest Irish fraternal societies in America, this is the venue for the famous St Cecelia Society Ball.

Across the street from the Mills House, the Historic Charleston Foundation works with Charleston's Board of Architectural Review (BAR) and the Preservation Society of Charleston to maintain Charleston's architectural integrity, to ensure its lasting beauty and preserve

Looking pretty: Charleston debutantes.

its historic environment. The preservation organizations run gift shops, and Historic Charleston produces the only historic reproduction gifts in the city.

Chalmers Street on the left along Meeting, near Broad Street, is the longest of some 10 cobblestone streets in the city. On it stands the **Fireproof Building**, home of the **South Carolina Historic Society**, and **Washington Square Park**, once lined with houses of ill repute. Also on Chalmers, the **Old Slave Mart Museum**, closed, served as an auction block for horses, steamships, and slaves, until 1856.

Many of the African-Americans in Charleston today are descendants of the first enslaved Africans, who were brought to the city for their expertise in rice cultivation, essential to the Charleston plantation system. Hired out as blacksmiths, masons, and artisans when not needed on the plantations, these slaves helped build the Charleston we know today, and their influence still permeates the city. It's seen in the growing number of African-American galleries around town; at the **Avery Research Center for African-American History and Culture** at 125 Bull Street; in piazza ceilings painted "haint blue" to ward off evil spirits; in the tight coils of the sweetgrass baskets which have been woven at the market and at Broad Street by the female descendants of slaves for the past 300 years; in the wrought-iron gates of the octogenarian African-American craftsman Philip Simmons; and during the **MOJA** arts festival held each October.

The "flying" staircase of the Nathaniel Russell House spirals unsupported for three floors.

Gullah residents: Traces of the heritage are also heard in the conversations of local people. Called Gullah (*see pages 118–19*), this distinctive Creole language developed from a blend of dialects and was spoken on many plantations. West African intonations pepper the English-derived language, and its idiomatic expressions make it sometimes difficult to understand. Pure Gullah is dying out now, but its presence is still heard in the streets of Chaa'stun, as they say.

At the intersection of Meeting and Broad streets rests the **Charleston County Courthouse**, **City Hall**, the **US Post Office** and **St Michael's Episcopal Church**, the oldest church building in the city. George Washington and Robert E. Lee worshipped here, and two signatories of the US Constitution are buried in the churchyard.

The intersection continues to be called **The Four Corners of Law** after the *Ripley's Believe It or Not* strip termed it so because each corner represented a different legal branch – city, state, federal, and God's law. It's the only place in the world where you can get married, divorced, pay your taxes, and pick up your mail all in the same place, or so the saying goes. Broad Street is called the "Wall Street of Charleston" because the city was originally a walled one surrounded by a moat, with Broad Street as its northernmost boundary. To the southwest of the Four Corners of Law stood a gatehouse with a drawbridge giving access from the land.

Broad Street, lined with palmettos, flagstone sidewalks, and Charleston's real estate, law, and banking offices, comprises the city's financial center. If you take a left off Meeting, then a right off Broad onto Church Street, you'll notice earthquake bolts on the sides of many of the buildings. Installed after the disastrous earthquake of August 31, 1886, each bolt stabilizes a metal rod running the length of the house between floors – a measure many Charlestonians used to reinforce their homes after the 7.5 Richter Scale quake destroyed more than 100 buildings and damaged 90 percent of the city.

Also down this portion of Church Street is **Cabbage Row** (*see page 119*), on which DuBose Heyward based Catfish Row in his novel *Porgy*, later made into the opera *Porgy and Bess* with music by George Gershwin. The pre-Revolutionary string of double tenements housed nearly 100 African-Americans who displayed cabbages for sale on their window sills. Heyward based his character Porgy on a crippled tenant, Sammy Smalls. Today the building houses gift shops.

Next door is the National Historic Landmark **Heyward-Washington House**, owned by the Charleston Museum. This was the 18th-century home of the prominent rice planter Daniel Heyward and his son Thomas, a signatory of the Declaration of Independence. The second part to the house's name honors the first president of the United States, who stayed here during his 1791 visit. If George Washington were to have ever stooped to graffiti, "Washington was here" would surely be carved into every wall in the city. Needless to say, Charleston was very dear to his heart.

Back on Meeting stands the Federal-style **Nathaniel Russell House** at No. 51. Both owned and operated by the Historic Charleston Foundation, this is one of America's most important neoclassical dwellings. Built in 1808, it features oval rooms, an impressive free-flying staircase which spirals unsupported for three floors, elaborate plasterwork ornamentation, and the kind of period furnishings that were favored by the merchant elite.

Cadets on parade, the Old Citadel.

The Nathaniel Russell House is one of the many museum houses in the city which have been bought, restored, and maintained by local preservation groups. There are so many of them that it's impossible to do more than touch on them here, but lists of them are available from the Visitor Center. Just because each Charleston home looks as if it could be a museum house doesn't mean it is. Most are private homes, a fact worth bearing in mind as you meander through the streets unguided.

And unguided is a good way to go. There seems to be something to see down every street. But even though it is rich in history, Charleston is a city of the present, and shoulders its fair share of crime. So don't let the beauty of the place make you forget your common sense, even though, thanks to the dedication of its police chief and his staff, it is said to be one of the safest cities in America.

The Battery: Continuing along Meeting or King in the direction of the water will bring you to **White Point Gardens** and The Battery. Shaded by massive live oak trees with a large white gazebo at its center, frequently used for weddings, White Point Gardens got its name from the mounds of oyster shells that once covered this southernmost tip of the peninsula. Stede Bonnet was hung for piracy not far from this park, and Anne Bonny, the first woman pirate – a Charleston debutante and subject of great local scandal – often enjoyed a good Cooper River skinny dip in the chilly water over the Battery wall. The cannons and statues in the park commemorate city and state heroes and the many wars in which Charleston has fought. The grand homes of **South Battery** that face the park catch the harbor breezes from their two-story piazzas.

Gracious homes on East Battery.

Walk along the promenade lining the Battery wall and stop at the brass marker laid in the curve of the sidewalk. From this point you can see **Fort Sumter National Monument** way out over the water at the mouth of the harbor. It is here that the Civil War – or "late unpleasantness" as Charlestonians call it – began on April 12, 1861 (*see pages 41 and 123*). When Union forces refused to vacate the fort, South Carolina troops of the Confederacy opened fire from **Fort Johnson** on James Island, starting a two-day bombardment that resulted in the surrender of Fort Sumter by Union forces. Johnny Reb held the fort until February 17, 1865, enduring one of the longest sieges in history.

And had President Abraham Lincoln accepted Fort Sumter's invitation to attend a flag ceremony on April 14, 1865, John Wilkes Booth would have been at a dead loss for a target at Ford's Theatre that night. Tours of Fort Sumter leave regularly from the **City Marina** on Lockwood Drive (enquire at the Visitor Center for times and details).

Also from this marker, Sullivan's Island can be seen to the left of Fort Sumter. Edgar Allen Poe used the island as the setting for *The Gold Bug* while he was stationed at Fort Moultrie during the Civil War. To the left of Sullivan's Island lie Isle of Palms and Wild Dunes. These barrier islands, along with Folly Beach out Folly Road and Kiawah Island Beachwalker County Park out Maybank Highway, remain some of the area's surprisingly undeveloped beaches. Isle of Palms is the most developed, with restaurants and shops lining its shore. *(For more about Fort Moultrie and the islands, see pages 306-7.)*

But before you spot Sullivan's Island from your position at the Battery, you are bound to see the World War II aircraft carrier ***Yorktown*** docked at **Patriot's Point Naval and Maritime Museum**, on the east banks of the Cooper River in Mount Pleasant. On display on the *Yorktown* are more than 20 vintage aircraft, and an exhibition of the history of naval aviation, as well as screenings of the Academy Award-winning film, *The Fighting Lady*.

From Patriot's Point, scan over to a smaller island in the harbor on which stands **Castle Pinckney**. The masonry fort, completed in 1809 to house Union prisoners of war, daily sinks a little more into the sand, its once tall entry arches now only a few feet high.

The harbor is permanently alive with sailboats skimming across the water, for sailing has always been a popular local tradition. The annual **Charleston Maritime Festival** celebrates America's rich maritime heritage, and the College of Charleston's nationally ranked sailing team can regularly be seen practicing in the waters of the Ashley and Cooper rivers. Each spring, two-hour joyrides on the 80-ft (24-meter) *Schooner Pride* start from the **Ripley Light Marina** at Albemarle Point on the Ashley River.

East Battery, called High Battery, is a picturesque street lined with grand mansions and the Regency-style **Edmondston-Alston House**, which is open to the public. Built in 1838 by the wealthy merchant Charles Edmondston and later bought by rice planter Colonel Charles Alston, it's the only museum house on the Battery. Farther along the same street is **Rainbow Row**, the longest row of pre-Revolutionary houses sharing the same wall in the US. It contains 14 residences, and is the most photographed scene in Charleston.

The Battery at night.

At the foot of Broad, the street turns into East Bay Street at **The Old Exchange and Provost Dungeon**. Constructed by the British during the Golden Age of Charles Towne, the building held imprisoned pirates and Indians in the lower level, and, in March 1776, South Carolina declared its independence from colonial rule on the Exchange steps. The building is now a museum, and there are two halls available for private events. Exchange employees tell tales of unaccountable voices echoing from the dungeon and an elevator that mysteriously operates on its own.

The place to go armed with an appetite is **East Bay Street** past the Old Exchange to one of the central dining spots in the city. The Moorish-designed **Saracen** provides contemporary international fare. **Unity Alley** off to the left is a little niche that boasts three culinary jewels. Owned by world-renowned chef José de Anacleto and local businessman William Gilliam, **Restaurant Millon** offers Relais and Chateaux-caliber meals; **The Long Room** has private dining where George Washington once ate; and **McCrady's** serves delicious, moderately priced cuisine in one of America's oldest taverns.

Off East Bay and down **Exchange Street** is the elegant but casual uptown bistro **Carolina's**, a restaurant often recommended by discerning Charlestonians. Further on down East Bay are the sister restaurants **Blossom Cafe** and **Magnolias**, featuring Mediterranean fare at the former and contemporary Southern cuisine at the latter.

Take a right at Vendue Range for a romp in one of the city's newer parks – **Charleston Waterfront Park**. When it was opened, the mayor called it "a place for people to dream." In the middle of the park, a giant pineapple-shaped fountain stands on the raised green frequented by dogs catching frisbees, children flying kites, lovers lounging, and friends picnicking.

The pier that extends through the spartina grass, or marsh grass, and over the pluff mud – responsible for that mucky odor at low tide – out into the Cooper River, contains a portico under which the swings and picnic tables never cease to be in demand. Bring your fishing rod because at the base of the pier you may want to drop a line – or cast a net as is the Low Country crabbing tradition.

Plantation paradise: Another Low Country tradition was for planters to pack up their bags and retreat to their townhouses in the city to escape the heat of Charleston summers. Today, their plantations, located on the Ashley and Cooper rivers anywhere from 10 to 30 miles (16 to 48 km) from Charleston, are open to the public and offer a glimpse into a different world.

Two of South Carolina's finest plantations were built by the same family of wealthy planters, the Draytons. Between 1738 and 1742, John Drayton built **Drayton Hall**, one of the finest examples of colonial architecture in America, and the only plantation house on the Ashley River to survive the Civil War intact. The house remained in the family until 1974, when it was purchased by the National Trust. Its style is charac-

Joggling board, a Charleston tradition, at Magnolia Gardens.

terized by the classical use of order, symmetry and bold detail; the two-story portico is believed to be the first of its kind in America. The National Trust has deliberately left the house unfurnished, giving added opportunity to study its fine architectural details.

Nearby **Magnolia Plantation and Gardens**, owned for over 10 generations by the Draytons, has one of the country's oldest and loveliest gardens (*circa* 1680), with year-round blooms and America's largest collections of azaleas and camellias. More than a century ago, tourists were climbing aboard steamboats and chugging up the river just to see the magnificent grounds.

Middleton Place is America's oldest landscaped garden (*circa* 1740). Although the house was burned during the "late unpleasantness," certain parts have been rebuilt. The stableyard features craftsmen practicing plantation trades. *(For a description of Boone Hall, see page 306.)*

Back to town: Down East Bay from Waterfront Park stands the **US Custom House** at the foot of the market. This is the place where the Provincial Congress met in 1775 to set up the first independent government established in America. If you're interested in jazz at **Henry's**, oysters at **A.W. Shucks**, a carriage tour, or any similar entertainment, then carry on up **North Market**.

This heavily populated area floods very easily, which is not surprising considering that the market used to be a tidal creek before it was filled in. In fact, the entire area near the market is jokingly referred to by Charlestonians as "the swamp district" because it used to be salt marsh. Actually, much of Charleston used to be salt marsh until colonists started the landfill process which continues today.

Notice the bumps in the road on Lockwood Drive, the sink holes dotting Calhoun Street, and the 18th-century ceramic shards scattered throughout the city. All are indications of a city built where it shouldn't have been – but most people today are extremely glad that the early settlers refused to give up.

Magnolia Gardens is one of America's oldest.

UPCOUNTRY AND THE MIDLANDS

Away from the cobbled streets of Charleston and its Atlantic coast beaches, South Carolina is a pleasant patchwork of orchards and farms, hills and rugged mountain foothills. The Chattooga River, where Burt Reynolds and Jon Voight battled whitewater rapids in John Boorman's 1972 movie *Deliverance*, rips along the state's northwestern border with Georgia. Around the state, hospitable rivers and streams and mammoth lakes welcome fishermen, swimmers and boaters.

Steeplechase: Football is king at Clemson University and the University of South Carolina; stock car racing rules at Darlington; and thoroughbred steeplechases and fox hunts are the chosen sports in Aiken and Camden. Some Upcountry towns are older than the state itself. They were battlegrounds during the Revolution and the Civil War.

South Carolina's state capital is the town of **Columbia**, on the Congaree River in the heart of the state. State workers and thousands of students on the University of South Carolina's main campus enhance the vitality of the old/new city with a metropolitan population of over 300,000. Founded in 1786, Columbia's many attractions include historical landmarks, a variety of museums, a planetarium, one of the nation's best zoos and a 50,000-acre (20,000-hectare) lake on its doorstep.

The **Columbia Metropolitan Visitor Center**, downtown at 1012 Gervais Street, is a good place to start. You can view the orientation film and pick up information on attractions, hotels, restaurants and tours. Then walk across the street to the Capitol.

The Italian Renaissance **State Capitol** was still under construction when it was shelled by General William T. Sherman's Union troops in May 1865. Bronze stars cover the cannonballs' scars. Civil War enthusiasts should be sure to see the flags, uniforms, weapons and soliders' personal effects in the **Confederate Relic Room and Museum** in the **War Memorial Building** on the neighboring **University of South Carolina** campus. The museum also exhibits 18th-and 19th-century women's fashions, money, stamps and everyday items. The **McKissick Museum** in the university's early 1800s Horseshoe complex highlights Southern folk arts, culture and natural history. The museum's historical artifacts include the **Howard Gemstone Collection** and the **Bernard Baruch Silver Collection**. In the same area, the **Robert Mills Historic House and Park**, built in 1823, commemorates the early 19th-century Columbia-bred architect of the Washington Monument in Washington, DC.

At the **Columbia Museum of Art** and **Gibbes Planetarium** you can see everything from contemporary, Medieval, Baroque and Renaissance paintings, sculpture and decorative arts, to a children's gallery and weekend planetarium shows.

Submarine: Also downtown, the **South Carolina State Museum** makes an interesting use of an 1890s textile plant. Four floors of the old Columbia Mills – one of the world's first totally electrified textile mills – are filled with historical displays and hands-on exhibits on transportation, communications, art, modern technology, science and natural history. Browsing through the dozens of exhibits, you can touch a 30-million-year-old great white shark's tooth, see a laser show or study a replica of the world's first submarine, a Confederate vessel that sank on its maiden voyage from Charleston.

Riverbanks Zoo takes a vicarious safari through rainforests and deserts, goes under the seas and then through a Southern farm. Ranked among the nation's best zoos, Riverbanks' natural habitats are home to more than 2,000 birds, reptiles and animals, many of them high on endangered species lists. Across the Saluda River from the zoo, the **Riverbanks Botanical Garden** boasts 70 acres (28 hectares) of woodlands, gardens, historic ruins and plant collections to explore.

After a busy day of sightseeing, the restaurants, nightclubs and unusual

Rural Carolina is prime horse country. Left, George "Bucky" Sallee, a fixture at Southern race meets.

shops in the **Five Points** neighborhood, near downtown and the university, offer a good evening out.

When Columbians want to unwind on water, they take a short drive west to **Lake Murray**. Around the lake's 540-mile (870-km) shoreline are marinas, fishing docks, full-service campgrounds, playgrounds, swimming and water skiing. Many recreational facilities and lodgings are in **Dreher Island State Park**, which is connected to the mainland by a causeway and bridges. Nature lovers may also enjoy an outing at **Congaree Swamp National Monument**, east of Columbia. The 22,000-acre (9,000-hectare) sanctuary teems with wildlife that can be viewed from two boardwalks. You can also go fishing, hiking, canoeing and camping.

In 1732, **Camden**, a half-hour east of Columbia, was chartered by King George II as the first official permanent settlement in South Carolina's interior. When the American Revolution broke out, Camdenites renounced their allegiance to the Crown, and in August, 1780, His Majesty's Commander in Chief in the Colonies, Lord General Charles Cornwallis, was sent to subdue the rebellious patriots. For nearly a year after winning the Battle of Camden, Cornwallis enjoyed the amenities of Camden's finest residence, the three-story Georgian-Colonial mansion built by wealthy merchant Joseph Kershaw. Burned during the Civil War, the **Kershaw-Cornwallis House** has been faithfully recreated, with some furnishings donated by Kershaw's descendants. The house is part of the 92-acre (37-hectare) **Historic Camden Revolutionary War Site**, which includes a powder magazine, log cabins, nature trails, picnic areas and a craft shop.

The **Camden Historic District** includes more than 60 homes, churches and buildings dotted around the picturesque town of 6,900 people. You can take self-guided walking and driving tours or arrange guided tours through the Kershaw County Chamber of Commerce. Virtually every building has a friendly spirit-in-residence.

The Kershaw-Cornwallis House in Camden ...

After the Civil War, Camden's mild climate attracted Northern horse breeders, who built beautiful in-town estates and fostered the passion for equestrian sports. The year's two big steeplechases are the Carolina Cup in late March and the Colonial Cup in late November. Both attract legions of serious horsefolk and a flood of partying tailgaters, who arrange their finest silver and china around the **Springdale Race Course** and partake of extensive picnics.

For races of a far different stripe, come to **Darlington**, east of Camden and north of Florence, when stock cars roar around the **Darlington Raceway**. If you can't make it for a race, you can see the champion cars in the Joe Weatherly **Stock Car Hall of Fame**.

Greenville and **Spartanburg** are two dynamic cities in the state's northwestern Upcountry. Greenville, population about 60,000, is proud of its more than 60 city parks and excellent zoo. Several blocks of Main Street downtown are a pedestrian mall lined with antique, apparel and gift shops. A short drive from the city, **Paris Mountain**, **Caesars Head** and **Table Rock** state parks have recreational lakes, picnic areas and campgrounds in the wooded Blue Ridge Mountain foothills. Table Rock State Park gets its name from the distinctive round dome of **Table Rock Mountain**, one of the Upcountry's best known landmarks. The two-lane, 130-mile (210-km) **Cherokee Foothills Scenic Highway** (SC 11), is a picture postcard route to those and other state parks, national forests, rivers and streams, historic sites and woodland hiking trails. The Scenic Highway loops north across the state from I-85 at the Georgia border to I-85 at Gaffney.

Greenville poses several options for art lovers. The **Greenville County Museum of Art** displays fine collections of Southern and American paintings, sculpture, photography and fabric art. The **Bob Jones University Gallery of Sacred Art and Bible Lands Museum and Planetarium** exhibits more than 400 religious paintings by Rembrandt, Titian, Rubens, Van Dyck and other European artists from the 13th to the 19th centuries. A free planetarium show linking science to sacred scripture is held on Sunday afternoons. Reflecting the Upcountry's growing international community, the **Nippon Center Yagoto** highlights traditional Japanese culture with tea ceremonies, festivals, illuminated gardens and a restaurant.

... is one of the oldest inland towns in the state.

Walnut Grove Plantation has graced the countryside near Spartanburg since 1765. The elegant main house has been restored and furnished with period antiques. Also situated in the grounds are a doctor's office, smokehouse, gristmill and family burial ground. Spartanburg's other historic shrines open to the public include the **Price House** (1795), and **Jammie Seay House** (1790).

The Cherokee Foothills Scenic Highway arcs eastward from Spartanburg to **Kings Mountain National Military Park** and **Cowpens National Battlefield**, two of the most important battle sites of the American Revolution's Southern theater. In September 1780, patriotic American mountainmen defeated a larger British force at Kings

Mountain, near the North Carolina/South Carolina border. At Kings Mountain National Military Park, off I-85, view the exhibits and dioramas in the Visitor Center, then follow a self-guided trail through the site.

In January 1781, the colonials followed up their Kings Mountain victory by routing the British at **Cowpens**, 18 miles (29 km) northeast of Spartanburg. At the battlefield's Visitor Center, you can follow the battle on a lighted map and see *Daybreak at the Cowpens*, a multimedia production. Then follow self-guided trails through the 893-acre (362-hectare) battle site.

The **Chattooga National Wild and Scenic River** provides a ticket to high adventure. Born high in the Blue Ridge Mountains, the river drops an average 49⅓ ft (15 meters) per mile as it forms a whitewater border beween northwestern South Carolina and northeastern Georgia. The river became internationally famous as the hair-raising setting for the film *Deliverance*, adapted from South Carolinian James Dickey's novel. Half-day, full-day and overnight excursions in six-person rubber rafts are offered by outfitters in **Long Creek** and **Mountain Rest**. Canoeing and kayaking trips are also available. When the water's high, and you're propelled through a chain of rambunctious rapids, you'll feel as though you've been shot from a giant slingshot. **Devil's Fork** and **Oconee State parks**, near the river, have furnished cabins, campgrounds, picnic areas, swimming, fishing and spectacular waterfalls.

Founded in 1790 by affluent coastal planters, **Pendleton**, southwest of Greenville and Spartanburg, seems like a page from an Early American album. Around the grassy **village green**, weathered brick buildings house antique shops, an eclectic mix of restaurants and other enterprises. When it was built in 1830, **Farmers Society Hall** at the south end of the green had the nation's third oldest agrarian association. Now it is known for its dining room, where gourmets gather for crab chops and lemonade pie.

Away from the green, Victorian and

Down on the farm.

saltbox cottages, tall-steepled churches and plantation houses hide behind boxwoods and stately live oak trees. Several historic residences are now restaurants, taverns and B&B inns. Two late-1820s residences – **Ashtabula**, and **Woodburn** – have been restored as house museums.

At **Clemson University**, 3 miles (5 km) from Pendleton, you can get maps and tour information in the **Tilman Hall Visitor Center** in order to explore museums, gardens and historic buildings on the wooded, 1,500-acre (600-hectare) campus. You can also stroll among the 2,200 varieties of ornamental plants in the sweet-smelling **State Botanical Garden**. Walkways lead by a Chinese pagoda, an arboretum, gristmill and lakeside teahouse. The Pioneer, Fern, Azalea and Camellia, Wildflower and Bog Gardens trails have Braille trails for the blind.

Fort Hill, on the campus, was the antebellum home of John C. Calhoun, US vice president under Andrew Jackson and John Quincy Adams and one of the South's most notable 19th-century statesmen. The mansion was part of the plantation land Calhoun's heirs donated to the state for its agricultural university. Before leaving the campus, stop at **Uniquely Clemson** in Newman Hall, to taste the delicious ice cream made on the university's dairy farm.

Abbeville, south of Pendleton and Clemson, is a charming time warp town, where it's possible to sit on a bench in the public square and relive 230 years of American history. The square was designed in oblong, 18th-century style by a homesick Frenchman who named the town for his own hometown. Attractively planted with seasonal flowers, the square's most imposing monument is a Confederate memorial obelisk. "**Old Bob**" is a cast-iron bell that has, over the years, summoned Abbevillians to all manner of happy and sad observances. Old Bob probably rang joyously in 1860, when South Carolina's first organized pro-secession rally was held in the square, but it must have tolled mournfully in May, 1865 – three weeks after

A girl's best friend.

the surrender at Appomattox – when Confederate President Jefferson Davis convened his war cabinet for the last time at the **Burt-Stark House**. The house is now a museum.

A stroll around the square takes you through a raft of antique shops, the 1842 **Trinity Episcopal Church**, the handsomely restored 1880s **Belmont Inn** and the turn-of-the-century **Opera House**. Once a forum for traveling vaudeville troupes – Fanny Brice, Al Jolson and Jimmy Durante graced its stage – the Opera House now hosts theatrical productions most weekends. Like the Opera House, the Belmont Inn has been returned to its Victorian glory. Guest rooms are furnished with antiques and reproductions, and in the lace-curtained dining room Southern, American and continental dishes are served.

Aiken, like Camden, is enamored of horses. Thoroughbreds have been training in Aiken's mild, pine-scented climate since the mid-19th century. Outstanding "graduates" include Kelso, Horse of the Year five years running in the 1960s; the 1981 Kentucky Derby winner, Pleasant Colony, and 1993 Derby champion Sea Hero. These and other Aiken-trained blue bloods are honored at the **Thoroughbred Racing Hall of Fame**. Located in a former carriage house at **Hopeland Gardens**, the hall salutes the champions with racing silks, photos, paintings, trophies and other memorabilia. After visiting, enjoy Hopeland's native trees and flowers, wetlands and outdoor sculptures. There's a Touch and Scent Trail for the visually impaired. On Monday evenings from May through August, the air is filled with jazz, bluegrass, classical and other musical sounds.

The city's horse mania reaches a feverish pitch three weekends in March when the Aiken Triple Crown fills historic **Aiken Mile Track** with harness, steeplechase and flat races. Needless to say, the "Triple" also puts Aiken's high society into high gear. Champagne brunches, teas, lunches, suppers and balls go on practically non-stop throughout the month. Even if you don't get an invitation to one of the gala events, be sure to take a driving tour through the **Aiken Winter Colony Historic Districts**, where "cottages" routinely have 50 to 90 rooms, and of course, stables. As you drive Whiskey Road, Easy Street and other paved roads and bridle paths, you'll pass many training farms and polo fields. These are especially active from November to April.

The **Aiken County Historical Museum**, in a 1930s Winter Colony mansion called **Banksia**, exhibits Indian artifacts, an old-timey drugstore and rooms furnished in period style. At **Aiken State Park**, 16 miles (26 km) east of the city, you can relax on four lakes and enjoy camping, swimming, boating and nature trails. There's also plentiful recreation to be had at the big lakes created by impoundments of the Savannah River on the South Carolina/Georgia border.

Lake Hartwell State Park, off I-85 at Fair Play, has campgrounds, boat ramps and picnic areas. Watersports beckon at **Lake Thurmond** and the **Richard B. Russell Dam and Lake**.

Left, tubing it on the lake. Right, just in time for dinner.

THE SOUTH CAROLINA COAST

If you listen to the accounts of those who grew up along South Carolina's coast, you'll discover a place rich in simplicity and close to the earth – a place in no hurry to catch up.

In his book, *The Prince of Tides*, author Pat Conroy writes: "To describe our growing up in the Low Country of South Carolina, I would have to take you to the marsh on a spring day, flush the great blue heron from its silent occupation, scatter marsh hens as we sink to our knees in the mud, open you an oyster with a pocketknife and feed it to you from the shell and say, 'There. That taste. That's the taste of my childhood.'"

Shrimp boats: For centuries, writers have found inspiration along the saltwater creeks, on the sheltered sea islands, and in the history-rich towns of South Carolina's coast. The coast is weather-worn cottages facing a shell-covered shore, shrimp boats heading out to sea. It is riverside plantations anchoring avenues of oak, and sea island blacks who keep alive the spirituals and Gullah language of their enslaved ancestors. The coast is a golden ribbon of tidal creeks and marshes kept alive by waves of green-and-gold spartina grass. It is a legacy comprised of earthquakes, hurricanes, tidal pools, wars, and a people too proud to give up.

The South Carolina coast is all these things. It is also sprawling golf-and-tennis resorts, oceanfront condominiums, theme parks, and outlet malls. Thanks to the Civil War, coastal residents have been "too poor to paint, too proud to whitewash" for generations. Perhaps this has been the area's greatest asset – along with a stubborn need to preserve the past.

Not until the 1950s did development really hit the area. Secluded beaches and islands remain, but the intrusion of the modern world has taken its toll on both wildlife and residents. Development may increase the standard of living for some, but for others, to simply have a plot of soil, a cast net, and the peace to roam an island without walls is more than enough to make life enriching. As you drive down the pre-colonial Indian trail that is now US 17, enjoy the South Carolina coast from the Grand Strand to the Low Country. When you experience its natural beauty, long-standing history, and distinct character, you'll know why residents call this fragile, somewhat threatened, oasis home.

The golf coast: Driving down **Myrtle Beach**'s **Ocean Boulevard** past the luxury high rises and campy motels, don't be surprised if a rowdy group of teenagers in a souped-up El Dorado challenges you to a drag race. For decades, this glitzy city by the sea has been the mecca for teenagers out for some mischief. In the 1940s, teens flocked to the beach to catch an earful of the black rhythm-and-blues music looked down upon by their white elders. Fittingly called beach music, these tunes spurred the creation of South Carolina's official dance, The Shag, a more refined version of the jitterbug.

Today, shaggers both young and old

Left, making a splash. **Right**, lighthouse on Hunting Island.

whirl about the dance floors of the **Myrtle Beach Pavilion and Amusement Park**, while thrill seekers race through the air on the famed Corkscrew. The most popular ride, though, is a vintage Herschel-Spillman Merry-Go-Round. Built in 1912, it is one of fewer than 100 hand-carved carousels still in existence in the US.

Back on Ocean Boulevard, Ripley's Believe It or Not Museum, the Myrtle Beach National Wax Museum, and the Motion Master Moving Theater offer different kinds of thrills. And the "horse-racing, whip-cracking, wagon-busting good time" of **Dixie Stampede** gives an Old South spark to the dinner theater experience. If you shy away from family-style spectacle, sample instead the area's famous calabash-style seafood on **Restaurant Row**.

Just one stop along the 60-mile (100-km) stretch of beach called the **Grand Strand** that runs from the northern tip of South Carolina down to Georgetown, Myrtle Beach has been called the "golf coast," with its more than 75 championship golf courses and resorts. And only 3 miles (5 km) to the south, the 312-acre (126-hectare) **Myrtle Beach State Park** is the most popular of South Carolina's state parks. No surprise, really, with around 350 campsites, a 730-ft (220-meter) fishing pier, and the popular **Sculptured Oak Nature Trail** to divert and entertain you.

Between the Grand Strand and the Low Country (the 200-mile/320-km area from Murrells Inlet south to the Savannah River), lies **Horry County**. Appropriately called **The Tidelands**, the region is as relaxed and meandering as the many rivers and tidal marshes that ribbon through it.

Around 18 miles (29 km) south of Myrtle Beach in Horry County, **Murrells Inlet** is the oldest fishing village in the state as well as the owner of the title "the seafood capital of South Carolina." Don't even think about leaving without sampling some of the seafood from one of the restaurants along this stretch of US 17. The catch is so fresh it practically swims into your plate.

Alternatively, why not picnic on the wide lawns and intimate alcoves at **Brookgreen Gardens**? The first public sculpture garden in America and a National Historic Landmark, Brookgreen features over 500 19th- and 20th-century sculptures, beginning, at the gate, with founder Anna Hyatt Huntington's *The Fighting Stallions*.

Famous for its locally hand-crafted hammocks, **Pawley's Island**, to the south past Litchfield, was used by 1800s plantation owners to escape the threat of malaria during the summer months. Although the hurricane of 1822 destroyed many of the earlier buildings, Pawley's remains the epitome of South Carolina beach towns, with its paint-peeled cottages standing watch over Myrtle Avenue. Pawley's does not appear to be ashamed of its weather-worn appearance. The slogan of the area is "arrogantly shabby."

Located at the confluence of the Waccamaw, Pee Dee, Black, and Sampit rivers, **Georgetown** is often overlooked as a tourist destination. The third oldest city in the state, this historic seaport's

Dionysus, Brookgreen Gardens, Murrells Inlet.

recently revitalized downtown area features a long **Harborwalk** on the Sampit River, and the town's **Historic District** keeps alive a vibrant past with more than 60 houses listed on the National Historic Register.

Ghost capital of the South: Many residents consider Georgetown to be a "little Charleston," complete with historic homes, sea-going vessels, and numerous B&B inns located both downtown and on Winyah Bay. Many regard Georgetown as the ghost capital of the South – nearly every historic home has a story to tell.

With the exception of the **Waterman-Kaminski House**, which boasts a collection of rare 18th-century antiques, many of Georgetown's homes are not open to the public but should be noted on any walking or driving tour. Other historic buildings, such as the **Rice Museum**, **Prince George-Winyah Episcopal Church** and the **Georgetown County Courthouse** do allow visitors to peek inside.

South of town, take SC 18 to **Belle Isle Plantation** on Winyah Bay for a look at the boyhood home of Francis Marion, South Carolina's Revolutionary War hero, otherwise known as "The Swamp Fox."

On the North and South Santee rivers back down US 17, **Hopsewee** and **Hampton** plantations offer a taste of luxurious Low Country plantation life.

The Swamp Fox trail: Bordered on the west by the Francis Marion National Forest and the south by the Cape Romain National Wildlife Refuge, the small fishing village of **McClellanville** still stands despite Hurricane Hugo's best efforts in 1989 to destroy it. Although the town was incorporated in 1926, its history dates back to a likewise hurricane-torn 1822 settlement.

The shrimp boats, clam dredges, and oyster boats moving in and out of the local shrimp docks hearken back to 1900 when McClellanville was the nation's largest exporter of oysters. Today, Charleston residents make the 45-minute drive to The Crab Pot just south of town for a taste of hand-picked crabs and locally caught shrimp.

Driving south toward Charleston on US 17 from McClellanville, you'll pass through **Francis Marion National Forest**, which covers over 250,000 acres (100,000 hectares). Hurricane Hugo destroyed more than three-fourths of the mature timber in this forest, and today logging companies fight with environmentalists over all that's still left. But don't get the wrong idea – thousands of acres have been preserved for the protection of endangered plants and animals, and hiking, camping, and canoeing facilities are reserved for lovers of the outdoors.

To experience more of Low Country South Carolina's wilderness, venture out SC 584 to **Moore's Landing**, where you can take an easy boat ride to **Cape Romain National Wildlife Refuge**. A 22-mile (35-km) stretch of barrier islands, Cape Romain encompasses 90 million acres (36 million hectares) of land and water populated only by dolphins, egrets, pelicans, herons, and other such wildlife viewed by boat, by nature trail, and by walking along the beach.

Southern comfort.

Back on US 17 just north of Charleston, **Mount Pleasant** (with its string of dockside seafood restaurants on Shem Creek) is the next town. Along the way there are many wooden roadside stands piled up with the Low Country's famous hand-woven sweetgrass baskets (*see page 84*). Passed down from mother to daughter through the generations, the Low Country art of basket weaving dates back to the time of slavery. Each basket's design represents its use in husking or storing the rice, which was grown on the area plantations, such as nearby Boone Hall.

Unlike plantations farther north, which can be austere and somewhat plain, **Boone Hall** is most people's idea of a genuine antebellum residence; it comes as no surprise to learn that the hall's breathtaking avenue of live oaks draped with Spanish moss inspired the plantation entrance for the movie version of *Gone With The Wind*.

What is more surprising to discover, however, is the fact that the present house was rebuilt only in 1935 in a style similar to the original hall. The surrounding buildings are much older, dating to around the mid-1700s, and include a smokehouse and a gin house. Of particular note are the nine original slave cabins. Boone Hall had on its premises a working brick- and tile-making yard, which made the bricks for these cabins. Taken together, these nine structures are considered to be one of the best-preserved "slave streets" still remaining (*see picture on page 118*).

Beach baby.

Continuing on US 17, take the East 526 exit to North SC 703 to **Sullivan's Island**. The drive winds through waves of whistling spartina grass and over the Intracoastal Waterway right onto the island's **Middle Street**, anchored by Dunleavy's Pub, Sully's Restaurant, and Bert's Bar. All establishments are as rough-and-tumble as the island itself, so don't worry about tracking in the sand.

Near the Sullivan's Island Lighthouse, is **Officer's Row**, a block of 10 houses along I'on Avenue. Originally constructed along the beach for Fort Moultrie field officers and their families, these sprawling residences feature pressed-tin ceilings and two-story verandahs unlike their more humble, whitewashed neighbors.

At the southern tip of the island facing Fort Sumter (where the first shots of the Civil War were fired, *see pages 41 and 123*) in Charleston Harbor, **Fort Moultrie** stands on the site of the original 1776 fort that held back British troops during the American Revolution with its bullet-absorbing palmetto-log construction – hence the palmetto-tree emblem on the state flag.

Head back the opposite direction on Middle Street to visit the more developed **Isle of Palms**. This residential and vacation community offers a wide array of activities including swimming, biking, beach combing, sailing, windsurfing, water skiing, canoeing, shrimping and crabbing.

The beachfront **Windjammer** is a popular nightspot that Charlestonians frequent – and they're not known for leaving the peninsula often. Located at the northeast end of the island, the world-renowned **Wild Dunes Resort** offers extensive golf-and-tennis facilities. While The Links features two finishing holes that hug the Atlantic Ocean, The Harbor Course actually has you hopping across islands.

South of Charlestown: Also known for its golfing facilities, **Kiawah Island** rests on the other side of Charleston – a well-preserved colonial seaport that mustn't be missed. Spend some time meandering about its streets before taking US 17 south out of town and heading down SC 20. Running through Johns Island, SC 20 takes you past the **Stono Marina** (once home of the Stono Indians), **Fenwick Hall** (whose proprietor was known to have entertained pirates), **St Johns Island Cafe** (the best sandwich and ice tea shack on the island), **Wadmalaw Island** (famous for the Charleston Tea Plantation – the only one in the United States), and **Rockville** (known as Wadmalaw Island's "Little Nantucket").

A man's castle is his home.

Once on Kiawah, head for **Beachwalker County Park** between Bohicket River and the ocean. Its wide boardwalk winds through a tangle of live oaks, pines, palmettos, and yucca plants before emptying onto an expansive, 10-mile (16-km) beach bordered by private condominiums. Most of Kiawah is private, but the oceanfront **Kiawah Island Inn** will guarantee you an enjoyable stay; Sunday Brunchis served at its Jasmine Porch restaurant.

As for golf, test your skills at **Turtle Point** as promoted by Jack Nicklaus; **Marsh Point** by Gary Player; **Osprey Point** by Tom Fazzio; and the famed **Ocean Course** by Pete Dye, which served as the site of the 1991 Ryder Cup Matches and was voted by *Golf Digest* as "The World's Toughest Resort Course."

And if that isn't enough, move on to **Seabrook Island** next door with 3 miles (5 km) of beaches, two championship golf courses, and over 200 villas. Outside its gates, **Bohicket Marina** on Bohicket Creek will satisfy your shopping needs amidst more than 300 consumer-ready vessels.

Follow US 17 south again for about

15 miles (24 km) to SC 174, which leads through a moss-covered archway of oak trees to **Edisto Island**, one of the oldest settlements in South Carolina.

Once home to the Edistow Indians and prosperous sea island cotton planters, the island still preserves remnants of the past. Visitors can find broken arrowheads, pottery, and sharks' teeth at an Indian shell mound on the beach (please leave what you find). The privately owned, **Windsor Plantation** (*circa* 1857) at the entrance to the island, stands as a typical representation of a sea-island home built up on piers to catch the cooling breeze and to avoid tempestuous tides.

On your way down US 17 toward Edisto Island, now a family vacation community, bordered by the Atlantic Ocean and St Helena Sound, stop in at the **Old Post Office Restaurant** for a casual but elegant meal. Actually located in an old post office, the Low Country cuisine of this restaurant is an area favorite.

Keep going and you'll pass **Edisto Island Presbyterian** church. Although the building is usually locked, the cemetery is worth a gander with its ornate tombstones marking the graves of sea island planters and the Legare Mausoleum sending a chill down the backs of islanders. As the story goes, a young woman who, finding herself prematurely buried, arose from her casket and tried to claw her way out of the tomb, but to no avail.

Where US 17 intersects with the Atlantic, **Edisto Beach State Park** on the left offers over a mile of prime, seashell-covered beach and 1,255 acres (505 hectares) of live-oak forest and salt marsh. On the right, **Palmetto Boulevard** gives the term "main drag" a new meaning. There's no traffic congestion or commercialization to be found on this oceanfront boulevard – only neatly kept seaside homes, manicured yards, and an uncluttered view of the ocean.

Walterboro: Back on US 17, head inland and north on SC 64 to the town of **Walterboro**, which boasts a main street typical of many small, Southern towns. Complete with a jail, courthouse, post office, pharmacy, barbershop, and a few specialty shops, Walterboro has no need for much more than the essentials.

Settled in 1784, the town has plenty of history and local culture to impart to visitors. Its prosperity as the largest railroad depot on the Savannah-to-Charleston line in the mid-1890s can still be seen in its luxurious, antebellum and Victorian homes shaded by plentiful hickory trees.

Churches dating back before the 18th century abound in Walterboro. The **Colleton Museum** and the **South Carolina Artisans Center** are both great places to view Low Country folk art. And the small-frame, Federalist-style **Walterboro Library Society Building**, or "Little Library," is so popular that, when the town was incorporated in 1826, city boundaries were defined as three-fourths of a mile in every direction from the building.

Of special note, the 133-ft (41-meter) landmark tower slit with narrow windows at the edge of town is not a former prison, but rather a 100,000-gallon

Pretty, historic Beaufort.

(380,000-liter) water tower. Don't let local tricksters lead you astray.

Take SC 303 back to US 17 and head south toward Beaufort through the ACE Basin, where the Ashepoo, Combahee, and Edisto rivers form one of the largest estuarine systems on the east coast. Travel down US 21 past the horse farms, marshlands, and vegetable farms of Port Royal Island. When you reach Beaufort itself, head down Boundary Street until you reach **Henry C. Chambers Waterfront Park** and nearby historic **Bay Street**, which is lined with specialty shops and boasts the town's favorite eatery and night-time hangout.

Established in 1711, **Beaufort** (pronounced *Bew-fort*) is the second oldest town in South Carolina. Its pre-Revolutionary homes are constructed of tabby and oyster shells, limestone, wooden pegs, and homemade nails. Its grand, antebellum homes point to a time of prosperity during the American Revolution. Their "Beaufort Style" design refers to their position facing due south on a raised basement to catch the breeze off their expansive porches. Perhaps the most famous of the Beaufort-style homes is **Tidalholm**, featured in Lawrence Kasdan's 1983 film *The Big Chill*.

Most of Beaufort's historic homes are privately owned, with the exception of the Federal-style **John Mark Verdier House**, built by a wealthy merchant in 1790. Along with Beaufort's historic churches (including the **Old Sheldon Church ruins** north of town), **The Arsenal** is worth a visit for its history as home of the Beaufort Voluntary Artillery – one of the oldest military units in the nation.

Just as Sullivan's Island inspired Edgar Allen Poe to write *The Gold Bug*, the Beaufort area inspired author Pat Conroy to write *The Prince of Tides*, which was made into a movie in 1991 by Barbra Streisand. *The Big Chill*, *The Prince of Tides*, and *Forrest Gump* are just a few of the movies that have been filmed, or part-filmed in the area. So, keep your eyes open, you might just see a movie in the works.

Take the bridge out of town to visit a

Hilton Head, site of one of America's first planned resorts.

couple of the 65 barrier islands that surround Beaufort. As you pass over **Lady's Island**, think about stopping in to **Whitehall Plantation Inn** for a waterfront sunset over continental cuisine. Or visit the Gullah House Restaurant on neighboring **St Helena's Island** to sample some traditional Low Country favorites. Frogmore on St Helena's is as famous for its Frogmore stew as it is for its legends of witchcraft.

The sea islands surrounding Beaufort feature semi-tropical wildland and carry overtones of a Gullah heritage still alive today. On St Helena's, the **Penn Center Historic District** is the site of the first school for freed slaves.

The 19th-century lighthouse on **Hunting Island** offers a sweeping view of the coastline and the 200-campsite state park below. Across **Port Royal Sound** on **Parris Island**, the US Marine Corps station adds a modern touch to the island's rich military history.

Hilton Head: Take SC 170 out of Beaufort heading south until you reach SC 278. Travel down this highway, past the historic town of **Bluffton**, the scenic **Pinckney Island National Wildlife Refuge**, and the popular Low Country **Factory Outlet Village** until you reach **Hilton Head Island**, 30 miles (48 km) south of Beaufort, and around the same distance from Savannah, Georgia.

Until the 1956 construction of a bridge linking the island to the mainland, Hilton Head resembled many of the other sea islands – isolated, rural, and poor with a population descended from slaves. In a region where change comes slowly, Hilton Head startled Low Country residents – not to mention Hilton natives, few of whom have prospered – with its sudden economic boon.

Around 12 miles (19 km) long and 5 miles (8 km) wide, Hilton Head boasts the nation's first master-planned resort and residential community, **Sea Pines**. Just one of the island's many resort "plantations" featuring golf, tennis and water sports, Sea Pines also encompasses a forest preserve most noted for its **Indian Shell Ring**, a refuse of oyster shells piled behind huts which once stood in a circle on the site. The resort's most popular attraction is its **Harbour Town Yacht Basin and Marina**, a luxurious affair with its numerous specialty shops and the relaxed, waterfront lounge, The Quarterdeck.

More than 800,000 rounds of golf are played annually on Hilton Head's 22 courses, and the island sports an international reputation for its high-profile professional and amateur golf events, including the MCI Classic at Harbour Town Golf Links. The island also possesses four of the nation's Top 50 tennis resorts, nine marinas, 300 shops, 200 restaurants, and 6,000 villas.

Bordered by loblolly pine, palmetto trees, and oak, Hilton Head's beaches are home to endangered, 200-lb (90-kg) loggerhead turtles, who bury their eggs in the soft sand on summer nights. Bottle-nosed dolphins are a common sight if you walk well away from the public-access **Coligny**, **Folly Field**, and **Burke's beaches**. The perfect place to see any of the nearly 200 species of birds that flock to Hilton Head each year is in the **New Hall Audubon Preserve**.

Left and right, Spanish moss is synonymous with coastal Carolina.

OLD SOUTH
CARRIAGE CO.
TOUR 262
VEHICLE

INSIGHT GUIDES

Travel Tips

Bozell

FOR THOSE WITH MORE THAN A PASSING INTEREST IN TIME...

Before you put your name down for a Patek Philippe watch *fig. 1*, there are a few basic things you might like to know, without knowing exactly whom to ask. In addressing such issues as accuracy, reliability and value for money, we would like to demonstrate why the watch we will make for you will be quite unlike any other watch currently produced.

"Punctuality", Louis XVIII was fond of saying, "is the politeness of kings."

We believe that in the matter of punctuality, we can rise to the occasion by making you a mechanical timepiece that will keep its rendezvous with the Gregorian calendar at the end of every century, omitting the leap-years in 2100, 2200 and 2300 and recording them in 2000 and 2400 *fig. 2*. Nevertheless, such a watch does need the occasional adjustment. Every 3333 years and 122 days you should remember to set it forward one day to the true time of the celestial clock. We suspect, however, that you are simply content to observe the politeness of kings. Be assured, therefore, that when you order your watch, we will be exploring for you the physical—if not the metaphysical—limits of precision.

Does everything have to depend on how much?

Consider, if you will, the motives of collectors who set record prices at auction to acquire a Patek Philippe. They may be paying for rarity, for looks or for micromechanical ingenuity. But we believe that behind each $500,000-plus bid is the conviction that a Patek Philippe, even if 50 years old or older, can be expected to work perfectly for future generations.
In case your ambitions to own a Patek Philippe are somewhat discouraged by the scale of the sacrifice involved, may we hasten to point out that the watch we will make for you today will certainly be a technical improvement on the Pateks bought at auction? In keeping with our tradition of inventing new mechanical solutions for greater reliability and better time-keeping, we will bring to your watch innovations *fig. 3* inconceivable to our watchmakers who created the supreme wristwatches of 50 years ago *fig. 4*.
At the same time, we will of course do our utmost to avoid placing undue strain on your financial resources.

Can it really be mine?

May we turn your thoughts to the day you take delivery of your watch? Sealed within its case is your watchmaker's tribute to the mysterious process of time. He has decorated each wheel with a chamfer carved into its hub and polished into a shining circle. Delicate ribbing flows over the plates and bridges of gold and rare alloys. Millimetric surfaces are bevelled and burnished to exactitudes measured in microns. Rubies are transformed into jewels that triumph over friction. And after many months—or even years—of work, your watchmaker stamps a small badge into the mainbridge of your watch. The Geneva Seal—the highest possible attestation of fine watchmaking *fig. 5*.

Looks that speak of inner grace *fig. 6*.

When you order your watch, you will no doubt like its outward appearance to reflect the harmony and elegance of the movement within. You may therefore find it helpful to know that we are uniquely able to cater for any special decorative needs you might like to express. For example, our engravers will delight in conjuring a subtle play of light and shadow on the gold case-back of one of our rare pocket-watches *fig. 7*. If you bring us your favourite picture, our enamellers will reproduce it in a brilliant miniature of hair-breadth detail *fig. 8*. The perfect execution of a double hobnail pattern on the bezel of a wristwatch is the pride of our casemakers and the satisfaction of our designers, while our chainsmiths will weave for you a rich brocade in gold *figs. 9 & 10*. May we also recommend the artistry of our goldsmiths and the experience of our lapidaries in the selection and setting of the finest gemstones? *figs. 11 & 12*.

How to enjoy your watch before you own it.

As you will appreciate, the very nature of our watches imposes a limit on the number we can make available. (The four Calibre 89 time-pieces we are now making will take up to nine years to complete). We cannot therefore promise instant gratification, but while you look forward to the day on which you take delivery of your Patek Philippe *fig. 13*, you will have the pleasure of reflecting that time is a universal and everlasting commodity, freely available to be enjoyed by all.

Should you require information on any particular Patek Philippe watch, or even on watchmaking in general, we would be delighted to reply to your letter of enquiry. And if you send us

fig. 1: The classic face of Patek Philippe.

fig. 2: One of the 33 complications of the Calibre 89 astronomical clock-watch is a satellite wheel that completes one revolution every 400 years.

fig. 3: Recognized as the most advanced mechanical regulating device to date, Patek Philippe's Gyromax balance wheel demonstrates the equivalence of simplicity and precision.

fig. 4: Complicated wristwatches circa 1930 (left) and 1990. The golden age of watchmaking will always be with us.

fig. 5: The Geneva Seal is awarded only to watches which achieve the standards of horological purity laid down in the laws of Geneva. These rules define the supreme quality of watchmaking.

fig. 6: Your pleasure in owning a Patek Philippe is the purpose of those who made it for you.

fig. 7: Arabesques come to life on a gold case-back.

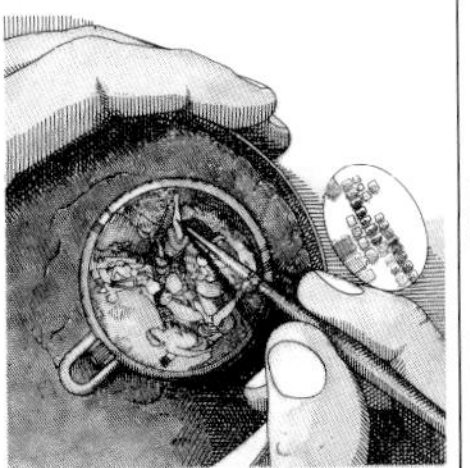

fig. 8: An artist working six hours a day takes about four months to complete a miniature in enamel on the case of a pocket-watch.

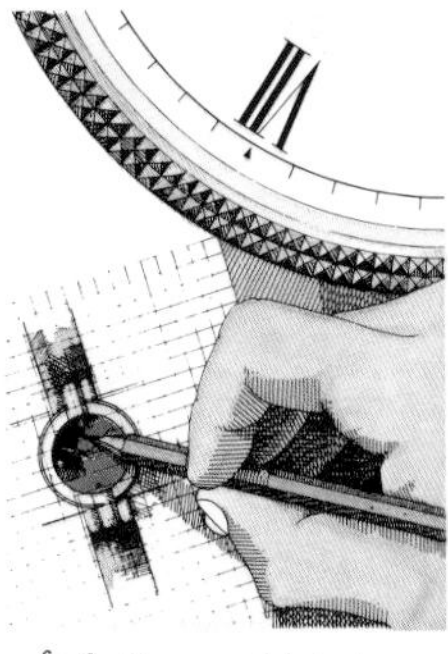

fig. 9: Harmony of design is executed in a work of simplicity and perfection in a lady's Calatrava wristwatch.

fig. 10: The chainsmith's hands impart strength and delicacy to a tracery of gold.

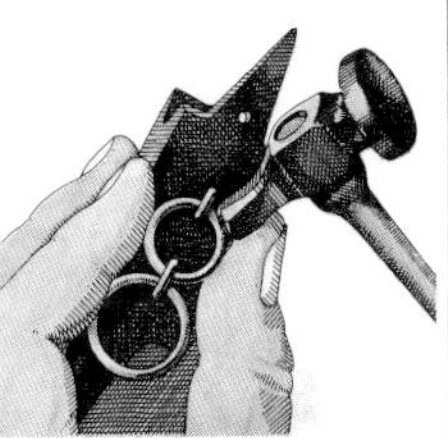

fig. 11: Circles in gold: symbols of perfection in the making.

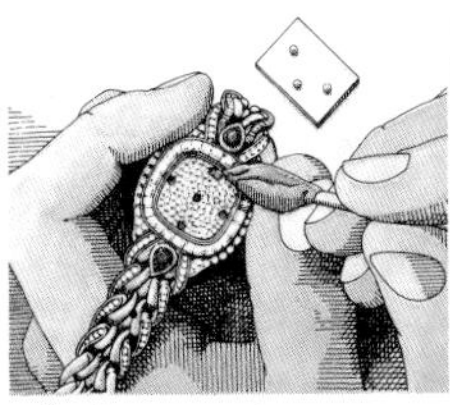

fig. 12: The test of a master lapidary is his ability to express the splendour of precious gemstones.

PATEK PHILIPPE
GENEVE

fig. 13: The discreet sign of those who value their time.

your card marked "book catalogue" we shall post you a catalogue of our publications. Patek Philippe, 41 rue du Rhône, 1204 Geneva, Switzerland, Tel. +41 22/310 03 66.

North America

160 Alaska
173 American Southwest
184I Atlanta
227 Boston
275 California
180 California, Northern
161 California, Southern
237 Canada
184C Chicago
184 Crossing America
243 Florida
240 Hawaii
275A Los Angeles
243A Miami
237B Montreal
184G National Parks of America: East
184H National Parks of America: West
269 Native America
100 New England
184E New Orleans
184F New York City
133 New York State
147 Pacific Northwest
184B Philadelphia
172 Rockies
275B San Francisco
184D Seattle
Southern States of America
186 Texas
237A Vancouver
184C Washington DC

Latin America and The Caribbean

150 Amazon Wildlife
260 Argentina
188 Bahamas
292 Barbados
251 Belize
217 Bermuda
127 Brazil
260A Buenos Aires
162 Caribbean
151 Chile
281 Costa Rica
282 Cuba
118 Ecuador
213 Jamaica
285 Mexico
285A Mexico City
249 Peru
156 Puerto Rico
127A Rio de Janeiro
116 South America
139 Trinidad & Tobago
198 Venezuela

Europe

155 Alsace
158A Amsterdam
167A Athens
263 Austria
107 Baltic States
219B Barcelona
1187 Bay of Naples
109 Belgium
135A Berlin
178 Brittany
109A Brussels
144A Budapest
213 Burgundy
122 Catalonia
141 Channel Islands
135E Cologne
119 Continental Europe
189 Corsica
291 Côte d'Azur
165 Crete
226 Cyprus
114 Czech/Slovak Reps
238 Denmark
135B Dresden
142B Dublin
135F Düsseldorf
149 Eastern Europe
148A Edinburgh
123 Finland
209B Florence
154 France
135C Frankfurt
135 Germany
148B Glasgow
279 Gran Canaria
124 Great Britain
167 Greece
166 Greek Islands
135G Hamburg
144 Hungary
256 Iceland
142 Ireland
209 Italy
202A Lisbon
258 Loire Valley
124A London
201 Madeira
219A Madrid
157 Mallorca & Ibiza
117 Malta
101A Moscow
135D Munich
158 Netherlands
111 Normandy
120 Norway
124B Oxford
154A Paris
115 Poland
202 Portugal
114A Prague
153 Provence
177 Rhine
209A Rome
101 Russia
130 Sardinia
148 Scotland
261 Sicily
264 South Tyrol
219 Spain
220 Spain, Southern
101B St. Petersburg
170 Sweden
232 Switzerland
112 Tenerife
210 Tuscany
174 Umbria
209C Venice
263A Vienna
267 Wales
183 Waterways of Europe

Middle East and Africa

268A Cairo
204 East African Wildlife
268 Egypt
208 Gambia & Senegal
252 Israel
236A Istanbul
252A Jerusalem-Tel Aviv
214 Jordan
270 Kenya
235 Morocco
259 Namibia
265 Nile, The
257 South Africa
113 Tunisia
236 Turkey
171 Turkish Coast
215 Yemen

Asia/Pacific

287 Asia, East
207 Asia, South
262 Asia, South East
194 Asian Wildlife, Southeast
272 Australia
206 Bali Baru
246A Bangkok
234A Beijing
247B Calcutta
234 China
247A Delhi, Jaipur, Agra
169 Great Barrier Reef
196 Hong Kong
247 India
212 India, South
128 Indian Wildlife
143 Indonesia
278 Japan
266 Java
203A Kathmandu
300 Korea
145 Malaysia
218 Marine Life in the South China Sea
272B Melbourne
211 Myanmar
203 Nepal
293 New Zealand
205 Pakistan
222 Philippines
250 Rajasthan
159 Singapore
105 Sri Lanka
272 Sydney
175 Taiwan
246 Thailand
278A Tokyo
255 Vietnam
193 Western Himalaya

THE OLD SOUTH

Getting Acquainted

Weights and measures

The US uses the Imperial system of weights and measures. Metric is rarely used. Below is a conversion chart.

1 inch = 2.54 centimeters
1 foot = 30.48 centimeters
1 mile = 1.609 kilometers
1 ounce = 28.4 grams
1 pound = .453 kilograms
1 yard = .9144 meters

Electricity

Standard American electric current is 110 volts. An adapter is necessary for European appliances, which run on 220–240 volts.

Planning the Trip

Entry Regulations

A passport, a visitor's visa, a health record, and evidence of intent to leave the US after your visit are required for entry into the US by most foreign nationals. Visitors from the UK and several other countries (including but not limited to Japan, Germany, Italy, France, Switzerland, Sweden and the Netherlands) staying less than 90 days may not need a visa if they meet certain requirements. All other foreign nationals must obtain a visa from the US consulate or embassy in their country. Exceptions are Canadians entering from the Western Hemisphere, Mexicans with border passes and British residents of Bermuda and Canada.

Visas are usually granted for six months. If you wish to remain in the country longer than six months, you must apply for an extension of stay at the **Immigration and Naturalization Service**, 2401 East St, Washington, DC 20520, tel: (202) 514-4330. If you lose your visa or passport, arrange to get a new one at your country's nearest consulate or embassy.

Health

Health care in the US is extremely expensive. It's therefore important for you to have some sort of insurance when traveling. If you don't already have insurance that is accepted in the US, ask your travel agent about a travel plan that, at the very least, covers emergency medical care.

Money

The basic unit of currency is the dollar, made up of 100 cents with coins in the denomination of 1¢, 5¢ ("a nickel"), 10¢ ("a dime'), 25¢ ("a quarter) and the rarely-seen 50¢ coin. There are also several denominations of paper money. They are: $1, $5, $10, $20, $50, $100 and, rarely, $2. Each bill is the same color, size and shape, so be sure to check the amount on the face of the bill.

It's advisable to arrive with at least $100 in cash (in small bills) in order to pay for ground transportation and other incidentals. It's always a good idea to carry internationally recognized traveler's checks rather than cash. These are usually accepted by retailers in lieu of cash. They can also be exchanged for cash at most banks. Be sure to take your passport.

Major credit cards are accepted at shops, restaurants, hotels and gas stations, although not all cards are accepted by every vendor. To be safe, carry at least two kinds. Some credit cards may also be used to withdraw cash from automatic teller machines (ATMs) located in most larger towns and cities. Out-of-town ATM cards may also work. Check with your bank or credit-card company for the names of the systems your card will operate.

Public Holidays

During the holidays listed below, post offices, banks, government offices and many shops and restaurants are closed.

New Year's Day
January 1
Martin Luther King Jr's Birthday
Third Monday in January
Presidents' Day
Third Monday in February
Easter Sunday
Memorial Day
Last Monday in May
Independence Day
July 4
Labor Day
First Monday in September
Columbus Day
Second Monday in October
Veteran's Day
November 11
Thanksgiving Day
Fourth Thursday in November
Christmas
December 25

Getting There

By Air

Perhaps one of the easiest and most convenient ways to reach the Old South is by plane. Certainly, the airports mentioned here are suitably placed, allowing you relatively easy access to the rest of the state you happen to arrive in. Airlines which service most of them include Delta, USAir, American, United and TWA.

VIRGINIA

Washington Dulles International Airport (IAD), tel: (703) 661-2700, 26 miles (42 km) west of the Washington, in Loudon County.

Newport News-Williamsburg International Airport (for Tidewater and Eastern Shore), Newport News.

KENTUCKY

Louisville Airport, tel: (502) 367-4636, 5 miles (8 km) from downtown Louisville.

TENNESSEE

Nashville Metropolitan Airport, 8 miles (13 km) south of Nashville.

NORTH CAROLINA

Charlotte-Douglas International Airport, tel: (704) 359-4000, west of the Charlotte, off I-85.

SOUTH CAROLINA

Charleston International Airport, tel: (803) 767-1100, 12 miles (19 km) west of Charleston, on I-26.

Myrtle Beach Jetport (for Myrtle Beach), tel: (803) 448-1589.

By Train

Amtrak, tel: (800) 872-7245, offer regular rail services from major towns and cities in the north, south and east of the US to numerous destinations in the Old South.

By Bus

Greyhound, tel: (800) 231-2222, also offer regular bus services from many towns and cities in the States to several destinations in the Old South.

By Car

Car Rentals

National car rental agencies are located at all airports, cities and large towns. In most places, you must be at least 21 years old (25 in some states) to rent a car, and you must have a valid driver's license and at least one major credit card. Foreign drivers must have an international driver's license.

Alamo
US (800) 327-9633
International +1-305-522 0000
Avis
US (800) 331-1212
International +1-918-664 4600
Budget
US (800) 527-0700
International +1-214-404 7600
Dollar
US (800) 800-4000
International +1-813-877 5507
Enterprise
US (800) 325-8007
International +1-314-781 8232
Hertz
US (800) 654-3131
International +1-405-749 4424
National
US (800) 227-7368
International +1-612-830 2345
Thrifty
US (800) 331-4200
International +1-918-669 2499

Useful Addresses

Tourist Information

For information on state chambers of commerce, consult the listings under individual states.

Travel South USA, 3400 Peachtree Rd NE, Suite 1517, Atlanta, GA 30326, tel: (404) 231-1790, fax: (404) 231-2364.

Southeast Tourism Society, PO Box 420308, Atlanta, GA 30342, tel: (404) 255-9472, fax: (404) 847-9518.

Where to Stay

Accommodation

National Hotels and Motels

The (800) numbers listed below are the main numbers that should be dialed in order to make a reservation. With the hotels, if you are unable to get through when using these numbers, then you should contact the local reservation center of that particular hotel chain in the region or country you happen to be in. The relevant telephone numbers will be available either from the telephone directory or from the operator.

The motels can only be contacted by dialing the numbers listed below. If you are unable to get through on these numbers, then make reservations once you are in the US.

Hotels

Best Western, tel: (800) 528-1234.
Hilton, tel: (800) HILTONS.
Holiday Inn, tel: (800) HOLIDAY
Marriot, tel: (800) 228-9290.
Quality Inn, tel: tel: (800) 228-5151.
Ramada, tel: (800) 2-RAMADA.
Sheraton, tel: (800) 325-3535.
Hyatt, tel: (800) 228-9000.
Stouffer Hotels and Resorts, tel: (800) HOTELS.
Trusthouse Forte, tel: (800) 225-5843.

Motels

Budget Host Inns, tel: (800) BUD-HOST.
Friendship Inns International, tel: (800) 453-4511.
Red Roof Inns, tel: (800) 843-7663.
Suisse Chalet International, tel: (800)258-1980.
Super 8, tel: (800) 800-8000.
Days Inns of America, tel: (800) 325-2525.

Food Terms

A–C

Ambrosia: A classic Southern sweet side dish blending oranges and coconut, it is rapidly falling from favor in all but the most traditional restaurants.

Barbecue: A traditional method of cooking that in most of the South means slowly smoking a whole pig over a slow wood fire sometimes set to burning in a pit. The meat is basted while it cooks, but not with barbecue sauce, as that would burn the spices and result in an acrid flavor. Barbecue sauces, ranging in styles from tomato-based to mustard-based to vinegar-pepper based and to dry-rubs, vary widely all over the South, with the passionate engaging in fervent arguments over its proper form.

Collards: A large, green-leafed vegetable popular throughout the South, it is traditionally served on New Year's Day with pork and black-eyed peas (see below) as a good-luck dish. Collards are also eaten throughout the year, often with a touch of hot pepper-flavored vinegar.

D–G

Doves: In the 19th century, upper-crust Southerners kept dovecotes in their back yards, making snagging supper easy. Today, smothered dove and other traditional dishes are the stuff of mainly hunters.

Eggplant casserole: A popular side dish that varies widely in seasoning and composition, but basically blends mashed, cooked eggplant (aubergine) with bread crumbs, eggs and seasonings to be baked in a flat pan.

Fritters: These deep-fried morsels, often served as side dishes or as desserts, may be made with vegetables, fruits, meats or seafood. The target foodstuff is surrounded with a light batter and deep-fried, and served hot.

Green tomatoes: After the film *Fried Green Tomatoes* was such a hit, the dish enjoyed a comeback in popularity. Sliced thin, green tomatoes are rolled in white cornmeal or flour and fried in hot fat. Crisp and sweet, they're a great side dish for all kinds of traditional meals.

H–K

Hush puppies: Round puffs of cornmeal mixed with minced onion and sometimes beer as the liquid, hush puppies are shaped with spoons and deep fried. Hush puppies are though to derive their name from the notion that the morsels were thrown to camp dogs to keep them quiet, that is to "hush" them with the admonition: "Hush, puppy" becoming the name of the treat itself. They are an essential element with fried fish.

Iced tea: In the South, if you ask for "tea", you'll get it on the rocks. Up North, the same request fetches you hot tea. Obviously, it's a climate-related matter. In the South, if you want hot tea, you must ask for hot tea. Iced tea (pronounced "ahs-tea," ignoring the participle's final d), is offered unsweetened, but the best way to enjoy it is presweetened with a wedge of fresh lemon.
Jam cake: A treat that's spread to most Southern states, jam cake, a layer cake, is usually thought of as coming from Tennessee and Kentucky. Incorporated into the cake batter, blackberry jam is the preferred flavor to use, and the cake may be finished with caramel icing.
Kale: One of many greens savored in the South, kale has a delightful bitter tang and, like most such greens, serious nutritional content.

L–N

Lady Baltimore Cake: Originating in South Carolina, not Baltimore, Maryland, Lady Baltimore Cake is a white layer cake covered with a nut-and-raisin studded white icing.
Moonshine: Distilled from corn, thus also known as corn liqueur, moonshine is produced both legally and illegally in most Southern states, and began in the early 19th century. Also called "white lightening," the bootlegged stuff, often containing impurities, can literally kill a person. Perfectly fine legal corn whiskey is available in reputable liqueur stores, and is best taken straight, as a digestif after dinner. It's strong stuff, somewhat reminiscent of grappa.
Nuts: In addition to pecans, probably the nut most associated with Southern cooking, hickory nuts, walnuts and black walnuts are traditional in Southern cooking for desserts.

O–R

Okra: From Africa, possibly via India, okra came to the New World with slaves, who hid seeds in their hair. A long pod with seeds inside, okra is best approached by the newcomer with some caution. Overcooked it can be slimy and disagreeable. Pickled, it's a delight. Rolled in cornmeal and fried, okra doesn't get its characteristic mucilaginous quality often obtained when it's abused by heat.
Pecans: Thomas Jefferson planted them at Monticello in Virginia, and called them "pacans." The origin of this nut, whose spectacular tree forms an eerie spectacle of gaunt forms against a fall sky, is lost in time. It appears in pecan pie, divinity, pralines (pronounced "praw-leens"), brittle and other traditional Southern delicacies.
Quail: Shooting birds is a favorite sport of the upper classes, but it also constitutes a serious means of sustaining a rural family. Quail frequently appears on the menus of fine restaurants, as well as on the home supper table. Methods for its preparation include grilling, frying, braising and roasting. It may be in a casserole, and it is not just limited to supper. Quail on the brunch buffet is not unusual.
Ribs: This ribs business, as an extension of the great barbecue argument, warrants serious discussion. Pork ribs, of course, are the mainstay of barbecue. In this instance, they're cooked slow over a low fire and brushed when done with barbecue sauce. They should be tender, not too fatty, and flavorful with or without sauce. No doubt about it, eating with the fingers is the most efficient methodology.

S–V

Spoon bread: Made from corn and baked like a custard, it is soft, so must be eaten with a spoon – hence the name. It is often served as a side dish with quail and fish.
Tomato pudding: Cubed, old bread, softened in juicy tomatoes, is covered with crumbs then baked. The dish is more likely to be seen at home than in a restaurant, and it is especially popular in Appalachia.
Upside Down Cake: A skillet cake with pineapple rings on the bottom that becomes the top when the finished cake is flipped out of the pan, this was a popular homemade cake until recent times.
Venison: An essential part of the Southern diet, venison, like other game, is enjoyed as much for the ritual of the hunt and the accompanying trophies as for its flavor. Unfortunately, many hunters today do not know proper field dressing, and such ignorance ruins much of the meat. Venison roasts, steaks, stews and even burgers are widely enjoyed.

W–Z

Wine: Southern wine is most often associated with Scuppernong and Muscadine, the traditional grapes of most home vineyards. But today, winemaking is on the comeback trail, especially in Virginia, which now has about 50 wineries. Norton, a grape developed in the 19th century to produce a claret-like red wine, yields terrific results in both Virginia and Tennessee, which has 16 wineries. In North Carolina, two wineries – Biltmore Estate at the chateauesque Vanderbilt Home in Ashville and Westbend near Winston-Salem – are producing excellent wines. Fruit wines based on apple, blackberry, elderberry, raspberry and strawberry are traditional in the South and being made in most Southern states with excellent results.
X: This stands for X-tra helpings, something Southerners tend to ask for right often.
Yams: Not to be confused with the South America sweet potato, another Southern staple, yams are of African origin. Whereas sweet potatoes, related botanically to the morning glory, are served either baked or in a casserole dish called soufflé, yams are usually served "candied," that is sliced and flavored with syrup and spices.
Z: Southerners wouldn't dream of eating anything starting with Z. Too non-traditional.

Leisure

Shopping

CLOTHING CHART

This table compares American, Continental European and British clothing sizes. It's a good idea to try clothes on before buying as sizes can vary.

Women's Dresses/Suits

American	European	British
6	38/34N	8/30
8	40/36N	10/32
10	42/38N	12/34
12	44/40N	14/36
14	46/42N	16/38
16	48/44N	18/40

Women's Shoes

American	European	British
4.5	36	3
5.5	37	4
6.5	38	5
7.5	40	6
8.5	41	7
9.5	42	8
10.5	43	9

Men's Suits

American	European	British
34	44	34
–	46	36
38	48	38
–	50	40
42	52	42
–	54	44
46	56	46

Men's Shirts

American	European	British
14	36	14
14.5	37	14.5
15	38	15.5
15.5	39	15.5
16	40	16
16.5	41	16.5
17	42	17

Men's Shoes

American	European	British
6.5	–	6
7.5	40	7
8.5	41	8
9.5	42	9
10.5	43	10
11.5	44	11

Movies

The following list of movies are a small selection of the many films where plots, characters and themes relate directly to the South.

The Beguiled, 1971
The Big Chill, 1983
The Color Purple, 1985
Deliverance, 1972
Driving Miss Daisy, 1989
Fried Green Tomatoes, 1991
The General, 1926
Glory, 1989
Gone With The Wind, 1939
The Good, The Bad, and The Ugly, 1966
The Prince of Tides, 1991
Rambling Rose, 1991
Steel Magnolias, 1989

Other Insight Guides

The 190 books in the *Insight Guides* series cover every continent and include 40 titles devoted to the US. Companion books to this title include:

Insight Guide: Atlanta. Stunning photography and local writers make the most out of the self-proclaimed "Capital of the New South."

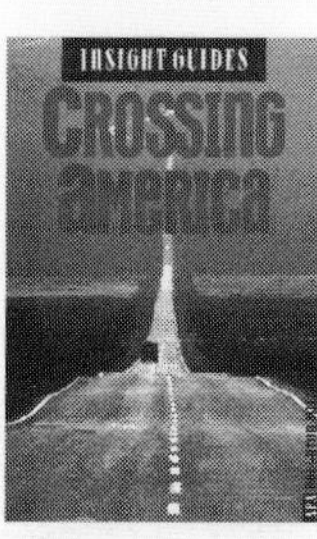

Insight Guide: Crossing America is for those restless souls who want to experience America by driving across it.

Insight Guide: New Orleans captures the essence of this alluring city, in the process explaining the origins of jazz, giving the best tips on places to eat, and delving into the history of the Mardi Gras.

VIRGINIA

Getting Acquainted

The Place

Known As: The Old Dominion.
Origin of Name: The Virgin Queen, Queen Elizabeth I.
Motto: *Sic Semper Tyrannis* – Thus Always to Tyrants.
Entered Union: 1788.
Population: 6½ million (12th largest in nation).
Population Density: 1,593 people per sq. mile (613 per sq. km).
Area: 40,815 sq. miles (105,710 sq. km).
Time Zone: Eastern Time Zone (GMT minus five hours).
Highest Point: Mount Rogers, 5,792 ft (1,765 meters).
Climate: Temperate, but with four distinct seasons. The spring and fall are the best seasons in which to visit. Summer is hot and humid in the lower areas, whilst winter can mean snow in the mountains. In central Virginia, temperatures range from 36°F/2°C in January to 78°F/26°C in July. In the mountains, they range from 29°F (-2°C) in January to 71°F/22°C in July.
Economy: Industries include trade, manufacturing, tourism, high technology, agriculture, government, military, chemicals and tobacco.
Local Government: Made up of 95 counties, 41 chartered cities, and 189 incorporated towns. Provides two senators and 11 representatives to US Congress.
Annual Visitors: More than 50 million.
Capital: Richmond.
Local Dialing Codes: (804) for the central and south eastern parts of the state; (703) for the western and northern areas; and (540) for the extreme western regions.
Famous Figures: Benjamin Harrison, Patrick Henry, William Henry, Thomas Jefferson, Robert E. Lee, James Madison, James Monroe, John Taylor, George Washington, Woodrow Wilson.

Useful Addresses

State Tourist Office

Virginia Division of Tourism, 901 East Byrd St, Richmond, VA 23219, tel: (804) 786-2051.

Local Tourist Offices

FREDERICKSBURG

Fredericksburg Department of Tourism, tel: (703) 373-1776 or (800) 678-4748, fax: (703) 372-6587.

NORFOLK

Norfolk Convention & Visitors Bureau, tel: (804) 441-5266 or (800) 368-3097, fax: (804) 622-3663.

RICHMOND

Metro Richmond Convention & Visitors Bureau, tel: (804) 782-2777 or (800) 365-7272, fax: (804) 780-2577.

ROANOKE

Roanoke Valley Convention & Visitors Bureau, tel: (703) 342-6025 or (800) 635-5535, fax: (703) 342-7119.

VIRGINIA BEACH

Virginia Beach Department of Convention & Visitor Development, tel: (804) 437-4700, fax: (804) 437-4747.

WILLIAMSBURG

Williamsburg Area Convention & Visitors Bureau, tel: (804) 253-0192 or (800) 368-6511, fax: (804) 229-2047.

Where to Stay

Accommodation

Abingdon

The Martha Washington Inn, 150 West Main St, 24210, tel: (540) 628-3161 or (800) 533-1014. An historic inn that's ideal as a base for southwest Virginia or at least a visit and meal. 61 rooms. $$

Alexandria

Alexandria Hotel Association, tel: (800) 296-1000. This hotel reservation service features many of Alexandria's finest hotels in a wide range of budgets and locations. $–$$$

Arlington

Ritz-Carlton Pentagon City, 1250 South Hayes St, 22202, tel: (703) 415-5000 or (800) 241-3333. The place to stay in Northern Virginia for an extra-special experience. 345 rooms. $$$–$$$$

Big Stone Gap

Country Inn, 627 Gilley Ave, 24219, tel: (540) 523-0374. Clean and convenient. 44 rooms. $

Charlottesville

Boar's Head Inn and Sports Club, Route 250 West, 22903, tel: (804) 296-2181 or (800) 476-1988. An elegant place to stay or just eat a meal in the midst of history and horse country. 173 rooms. $$

Guesthouses B&B Reservation Service, tel: (804) 979-7264. This company features a wide array of B&Bs, suites, and cottages. $–$$$

The Inn at Monticello, Route 19, 22902, tel: (804) 979-3593. This cozy country inn is close to Monticello and many other Charlottesville attractions. 5 rooms. $$

Chincoteague

Channel Bass Inn, 6228 Church St, 23336, tel: (804) 336-6148 or (800) 249-0818. This is one of the Eastern Shore's finest inns, with Victorian elegance and Eastern Shore charm. It serves good food, too. 5 rooms. $$$

Danville

Stratford Inn, 2500 Riverside Dr., 24540, tel: (804) 793-2500 or (800) 326-8455. This older property is convenient and has an excellent local restaurant. 160 rooms. $

Fredericksburg

Fredericksburg Colonial Inn, 1707 Princess Anne St, 22401, tel: (540) 371-5666. Pretty hotel reminiscent of an earlier time. 30 rooms. $

Kenmore Inn, 1200 Princess Anne St, 22401, tel: (540) 371-7622 or (800) 437-7622. B&B. Huge old 1796 house. 12 rooms. $$

Harrisonburg

Joshua Wilton House, 412 South Main St, 22801, tel: (540) 434-4464. This wonderful Victorian B&B inn can serve as a perfect Shenandoah Valley base. Good food, too. 5 rooms. $$

Hot Springs

The Homestead, 24445, tel: (800) 838-1766. This historic four-season resort features a wide array of outdoors activities, including golf, tennis, shooting, fishing, hiking, biking, skiing, and much more. 521 rooms. $$–$$$$

Irvington

The Tides Inn, King Carter Dr., 22480, tel: (804) 438-5000 or (800) 843-3746. One of Virginia's most beloved resorts, located right on a peaceful river. 110 rooms. $$–$$$

Leesburg

Carradoc Hall Hotel, 1500 East Market St, 22075, tel: (703) 771-9200 or (800) 552-6702. This converted old mansion is a quaint choice right in the heart of Leesburg. 120 rooms. $

Lansdowne Conference Resort, 44050 Woodbridge Pkwy, 22075, tel: (703) 729-8400 or (800) 541-4801. This elegant resort, with golf and much more, is in the country, but near bustling Northern Virginia. 305 rooms. $$

Lexington

Alexander-Witherow House, 11 North Main St, 24450, tel: (540) 463-2044. This 18th-century B&B inn is situated right in Lexington's historic district. 7 rooms. $$

Luray

Luray Caverns Motel, Route 211, 22835, tel: (540) 743-6551. Locally owned, clean, and convenient to the caverns. 19 rooms. $

The Mimslyn, 401 West Main St, 22835, tel: (504) 743 5105 or (800) 296-5105. A handsome hotel set high on a hill in its own grounds. Sweeping dining room, rooftop solarium and secluded nooks and crannies convey an elegance not reflected in the price. Suites also available. $–$$

Manassas

Holiday Inn Manassas Battlefield, 10800 Vandor Lane, 22110, tel: (703) 335-0000 or (800) HOLIDAY. Modern and convenient, with Civil War tour packages.160 rooms. $–$$

Middleburg

Red Fox Inn, 2 East Washington St, 22117, tel: (540) 687-6301 or (800) 223-1728. This historic inn was built in 1728 and is a popular place for regional cooking, too. 24 rooms. $$–$$$

Middletown

Wayside Inn, 7783 Main St, 22645, tel: (540) 869-1797. Historic inn and restaurant, featuring southern hospitality and cuisine. 24 rooms. $

Mountain Lake

Mountain Lake, 24136, tel: (800) 346-3334. An historic mountain resort featuring 2,600 acres (1,050 hectares) of tall trees, stunning mountain scenery, dining rooms overlooking a clear mountain lake, and a wide variety of accommodation. 66 rooms. $–$$$

Newport News

The Inn at Kiln Creek, 1003 Brick Kiln Blvd, 23602, tel: (804) 874-2600. Pretty golf resort with adjoining hotel. 16 rooms. $–$$

Norfolk

Omni International Hotel, 777 Waterside Dr., 23510, tel: (804) 622-6664 or (800) THE OMNI. Modern hotel situated right next to Waterside and overlooking the water. 442 rooms. $$

Plantation Country

Edgewood Bed and Breakfast, 4800 John Tyler Memorial Hwy, 23030, tel: (804) 829-2962 or (800) 296-EDGE. B&B. A fine mid-19th-century plantation home. 8 rooms. $$–$$$

Petersburg

Petersburg Ramada, 380 East Washington St, 23803, tel: (804) 733-0000 or (800) 473-0005. Modern and convenient to Old Towne Petersburg. 200 rooms. $

Portsmouth

Holiday Inn Waterfront, 8 Crawford Pkwy, 23704, tel: (804) 393-2573 or (800) HOLIDAY. This waterfront hotel is convenient to everything in the Tidewater area. 232 rooms. $

Richmond

The Berkeley Hotel, 1200 East Cary St, 23219, tel: (804) 780-1300. Located in the Shockoe Slip warehouse district, this elegant hotel is convenient to everything in downtown Richmond. 55 rooms. $$

The Jefferson Hotel, Franklin and Adams Sts, 23220, tel: (804) 788-8000 or (800) 424-8014. Originally opened in 1895, this is Richmond's finest hotel and well worth a visit or a stay. 274 rooms. $$–$$$

Linden Row Inn, 101 North 1st St, 23219, tel: (804) 783-7000 or (800) 348-7424. Centrally-located in the downtown area and combines the best of a hotel and B&B stay. 71 rooms. $$

Roanoke

Radisson Patrick Henry Hotel, 617 South Jefferson St, 24011, tel: (540) 345-8811 or (800) 833-4567. This conveniently located historic landmark is the ideal base in downtown Roanoke. 125 rooms. $$

Staunton

Belle Grae Inn, 515 West Frederick St, 24401, tel: (540) 886-5151. This city B&B inn features rooms in the main building and many outbuildings. 12 rooms. $–$$

Frederick House, 28 North New St, 24401, tel: (540) 885-4200 or (800) 334-5575. Located in the downtown area, this historic building houses a European-style B&B inn. 14 rooms. $

Strasburg

Hotel Strasburg, 201 Holliday St, 22657, tel: (540) 465-9191 or (800) 348-8327. This old home served as a hospital before becoming an inn, serving interesting Southern-style food. A stay here is a highlight of a Shenandoah Valley visit. 25 rooms. $

Tangier Island

Hilda Crockett's Chesapeake House, Box 194 (Main St), 23440, tel: (804) 891-2331. Basic rooms, including packages with a family-style dinner and breakfast. Seafood meals are available to the public. 7 rooms. $

Virginia Beach

The Cavalier, 42nd St and Oceanfront, 23451, tel: (804) 425-8555 or (800) 980-5555. This pretty property is a Virginia Beach legend. The old section offers historic rooms with meals, while the new section provides modern options. 400 rooms. $–$$

Washington

The Inn at Little Washington, Middle and Main Sts, 22747, tel: (540) 675-3800. This special Northern Virginia property features some of the finest accommodations and French meals in the state. 12 rooms. $$$$

Williamsburg

Kingsmill Resort, 1010 Kingsmill Rd, 23185, tel: (804) 253-1703 or (800) 832-5665. Located just 15 minutes from Colonial Williamsburg, this full-service resort is a popular getaway for relaxation, golf, and other sporting activities. 407 rooms. $$–$$$$

Williamsburg Inn, Francis St at South England St, 23187, tel: (804) 229-1000 or (800) HISTORY. If you want perfect elegance right in the historic district, then plan to stay here. 235 rooms. $$$–$$$$

Wintergreen

Trillium House, Wintergreen Resort, 22958, tel: (804) 325-9126 or (800) 325-9126. Located at the top of the mountain at Wintergreen Resort, this popular country B&B inn is an ideal mountain getaway anytime of the year. Meals featuring regional dishes available to non-guests. 12 rooms. $$

Wintergreen Resort, 22958, tel: (804) 325-2200 or (800) 325-2200. This 11,000-acre (4,500-hectare) four-season resort features a wide range of accommodations and activities, including golf, tennis, hiking, biking, horseback riding, skiing, and much more. Elegant dining overlooking the mountains. 320 rooms. $–$$$

Yorktown

Duke of York Motor Inn, 508 Water St, 23690, tel: (804) 898-3232. Located right on the York River waterfront, this is an ideal base for exploring Yorktown and the rest of the Historic Triangle. 57 rooms. $

Eating Out

Where to Eat

Many of the resorts and inns in "Where to Stay" also serve meals to non-guests.

Abingdon

The Tavern, 222 East Main St, tel: (540) 628-1118. This original restored tavern features creative regional cuisine in a casual historic setting. $$

Alexandria

The Chart House, 1 Cameron St, tel: (703) 684-5080. Seafood, steaks, and river views are the highlights at this local favorite. $$–$$$

The Fish Market, 105 King St, tel: (703) 836-5676. This casual bar and restaurant features Chesapeake Bay seafood. $$

Gadsby's Tavern, 138 North Royal St, tel: (703) 548-1288. If you're looking for a meal to match the historic ambiance of Old Town, this is a perfect choice. The interior and the menu both recall 18th-century living. $$

Seaport Inn, 6 King St, tel: (703) 549-2341. This historic inn, built in 1765, features river views, an elegant setting, and excellent seafood. $$

Arlington

Bardo Rodeo, 2000 Wilson Blvd, tel: (703) 527-9399. This huge, casual brewpub claims to be the largest brewery restaurant in the US. $

Cafe Dalat, 3143 Wilson Blvd, tel: (703) 276-0935. Cosmopolitan Arlington features many ethnic restaurants and the Little Saigon area leads the way. This is one of the best Vietnamese choices. $

Charlottesville

C&O Restaurant, 515 East Water St, tel: (804) 971-7044. This popular local spot features regional cuisine in both the casual downstairs dining room and the more formal space upstairs (jackets required). $–$$

Court Square Tavern, 5th and East Jefferson Sts., tel: (804) 296-6111. Authentic pub fare and a large selection of beers. $

Michie Tavern, Route 53, tel: (804) 977-1234. This historic inn features country cooking in a rustic atmosphere. $–$$

Chincoteague

Landmark Crab House, Landmark Plaza, tel: (804) 336-5552. The best spot for a wide variety of fresh seafood and great views of the bay. $–$$

Fredericksburg

The Smythe's Cottage and Tavern, 303 Fauquier St, tel: (540) 373-1645. This tavern, located in the historic district, offers Colonial and regional cooking at its Virginia finest. $

Hampton

Fisherman's Wharf, 14 Ivy Home Rd, tel: (804) 723-3113. This waterfront restaurant features some of the area's best seafood, including a huge seafood buffet. $$

Leesburg

Tuscarora Mill, 203 Harrison St SE, tel: (703) 771-9300. Located in an 1899 mill, this popular downtown restaurant offers American cuisine and a lengthy wine list in a rustic and casual atmosphere. $–$$

Lexington

The Palms, 101 West Nelson St, tel: (540) 463-7911. This casual restaurant is frequented by college students, professors, and lots of locals, thanks to interesting American cuisine and cold drinks. $

Luray

Parkhurst Restaurant, Route 1, tel: (540) 743-6009. This popular restaurant features international cuisine with many local touches, as well as an award-winning wine list. $–$$

Norfolk

Doumar's, 1900 Monticello Ave, tel: (804) 627-4163. The legendary local place for barbecue sandwiches and curbside service at the state's first drive-in restaurant. $

Philips Seafood Restaurant, 333 Waterside Dr., tel: (804) 627-6000. This waterfront seafood restaurant in the Waterside complex is a great place to enjoy succulent Chesapeake Bay seafood close to the source. $$

Ships Cabin, 4110 East Ocean View Ave, tel: (804) 362-2526. Overlooking the Chesapeake Bay, this is a great place for seafood in the Tidewater area. $$

Plantation Country

Indian Fields Tavern, Route 5, tel: (804) 829-5004. Try to plan your plantation drive around a lunch or dinner of regional specialties at this well-established Route 5 restaurant. $$

Petersburg

King's Barbeque, 3221 West Washington Rd, tel: (804) 732-5861. King's has been the king of barbecue for central Virginia (since 1946). $

Richmond

Joe's Inn, 205 North Shields Ave, tel: (804) 355-2282. One of the historic Fan District's many excellent restaurants, featuring a wide array of American and Italian specialties in a casual neighborhood atmosphere. $

Strawberry Street Cafe, 421 North Strawberry St, tel: (804) 353-6860. A Fan District favorite, with American fare and an unusual bathtub salad bar. $$

Tobacco Company Restaurant, 12th & Cary Sts, tel: (804) 782-9431. Located in the restored Shockoe Slip warehouse district, this large and popular downtown restaurant offers a wide array of American entrees. $$

Roanoke

The Library, 3117 Franklin Rd SW, tel: (540) 985-0811. One of Roanoke's all-time local favorites, with an elegant atmosphere and outstanding French and Continental cuisine. $$

Virginia Beach

Capt. George's Seafood Restaurant, 1956 Laskin Rd, tel: (804) 428-3494, or 2272 Old Pungo Ferry Rd, tel: (804) 721-3463. With two locations and a following with tourists and locals, Capt. George's is the king of seafood buffets in the Virginia Beach area. $$

Le Chambord, 324 North Great Neck Rd, tel: (804) 498-1234. The best French restaurant in the area. $$–$$$

The Lighthouse, 1st and Atlantic Ave, tel: (804) 428-7974. Located directly on pretty Rudee Inlet, this is a perfect place for a seafood buffet or one of their seafood specials. $$–$$$

Wakefield

The Virginia Diner, Route 460, tel: (804) 899-3106 or (800) 868-6887 (NUTS). This unusual restaurant, located between Richmond and Norfolk, is surely the state's peanut mecca. You can buy a load of Virginia peanuts here, but you can also enjoy some excellent southern cooking in a friendly atmosphere. $

Williamsburg

Chowning's Tavern, Duke of Gloucester St, tel: (804) 229-2141. Offering Colonial food and drink, this is one of several historic district taverns that features period food and atmosphere.

Other good choices nearby include **Christina Campbell's Tavern**, **Kings Arms Tavern**, and **Shields Tavern**. $$

The Trellis, Merchants Square, tel: (804) 229-8610. This award-winning restaurant and the owner/chef have been hosting Williamsburg guests for many years, offering unusual regional cuisine in a casual setting. $$–$$$

Winchester

Old Post Office Restaurant & Lounge, 200 North Braddock St, tel: (540) 722-9881. Located in Winchester's original 1910 post office, this downtown restaurant serves American fare in an historic setting. $–$$

Attractions

Places of Interest

Alexandria

Alexandria Archaeology, 105 North Union St, tel: (703) 838-4399. An active museum and laboratory.

Alexandria Black History Resource Center, 628 North Alfred St, tel: (703) 838-4356.

Carlyle House, 121 North Fairfax St, tel: (703) 549-2997. The 18th-century home of a wealthy landowner and merchant.

Christ Church, 118 North Washington St, tel: (703) 549-1450. The church, built in 1773, where Robert E. Lee, George Washington, and many others worshipped.

Gadsby's Tavern Museum, 134 North Royal St, tel: (703) 838-4242. George Washington drank and ate here.

The Lyceum, 201 South Washington St, tel: (703) 838-4994. The city's history museum.

Ramsey House Visitors Center, 221 King St, tel: (703) 838-4200. This helpful visitors center is located in an historic house.

Stabler Leadbetter Apothecary Museum, 105–107 South Fairfax St, tel: (703) 836-3713. This manufacturing apothecary operated from 1792 to 1933.

Torpedo Factory Art Center, 105 North Union St, tel: (703) 838-4565. A highly successful venue, located in an old torpedo munitions factory, where artists create, exhibit, and sell their work.

Arlington

Arlington National Cemetery, George Washington Memorial Pkwy, tel: (703) 692-0931. The nation's cemetery, including the Tomb of the Unknowns, Kennedy's grave, and Robert E. Lee's home, the Ramsey House.

Pentagon Tours, George Washington Memorial Pkwy, tel: (703) 695-1776. Tours of the huge US Armed Forces facility.

US Marine Corps War Memorial – Iwo Jima, George Washington Memorial Pkwy, tel: (703) 285-2598. Dedicated to all US Marines who have given their lives.

Appomattox

Appomattox County Historic Museum, Route 4, tel: (804) 352-7510. The county's historic museum located in a former jail.

Big Stone Gap

Harry W. Meador Jr Coal Museum, East Third St and Shawnee Ave, tel: (540) 523-4950. The town is known as the "Gateway to the Coalfields" and this museum depicts the lives and events of this coal region.

John Fox Jr Museum, 117 Shawnee Ave, tel: (540) 523-1235. The house of the author of *Trail of the Lonesome Pine*.

Southwest Virginia Museum, 10 West First St, tel: (540) 523-1322 or (800) VA-BYWAY. Exhibits covering the history of this interesting region.

Cape Charles

Cape Charles Historic District, tel: (804) 331-2304. This once-bustling seaport and railroad town is returning to its former glory.

Chesapeake Bay Bridge and Tunnel District, tel: (804) 624-3511. A 17.6-mile (28.3-km) engineering wonder.

Eastern Shore of Virginia National Wildlife Refuge, 5003 Hallet Circle, tel: (804) 331-2760. Hiking and wildlife tours.

Charlottesville

Ash Lawn-Highland, James Monroe Pkwy, tel: (804) 293-9539. President Monroe's mansion.

Montdomaine Cellars, Route 6, tel: (804) 971-8947. Popular award-winning winery.

Monticello, Route 53, tel: (804) 984-9822. Thomas Jefferson's estate.

Oakencroft Vineyard and Winery, Route 5, Barracks Rd, tel: (804) 296-4188. Award-winning winery.

The Rotunda, University of Virginia, tel: (804) 924-1019. Designed by Thomas Jefferson.

Chincoteague

Assateague National Seashore, Tom's Cove Visitor Center, tel: (804) 336-6577. Seashore hiking, biking, camping, programs, and much more.

Oyster & Maritime Museum, 7125 Maddox Blvd, tel: (804) 336-6117. Displays and exhibits concerning the oyster and other maritime history in the area.

Danville

Danville Museum of Fine Arts & History, 975 Main St, tel: (804) 793-5644. Regional history and art museum.

Duffield

Natural Tunnel State Park, tel: (540) 940-2674. A huge underground tunnel formed more than one million years ago from the dissolving of limestone and dolomitic bedrock by groundwater bearing carbonic acid.

Fredericksburg

James Monroe Law Office and Museum, 908 Charles St, tel: (540) 899-4559. The law office for the young lawyer, Monroe would eventually hold more high offices than any other US president.

Kenmore, 1201 Washington Ave, tel: (540) 373-3581. This was the elegant 18th-century plantation home of George Washington's only sister, Betty.

Mary Washington House, 1200 Charles St, tel: (540) 373-1569. Many of the belongings of George's mother remain, as well as a beautiful English garden in the back.

Mercer Apothecary Shop, 1020 Caroline St, tel: (540) 373-3362. Opened in 1771, this is one of the oldest apothecary shops in the nation and still has Dr. Mercer's medicine bottles, pills, and prescriptions.

Rising Sun Tavern, 1306 Caroline St, tel: (540) 371-1494. This was the social and political center of early life in Fredericksburg.

Galax

Galax Mountain Music Jamboree, tel: (540) 236-0668. Traditional mountain music and events.

Hampton

African-American Heritage Tour, 710 Settlers Landing Rd, tel: (804) 727-1102 or (800) 800-2202. Seven African-American sites on a self-guided tour.

Air Power Park, 413 West Mercury Blvd, tel: (804) 727-1163. A wide array of military aircraft, rockets, and missiles, great for the entire family.

Hampton Fleet, 710 Settlers Landing Rd, tel: (804) 727-1102 or (800) 244-1040 in Virginia. Harbor tours.

Virginia Air and Space Center and Hampton Roads History Center, 600 Settlers Landing Rd, tel: (804) 727-0800 or (800) 296-0800. Huge collection of spacecraft and aircraft.

Irvington

Historic Christ Church, Route 3, tel: (804) 438-6855. 1735 historic church.

Leesburg

Morven Park, Route 3, tel: (703) 777-2414. An elegant mansion, fox hunting and carriage museums, gardens, and more.

Oatlands, Route 2, tel: (703) 777-3174. This 1803 plantation features excellent tours and historic formal gardens.

Lexington

Virginia Military Institute, tel: (540) 464-7000. Founded in 1839, it is the oldest state-supported military college in the nation.

Washington and Lee University, tel: (540) 463-8400. Named for George Washington and Robert E. Lee.

Luray

Luray Caverns, Route 211, tel: (540) 743-6551. Large and popular caverns and tours.

Lynchburg

Lynchburg Museum, Old Court House, tel: (804) 847-1459. Regional history exhibits in a restored 1855 courthouse.

Middleburg

Meredyth Vineyards, Route 628, tel: (540) 687-6277. Tours and tastings.

Piedmont Vineyards & Winery, Route 626, tel: (540) 687-5528. Tours and tastings.

Swedenburg Estate Vineyard, Route 50 East, tel: (540) 687-5219. Tours and tastings.

Middletown

Wayside Theatre, 7835 Main St, tel: (540) 869-1776. Historic theatre venue and productions.

Mount Vernon

Mount Vernon, George Washington Memorial Pkwy, tel: (540) 780-2000. The home and burial places of George and Martha Washington.

Natural Bridge

Caverns of Natural Bridge, Route 11, tel: (540) 291-2121 or (800) 533-1410. Underground rock formations.

Natural Bridge, Route 11, tel: (540) 291-2121 or (800) 533-1410. This huge natural bridge is one of the natural wonders of the world.

Natural Bridge Wax Museum and Factory Tour, Route 11, tel: (540) 291-2426 or (800) 343-8843. A wide variety of wax figures and a factory tour that shows how it's done.

Natural Bridge Zoological Park, Route 11, tel: (540) 291-2420. Many animals to view and pet.

Newport News

Harbor Cruises at Waterman's Wharf, 917 Jefferson Ave, tel: (804) 245-1533. Hampton Roads harbor tours.

Mariners' Museum, 100 Museum Dr., tel: tel: (804) 596-2222. Wide variety of international marine history.

Virginia Living Museum, 524 J. Clyde Morris Blvd, tel: (804) 595-1900. Animals in their natural habitats.

War Memorial Museum of Virginia, 9285 Warwick Blvd, tel: (804) 247-8523, Newport News, 23607. Huge military history collection.

Norfolk

Carrie B. Harbor Tours, Waterside, tel: (804) 393-4735. Popular shipyard and harbor tours.

Chrysler Museum, 245 West Olney Rd, tel: (804) 664-6200. One of the region's top art museums.

Nauticus, 1 Waterside Dr., tel: (804) 664-1000. Hugely popular maritime center.

Norfolk Naval Base, tel: (804) 640-6300. The world's largest naval base, with tours available.

Virginia Zoological Park, 3500 Granby St, tel: (804) 441-2706. Large zoo, with more than 300 animals.

Northern Neck

George Washington's Birthplace National Monument, RR 1, Washington Birthplace, VA 22443, tel: (804) 224-1732. This Colonial farm was the site of Washington's birth.

Reedville Fishermen's Museum, Box 306, Reedville, VA 22539, tel: (804) 453-3430. A monument and museum to the fishermen of the area.

Tangier and Chesapeake Cruises, Route 1, Box 1332, Reedville, VA 22539, tel: (804) 453-2628. Cruises to Tangier Island.

Onancock

Hopkins & Bros. Store, 2 Market St, tel: (804) 787-4478. Still in operation, one of the oldest general goods stores in the region.

Kerr Place, 69 Market St, tel: (804) 787-8012. The Eastern Shore Historical Society's collection and exhibits.

Orange

James Madison Museum, 129 Caroline St, tel: (540) 672-1776. Museum dedicated to the 4th president.

Montpelier, Montpelier Station, VA 22957, tel: (540) 672-2728. House and archaeological dig tours.

Portsmouth

Children's Museum of Virginia, 221 High St, tel: (804) 393-8983. A modern children's museum.

Portsmouth Lightship Museum, London Slip, tel: (804) 393-8741. On a restored Coast Guard lightship.

Richmond

Agecroft Hall, 4305 Sulgrave Rd, tel: (804) 353-4241. A completely restored and relocated 15th-century English manor house.

Chesterfield Museum, Route 10, Chesterfield Courthouse, VA 23832, tel: (804) 748-1026. County history in an historic courthouse.

Edgar Allan Poe Museum, 1914 East Main St, tel: (804) 648-5523. Richmond's oldest house houses a huge collection of Poe material.

Federal Reserve Bank Money Museum, 7th and Byrd Sts, tel: (804) 697-8108. A regional bank museum detailing the history and making of US currency.

John Marshall House, 818 East Marshall St, tel: (804) 648-7998. Chief Justice John Marshall's house, built in 1790.

Lewis Ginter Botanical Garden, 1800 Lakeside Ave, tel: (804) 262-9887. Pretty year-round gardens and house.

Maggie Walker National Historical Site, 110 1/2 East Leigh St, tel: (804) 780-1380. Home of the African-American banker and leader.

Magnolia Grange, Route 10, Chesterfield Courthouse, VA 23832, tel: (804) 796-1479. Tours of an 1822 plantation home.

Maymont, 1700 Hampton St, Richmond, 23220, tel: (804) 358-1766. A huge Victorian estate, petting zoo, grounds, and gardens.

Paramount's Kings Dominion, I-95, tel: (804) 876-5000. An amusement park with more than 40 rides and dozens of attractions.

Richmond Children's Museum, 740 Navy Hill Dr., tel: (804) 788-4949. Exhibits and programs for the kids.

Science Museum of Virginia, 2500 West Broad St, tel: (804) 367-1013. More than 200 hands-on exhibits and programs, as well as the Ethyl UNIVERSE Theater featuring OMNIMAX films and a planetarium.

St John's Church, 2401 East Broad St, tel: (804) 648-5015. Tours and programs at the locations of Patrick Henry's famed "Liberty or Death" speech.

Tuckahoe Plantation, 12601 River Rd, tel: (804) 784-5736. Jefferson's boyhood home.

Valentine Court End & Wickham House, 1015 East Clay St, tel: (804) 649-0711. Richmond's city history museum.

Virginia Aviation Museum, Richmond International Airport, 5701 Huntsman Rd, tel: (804) 236-3622. A wide range of the state's aircraft.

Virginia Fire and Police Museum, 200 West Marshall St, tel: (804) 644-1849. One of the oldest firehouses in the US, housing the state's fire and police history.

Virginia Historical Society, 428 North Blvd, tel: (804) 358-4901. A huge offering of Virginia-oriented exhibits and programs.

Virginia Museum of Fine Arts, 2800 Grove Ave, tel: (804) 367-0844. One of the finest modern collections in the nation.

Roanoke

Center in the Square, One Market Square, tel: (540) 342-5700. Located in the historic downtown district, these renovated warehouses now house the Art Museum of Western Virginia, the Arts Council of the Blue Ridge, Mill Mountain Theatre, the Roanoke Valley History Museum, and the Science Museum of Western Virginia.

Mill Mountain Zoological Park, Mill Mountain, tel: (540) 343-3241. Many animals, exhibits, and programs.

Virginia Museum of Transportation, 303 Norfolk Ave SW, tel: (540) 342-5670. Dozens of trains, cars, trucks, exhibits, and much more.

Shenandoah County

Shenandoah Caverns, Route 11, tel: (540) 477-3115. An elevator leads down to many spectacular formations.

Staunton

Museum of American Frontier Culture, I-81, tel: (540) 332-7850. Reconstructed homes from the 17th, 18th, and 19th centuries that demonstrate life on the Virginia frontier.

Woodrow Wilson Birthplace and Museum, 18 North Coalter St, tel: (540) 885-0897. Exhibits and programs concerning President Wilson.

Tangier Island

Tangier and Chesapeake Cruises, Route 1, Box 1332, Reedville, VA 22539, tel: (804) 453-2628. Ferry service to and from Tangier Island.

Tangier Island Cruises, 1001 West Main St, Crisfeld, MD 21817, tel: (410) 968-2338. Ferry service to and from Tangier Island.

Tangier Mail & Freight Service, 16458 West Ridge Rd, Tangier, VA 23440, tel: (804) 891-2240. Ferry service to and from Tangier Island.

Virginia Beach

Association for Research and Enlightenment, 67th St and Atlantic Ave, tel: (804) 428-3588. Headquarters, school and museum concerning the work of psychic Edgar Cayce.

Discovery Cruise, 600 Laskin Rd, tel: (804) 422-2900. Inland waterway tour.

Life-Saving Museum of Virginia, 24th and Atlantic Ave, tel: (804) 422-1587. This former life-saving station now houses an interesting museum about shipwrecks and rescues.

Ocean Breeze Fun Park, 849 General Booth Blvd, tel: (804) 422-4444. A wide variety of amusement park activities for the entire family.

Old Cape Henry Lighthouse, Fort Story, tel: (804) 422-9421. This 1791 lighthouse is open from the spring until the fall.

Virginia Marine Science Museum, 717 General Booth Blvd, tel: (804) 437-4949. Huge aquariums, exhibits, and dolphin-watching trips.

Warrenton

Old Jail Museum, Courthouse Square, tel: (540) 347-1545. One of the oldest continuously used jails in Virginia.

Waynesboro

Moss Museum, 2150 Rosser Ave, tel: (703) 949-6473. Exhibits and sale of the work of artist P. Buckley Moss.

Williamsburg

Busch Gardens, One Busch Gardens Blvd, tel: (804) 253-3350. Theme park featuring amusement park rides and various European-themed villages.

Colonial Williamsburg, tel: (804) 220-7645 or (800) HISTORY. A restored 18th-century colony.

Winchester

Abram's Delight Museum, 1340 South Pleasant Valley Rd, tel: (540) 662-6519. Historic limestone house built in 1754.

George Washington's Office Museum, 32 West Cork St, tel: (540) 662-4412. The surveying office used by Washington in 1755.

Yorktown

Colonial National Historic Park, Colonial Pkwy, tel: (804) 898-3400. Self-guided tours and exhibits.

Watermen's Museum, 309 Water St, tel: (804) 887-2641. History and exhibits concerning local watermen.

Yorktown and the **Yorktown Battlefield**, Colonial National Historical Park, tel: (804) 898-3400. The site where independence was won.

Yorktown Victory Center, Route 238 and Colonial Pkwy, tel: (804) 253-4838. Modern exhibits and recreations describe the story of the American Revolution.

Civil War Sites

Historic Places

Civil War Sites are located throughout the state. Among the most interesting are the following:

Alexandria

Boyhood Home of Robert E. Lee, 607 Oronoco St, tel: (703) 548-8454. Furnished with period pieces, Lee lived here between the ages of 5 and 18.

Fort Ward Museum & Historic Site, 430 West Braddock Rd, tel: (703) 838-4848. A Civil War fort for the Union forces.

Lee-Fendall Museum, 614 Oronoco St, tel: (703) 548-1789. Lee's family home and garden.

Appomattox

Appomattox Court House National Historic Park, tel: (804) 352-8987. The site of Lee's surrender to Grant at the conclusion to the Civil War.

Fredericksburg

Chancellorsville Battlefield Visitor Center, Route 3, tel: (540) 786-2880. The battlefield site of Lee's greatest Civil War victory.

Fredericksburg Battlefield Visitor Center, 1013 Lafayette Blvd, tel: (540) 373-6122. Another interesting Civil War battle site, located along Sunken Road.

Hampton

Casemate Museum, Fort Monroe, tel: (804) 727-3391. Civil War exhibits.

Lexington

Stonewall Jackson House, 8 East Washington St, tel: (540) 463-2552. The house where Jackson lived before the Civil War.

Stonewall Jackson Memorial Cemetery, South Main St, tel: (540) 463-3777. Two Virginia governors, more than 100 Confederate soldiers, Jackson, and many of his family members are buried here.

Manassas

Manassas National Battlefield Park, 6511 Sudley Rd, tel: (540) 361-1339. The site of two major Civil War battles.

Middletown

Cedar Creek Battlefield Foundations Visitors Center and Book Shop, Route 11, tel: (540) 869-2064. Civil War battlefield site.

New Market

New Market Battlefield Historical Park, tel: (540) 740-3101. Major Civil War battlefield, with emphasis on the role of the VMI Corps of Cadets.

Northern Neck

Stratford Hall Plantation, Stratford, VA 22558, tel: (804) 493-8038. Robert E. Lee's birthplace.

Petersburg

Petersburg National Battlefield, Route Route 36, tel: (804) 732-3531. Tours concerning the 1864-65 siege of Petersburg during the Civil War.

Richmond

The Museum and White House of the Confederacy, 1201 East Clay St, Richmond, 23219, tel: (804) 649-1861. Huge Confederate collection and tours of the restored White House.

Richmond National Battlefield Park, 3215 East Broad St, tel: (804) 226-1981. Many Civil War battles took place around Richmond.

Winchester

Stonewall Jackson's Headquarters Museum, 415 North Braddock St, tel: (540) 667-3242. Served as Jackson's headquarters in 1861 and 1862.

KENTUCKY

Getting Acquainted

The Place

Known as: The Bluegrass State for the grass that covers much of the central region; the grass is not blue, but when it flowers in early spring, gives that appearance.

Origin of Name: *Kain-tuck-ee* is an Indian word which has been variously translated as the Shawnee's "head of a river;" or, an Iroquoian term meaning, "place of meadows," and the Wyandot's, "land of tomorrow."

Motto: "United We Stand, Divided We Fall."

Entered Union: 1792.

Population: 3.7 million.

Population Density: 93 people per sq. mile (36 people per sq. km).

Area: 40,395 sq. miles (104,622 sq. km).

Time Zones: Kentucky is split into two time zones: central and eastern.

Highest Point: Big Black Mountain, 4,145 ft (1,275 meters).

Climate: A temperate climate with four distinct seasons. Mean annual temperatures range from 54°F (12°C) in the northeast to 58°F (15°C) in the southwest; Annual precipitation averages 48 inches (122 cm) including an average snowfall of 14 inches (36 cm). Spring and summer are the wettest seasons. January temperatures range between 23/40°F (4/5°C); July's, 66/86°F (19/30°C).

Economy: The manufacture of automobile, truck and consumer appliances, and oil refining top the list, followed by the horse and coal industries and agriculture (primarily tobacco cultivation).

Local Government: 120 counties, each with a local seat of government.

Annual Visitors: over 17.4 million.

Capital: Frankfort.

Local Dialing Codes: (606) covers the state eastward from Covington and Lexington south, (502) covers the remainder.

Famous Figures: Muhammad Ali, who as Cassius Clay, won the Heavyweight boxing Olympic gold medal in 1960; Rosemary Clooney, singer; Jefferson Davis, President of the Confederacy; D. W. Griffith, film director; John "Casey" Jones, railroad engineer immortalized in song; Abraham Lincoln, 16th US president; Patricia Neal, actress; Diane Sawyer, television broadcaster; Adlai Stevenson, two-time US presidential candidate and ambassador to the United Nations; Frederick Moore Vinson, US Supreme Court chief justice; Robert Penn Warren, writer, and only winner of the Pulitzer prize for poetry and for prose; Dr Whitney M. Young, civil rights leader.

Useful Addresses

State Office

Kentucky Department of Tourism Development, Capital Plaza Tower, 500 Mero St, Frankfort, 40601-1968, tel: (502) 564-4930 or (800) 225-TRIP, fax: (502) 564-5695.

Local Offices

BOWLING GREEN

Bowling Green-Warren County Tourist & Convention Commission, tel: (502) 782-0800 or (800) 326-7465, fax: (502) 782-0800.

LEXINGTON

Greater Lexington Convention & Visitors Bureau, tel: (606) 233-1221, fax: (606) 254-4555.

LOUISVILLE

Louisville and Jefferson County Convention & Visitors Bureau, tel: (502) 584-2121 or (800) 633-3384 (KY), (800) 626-5646 (US); fax: (502) 584-6697.

Where to Stay

Accommodation

The **Bed & Breakfast Association of Kentucky** (tel: 800/292-2632) lists over 200 B&Bs across the state. They do not make reservations, but will send brochures.

Allensville

The Pepper Place (B&B), Hwy 102, PO Box 95, 42204. This blue clapboad house has three rooms; built around 1864. Guests may also find themselves spectators at a wedding reception as the house is a popular place for local festivities. $$

Auburn

Auburn Guest House (B&B), 421 West Main St, 42206, tel: (502) 542-6019 (call after 3pm). This five-room B&B is famous for the southern breakfasts it offers. The colonial style mansion is within walking distance of antique shops in town. $$

Augusta

The Lamplighter Inn, 103 West Second St, 41002, tel: (606) 756-2603. This charming inn has nine bedrooms with private facilities. Evening meals served. $$$

Riverside House 1860 (B&B), tel: (606) 756-2458. Located on the Ohio River, this B&B is a perfectly restored Victorian period piece. Each of the bedrooms is individually decorated. $$$

Bardstown

Jailer's Inn (B&B), 111 West Stephen Foster Ave, 40004, tel: (502) 348-5551. Four of the rooms in the city's former jail have been decorated in antiques, the fifth re-creates a cell. Located in the city center. Open March–December. $$$

1790 House (B&B), 110 East Broadway, 40004, tel: (502) 348-7072. A charming residence in the heart of the historic district. $$$

Sherwood Inn, 138 South Main St, New Haven 40051, tel: (502) 549-3386. Located 10 miles (16 km) south of Bardstown, the inn has been operated by the same family since 1875. Full service restaurant. $$

Berea

Boone Tavern Hotel, Main and Prospect Sts, Berea College, 40404, tel: (606) 986-9358 or (800) 366-9358. Founded in 1909 as a guest house for the college, the hotel has 57 rooms. Local restrictions include a ban on alcohol, cigarettes and tipping. There is a dress code for dinner. $$

Big South Fork National Recreational Area

Marcum-Porter House (B&B), Hwy 1561, PO Box 369, Stearns, 42647, tel: (606) 376-2242. Charming early 20th-century house in scenic beauty site. Closed November–March. $$

Brandenburg

Doe Run Inn, 500 Coleman Lane, 40108, tel: (502) 422-2042. Located 38 miles (61 km) southwest of Louisville, the inn was originally built as a fieldstone mill in 1816. $$

Carrollton

Carrollton Inn, 218 Main St, 41008, tel: (502) 732-6905. Built in 1812, the fully restored inn has 10 double bedrooms. The restaurant's menu is filled with regional specialties. $$

Covington

Ames Shinkle Townhouse (B&B), 215 Gerrard St, 41001, tel: (606) 431-2118. There are seven double rooms in this 1850s townhouse and adjacent carriage house in the Riverside Historic District. $$$

Sanford House (B&B), 1026 Russell St, 41001, tel: (606) 291-9133. Just a 5-minute walk from Covington Landing, it was built in 1820 and completely remodeled in 1990. $$$

Weller Haus (B&B), 319 Popular St, Bellevue 41073, tel: (606) 431-6829. Located in an 1880s Victorian house, just 5 minutes from Covington's city center. Five individually decorated rooms. $$$

Cumberland Falls State Park

Dupont Lodge, 7351 Hwy 90, Corbin 40701-8814, tel: (606) 528-4121 or (800) 325-0063. This older, traditional hotel has long been a favorite with people visiting Cumberland Falls and the Big South Fork Recreation Area. Good country cooking. $$$

Lake Cumberland State Resort, PO Box 380, Jamestown, 42629, tel: (502) 343-3111 or (800) 325-1709. Set on the edge of the lake, the resort offers excellent facilities for the sportsman and nature lover. 77 rooms and three suites in the lodge and 30 cottages with fully equipped kitchens. $$–$$$

Cumberland Lake Area

Annie's of Lake Cumberland, 908 Waitsboro Rd, PO Box 246, Bronston, 42518, tel: (606) 561-0066. Walk to the lake to swim or fish, or enjoy doing nothing in the relaxed country atmosphere. $$

Danville

The Empty Nest (B&B), 111 East Lexington Ave, tel: (606) 236-3339. In the historic district and set amid dogwood and magnolia trees, each bedroom has private facilities. $$

The Cottage (B&B), 2826 Lexington Rd, tel: (606) 236-9642. For a taste of rural life, spend a night at this old farmhouse. A 2-mile (3-km) drive from Danville. $$$

Twin Hollies (B&B), 406 Maple Ave, 40422, tel: (606) 236-8954. The landmark house is on Danville's walking tour. $$$

Elizabethtown

The Olde Bethlehem Academy Inn, 7051 St John Rd, 42701, tel: (502) 862-9003 or (800) 662-5670. A former Catholic girls' school which was renowned for the education it offered young ladies in the 19th century. Full restaurant service. $$

Harrodsburg

Beaumont Inn, 638 Beaumont Dr., 40330, tel: (606) 734-3381. Nationally recognized as one of the South's finest inns and restaurants. Formerly a girls' college, the buildings date to 1845. 35 rooms; open mid-March to mid-December. $$$

Canaan Land Farm (B&B), 4355 Lexington Rd, 40330, tel: (606) 734-3984. Late 1700s farmhouse exudes charm. Near Shakertown. $$$

The Jailhouse (B&B), 320 South Chiles St, 40330, tel: (606) 734-7012. Circa-1830s jail has been delightfully renovated. Town sightseeing within walking distance. $$

Shaker Village, Pleasant Hill, 3500 Lexington Rd, 40330, tel: (606) 734-5411. 80 rooms are spread throughout the Pleasant Hill complex in the restored buildings. Each one is impeccably furnished with reproduction Shaker furniture. Dine at the Trustees' Inn. Reservations always a must. $$–$$$$

Hindman

Quilt Maker Inn, Main St, PO Box 973, 41822, tel: (606) 785-5622 or (606) 785-1902. Mountain crafts and artifacts adorn the 15 traditionally decorated rooms. $

Lexington

Cherry Knoll Farm (B&B), 3975 Lemon Mill Rd, 40511. The 1855-built Greek Revival home is set amid horse country. $$

French Quarter Suites, 2601 Richmond Rd, 40508, tel: (606) 268-0600 or (800) 262-3774. For luxury married to the charm of New Orleans-inspired architecture, stay here. 155 rooms. $$$–$$$$

Gratz Park Inn, 120 West Second St, 40501, tel: (606) 231-1777 or (800) 227-4362. This small, elegant downtown hotel was built in 1916, but the interior was gutted in the late 1980s and impeccably restored. 38 rooms, six suites. $$$–$$$$

Homewood Farm (B&B), 5301 Bethel Rd, 40511, tel: (606) 255-2814. For those who want the peace of a country setting with the joys of all modern conveniences. $$–$$$

Springs Inn, 2020 Harrodsburg Rd, 40516, tel: (606) 277-5751 or (800) 354-9503. One of the city's traditional hotels, it truly exudes Southern charm. The dining room is noted for its southern breakfasts; the staff for excellent service. $$

Louisville

The Brown Hotel, Fourth and Broadway, 40202, tel: (502) 583-1234 or (800) 866-ROOM. A large downtown hotel, recently restored to its 1920s English country home glamour. One of Louisville's best. $$$$

Inn at the Park (B&B), 1332 South Fourth St, 40203. Built in 1886 for a founder of the L&N railroad, the Richardsonian Romanesque building has been splendidly restored. $$–$$$

Old Louisville Inn (B&B), 1359 South Third St, 40208, tel: (502) 635-1574. Built as a private residence in 1901, the rooms are individually decorated in period furniture. Great downtown location. $$–$$$$

Seelbach Hotel, 500 Fourth Ave, 40202, tel: (502) 585-3200 or (800) 333-3399. Another *grande dame* rescued from the depths of dinginess. The 332 rooms and public spaces have been restored to their former 1905 opulence. $$$$

Middlesborough

The Ridge Runner (B&B), 208 Arthur Heights, 40965, tel: (606) 248-4299. The 1890s-built Victorian house sits on a ridge overlooking the Cumberland Mountains. $$

Midway

Holly Hill Inn, North Winter St, 40347, tel: (606) 846-4732. Built in 1830, this Greek-Revival mansion was recently restored to its original glory. The rooms are individually decorated and the kitchen is excellent. Reservations for non-guests are a must. $$

Murray

The Diuguid House (B&B), 603 Main St, 42071, tel: (502) 753-5470. This cosy, Victorian house is listed on the National Register of Historic Homes. $

Owensboro

WeatherBerry (BB), 2731 West Second St, 42301, tel: (502) 684-US 60. This 1840s Greek-Revival house is named after the family who owned it for over 100 years, the Berrys, and for its previous tenant, the US Weather Service. Countryside setting. $$

Perryville

Elmwood Inn (B&B), 205 East Fourth St, 40468, tel: (606) 332-2400. This beautifully decorated Greek-Revival building was a hospital during the Civil War. $$$

Russellville

The Washington House (B&B), 283 West Ninth St, 42276, tel: (502) 726-7608 or (502) 726-3093. George may not have slept here, but his third cousin, John Whitting Washington, did, building this Federal-style house in 1824. $$

Sandy Hook

Charlene's Country Inn (B&B), Hwy 7 & 32, HC 75, Box 265, Sandy Hook 41171, tel: (606) 738-6674 or (606) 738-5712. Situated in the Appalachian foothills near four scenic recreation areas. $$$

Simpsonsville

Old Stone Inn, Route 60 East, 40347, tel: (502) 722-8882. The fieldstone building was built in 1820 to serve as a coaching inn. For years the local landmark was known primarily for its food. New owners added four bedrooms with private facilities. $$

Shelbyville

The Marcardin Inn (B&B), 115 Old Mount Eden Rd, 40065, tel: (502) 633-7759. Five rooms, each individually furnished in a beautifully restored white-frame Victorian house. Full service breakfast; evening beverages and snacks included in cost. $$$

The Wallace House (B&B), 613 Washington St, 40065, tel: (502) 633-2006. Situated adjacent to historic Science Hill Inn, the bright yellow building was constructed in the 1830s. $$

Springfield

Glenmar Plantation (B&B), 2444 Valley Hill Rd, 40069, tel: (606) 284-7791. Imposing is the word for this elegant 1785-built brick mansion. Evening meals served. $$$–$$$$

Maple Hill Manor (B&B), 2941 Perryville Rd, 40069, tel: (606) 336-3075. This Greek-Revival antebellum home is as beautiful on the inside as its outward appearance suggests. One of the most striking residences in the vicinity, it offers peace and serenity. $$$

Versailles

Shepherd Place (B&B), 31 Heritage Rd, 40383, tel: (606) 873-7843. An unusual bonus of staying here is the ability to admire Sylvia's pet sheep and then order a custom-designed sweater made from their wool. The 1820-renovated Federal house sits in the middle of 5 acres (2 hectares). $$

Sills Inn (B&B), 270 Montgomery Ave, 40383, tel: (606) 873-4478 or (800) 526-9801. From the exterior to the perfectly appointed rooms, this 1911 Victorian frame house is a perfect period piece. $$–$$$

State Park Resorts

Kentucky has 15 resort state parks scattered through it from the mountainous east to the Land Between the Lakes. All have a lodge with dining room and most offer cottages for family groups. Marina facilities, tennis, pools, golf, riding and hiking are among the available sports facilities. Most are open all year, rates are very reasonable and reservations are a must. For details, tel: (800) 255-PARK or (502) 564-2172. Or, write to: **Kentucky Department of Parks**, 500 Mero St, 11th Floor, Frankfort, 40601-1974.

Eating Out

Where to Eat

Anchorage

The Train Station, 1500 Evergreen Rd, tel: (502) 245-7121. A bright and breezy place which is an easy drive from the center of Louisville. $$$

Bardstown

The Bardstonian, 521 North Third St, tel: (502) 349-1404. Dine in a pre-Civil War home turned into an elegant restaurant. $$

Nathan's Cafe Americana, 885 Pennsylvania Ave, tel: (502) 348-3946. An imaginative decor and menu. $$

Old Talbott Tavern, 107 West Stephen Foster Ave and **McLean House (B&B)**, Court Square, 40004, tel: (502) 348-3494 for reservations at both. Built in 1779, the Tavern still retains its Colonial air. Around the corner, McLean House has seven individually decorated rooms. Meals: $$. B&B: $$–$$$

Bowling Green

Parakeet Cafe, 951 Chestnut St, tel: (502) 781-1538. A delightful restaurant in a refurbished blacksmith shop. Pasta dishes a specialty. $$

440 Main Restaurant, 440 East Main St, tel: (502) 793-0450. Dine in a restored historic building overlooking Fountain Square. $$

Covington

Dee Felice Cafe, 529 Main St, tel: (606) 261-2365. Owned by the jazz musician of the same name, musicians entertain diners on the weekend. The Raw Seafood Bar is a specialty. $$$

The Mike Fink, on the river at the foot of Greenup St, tel: (606) 261-4212. Dine on a converted riverboat and watch the sun set behind Cincinnati's skyline. Seafood a specialty. $$$

Danville

Sweet Difference, 132 Church St, tel: (606) 236-9847. This is like walking into a garden. Lunch and Friday evenings only. $

The Tea Leaf, 230 West Broadway, tel: (606) 236-7456. Situated in a renovated church and antique mall. Open for lunch and tea only. $

Frankfort

Bullfrog's, 243 West Broadway, tel: (502) 875-0090. Charcoal-grilled food with an open kitchen. Overlooks the Old State Capitol. $$

Gabriel's at the Holiday Inn, Capitol Plaza, 405 Wilkinson Blvd, tel: (502) 227-5100. Pols gather here to enjoy the Kentucky Bourbon Ribs. $$

Jim's Seafood, 950 Wilkinson Blvd, tel: (502) 223-7448. Outside seating overlooking the Kentucky River. $$

Glendale

The Whistle Stop, 216 East Main, tel: (502) 369-8586. Delightful restaurant in a turn-of-the century town. $$

The Depot, 200 Main St, tel: (502) 369-6000. An old train station has been turned into a museum, shop area and restaurant. $$

Grand Rivers

Patti's 1880 Settlement, 1793 J.H. O'Bryan Ave, tel: (502) 362-8844. A recreated 1880s village of shops, historic sites and restaurants. Reservations for the restaurants advised. $$

Hopkinsville

Bartholomew's, 914 South Main St, tel: (502) 886-5768. The open, airy restaurant is in an 1890s building. Fresh ingredients and unusual food combinations. $$

Lexington

à la Lucie, 159 North Limestone, tel: (606) 252-5277. One of the best restaurants in the downtown area, it conveys the feel of a bistro in Paris. Reservations a must. $$$

Billy's Bar B-Q, 101 Cochran Rd. This was the first Lexington-area place to serve western Kentucky-style hickory pit barbecue, and to many residents, still the best. $$

Buffalo & Dad's, 805 North Broadway, tel: (606) 252-9325. More tavern than restaurant, the menu is diverse, ranging from fried bologna sandwiches to blackened swordfish. Gathering place for local jocks; much fun. $$

Campbell House, 1375 Harrodsburg Rd, tel: (606) 255-4281. The doyen of Lexington restaurants serves continental cuisine as well as some regional specialties. $$$

deSha's, 101 North Broadway, tel: (606) 259-3771. The restaurant occupies one corner of Victorian Square and it takes wonderful advantage of the building's architecture. House specialties include cornbread with honey butter which is served with all dinners. Reservations a must; easiest time (and the quietest) to get a table is while the University of Kentucky basketball team is playing. $$$

Dudley's, 380 South Mill St, tel: (606) 252-1010. When the weather is favorable, the patio of this restaurant is the place to eat. Carved from part of the historic Dudley School, it offers a varied menu. Reservations advised. $$$

Merrick Inn, 3380 Tates Creek Rd, tel: (606) 269-5417. Elegance is the decorating by-word in the Colonial-inn atmosphere; excellent food is the kitchen's contribution. Regional and continental cuisines. Reservations a must. $$$

Louisville

Bobby J's, 3220 Frankfort Ave (502) 899-7142. The art work is eclectic and the mix of cuisines – American south, Caribbean and Indonesian – is equally diverse. But it works. $$

Captain's Quarters, 5700 Captain's Quarter Rd, tel: (502) 228-1651. On the river with a choice of casual, outdoor dining, or dress-up and have a good-time evenings. $$–$$$$

Deitrich's, 2862 Frankfort Ave, tel: (502) 879-6076. The place for movie buffs who enjoy excellent food. The restaurant is in a converted movie theater and the open kitchen is in full view: it's where the screen used to be. $$$$

English Grill, Brown Hotel, Fourth and Broadway (502) 583-1234. Like having dinner in an English country restaurant. One of the best restaurants in the city. $$$$

Jay's Cafeteria, 1812 West Muhammad Ali Blvd (502) 583-2634. The best soul food in town. Only one complaint: it's only open Monday to Thursday. $

Le Relais, Bowman Field, tel: (502) 451-9020. Jackets are required inside this glorious art deco restaurant. Fortunately, the quality of the food matches the decor. Reservations recommended. $$$$

Lilly's, 1477 Bardstown Rd, tel: (502) 451-0447. It is owned by one of Louisville's best-known chefs. The food lives up to Kathy Cary's reputation. $$$$

Lynn's Paradise Kitchen, 894 Barret Ave, tel: (502) 583-3447. Contemporary American cuisine in a kitsch-filled setting. Unusually, it's also open for breakfast everyday except Monday, as well as for lunch and dinner. $$

Shariat's, 2901 Brownsboro Rd, tel: (502) 899-7878. Vegetarians who want to dine elegantly will enjoy this restaurant. $$$$

Vincenzo's, 150 South Fifth St (502) 580-1350. Whether it's a quick meal before the theater (it's near the Kentucky Center for the Performing Arts), or a leisurely dinner, this is probably Louisville's finest Italian restaurant. Reservations a must; so are jackets and ties for men. $$$$

Mayfield

The Happy House, 236 North Eighth St, tel: (502) 247-5743. Originally the home of the city's richest man, each of the rooms has been decorated to make diners "happy." Regional dishes a specialty. $$

Owensboro

Moonlite Bar-B-Que, 2840 West Parrish Ave, tel: (502) 684-8143. In a city which bills itself as the Bar-B-Q capital of the world, aficionados consider this place the best of the best. $

Barney's Callas Grill, 420 Frederica St, tel: (502) 683-2363. The art deco interior and the 1940s porcelain facade in the 1920s landmark building are intact; but it's the "real" food that draws the crowds. Lunch only. $

Paducah

Cynthia's, 127 Market House Square, tel: (502) 443-3319. In the heart of the downtown historic district, three blocks from the Ohio River. $$

The Ninth Street House, 323 Ninth St, tel: (502) 442-9019. Classic Southern cooking is the restaurant's pride. The Victorian house has been restored and furnished with period antiques. $$

C.C. Cohen, 101 South Second St, tel: (502) 442-6391. The site was adapted from a former department store. Unusual drinks and "theatrical" coffees are a specialty of this local landmark. $$

Paris

Amelia Field's Country Inn, 617 Cynthiana Rd, tel: (606) 987-5778. Situated in a pretty country house, the menu is redolent with the smells of southern France and Provence. Limited seating. Reservations a must. $$$$

Shelbyville

The Bistro, 535 Main St, tel: (502) 633-4147. Regional specialties; good food; excellent service. $–$$

Science Hill Inn, 525 Washington St, tel: (502) 633-2825. Situated in the former dining room of a girls' school which was founded in 1825. Antebellum elegance. $$

Washington

Broderick's Tavern, Main St, tel: (606) 759-7934. Serving good "country cooking." $$

Drinking Laws

Kentucky allows cities and counties the right to pass local ordinances concerning liquor sales and consumption. Consequently, the state is a patchwork of laws which can be confusing to the tourist who may enjoy a cocktail in one city, but finds it impossible to have the same refreshment a short distance, but a county line, away. Some hotels and restaurants allow diners to "brown bag" it, bringing their own booze and discreetly serving themselves. (Sometimes a modest "corkage" or "ice" fee is charged.) In other places, nothing alcoholic is allowed in public view. If a tipple before (or with) meals is desired, learn which Kentucky counties fall into which category. (Most "wet" counties advertise that fact with signs indicating a last chance to "stock up" before crossing the county line.) *For a list of distilleries, see "Attractions."*

Attractions

Places of Interest

Ashland

The Kentucky Highlands Museum, 1620 Winchester St, tel: (606) 329-8888.

Paramount Arts Center, 1300 Winchester Ave, tel: (606) 324-3175. Free guided tours.

Bardstown

See Bardstown's historic sites by **walking tour** or **tourmobile** (June–August 9.30am & 1.30pm). Horse-drawn carriage rides in the evening May–October, tel: (502) 348-0331. Both start at the **Visitor Center** at 107 East Stephen Foster, tel: (800) 638-4877.

America's Miniature Soldier Museum, 804 North Third St, tel: (502) 348-4879. Over 10,000 toy soldiers from all over the world on display.

The Boll Cottage, 213 Est Stephen Foster Ave, tel: (502) 348-8210. Hundreds of dolls on display.

Kentucky Railway Museum, Bluegrass Pkwy exit 10 or 1-65 exit 105, tel: (800) 272-0152. Twelve miles (19 km) south of Bardstown via US 31E near New Haven. It also offers train rides to Boston. Depot open 1 hour prior to boarding. No restrooms on train.

My Old Kentucky Dinner Train, 602 North Third, tel: (502) 348-7300. Enjoy an elegant four-course meal aboard vintage 1940s railroad cars.

My Old Kentucky Home State Park, on US 150, tel: (502) 348-3502. Known throughout the world because of the song written by Stephen Foster.

Spalding Hall: The **Oscar Getz Museum of Whiskey History**, 114 North Fifth, tel: (502) 348-2999. Displays include an authentic moonshine still.

"The Stephen Foster Story", My Old Kentucky Home State Park Amphitheater, tel: (800) 626-1563. Outdoor musical featuring more than 50 Foster songs, colorful period costumes and lively choreography.

Wickland, US 62, a short drive east of Court Square, tel: (502) 348-5428. Completed in 1817 and the home of three governors, this mansion is one of the finest examples of Georgian architecture in the country.

Big South Fork Area

Stearns Museum, off US 27 downtown, tel: (606) 376-5730. Contains lumber and mining clothes, and equipment highlighting the area's history. A country store room contains the original post office.

Big South Fork Scenic Railway, US 27 to KY 92, tel: (800) GO-ALONG. The 11-mile (18-km), narrated open-air excursion follows the original coal train route through the gorge, stopping at the **Blue Heron Mining Community**. Accessible to wheelchairs.

Bowling Green

GM Corvette Plant, Off 1-65 exit 28, tel: (502) 745-8419. See the step-by-step production of the famous Corvette sports car. Tours are subject to cancellation due to production schedules and model changes. No cameras allowed.

Kentucky Museum, Kentucky St, Western Kentucky University, tel: (502) 745-2592. Successfully preserves Kentucky's cultural heritage with a collection of photographs, manuscripts and other artifacts.

National Corvette Museum, 350 Corvette Dr., tel: (502) 781-7973, fax: (502) 781-5286. Offers a look at vintage Corvettes and memorabilia.

Riverview – The Hobson House, 1100 West Main, tel: (502) 843-5565. Elegant, 1872 Italianate home recreates Victorian family life from 1860 to 1890.

Carrollton

Masterson House, US-42 east, Highland Ave, tel: (800) 325-4290. Built in 1790. Free guided tours. Stop by the **Markland Locks & Dam** (US-42, tel: 606/567-7661) near Warsaw to watch river traffic on the Ohio. Observation deck, picnic area.

Cumberland Falls

See the falls close up on the **Cumberland Falls Rainbow Mist Ride**, tel: (800) 541-RAFT. Rafts leave every hour from the state park.

Danville

The McDowell House & Apothecary Shop, 125 South Second, tel: (606) 236-2804. This belonged to Dr Ephraim McDowell who performed the first successful removal of an ovarian tumor in 1809. Guided tours.

Isaac Shelby Cemetery State Historic Site, off US 127, tel: (606) 236-5089. Situated 5 miles (8 km) south of Danville, this is the burial place of Kentucky's first governor.

William Whitley House State Historic Site, On US 150 between Stanford and Crab Orchard, tel: (606) 355-2881. This late 1780s home was used as a refuge by settlers on Kentucky's frontier.

Elizabethtown

Schmidt's Museum of Coca-Cola Memorabilia, on US-31W at 1201 North Dixie Hwy, tel: (502) 737-4000. In **Freeman Lake Park** is the **Lindoln Heritage House**, the **Sarah Bush Johnston Lincoln Memorial** and a restored **One-Room School House**, first opened in 1892. Tel: (800) 437-0092.

Emma Reno Connor's Black History Gallery, off US 31W at 602 Hawkins, tel: (502) 769-5204. Features pictures, articles, biographies, magazine and newspaper prints.

Fort Knox

Patton Museum of Cavalry & Armor, Fayette Ave near the Chaffe Ave entrance, tel: (502) 624-3812.

Frankfort

Fish & Wildlife Game Farm, 3 miles (5 km) west on US 60, tel: (502) 564-5448. The 150-acre (60-hectare) game farm features native wildlife such as buffalo, bobcats, black bears, cougars, coyotes, otters and deer. Also two fishing lakes (license required).

Frankfort Cemetery, 215 East Main, tel: (502) 227-2403. The grave sites of Daniel and Rebecca Boone.

Frank Lloyd Wright's Zeigler House, 509 Shelby St, tel: (502) 227-7164. The only Frank Lloyd Wright building in Kentucky.

Governor's Mansion, East end of State Capitol, tel: (502) 564-3000. The official governor's residence was modeled after the Petit Trianon, Marie Antionette's summer villa. Free guided tours.

Kentucky History Museum, Broadway at Saint Clair Mall, tel: (502) 564-3016. This museum depicts Kentucky's political, social and economic history.

Kentucky Vietnam Veterans Memorial, Coffee Treet Rd in front of Libraries & Archives, tel: (502) 875-8687. The granite plaza contains 1,093 names.

Old Governor's Mansion, 420 High St, tel: (502) 564-3000. Now the official residence of the lieutenant governor. Free guided tours.

Old State Capitol, Broadway at Saint Clair Mall, tel: (502) 564-3016. Free guided tours feature the unique self-supporting stone circular stairway held together by precision and pressure.

Rebecca-Ruth Candies, 112 East Second St, tel: (502) 223-7475. Where the famous Kentucky Colonel 100-proof bourbon candy is made. Free guided tours.

State Capitol, Capital Ave, tel: (502) 564-3000. Houses the First Lady Doll Collection. Outside is the giant Floral Clock.

Georgetown

Toyota Manufacturing Plant, 1-75 exit 126, tel: (502) 868-3027. Free tours via motorized tram ride. Reservations required; no children under 8.

Great River Road Area

Wickliffe Mounds, north of US 51/60/62 at the confluence of the Ohio and Mississippi rivers, tel: (502) 335-3681.

Warren Thomas Museum, Moulton St, tel: (502) 236-2553. The history of the local African-American community is preserved here.

Harrodsburg

The Gathering Place, across from Old Fort Harrod, tel: (606) 734-4189.

Old Fort Harrod State Park, US 127, tel: (606) 734-3314. The park also includes a pioneer cemetery, the cabin believed to be the one where Abraham Lincoln's parents were married, and the 1830 Mansion Museum with Indian and Civil War artifacts.

Shakertown at Pleasant Hill, US 68, tel: (606) 734-5411. Site of the largest Shaker community in Kentucky. 14 buildings open; many contain authentic Shaker furniture. Craftpeople demonstrate Shaker crafts; costumed docents explain the lifestyle. Dine at the Trustees Inn; B&B rooms available.

The Legend of Daniel Boone, tel: (606) 734-3346. Outdoor drama recreates the comedy, romance, danger and adventure of the Kentucky frontier.

Hodgenville

Abraham Lincoln Birthplace National Historic Site, 3 miles (5 km) south of town on US 31E, tel: (502) 358-3874. Features an audiovisual presentation on Lincoln's years in Kentucky.

Lincoln's Boyhood Home, 6 miles (10 km) east of town on US 31E, tel: (502) 549-3741. Guided tours, museum and picnic area.

Lincoln Museum, 66 Lincoln Square, tel: (502) 358-3163. Situated in downtown Hodgenville, this museum features 12 scenes of importance in his life and our nation's history.

Hopkinsville

Trail of Tears Commemorative Park, US-41 North/Pembroke Rd, tel: (502) 886-8033. In 1838, this was a Cherokee campground during the tribe's forced march to Oklahoma. Today, there are statues at the gravesites of two Cherokee chiefs who died here, an information wall and a 151-year old log cabin with displays of Cherokee culture. Also hiking trails and picnic area.

Don F. Pratt Museum, Wickham Hall, 26th and Tennessee Sts, tel: (502) 798-3215. Highlights the 101st Airborne "Screaming Eagles" Division. Outdoor exhibits include C-119 and C-47 aircraft and helicopters.

Jefferson Davis Monument State Historic Site, 10 miles (16 km) east of Hopkinsville on US 68, tel: (502) 886-1765. Ride to the top of the 351-ft (107-meter) memorial. Picnic area, playground.

Land Between The Lakes

Kentucky Lake and Lake Barkley, connected by a canal, together form one of the largest manmade bodies of water in the US. Featured here are the **Golden Pond Visitor Center** and **Planetarium, Homeplace-1850** as well as a **Nature Center**. For information write to: Land Between The Lakes, 100 Van Morgan Dr., Golden Pond, KY 42211-9001, or telephone (502) 924-5602.

Lexington

American Saddle Horse Museum, 4093 Iron Works Pike, 1-75 exit 120, tel: (606) 259-2746. Situated at the Kentucky Horse Park, this museum features the only breed of horse which originated in Kentucky.

Ashland, Henry Clay's Estate, Richmond Rd at Sycamore, tel: (606) 266-8581. House surrounded by gardens on 20 wooded acres (8 hectares).

Horse Farm Tours, tel: (800) 848-1224. No visit to the Bluegrass State would be complete without seeing the horse farms. Call for details.

Kentucky Horse Center, 3380 Paris Pike, tel: (606) 293-1853. Take a guided tour of a thoroughbred training complex.

Mary Todd Lincoln House, 578 West Main, tel: (606) 233-9999. The girlhood home of Abraham Lincoln's wife features personal articles of the Lincoln-Todd families.

Star of Lexington, 1-75 exit 99, tel: (606) 263-STAR. Riverboat cruises through beautiful Kentucky river palisades. Luncheon, dinner, sightseeing and moonlight cruises.

Louisville

Actors Theatre, 316 West Main, tel: (502) 585-1210. This Tony Award-winning company is recognized internationally for the Humana Festival of New American Plays.

American Printing House for the Blind, 1839 Frankfort Ave, tel: (502) 895-2405. A totally different way of publishing. Tour the oldest national non-profit agency for the visually impaired in the US.

Belle of Louisville, Fourth and River Rd, tel: (502) 625-BELL. Cruise the Ohio River on one of the last authentic sternwheelers in the country.

Courier-Journal Newspaper, 525 West Broadway, tel: (800) 765-4011 x4545. Free guided tours of the newsroom, composing room and press room include a slide show on the newspaper's history.

Ford Kentucky Truck Plant, 3001 Chamberlain Lane, tel: (502) 429-2146. Largest truck plant in the world.

Hadley Pottery, 1570 Story Ave, tel: (502) 584-2171. Free guided tours (no tours if over 85°F (30°C).

Kentucky Center for the Arts, Main St between 5th & 6th, tel: (502) 562-0100; or (800) 283-7777 (box office). Tours of the building and sculpture collection. Check paper for schedule of performances.

Locust Grove, 561 Blankenbaker Lane, tel: (502) 897-9845. The last home of Louisville's founder, Gen. George Rogers Clark.

Museum of History and Science. 727 West Main, tel: (502) 561-6100. The museum features a four-story IMAX Theater.

Thomas Edison's Butchertown House, 729 East Washington St, tel: (502) 585-5247. Features inventions and memorabilia.

Mammoth Cave National Park

Cave tours are offered year round. Tickets are available through Mistix

(800) 365-2267. Or, write to: Mammoth Cave NP, Mammoth Cave, KY 42259 or telephone (502) 758-2328. Above ground, the Green River winds its way through the park and offers some of the best canoe runs in the state. The ***Miss Green River II*** (tel: 502/758-2243) cruise boat is a great way to enjoy the scenery and wildlife.

Murray

National Scouting Museum, 16th & Calloway Sts, tel: (502) 762-3383. Scouting memorabilia. Be sure to see the 54 original paintings and drawings by Norman Rockwell.

Paducah

Alben Barkley Museum, Madison at Sixth, tel: (502) 554-9690. Barkley was the 35th vice president, serving with Harry S. Truman. Memorabilia is featured in the 1852 Greek-Revival home.

The Market House at 200 Broadway: the **Yeiser Art Center** (tel: 502/442-2453) features changing exhibits of traditional and contemporary art; the **Market House Museum** (tel: 502/443-7759) houses the complete interior of a local 1877 drugstore; and the **Market House Theatre** (tel: 502/444-6828) offers 12 productions throughout the year and free tours.

Museum of the American Quilter's Society, 215 Jefferson, tel: (502) 442-8856. Antique and contemporary quilts from the museum's collection are on display in three galleries.

Paducah Jubilee, Broadway at the river, tel: (502) 443-8874 or (800) 788-1057. Cruise the Ohio and Tennessee rivers aboard this authentic paddlewheeler for a variety of sightseeing, dining and entertainment cruises.

Paris

Duncan Tavern, 323 High St, tel: (606) 987-1788. Founded in 1788, this establishment hosted such notables as Daniel Boone and Simon Kenton. Seven miles (11 km) east of Paris is the 1791 **Cane Ridge Meetinghouse** (US 460 to KY 537, tel: 606/987-5350), the birthplace of the Disciples of Christ Church in 1804.

Richmond

Fort Boonesborough State Park, 1-75 exit 95 on KY 627, tel: (606) 527-3131. Craftsmen demonstrate skills on 18th-century antiques. Also pool, camping.

White Hall State Historic Site, 1-75 exit 95 on US 25/421, tel: (606) 623-9178. Home of Cassius Marcellus Clay.

Russellville

Bibb House, 183 West Eighth, tel: (502) 726-2508. Circa 1822 Georgian mansion.

Shakertown at South Union, 15 miles (24 km) east of Russellville, is the site of the last western Shaker community, 1807–1922. **The Shaker Tavern** serves lunch (reservations, tel: 542-6801). Special events include the **Shaker Festival** (US 68, tel: 502/542-4167) in late June, featuring Shaker crafts, music and foods.

Springfield

Lincoln Homestead State Park, KY-528, tel: (606) 336-7461.

Distilleries

Ancient Age, Wilkinson Blvd, Frankfort, tel: (502) 223-7641. This has been distilling bourbon whiskey since 1869. Free tours offered.

Jim Beam Distillery, near Bardstown, tel: (502) 543-9877. Free tours offered seven days a week at the company's American Outpost (the distillery itself is not open to tourists). Blue Grass Parkway exit 25, then KY 245 for about 20 miles (32 km). From I-65, take exit 112, follow signs.

Heaven Hill Distilleries, KY 49, Bardstown, tel: (502) 348-3921. The home of Heaven Hill, Elijah Craig and Evan Williams bourbons is the largest family-owned distillery in the country. The free guided tour includes emptying aged bourbon from the white-oak barrels, the bottling operation, and a bourbon cookbook.

Makers Mark Distillery. Loretto, south of Bardstown. Take Ky 49 from Bardstown to Loretto; then KY 152 and follow signs; tel: (502) 865-2099. Called the prettiest distillery in the nation, visitors are greeted by charcoal grey buildings with red shutters rising above neat flower beds. The product certainly matches the package; connoisseurs call Makers Mark the finest bourbon in the nation. A small establishment, only 38 barrels are produced each day. A tour highlight is watching the bottle tops being hand-dipped into the red sealing wax which gives Maker's Mark its distinctive touch. Free tours on the half hour.

Wild Turkey Distillery, Lawrenceburg, tel: (502) 839-4544. The plant produces 8-year-old, 101-proof (52% alcohol content) bourbon. Free tours. Blue Grass Parkway exit 59, Ky 150 north. Follow signs.

Civil War Sites

Historic Places

Columbus-Belmont Battlefield State Park, 15 miles (24 km) south at KY-58 & KY-123/80, tel: (502) 677-2327. This is the site of a massive chain and anchor used to block the passage of Union gunboats during the Civil War. There is also a Confederate cannon and a network of earthen trenches. Museum, campground, mini-golf, historic hiking trail.

Perryville Civil War Battlefield State Historic Site, Off US 68 & US 150, tel: (606) 332-8631. Situated 10 miles (16 km) west of Danville, this is site of the largest battle of the Kentucky campaign, fought on October 8, 1862. The annual re-enactment is held the weekend closest to the battle date.

TENNESSEE

Getting Acquainted

The Place

Known as: The Volunteer State from the War of 1812 when volunteer soldiers from Tennessee under General Andrew Jackson displayed great valor during the Battle of New Orleans.

Motto: "Agriculture and Commerce", words which are also prominent on the Great Seal of the State of Tennessee.

Entered Union: June 1, 1796 as the 16th of the United States. The state was formed from land ceded to the federal government by North Carolina in 1784 and originally known as The Territory of the United States South of the River Ohio.

Population: 5.2 million.

Population Density: More than half of the state's residents live in rural areas. The four major urban areas in order of size are: Memphis, Nashville, Knoxville and Chattanooga.

Area: 42,244 sq. miles (109,412 sq. km).

Time Zones: Central Time Zone (GMT minus 6 hours).

Highest Point: Clingman's Dome, 6,643 ft (2,025 meters).

Climate: Moderate with four distinct seasons. Spring and fall are seasons of pleasantly warm days and cool nights. Summer daytime temperatures are generally in the 80–90°F (27–32°C) range, although they can occasionally reach 100°F (38°C) on ver y hot days. Winter daytime temperatures are generally in the 30–40°F (-1–4°C) range, very occasionally dropping to near zero or below.

Economy: Agriculture is the state's largest single economic base. Tobacco, cotton and soybeans are among the leading crops. Manufacturing, banking, printing, and insurance are mainstays of the urban economy. The breeding of Tennessee Walking Horses is a major industry in Middle Tennessee.

Local Government: Made up of 95 county governments which hold the primary responsibility for such items as education and law enforcement. City governments are usually separate, although some cities have combined county and city operations into a single metro form of government.

Capital: Nashville.

Local Dialing Codes: 423 (East Tennessee), 615 (Middle Tennessee) 901 (West Tennessee).

Famous Figures: Andrew Jackson (7th President), James K. Polk (11th President), Andrew Johnson (17th President), frontiersman Davy Crockett, Union Admiral David Farragut, Confederate Cavalry General Nathan Bedford Forrest, World War I hero Sergeant Alvin York, Nobel Peace Prize winner Cordell Hull, Pulitzer-prize winning author Alex Haley.

Useful Addresses

State Office

Tennessee Department of Tourism Development, PO Box 23170, Nashville, TN 37202-3170, tel: (615) 741-2158.

Local Offices

CHATTANOOGA

Chattanooga Area Convention & Visitors Bureau, tel: (615) 756-8687 or (800) 322-3344, fax: (615) 265-1630.

GATLINBURG

Gatlinburg Visitors & Convention Bureau, tel: (615) 436 2392 or (800) 343-1475, fax: (615) 436-3704.

KNOXVILLE

Knoxville Convention & Visitors Bureau, tel: (615) 523-7263 or (800) 727-8045, fax: (615) 673-4400.

MEMPHIS

Memphis Convention & Visitors Bureau, tel: (901) 543-5300, fax: (901) 543-5350.

NASHVILLE

Nashville Convention & Visitors Bureau, tel: (615) 259-4730 or (615) 259 4760 (asst), fax: (615) 244-6278, tlx: 757599.

Where to Stay

Accommodation

Chattanooga

Chattanooga Choo Choo Holiday Inn, 1400 Market St, tel: (615) 266-5000. An elegantly restored railroad depot. The depot won design awards around the turn-of-the century. 361 rooms, including several former passenger cars now converted into Victorian splendor. $$$

Radison Read House Hotel, M.L. King Blvd at 9th St, tel: (615) 266-4121. One of Chattanooga's oldest downtown hotels restored to prime condition. $$

Chattanooga Marriot, 2 Carter Plaza, tel: (615) 756-0002. 343 rooms. Good downtown location. $$

Gatlinburg

Best Western Zoder's Inn, 402 Pkwy, tel: (615) 436-5681. One of the best one in a resort city full of hotels and motels. 90 rooms $$

Brookside Resort, 463 East Pkwy, tel: (615) 436-5611. Wooded landscape with a mountain stream. 225 rooms, most with wood-burning fireplaces. $

Gatlinburg Inn, 755 Pkwy, tel: (615) 436-5133. One of the city's oldest resort hotels. 67 rooms. $$

Jackson

Garden Plaza Hotel, 1770 Hwy 45 Bypass, tel: (901) 664-6900. 168 rooms, pool, lounge. $

Knoxville

Hyatt Regency Knoxville, 500 Hill Ave, tel: (615) 637-1234. 387 rooms. $$$

Holiday Inn World's Fair, 523 Henley St, tel: (615) 522-2800. On the site of the 1982 Knoxville World's Fair. $$

Hilton Knoxville, 501 West Church, tel: (615) 523-2300. Good downtown location. 317 rooms. $$

Memphis

The Peabody Hotel, 149 Union Ave, tel: (901) 529-4000 or (800) PEABODY, fax: (901) 529-3600. One of the South's most elegant hotels with 458 rooms on 12 floors, including 15 suites. Four major restaurants, including Dux, named in honor of the famous Peabody Marching Ducks. High tea in the grand lobby. Shops, athletic club with indoor pool. Outstanding downtown location one block from Beale St. Don't miss the daily "Duck Ceremony" or a visit to The Duck Palace on the hotel roof. $$$

Adam's Mark Hotel, 939 Ridge Lake Blvd, tel: (901) 584-6664 or (800) 444-ADAM, fax: (901) 762-7411. 380 rooms on 27 floors. A luxury hotel with live music in the lounge and a full-service restaurant featuring American and Italian cuisine. $$$

Crowne Plaza Memphis, 250 North Main St, tel: (901) 527-7300 or (800) 3-CROWNE, FAX: (901) 526-1561. The Holiday Inn chain began in Memphis, so it is fitting that the city boasts one of the chain's finest hotels. 402 rooms on 18 floors with a full-service restaurant, a lounge with live music, indoor pool, health club, whirlpool and sauna. $$$

East Memphis Hilton, 5069 Sanderlin Ave, tel: (901) 767-6666 or (800) 445-8667, fax: (901) 767-6666. 264 rooms on eight floors. King-sized bedrooms are also available, along with a full-service restaurant, lounge, exercise room and indoor/outdoor pool. $$

Memphis Marriot, 2625 Thousand Oaks Blvd, tel: (901) 362-6200 or (800) 627-3587, fax: (901) 362-7221. 320 rooms. Lounge, full-service restaurant, indoor/outdoor pools, sauna, whirlpool and weight room. $$

Brownstone Hotel, 300 North Second St, tel: (901) 525-2511 or (800) 468-3515, fax: (901) 525-2511. 243 rooms on 11 floors with a full-service restaurant serving Southern-style menus. Lounge, lobby bar and outdoor pool. $$

Holiday Inn Memphis East, 5795 Popular Ave, tel: (901) 682-7881, fax: (901) 682-7881. 243 rooms on ten floors. Lounge. Health club, indoor pool, whirlpools and sauna. Superior Holiday Inn award winner in two consecutive years, no small feat in the city where Holiday Inn originated. $$

Radisson Hotel Memphis, 185 Union Ave, tel: (901) 528-1800 or (800) 333-3333, fax: (901) 526-3226. 280 rooms on ten floors. Located in the heart of downtown Memphis within walking distance of Beale St. Southern specialties featured in the Veranda restaurant. Try a frozen dessert at Scoops Ice Cream Parlor. Outdoor pool, whirlpool and sauna. $$

Ramada Plaza Hotel,160 Union Ave, tel: (901) 525-5491 or (800) 2RAMADA, fax: (901) 525-5491. 187 rooms on multiple levels in the downtown area. Conveniently located to Mud Island, Beale St and The Pyramid. Full-service restaurant, lobby bar and terrace pool. $

Wilson World Graceland, 3677 Elvis Presley Blvd, tel: (901) 332-1000 or (800) WILSONS. Convenient for visitors to Elvis Presley's Graceland Mansion. Spacious rooms. Suites are also available. $

Monteagle

Jim Oliver's Smokehouse Restaurant & Lodge, US Hwy 70S off I-24, tel: (615) 484-9566. 48 rooms and an excellent country-style restaurant with a winery across the street. $

Murfreesboro

Garden Plaza Hotel, 1855 South Church St, tel: (615) 895-5555. 170 rooms. $

Nashville

Opryland Hotel, 2800 Opryland Dr., tel: (615) 883-2211, fax: (615) 871-5728. Wow! With 1,891 rooms, this stunner is one of the largest hotels in the United States. Two wings of the hotel are built around incredible indoor gardens. "The Conservatory" features both an elevated walkway and paths through the jungle. "The Cascades" features a 40-ft (12-meter) waterfall as the centerpiece. There are several excellent restaurants and live music everywhere. $$$

Sheraton Music City, 777 McGavock Pike, tel: (615) 885-2200, fax: (615) 871-0926. It is hard to match the elegance of Opryland, but this hotel comes close. There are 412 rooms on four floors. $$$

Fiddlers Inn North, 2410 Music Valley Dr., tel: (615) 885-1440, fax: (615) 883-6477. 202 rooms located in the center of the Opryland area. $$

Ramada Inn Across From Opryland, 2401 Music Valley Dr., tel: (615) 889-0800, fax: (615) 883-1230. The name says it all, and you can walk across to the Opryland Hotel to see how the wealthy people live – or those with expense accounts. 307 rooms. $$

The Hermitage Hotel, Corner of 6th and Union, tel: (615) 244-3121, fax: (615) 254-6909. One of Nashville's oldest hotels, the Hermitage has been restored to the elegance it once enjoyed. There are excellent views of the Tennessee State Capitol from some of the 120 rooms. $$$

Stouffer Renaissance Nashville Hotel, 611 Commerce St, tel: (615) 255-8400, fax: (615) 255-8202. The hotel adjoins the city's Convention Center and is within walking distance of the Second Avenue Historic District and Printers Alley. 623 rooms. $$$

Union Station Hotel, 1001 Broadway, tel: (615) 726-1001, fax: (615) 248-3554. Once Nashville's major railroad station, the old depot was saved from the wrecking ball and converted into an elegant 124-room hotel. $$$

Regal Maxwell House Hotel, 2025 Metrocenter Blvd, tel: (615) 259-4343, fax: (615) 313-1327. Maxwell House Coffee originated at this hotel – or at least a previous incarnation of it. It was President Theodore Roosevelt who said it was "good to the last drop" during a stay at the old Maxwell House hotel. This 269-room version of the hotel also features the award-winning Crown Court gourmet restaurant. $$$

Lowe's Vanderbilt Plaza Hotel, 2100 West End Ave, tel: (615) 320-1700, fax: (615) 320-5019. Located across from Nashville's prestigious Vanderbilt University, this 338-room hotel is a study in classic elegance. $$$

Pickwick

Pickwick Landing State Park Inn, Hwy 57, tel: (901) 689-3135. A popular West Tennessee resort park on Kentucky Lake at Pickwick Dam. Golf course and a superb restaurant. $

Pigeon Forge

Grand Resort Hotel & Convention Center, 3171 Pkwy, tel: (423) 453-1000. 425 rooms. $$

Pikeville

Fall Creek Falls State Resort Park, Hwy 284, tel: (423) 881-5241. One of Tennessee's most popular state parks surrounded by wilderness and on the shores of an excellent fishing lake. Hiking, biking and nature trails. Recreational facilities. Has excellent restaurant. $

Red Boiling Springs

Donoho Hotel, 500 East Main St, tel: (615) 699-3141. Once a famous resort hotel for visitors taking the mineral waters of this resort town. 32 rooms. $

Rogersville

Hale Springs Inn, Town Square, tel: (423) 272-5121. Tennessee's oldest continuously operating lodging establishment opened its doors in 1824. Gorgeously restored by a descendant of the original builder. $

Savannah

Savannah Lodge, 420 Pickwick Rd, tel: (901) 925-8586. 41 rooms. $

Townsend

Highland Manor Motel & Conference Center, 7766 East Lamar Alexander Pkwy, tel: (423) 448-2211. 50 rooms. $$

Talley-Ho Inn, 8314 State Hwy 73, tel: (423) 448-2465. 48 rooms. Excellent restaurant next door.

Eating Out

Where to Eat

Cracker Barrel

Cracker Barrel is a Tennessee-based chain of restaurants located all over the South, usually on Interstate Highway exits. Restaurants vary in quality, but strict quality control makes this chain universally outstanding. For Southern-style cooking at this type of eatery, Cracker Barrel is as good as it gets. $

Chattanooga

Fehn's, 5435 Hwy 153, tel: (615) 877-1615. Hamburger steak is the specialty and it's easy to see why. $$

The Loft, 328 Cherokee Blvd, tel: (615) 266-3601. Outstanding steaks and beef. $$$

Mt Vernon, 3509 South Broad St, tel: (615) 266-6591. Southern specialties, streak and seafood. $$

Town and Country, 110 North Market St, tel: (615) 267-8544. A Chattanooga institution for good food. $$

212 Market, 212 Market St, tel: (615) 265-1212. One of Chattanooga's best restaurants across the street from the Tennessee Aquarium. $$$

Gulas, 5665 Brainerd Rd, tel: (615) 894-2241. Good food has made this restaurant one of Chattanooga's most established. $$

Franklin

Choices, 108 Fourth Ave, tel: (615) 791-0001. The restoration of a historic downtown building for this restaurant led to a major restoration of much of this antebellum town. The food is excellent too. $$$

Uncle Bud's Catfish, 1214 Lakeview Dr., tel: (615) 790-1234. Catfish and all the fixin's made the restaurant's reputation and led to other Uncle Bud's in other cities. But this is the original and still the best. $$

Gatlinburg

Brass Lantern, 710 Pkwy, tel: (615) 436-4168. One of the best in this resort city full of restaurants. $$

The Burning Bush, Parkway at Park Entrance, tel: (615) 436-4669. The Bountiful Breakfast is of special note with such unusual delicacies as quail and Smoky Mountain trout on the menu. $$$

Heidelberg Restaurant, 148 Pkwy, tel: (615) 430-3094. The restaurant is actually on top of a mountain ski resort overlooking the city. Take the aerial tram from downtown. German food and a rousing floor show. $$

The Open Hearth, 1138 Pkwy, tel: (615) 436-5648. Steaks and prime ribs are the specialties and extremely well done. $$

Smoky Mountain Trout House, 410 Pkwy, tel: (615) 436-5416. Fresh Smoky Mountain trout is obviously the specialty of the house, but there is more on the menu. $$

Jackson

Brooks Shaw & Son Old Country Store, Casey Jones Lane off I-40 exit 81, tel: (901) 668-1223. Buffet-style southern cooking. Lots of choices. $

Jonesborough

The Parson's Table, 102 Woodrow Ave, tel: (423) 753-8002. The building was once a church; now it's a superlative restaurant. $$$

Kingsport

Skoby's, 1001 Konnarock Rd, tel: (423) 247-5629. Even if the food wasn't excellent, it would be worth the trip just to look at the eclectic decor of this unusual restaurant. $$

Knoxville

Calhoun's on The River, 400 Neyland Dr., tel: (615) 673-3355. Barbecue, the East Tennessee variety, is the specialty and Calhoun's has won many awards for its version of this Southern delight. $$. There's also one at 10020 Kingston Pike, tel: (615) 673-3444; and one in Nashville, 96 White Bridge Rd, tel: (615) 356-0855.

Chesapeake's, 500 Henley St, tel: (615) 673-3433. Seafood, steaks and chicken. Blue crab and lobster are the specialties. $$

Copper Cellar, 386B Kingston Pike, tel: (615) 673-3411. Near the University of Tennessee, a popular spot for generations of college students and local professionals. $$

The Orangery, 5412 Kingston Pike, tel: (615) 588-2964. French cuisine and Old World ambiance. Contemporary American is also served. Orange is the school color of the University of Tennessee. $$$

Regas The Restaurant & The Gathering Place, 318 Gay St, tel: (615) 637-9805. One of Knoxville's best restaurants for more than half a century. Wendy's hamburger chain founder Dave Thomas learned the business working at Regas. $$$

Great American Steak and Buffet, 4310 Chapman Hwy, tel: (615) 579-6002; 900 Merchants Dr., tel: (615) 687-8773. Almost anything you can imagine is probably on one of the buffet tables, and it's all good. $

Patrick Sullivan's, 100 North Central St, tel: (615) 522-4511. One of the most popular of several restaurants in the center of Knoxville's restored Old Town entertainment district. $$

Lynchburg

Miss Bobo's Boarding House, tel: (615) 759-7394. Situated a stone's throw away from the famous Jack Daniel's Distillery. Standard fare includes an assortment of meats and vegetables, breads, beverage and dessert.

Memphis

Chez Philippe, 149 Union Ave (The Peabody), tel: (901) 529-4188. The finest Memphis has to offer according to many customers. Master Chef Jose Gutierrez has made this French-style restaurant a Four Star gourmet award winner. $$$

Maxwell's, 948 South Cooper St, tel: (901) 725-1009. Extraordinary fresh eclectic food with Mediterranean and Indian influences. Voted "Best New Restaurant" by *Memphis* magazine when it started out. The work of area artists is also featured. $$$

Paulette's, 2110 Madison Ave, tel: (901) 726-5128. Cozy old-world ambiance, filet mignon, salmon, shrimp and European specialities, plus live music, make this a very popular Memphis dining spot. $$$

Automatic Slim's Tonga Club, 83 South Second St, tel: (901) 525-7948. Where Memphis meets Manhattan. Southwestern and Caribbean inspired cuisine. $$

Bravo! Ristorante, 939 Ridge Lake Blvd (Adam's Mark Hotel), tel: (901) 684-6664. If Memphis can have a pyramid, it can also have a bit of Italy. Professionally trained singers serve up regional specialties and a serving of opera, operetta and Broadway. $$$

The Rendezvous, 52 South Second St – Rear, tel: (901) 523-2746. Barbecue ribs are what Memphis is most famous for, and The Rendezvous is one reason why. These are the dry variety. Ambiance? The place is downstairs in an alley, but who cares? Everyone in Memphis knows where it is. $

Public Eye, 2740 Bartlett Rd, tel: (901) 386-3300. More ribs, a different style of cooking. Fried green tomatoes and pickles are also specialities of the house. $$

Interstate Bar-B-Q, 2265 South Third St, tel: (901) 775-2304. Okay, so Memphis is literally full of good barbecue joints, but this one was rated Number 2 in the United States by *People* magazine and as The Best Little Pork House in Memphis by the *Commercial-Appeal* newspaper. There's more than just ribs to be had. BBQ spaghetti? It's on the menu. $

B.B. King's Blues Club and Restaurant, 143 Beale St, tel: (901) 624-KING. More barbecue, but lots of other good choices, too. The restaurant also showcases memorabilia from the famous blues artist who has been known to play here himself. Usually, though, it's musicians passing through who like to jam with the smokin' hot house band. Try the fried dill pickles. $$

Monteagle

Jim Oliver's Smokehouse, 850 West Main St, tel: (615) 924-2268. Southern-style cooking. $

Nashville

Arthur's. 1001 Broadway, tel: (615) 255-1494. A four star award-winning restaurant located in the historic Union Station Hotel. $$$

Merchant's, 401 Broadway, tel: (615) 254-1892. It used to be a hotel, then it was one of Nashville's toughest cowboy bars, now it's a great restaurant. It's also just a block away from the Second Avenue Historic District. $$$

Mere Bulles, 152 Second Ave North, tel: (615) 256-1946. Right in the heart of Nashville's Second Avenue Historic District, this restaurant is also one of the area's top music clubs. $$$

Mario's Ristorante, 2005 Broadway, tel: (615) 327-3232. Mario has been in Nashville long enough to become an institution, but he makes frequent trips home to Italy, presumably to brush up on the latest cuisine techniques. It must work because his food is outstanding. $$$

The Stockyard, 901 Second Ave North, tel: (615) 255-6464. Steaks are the specialty, but there is lots more on the menu and The Bull Pen Lounge downstairs is one of Nashville's top spots for live country music and dancing. $$$

Cooker Bar and Grill, 2609 West End Ave, tel: (615) 327-2925; 1211 Murfreesboro Rd, tel: (615) 361-4747. Southern and regional cuisines like meat loaf, pot roast, country fried steak and fried okra are the specialties of the house. The outstanding service also deserves a mention. $

Pigeon Forge

Duff's Famous Smorgasbord, 3960 Pkwy, tel: (423) 429-3463. Be sure to bring a big appetite because there's a lot to sample. $

Santos, 3270 Pkwy, tel: (423) 428-5840. Fine Italian restaurant in the heart of southern fried country. $$

Trotters, 3718 Pkwy, tel: (423) 453-3347. American style with an outstanding homey atmosphere. $–$$

Sevierville

Applewood Farmhouse Restaurant, 240 Apple Valley Rd, tel: (423) 428-1222. This is actually an orchard with a huge gift shop selling apples, apple cider, apple pies – anything to do with apples. There is also a winery specializing in apple wines. Meals begin with a basket of wonderful apple fritters and end with such delights as apple cider sour cream pie. $$

Attractions

Places of Interest

Adamsville

Buford Pusser Home & Museum, 342 Pusser St, tel: (901) 632-4080. The home of Tennessee's famed sheriff profiled in three *Walking Tall* movies. Original furnishings and memorabilia.

Big South Fork National River & Recreation Area

Park Headquarters at Oneida, tel: (615) 879-3625. A 105,000-acre (40,000-hectare) scenic wilderness administered by the National Park Service. Horseback riding, mountain biking, canoeing, whitewater rafting.

Camden

Tennessee River Folklife Center, Nathan Bedford Forrest State Park, tel: (901) 584-6356. Exhibits and displays tell the story of the people and life on the Tennessee River.

Chattanooga

Lookout Mountain Incline Railway, 827 East Brow Rd, tel: (615) 821-4224. Part of the Chattanooga public transportation system, the Incline reaches a grade of more than 70 percent as it climbs the steep slope of Lookout Mountain.

National Knife Museum, 7201 Shallowford Rd, tel: (615) 892-5007. Owned and operated by the National Knife Collectors Association, the museum features thousands of knives, swords, razors and other types of cutlery.

Rock City Gardens, 1400 Patton Rd, tel: (615) 820-2531. Spectacular city of rock formations and native plants utilizing the natural rock formations of Lookout Mountain.

Ruby Falls, Lookout Mountain Scenic Hwy, tel: (615) 821-2544. Spectacular 120-ft (40-meter) waterfall located 1,120 ft (340 meters) below the point of Lookout Mountain.

Tennessee Aquarium, One BRd St, tel: (615) 265-0695. The nation's only aquarium dedicated to freshwater species follows the course of a single drop of water from the Great Smoky Mountains to the Gulf of Mexico. Live fish, river otters, birds and mammals are showcased in exhibits.

Tennessee Valley Railroad, 4119 Cromwell Rd, tel: (615) 894-8028. A fully operational railroad running between a 1920s frame depot and a 1940s brick station. Steam locomotives, passenger cars, office cars and all type of railroad equipment and memorabilia.

Columbia

James K. Polk Ancestral Home, 301 West Seventh St, tel: (615) 388-2354. From this home built by his parents in 1816, Polk began his legal and political career which climaxed with his election as the 7th President of the United States.

Dayton

Scopes Museum, 1475 Market St, tel: (423) 775-7801. Located in the historic Rhea County Courthouse where the famous evolution trial took place in 1925 pitting noted attorneys William Jennings Byran and Clarence Darrow. The courthouse and courtroom have been restored.

Gatlinburg

Great Smoky Mountains National Park, 107 Park Headquarters Rd, tel: (615) 436-1200. With more than 500,000 acres (200,000 hectares) of wilderness and 16 peaks above 6,000 ft (1,800 meters) in height, the Smokies is the nation's most visited national park. In addition to a huge variety of animal and plant life, the park is also a showcase for southern Appalachian Mountain culture.

Henning

Alex Haley House Museum, 200 South Church St, tel: (901) 738-2240. Boyhood home of the Pulitzer-prize winning author of *Roots*.

Jackson

Casey Jones Home & Railroad Museum, 1-40 at Hwy 45 Bypass East. Historic 1890s home of the railroad engineer killed in America's most famous train accident.

Jonesborough

Jonesborough Historic District, Visitor Center, tel: (423) 753-5961. Tennessee's oldest town founded in 1779. A remarkably preserved and restored collection of frontier architecture. Original buildings include the Chester Inn on Main St. Visitor Center museum.

Knoxville

Blount Mansion, 200 West Hill Ave, tel: (615) 525-2375. The 1792 residence of Territorial Governor William Blount. It is thought to be the first frame house west of the Appalachian Mountains.

James White Fort, 205 West Hill Ave, tel: (615) 525-6514. Historical fort consisting of several buildings, some dating from the original 1786 complex.

Land Between The Lakes

A 170,000-acre (70,000-hectare) recreation area between Kentucky and Barkley Lakes. Attractions include The Homeplace – 1850, a working farm of the period. For information, tel: (615) 924-5602.

Lynchburg

Jack Daniel's Distillery, tel: (615) 759-6180. There's nothing in Lynchburg except for the world-famous distillery.

McMinnville

Cumberland Caverns, tel: (615) 668-4396. One of America's largest caverns with impressive hallways, galleries and formations.

Memphis

Beale Street Blues Museum, 329 Beale St, tel: (901) 527-6008. Housed in the old Daisy Theater with its distinctive facade, the museum focuses on the part played by "the street" in the history of the blues.

Center for Southern Folklore, 130 Beale St, tel: (901) 525-3655. Intimate informal folklife center presenting the people, music and traditions of Beale Street and the South in general.

Chucalissa Archaeological Museum, 1987 Indian Village Dr., tel: (901) 785-3160. Museum includes artifacts of Indians of the mid-South region and a reconstructed 15th-century village of thatched houses and mounds.

Graceland, 3734 Elvis Presley Blvd, tel: (901) 332-3322 or (800) 238-2000. The mansion home of the "King of Rock 'n' Roll." Guided tours of the house and grounds. Other attractions include the automobile museum, and two of the entertainer's private jets.

Memphis Hall of Fame, 97 South Second St, tel: (901) 525-4007. Rare blues recordings, vintage posters, video exhibits and photos.

Memphis Pink Palace Museum and Planetarium, 3050 Central Ave, tel: (901) 320-6320. Prize-winning exhibits of the cultural and natural history of the mid-South. The Pink Palace mansion was the home of Clarence Saunders, creator of the supermarket which became the Piggly Wiggly chain.

Mississippi River Museum, On Mud Island, tel: (901) 576-7230. Impressive displays of the cultural and natural history of the Mississippi River include a full-size 19th-century packet boat and a Union gunboat of the Civil War era.

The National Civil Rights Museum, 406 Mulberry St, tel: (901) 521-9699. Located at the Lorraine Motel, the site of the 1968 assassination of Dr Martin Luther King, Jr, the museum is the first of its kind in the nation.

National Ornamental Metal Museum, 374 California Ave, tel: (901) 774-6380. The nation's only museum dedicated exclusively to the art and craft of metalwork.

Sun Studio, 706 Union Ave, tel: (901) 521-0664. One of the most famous recording studios in America. 1950s sessions launched the careers of Elvis Presley, Jerry Lee Lewis, Carl Perkins, Roy Orbison, Johnny Cash, B.B. King and others.

W. C. Handy Museum and Gallery, 352 Beale St, tel: (901) 522-8300. The actual home of the musician known as "The Father of the Blues."

Woodruff-Fontaine House, 680 Adams Ave, tel: (901) 526-1469. The centerpiece of Memphis's Victorian Village Historic District, this 1870s Second Empire home contains a fine collection of 18th and 19th century antiques and clothing.

Libertyland, 940 Early Maxwell Blvd, tel: (901) 274-1776. A historical, educational and recreational theme park with rides and live music shows.

Nashville

Country Music Hall of Fame and Museum/Studio B, 4 Music Square East, tel: (615) 256-1639. Exhibits, artifacts and personal mementoes of past and present country music stars. Nearby Studio B was one of the original Nashville recording studios.

Grand Ole Opry, 2804 Opryland Dr., tel: (615) 889-3060. Famous live country music radio show that has been preformed every weekend since 1925. Performances Friday and Saturday evenings. Matinees and Sunday shows during the summer.

The Hermitage, 4580 Rachel's Lane, tel: (615) 889-2941. The elegant home of Andrew Jackson, the 7th President of the United States. Tours also feature the original cabins, smokehouse and spring house, Old Hermitage Church and nearby Tulip Grove Mansion.

Opryland USA, 2802 Opryland Dr., tel: (615) 889-6611. A family-oriented theme park showcasing all forms of American music in live shows. Rides, shops, game areas, and a petting zoo.

The Parthenon, Centennial Park on West End Ave, tel: (615) 862-8431. Full-sized replica of the famous Greek structure built for Tennessee's 1896 centennial celebration has a 40-ft (12-meter) statue of the goddess Athena. It also houses an art gallery.

Tennessee State Capitol, Charlotte Ave, tel: (615) 741-2692. Designed by architect William Strickland who is buried within its walls. One of the oldest state capitol buildings in the US.

Tennessee State Museum, 505 Deaderick St, tel: (615) 741-2692. Exhibits detail the history of Tennessee from pre-historic Indian times through the early 1900s.

Norris

Museum of Appalachia, Hwy 61 off I-75, tel: (423) 494-7680. Perhaps the most complete and authentic replica pf pioneer Appalachian Mountain life in the world. The complex contains more than 30 authentic log structures and more than 250,000 artifacts.

Oak Ridge

American Museum of Science and Energy, 300 South Tulane Ave, tel: (423) 576-3200. Free museum dedicated to all forms of energy and energy use. Of special interest is an exhibit of The Oak Ridge Story detailing the World War II Manhattan Project to develop the atomic bomb.

Graphite Reactor, Bethel Valley Rd, tel: (423) 574-4160. The world's oldest nuclear reactor built during World War II as part of the Manhattan Project.

Pigeon Forge

Dollywood, 1020 Dollywood Lane, tel: (423) 428-9488. Rides, music and shows are the theme of an entertainment complex developed by Dolly Parton near her girlhood home.

Rugby

Historic Rugby, State Hwy 52, tel: (423) 628-2441. Historic 1880s English colony founded by author Thomas Hughes. 17 of the original Victorian buildings remain today, including the Hughes Public Library and Christ Church Episcopal.

Smithville

Joe L. Evins Appalachian Center for Crafts, State Hwy 56, tel: (615) 597-6801. Both a full-scale university and a retail outlet for craftsmen from throughout the 13 state Appalachian region. Working artists in wood, metal, fiber, glass and clay.

Sweetwater

The Lost Sea, 140 Lost Sea Rd, tel: (423) 337-6616. Large and historic cavern which includes a 4½-acre (2-hectare) lake listed by the *Guinness Book of World Records* as the world's largest underground lake.

Tullahoma

George A. Dickel Distillery, Cascade Hollow Rd, tel: (615) 857-3124. There are only two Tennessee sour-mash whiskeys. Jack Daniel's is one, George Dickel is the other.

Civil War Sites

Historic Places

Chattanooga

Chickamauga-Chattanooga National Military Park, US Hwy 27 at Fort Oglethorpe, Georgia, tel: (615) 866-9241. The nation's oldest and largest National Military Park contains five separate areas, including the Chickamauga Battlefield at nearby Fort Oglethorpe, Georgia, which claimed 48,000 Union and Confederate casualties, as well as Lookout Mountain, Signal Mountain, Missionary Ridge and Orchard Knob in Chattanooga. Visitor center/museums are located at Chickamauga and Lookout Mountain.

Chattanooga National Cemetery, Bailey Ave, Chattanooga. Burial site for many of the dead from the battles of Chickamauga, Lookout Mountain and Missionary Ridge.

Dover

Fort Donelson National Battlefield, Off US Hwy 79, tel: (615) 232-5706. The site of the first major Union victory of the Civil War. The earthen fort, river batteries and outer earthworks remain. Tours begin at the visitor center, which includes a museum and a slide presentation describing the battle. A 6-mile (10-km) self-guided auto tour includes the National Cemetery and the preserved Dover Hotel where the surrender of the fort to Union forces under General Ulysses Grant was signed.

Franklin

Historic Carnton Plantation, 1345 Carnton Lane, tel: (615) 794-0903. A beautifully preserved antebellum mansion which served as a field hospital during the Civil War Battle of Franklin.

The Carter House, 1140 Columbia Ave, tel: (615) 791-1861. Historic 1830s house now designated as a National Landmark. The house was at the center of the Civil War Battle of Franklin. Tours include a museum, video presentation and guided tour of the house and grounds.

Greeneville

Andrew Johnson National Historic Site, College and Depot Sts, Greeneville, tel: (423) 638-3551. Museum, home and tailor shop of the 17th President of the United States who took office following the assassination of President Abraham Lincoln.

Harrogate

Abraham Lincoln Museum, Cumberland Gap Pkwy, Harrogate, tel: (423) 859-6235. Outstanding museum of Lincoln memorabilia on the campus of Lincoln Memorial University. The university and the museum were established in recognition of the strong Union support provided by residents of East Tennessee.

Murfreesboro

Stones River National Battlefield, 3501 Old Nashville Hwy, tel: (615) 893-9501. More than 83,000 soldiers took part in this Union offensive to trisect the Confederacy. With 23,000 casualties, it was one of the bloodiest battles fought in the western theater of the war.

Oaklands Historic House Museum, 900 North Maney Ave, Murfreesboro, tel: (615) 983-0022. An antebellum plantation house. Site of Nathan Bedford Forrest's raid on Murfreesboro in July, 1862.

Nashville

Belle Meade Plantation, 5035 Harding Rd, Nashville, tel: (615) 356-0501. Renown thoroughbred horse farm of the 19th century. A focal point of the Battle of Nashville. Marks left by Civil War bullets can still be seen on the mansion's columns.

Savannah

Shiloh National Military Park, State Hwy 22, tel: (901) 689-5696. The site of the first epic battle of the Civil War where combined Union and Confederate casualties totaled almost 24,000.

Smyrna

Sam Davis Home, 1399 Sam Davis Rd, Smyrna, tel: (615) 459-2341. Home and museum tell the story of Confederate hero Sam Davis, a scout who was caught with incriminating documents hidden in his boot and hanged as a spy after refusing to divulge the source of the documents.

NORTH CAROLINA

Getting Acquainted

The Place

Known as: The Tar Heel State because North Carolina soldiers stuck in battle during a fierce Civil War battle like tar sticks to heels.

Origin of Name: The name Carolina was given to a vast colonial territory by Sir Robert Heath in honor of King Charles I. When the area was carved into states, what remained of Carolina was divided into two states: North Carolina and South Carolina.

Motto: "*Esse Quam Videri*" – To Be Rather Than to Seem.

Entered Union: The 12th state entered the Union on November 12, 1789.

Population: 6.7 million.

Population Density: Half the population lives in rural areas, while the other half is scattered in nine metropolitan areas, none of which has more than 450,000 residents.

Area: 52,712 sq. miles (136,524 sq. km).

Time Zones: Eastern Time Zone (GMT minus five hours).

Highest Point: Mount Mitchell, 6,684 ft (2,037 meters).

Climate: Four seasons. Temperatures normally range from 22°F (-6°C) to 92°F (33°C). Annual pr ecipitation averages 44 inches (112 cm); annual snowfall 5 to 6 inches (13 to 15 cm).

Economy: Main industries are tobacco, textiles, and tourism, with banking and high-tech companies having a high profile. Has one of the nation's lowest unemployment rates.

Local Government: Made up of 100 counties and 525 municipalities. Provides two senators and 12 representatives to US Congress.

Annual visitors: 8½ million, including an estimated 746,000 international visitors.

Capital: Raleigh.

Local Dialing Codes: (919) and (910) cover the eastern regions; (704) covers the western.

Famous Figures: President Andrew Johnson, Daniel Boone, Dr Billy Graham, Ava Gardner.

Useful Addresses

State Offices

North Carolina Travel and Tourism Division, Department of Commerce, 430 North Salisbury St, Raleigh, North Carolina 27603, tel: (800) VISIT-NC or (919) 733-4171.

Outer Banks Chamber of Commerce, Ocean Bay Blvd at Mustian St, tel: (919) 441-8144. Information on the string of narrow coastal islands that lie between the Atlantic Ocean and the North Carolina mainland.

Local Offices

ASHEVILLE

Asheville Area Convention & Visitors Bureau, tel: (704) 258-6111 or (800) 257-1300, fax: (704) 251-0926.

CHARLOTTE

Charlotte Convention & Visitors Bureau, Inc, tel: (704) 334-2282 or (800) 231-4636, fax: (704) 342-3972.

OUTER BANKS

Dare County Tourist Bureau, tel: (919) 473-2138 or (800) 446-6262, fax: (919) 473-5106.

RALEIGH

Greater Raleigh Convention & Visitors Bureau, tel: (919) 834-5900 or (800) 849-8499, fax: (919) 831-2887.

WINSTON-SALEM

Winston-Salem Convention & Visitors Bureau, tel: (910) 725-2361 or (800) 331-7018, fax: (910) 773-1404.

Where to Stay

Accommodation

Asheville

The Grove Park Inn Resort, 290 Macon Ave, 28804, tel: (704) 252-2711 or (800) 438-5800. A full-service mountain resort, dating to 1913, offering everything from afternoon tea to golf. 510 rooms. $$–$$$

Richmond Hill Inn, 87 Richmond Hill Dr., 28806, tel: (704) 252-7313. An historic country inn known for gourmet dining and croquet. 21 rooms. $$–$$$

Atlantic Beach

Sea Hawk Motel, Salter Path Rd, PO Box 177, 28512, tel: (919) 726-4146. A two-story beachfront motel that's open from April through October. 36 rooms. $

Bald Head Island (near Wilmington)

Bald Head Island Resort, PO Box 3069, Bald Head Island, 28461, tel: (910) 457-5000 or (800) 234-1666. Accessible only by ferry, this luxurious island resort is home to loggerhead turtles. Has 100 condos, cottages, and villas. $$–$$$$

Banner Elk

The Banner Elk Inn, Route 3, Box 1134, 28604, tel: (704) 898-6223. B&B. Restored 1912 home, furnished in antiques, serves breakfast. 4 rooms. $

Bath

Bath Guest House, 215 South Main St, 27808, tel: (919) 923-6811. 5 rooms. B&B. You can enjoy history as well as bicycling, lawn games, canoeing, and other activities. $

Beech Mountain

Slopeside Chalet Rentals, Inc. 503 Beech Mountain Pkwy, 28604, tel: (704) 387-4251 or (800) 692-2061. Mile-high lodging near the ski slopes. Has 30 condos and 40 chalets. $–$$

Beaufort

Beaufort Inn, 101 Ann St, 28516, tel: (919) 728-2600. A waterside motel. Breakfast included. 41 rooms. $

Langdon House Bed & Breakfast, 135 Craven St, 28516, tel: (919) 728-5499. B&B. A well-kept colonial house with a charming host. 4 rooms. $–$$

Blowing Rock

Hillwinds Inn, Sunset Dr. & Ransom St, PO Box 649, 28605, tel: (704) 295-4300. An immaculate village motel that's convenient to restaurants and shops. $

Westglow Spa, Hwy 221 South, PO Box 1083, 28605, tel: (704) 295-4463 or (800) 562-0807. An artist's private mountain home now welcomes guests, and a European-style spa occupies his studio site. Has 6 rooms and 2 cottages. $$–$$$$

Boone

Lovill House Inn, 404 Old Bristol Rd, 28607, tel: (704) 264-4204 or (800) 849-9466. An historic mountain B&B offering breakfast and bicycles. (Closed during March and two weeks in September.) 5 rooms. $

Bryson City

Nanatahala Outdoor Center, 13077 US 19 West, 28713, tel: (704) 488-2175 or (800) 232-7238. Rustic rooms and cabins convenient to whitewater activities and other sports.

Chapel Hill

The Carolina Inn, 211 Pittsboro St, 27514, tel: (919) 933-2001 or (800) 962-8519. A renovated historic inn that's close to the university and shopping. Has 124 rooms and 16 suites. $–$$

The Fearrington House Inn, 2000 Fearrington Village Center, Fearrington, 27312-6502, tel: (919) 542-4202. A member of Relais & Chateaux, this luxurious inn in the middle of the country offers lodging, gourmet dining, and shopping. 25 rooms. $$$–$$$$

Charlotte

The Dunhill Hotel, 237 North Tryon St, 28202, tel: (704) 376-4117. The city's only historic hotel caters to individuals and business travelers. 60 rooms. $–$$

The Homeplace, 5901 Sardis Rd, 28270, tel: (704) 365-1936. B&B. A delightful turn-of-the-century country home in the suburbs with congenial hosts. 3 rooms. $

Morehead Inn, 1122 East Morehead St, 28204, tel: (704) 375-3357. Formerly a private home, this Dilworth inn offers many extras. Has 11 rooms and 1 apartment. $–$$

The Park Hotel, 2200 Rexford Rd, 28211, tel: (704) 364-8220. A luxury hotel near SouthPark with an impeccable reputation for food and service. Has 190 rooms and 4 suites. $$$$

Duck (on the Outer Banks)

The Sanderling Inn Resort, 1461 Duck Rd, 27949, tel: (919) 261-4111. A luxurious seaside inn where guests are spoiled with pampering and good food. Has 46 rooms and 5 suites. $$–$$$$

Durham

Washington Duke Inn & Golf Club, 3001 Cameron Blvd, 27706, tel: (919) 490-0999. A luxury hotel near Duke University that overlooks the golf course. 171 rooms. $$

Franklin

The Franklin Terrace, 67 Harrison Ave, 28734, tel: (704) 524-7907 or (800) 633-2431. B&B. Open April through mid-November, this gracious home is known for its hospitality and great food. Has 9 rooms and 1 cabin. $

Greensboro

The Biltmore Greensboro Hotel, 111 Washington St, 27401, tel: (910) 272-3474 or (800) 332-0303. A downtown luxury hotel that's loaded with history and charm. 29 rooms. $–$$

Greenville

East Carolina Inn, 2095 Stantonsburg Rd, 27834, tel: (919) 752-2122. Close to the medical center, this motel offers above-average rooms. 53 rooms. $

Hendersonville (near Flat Rock)

The Waverly Inn, 783 North Main St, 28792, tel: (704) 693-9193 or (800) 537-8195. B&B. A restored turn-of-the-century charmer offering all the comforts of home. 14 rooms. $–$$

Highlands

The Highlands Inn, East Main St, PO Box 1030, 28741, tel: (704) 526-9380. Located in the heart of the village, this restored mountain inn is a decorator's dream. Has 20 rooms and 10 suites. $

Hillsborough

Colonial Inn, 153 West King St, 27278, tel: (919) 732-2461. A colonial inn offering overnight lodging and meals in the heart of historic Hillsborough. 8 rooms. $

Lake Lure (near Chimney Rock)

The Lodge on Lake Lure, Charlotte Dr., PO Box 529A, 28746, tel: (704) 625-2789 or (800) 733-2785. Formerly a state highway patrol lodge, this lakeside B&B charms visitors from February through December. $–$$

Linville

Eseeola Lodge, 175 Linville Ave, Box 99, 28646, tel: (704) 733-4311 or (800) 742-6717. Open mid-May through late October, this mountain inn has been going strong since the 1890s. Breakfast and dinner are included in the tariff. 31 rooms. $$$$

Maggie Valley

Cataloochee Ranch, Fie Top Rd, Route 1, Box 500, 28751, tel: (704) 926-1401 or (800) 868-1401. A family-owned dude ranch and ski resort next to the Great Smoky Mountains National Park. Has 21 rooms in lodges and 8 log cabins. $$–$$$$

Manteo (on the Outer Banks)

The Tranquil House Inn, 405 Queen Elizabeth St, 27954, tel: (919) 473-1404. Located in the heart of the village, this inn overlooking the harbor serves breakfast and dinner. 25 rooms. $–$$

Nags Head (on the Outer Banks)

First Colony Inn, 6720 South Virginia Dare Tr., 27959, tel: (919) 441-2343. B&B Originally built in 1932, this weathered beach structure is decorated with antiques and period furnishings. 26 rooms. $$–$$$

New Bern

Harmony House Inn, 215 Pollock St, 28560, tel: (919) 636-3810. This Greek Revival B&B in the heart of the historic district offers a delightful breakfast. 9 rooms. $

Ocracoke Island (on the Outer Banks)

The Berkley Center, a block east of Cedar Island Ferry, PO Box 220, 27960, tel: (919) 928-5911. No phones or TVs will intrude at this rustic B&B that's within walking distance of the village. 9 rooms. $

Pinehurst

Holly Inn, 2300 Cherokee Rd, 28374. tel: (910) 295-0968. Pinehurst's first hotel has been renovated to serve the needs of modern-day travelers. 76 rooms. $$

Pinehurst Resort & Country Club, Route 2, PO Box 4000, 28374, tel: (910) 295-6811. A renowned resort in the heart of the village offering golf, tennis, croquet, trap and skeet shooting, water sports, carriage rides, and fine dining. 299 rooms. $$–$$$

Raleigh

The Oakwood Inn Bed & Breakfast, 411 North Bloodworth St, 27604, tel: (919) 832-9712 or (800) 267-9712. B&B A restored Victorian home near the Capitol that serves breakfast. 6 rooms. $

Velvet Cloak Inn, 1510 Hillsborough St, 27605, tel: (919) 828-0333. Close to NC State University, this is where the movers and shakers of Raleigh do business. 172 rooms. $

Smithfield

Log Cabin Motel, US 70 Business, 27577, tel: (919) 934-1534. Quiet and secluded, this motel offers roomy units with a country decor, plus a restaurant. 61 rooms. $

Southern Pines

Mid-Pines – A Clarion Resort, 1010 Midland Rd, 28387, tel: (910) 692-2114 or (800) 323-2114. A golf resort dating to the 1920s. 118 rooms. $–$$

Pine Needles Golf Resort, Ridge Rd, PO Box 88, 28387, tel: (910) 692-7111. Owned by golf legend Peggy Kirk Bell and her family, the resort built its reputation on Golfarias and Learning Centers. 71 rooms. $$–$$$$

Sparta

Mountain Hearth Lodge & Restaurant, Route 1, Box 288-E, 28675, tel: (910) 372-8743. B&B. Comfortable lodgings and good food are offered at this log lodge, open to guests from April through November. Has 5 rooms and 2 cabins. $

Waynesville

The Swag, Route 2, Box 280-A, 28786-9624, tel: (704) 926-0430 or 926-3119. A mile-high inn with gracious hosts and wonderful food. Has 12 rooms and 2 cabins. $$$–$$$$

Wilmington

Catherine's Inn on Orange, 410 Orange St, 28401, tel: (910) 251-0863 or (800) 476-0723. B&B A home away from home that's filled with antiques. 3 rooms. $

The Inn at St Thomas Court, 101 South Second St, 28401, tel: (910) 343-1800 or (800) 525-0909. A small, luxury hotel close to the Riverwalk and the business district. 23 suites. $–$$

Winston-Salem

Augustus T. Zevely Inn, 803 South Main St, 27101, tel: (910) 748-9299. B&B. In the heart of Old Salem, this historic inn offers charming, quaint rooms with homey touches. 12 rooms. $–$$

The Brookstown Inn, 200 Brookstown Inn, 27101, tel: (910) 725-1120 or (800) 845-2462. An old textile and flour mill dating to 1856 now offers overnight accommodations with breakfast and an afternoon wine reception. Has 39 rooms and 32 suites. $–$$

Wrightsville Beach

Blockade Runner Beach Resort, 275 Waynick Blvd, 28480, tel: (910) 256-2251 or (800) 541-1161. A favorite beach resort for families and groups, offering swimming, water sports, and golf packages, plus dining. 150 rooms. $–$$

Eating Out

Where to Eat

Asheville

Blue Moon Bakery, 60 Biltmore Ave, tel: (704) 252-6063. Downtown bakery serving breakfast and lunches all day, plus various blends of coffee. $

23 Page at Haywood Park, 1 Battery Park, tel: (704) 252-3685. Nouvelle cuisine served in an elegant atmosphere. $$–$$$

Atlantic Beach

Trattoria Da Francois, Fort Macon Rd & Kinston Ave, tel: (919) 240-3141. Northern and Italian cuisine are offered at this popular Italian eatery. $

Beaufort

The Beaufort Grocery, 117 Queen St, tel: (919) 728-3899. You can dine with the locals at this restaurant, which occupies a former grocery store. Lunch features soups, salads, and sandwiches; dinner, a variety of seafood, beef, and poultry entrees. $

Beech Mountain

Fred's Backside Deli, Beech Mountain Pkwy, tel: (704) 387-9331. Eat in or carry out breakfast foods, sandwiches, soups, and salads at this restaurant, located in a country store. $

Blowing Rock

The Blowing Rock Cafe, 321 Sunset Dr., tel: (704) 295-9474. Locals and visitors alike love the food and ambiance of this cozy little cafe. $

Brevard

Oh! Susanna's, 230 West Main St, tel: (704) 883-3289. Great sandwiches and daily specials are served at this homelike restaurant. $

Bryson City

Hemlock Inn, US 19, tel: (704) 488-2885. Open to the public by reservation, this well-established mountain inn serves breakfast and dinner from mid-April through mid-November and weekends only mid-November through mid-December. $–$$

Chapel Hill

Il Palio, Hotel Siena, 1505 East Franklin St, tel: (919) 929-4000. Mediterranean cuisine, including Italian, is served in this hotel restaurant. $–$$

The Fearrington House, Fearrington Village, tel: (919) 542-2121. Gourmet cuisine, beautiful to the eye and the palate, is served in a restored farm house. $$$

Charlotte

Bravo Ristorante, Adams Mark Hotel, 555 McDowell St, tel: (704) 372-4100. Professional singers not only serenade you but act as your servers at this classic Italian restaurant, the best place in Charlotte to celebrate special occasions. $$–$$$

Morton's of Chicago, 227 West Trade St tel: (704) 333-2602. Thick beefsteaks and lobsters flown in from the source, plus the freshest vegetables and delectable desserts, are standard fare at this Chicago-based restaurant chain. $$$–$$$$

Providence Cafe, 110 Perrin Pl. tel: (704) 376-2008. Innovative cuisine, including sandwiches prepared on focaccia crust and wondrous desserts, make this a favorite stop for lunch, dinner, or after-hours. $$–$$$$

Dillsboro

The Jarrett House, 100 Haywood St, tel: (704) 586-0265 or (800) 972-5623. Dine on fried chicken, country ham, fresh vegetables, fried applies, homemade biscuits, and all the trimmings at this mountain inn and then rock it off on the front porch. $

Durham

Anotherthyme Restaurant, Brightleaf Square, 109 North Gragson St, tel: (919) 682-5225. Healthy cuisine, including many vegetable dishes, are served in the casual atmosphere of a converted tobacco warehouse. $

Bullock's Bar-B-Que, 3330 Wortham St, tel: (919) 383-3211. Diners queue up early for chopped pork barbecue and Brunswick stew at this local favorite. $

Franklin

Hickory Ranch Restaurant, US 441 Business, tel: (704) 369-9909. Barbecue ribs and chicken, homemade soups, breads, and desserts, plus an ice cream parlor, make this a popular place to eat. (Closed late November through December.) $

Greenville

Parker's Barbecue # 1, 3109 South Memorial Dr., tel: (919) 756-2388. The place to get authentic Eastern-style North Carolina pork barbecue.$

Hickory

The Vintage House Restaurant, 271 3rd Ave, tel: (704) 324-1210. Italian cuisine and fresh seafood are served in a restored historic home. $$

Highlands

Louie Michaud's Fine Dining, Mountain Brook Center, US 64., tel: (704) 526-3573. You can count on the chef's original dishes at this gourmet restaurant. $

Hillsborough

The Colonial Inn, 153 King St, tel: (919) 732-2461. This old inn dating to 1759 serves Southern cuisine. $

Lake Lure

Lake Lure Inn, US 64 and 74, tel: (704) 625-2525. Fine dining is offered every day but Monday at this refurbished lakeside inn. Brunch is served on Sunday. $

Lexington

Lexington Barbecue #1, Business 85 & US 64, tel: (910) 249-9814. This 1950s-style roadside restaurant sets the benchmark for North Carolina barbecue, cooked over hot coals and served with red slaw and hush puppies. $

Manteo

Clara's Seafood Grill, 400 East Queen Elizabeth Hwy, tel: (919) 473-1727. Fresh seafood is served any way you like it at this waterside restaurant. $

Morehead City

Sanitary Fish Market & Restaurant, 501 Evans St, tel: (919) 247-3111. The tradition of fine seafood, spanning over half a century, continues at this waterside restaurant overlooking Bogue Sound. $

Nags Head

Kelly's Outer Banks Restaurant & Tavern, 2316 South Croatan Hwy, tel: (919) 441-4116. Fresh seafood, steaks, and prime rib are served in this well-established restaurant. $–$$

Owens' Restaurant, 7114 South Virginia Dare Tr., tel: (919) 441-7309. The freshest seafood found on the Outer Banks is offered at this family-owned restaurant. $–$$

New Bern

The Harvey Mansion Restaurant & Lounge, 216 Pollock St, tel: (919) 638-3205. Owned by a Swiss chef, this upscale restaurant offers international cuisine in a restored historic structure dating to 1797. $–$$

Ocracoke Island

Back Porch, Route 1324, tel: (919) 928-6401. Fresh seafood is served in a porch atmosphere. $

Raleigh

The Angus Barn, Raleigh-Durham Hwy at Airport Rd, tel: (919) 787-3505. Known for its steaks and seafood, as well as its extensive winelist, this is a dining tradition in Raleigh. $–$$

42nd St Oyster Bar & Seafood Grill, 508 West Jones St, tel: (919) 831-2811. Located in a restored warehouse, this seafood restaurant is a popular watering hole for locals and politics. $–$$

Irregardless, 901 West Morgan St, tel: (919) 833-8898. Vegetable dishes and other health-conscious foods are the order of the day at this bistro. $

Smithfield

Becky's Log Cabin Restaurant, 2491 US 70, tel: (919) 934-1534. Beef and seafood are served in a rustic cabin. $

Southern Pines

Whiskey McNeill's, 181 North Broad St, tel: (910) 695-8822. Soups, salads, sandwiches, and light meals delight patrons in this former filling station that's been converted into a restaurant. $

The Lob Steer Inn, US 1. tel: (910) 692-3503. This local favorite serves Angus beef and fresh seafood, along with a delightful salad bar. $

Sparta

Mountain Hearth Lodge & Restaurant, Route 1, tel: (910) 372-8743. Fresh homemade bread comes with all the meals at this mountain lodge. $

Valle Crucis

Mast Farm Inn, tel: (704) 963-5857. Breakfast and dinner are served in the dining room January through early March and late April through early November. Reservations are advised. $

Wayneville

Grandview Lodge, 809 Valley View Circle Rd, tel: (800) 255-7826 or (704) 456-5212. The well-prepared food is something to write home about at this well-kept mountain lodge. (Overnight guests have priority.) $–$$

Wilmington

Elijah's, Candler's Wharf, 2 Ann St, tel: (910) 343-1448. Classic American cuisine, including seafood dishes, is served overlooking the Cape Fear River. $–$$

The Pilot House, Candler's Wharf, 2 Ann St, tel: (919) 343-0200. A variety of entrees is offered at this waterside restaurant. $–$$

Winston-Salem

Leon's Cafe, 924 South Marshall St, tel: (919) 725-9593. Innovative cuisine is the standard in this neighborhood restaurant close to Old Salem. $

Salem Tavern Dining Room, 736 South Main St, tel: (919) 748-8585. Costumed servers tend to all your needs at this colonial restaurant, known for its chicken pot pie. $

Attractions

Places of Interest

Asheville

Biltmore Estate, US 25 (I-40, Exit 50), tel: (704) 255-1700 or (800) 543-2961. This 8,000-acre (3,200-hectare) private estate features a 255-room French Renaissance chateau, gardens, and a winery.

Blue Ridge Parkway, Headquarters, 200 BB & T Bldg, 1 Pack Square, tel: (704) 298-0398. This scenic crestline highway begins in North Carolina at the Virginia stateline and ends near the eastern entrance to the Great Smoky Mountains National Park at Cherokee. It intersects Asheville at Highways 25, 70, and 74.

Folk Art Center, Milepost 382, Blue Ridge Pkwy, tel: (704) 298-7928. Museum galleries, craft exhibits, demonstrations, and a shop offer authentic mountain-made crafts.

Pack Place – Education, Arts and Science Center, 2 South Pack Square, tel: (704) 257-4500. The downtown complex includes the Asheville Art Museum, Colburn Gem & Mineral Museum, Health Adventure, and YMI Cultural Center, plus a 520-seat theater.

Thomas Wolfe Memorial, 48 Spruce St, tel: (704) 253-8304. The novelist's boyhood home and the inspiration for *Look Homeward, Angel*, is open for tours.

Banner Elk

Hawksnest Golf & Ski Resort, off NC 105 at Seven Devils, tel: (704) 963-6561 or (800) 822-HAWK. Known for its night skiing, this resort offers 12 slopes, including a fabulous Black Diamond slope.

Sugar Mountain Resort, off NC194, tel: (704) 898-4521 or (800) 784-2768. Eighteen slopes and a 1½-mile (2.5-km) run, plus easy access, make this a popular resort.

Woolly Worm Festival, Banner Elk Elementary School grounds, tel: (704) 898-5605. An annual festival in mid-October where wise mountaineers predict the winter weather by the colored bands on the woolly worm. The event features woolly worm races, crafts, food, and entertainment.

Bath

Historic Bath, Route 92, tel: (919) 923-3971. The oldest chartered settlement in North Carolina includes several historic structures.

Beaufort

Historic Beaufort, 100 block of Turner St, tel: (919) 728-5225. The historic site contains 18th- and 19th-century homes, a courthouse, jail, apothecary's shop, and doctor's office. Living history demonstrations are often presented.

North Carolina Maritime Museum, 315 Front St, tel: (919) 728-7317. Beaufort's maritime history is told through exhibits, special programs, and boat building demonstrations.

Beech Mountain

Ski Beech, Beech Mountain Pkwy, tel: (704) 387-9283 or (800) 438-2093. Offering 14 slopes centered around an alpine village with shops and an outdoor ice rink.

Blowing Rock

Appalachian Ski Mountain, off US 321, tel: (704) 295-7858 or (800) 322-2373. The oldest ski resort in the High Country is known for its ski instruction.

Tweetsie Railroad, US 321 between Blowing Rock and Boone, tel: (704) 264-9061 or (800) 526-5740. Narrow-gauge train rides, live shows, and a petting zoo are a part of this fun-filled theme park, open spring, summer, and fall.

Boone

Appalachian Cultural Museum, US 321, tel: (704) 262-3117. The history and culture of the mountains are portrayed at this Appalachain State University museum.

An Appalachian Summer Festival, Appalachian State University, tel: (800) 841-ARTS. Music, dance, theater, visual arts, films, and educational programs are standard fare at this annual summer festival.

***Horn in the West* amphitheater**, off US 421, tel: (704) 264-2120. This summer outdoor drama portrays the life of early pioneer, including explorer Daniel Boone.

Brevard

Brevard Music Center, PO Box 592, 28712, tel: (704) 884-2019. An annual summer event featuring top musicians, singers, and performers.

Cradle of Forestry, on US 276 in Pisgah National Forest, tel: (704) 877-3130. Exhibits, films, photographs, and guided tours of historic buildings and a steam locomotive explain America's first forestry school.

Sliding Rock, on US 276 in Pisgah National Forest, tel: (704) 877-3130. Wear old jeans and sneakers to ride down this natural waterslide.

Bryson City

Nantahala Outdoor Center, US 19/74 West, tel: (704) 488-6900 or (800) 232-7238. This large outfitter offers guided and self-guided raft trips on the Nantahala River, plus other programs.

Burlington

Burlington Manufacturers Outlet Center, (I-85, Exit 45-B), tel: (910) 227-2872. More than 100 stores offer discounts on clothing, shoes, and household goods.

Chapel Hill

Morehead Planetarium, UNC, East Franklin St, tel: (919) 962-1247. The planetarium features a Zeiss Model VI projector revealing approximately 8,900 stars.

North Carolina Botanical Garden, Old Mason Farm Rd, tel: (919) 962-0522. This 600-acre (240-hectare) garden includes nature trails, carnivorous plants, plant collections, aquatics, and herb gardens.

Charlotte

African-American Cultural Center, 401 North Myers St, tel: (704) 374-1565. Special exhibits and events relating to the African-American experience are the focus of this center.

Charlotte Motor Speedway, off I-85 at Concord, tel: (704) 455-3200. Home of the Coca-Cola 600, the NASCAR facility also offers tours.

Discovery Place, 301 North Tryon St, tel: (704) 372-6261 or (800) 935-0553 . One of the nation's top hands-on science museums offers an OMNIMAX theatre, planetarium and exhibits.

Historic Latta Plantation, 5225 Sample Rd, Huntersville, tel: (704) 875-2312. The restored plantation home of James Latta offers tours, an equestrian center, and other activities.

Mint Museum of Art, 2730 Randolph Rd, tel: (704) 333-6468. Formerly a US Mint, the museum offers outstanding collections and rotating exhibits.

Paramount's Carowinds, I-77 & Carowinds Blvd, tel: (704) 588-2606 or (800) 888-4FUN. Rides, shows, shops, camping, and a amphitheatre offering big-name entertainment are offered at this movie themepark, open from early June through mid-October.

Radisson Grand Resort, 3000 Heritage Pkwy, Fort Mill, SC, tel: (800) 374-1234. This family resort features a huge waterpark and other recreational choices, plus tours of Billy Graham's boyhood home.

Reed Gold Mine State Historic Site, 9621 Reed Mine Rd, Stanfield, tel: (704) 786-8337. The site of the first discovery of gold in America offers a museum, mine tours, gold panning, hiking, and picnicking.

Richard Petty Driving Experience, 6022 Victory Ln., Harrisburg, tel: (704) 455-9443. Experience the thrill of stock car racing with a pro.

Cherokee

Cherokee Indian Reservation, tel: (800) 438-1601. Home to the Eastern Band of the Cherokee Indians, this 56,000-acre (23,000-hectare) reservation offers several attractions, including the Museum of the Cherokee Indian, Oconaluftee Indian Village, and "Unto These Hills" outdoor drama.

Great Smoky Mountains National Park, tel: (615) 436-1200. America's most visited park, which straddles the North Carolina/Tennessee border, is a protected forest offering historic sites, camping, fishing, horseback riding, hiking, picnicking, nature programs, and more.

Chimney Rock

Chimney Rock Park, US 64/74, tel: (704) 625-9611 or (800) 277-9611. A 26-story elevator ride takes you to the top of the summit for breathtaking views of Hickory Nut Gorge.

Dillsboro

Great Smoky Mountains Railway, tel: (704) 586-8811 or (800) 872-4681 . Offering excursions through the Nantahala Gorge and other scenic areas, the train departs from Dillsboro, as well as Bryson City, Andrews, and Murphy, from late March through December.

Durham

Duke Homestead Historic Site and Tobacco Museum, 2828 Duke Homestead Rd, tel: (919) 477-5498. Tobacco museum and original home and barns of the Duke family.

Duke University Chapel, West Campus Chapel Dr., tel: (919) 684-2572. Gothic cathedral offering pipe organ concerts, carillon, and nondenominational worship services on Sunday.

Edenton

Historic Edenton, PO Box 474, 27932, tel: (919) 482-2637. Located on Edenton Bay, this colonial town dating to 1722 offers an extensive historic district. Guided tours are available.

Fayetteville

Marquis de Lafayette Collection, Methodist College, 5400 Ramsey St, tel: (919) 630-7123. Letters, books, and artifacts pertaining to the famous French general are displayed in the Lafayette Room.

Flat Rock

Carl Sandburg National Historic Site, Little River Rd, off I-26, tel: (704) 693-4178. A 263-acre (106-hectare) goat farm where the author spent the last years of his life with his family.

Greensboro

Eastern Music Festival, Guilford College, Friendly Rd, tel: (910) 333-7450. An annual summer music festival featuring top performers.

Greensboro Historical Museum, 130 Summit Ave, tel: (910) 373-2043. Exhibits on short-story writer O.Henry, Dolley Madison, and the Woolworth sit-ins, plus early settlement, military history, and transportation.

Weatherspoon Art Gallery, UNC-G Campus, Tate and Spring Garden Sts, tel: (910) 334-5770. Six galleries showcase an outstanding collection of 20th-century American art.

High Point

Furniture Discovery Center, 101 West Green Dr., tel: (910) 887-3876. Furniture production, from start to finish, is explained in this unique museum, the only one of its kind in the country. (A list of furniture outlets is available from the High Point Convention and Visitors Bureau, 300 South Main St, tel: (910) 884-5255.)

Kannapolis

Cannon Village, 200 West Ave, tel: (704) 938-3200. Namebrands are discounted at outlet stores in the village, which also features a free textile museum and show.

Kill Devil Hills

Wright Brothers National Memorial, Milepost 8 on US 158 Bypass, tel: (919) 441-7430. Two Ohio bicycle mechanics called Wilbur and Orville Wright successfully lifted their crude flyer off the ground on December 17, 1903, marking man's first flight.

Level Cross (near Randleman)

Richard Petty Museum, 311 Branson Mill Rd, tel: (910) 495-1143. Race cars, awards, and photos honor the seven-time Winston Cup Series Champion, considered the "King of NASCAR racing."

Lexington

Lexington Barbecue Festival, tel: (800) 222-5579. Held the last weekend of October, the festival features barbecue, a pig parade, music, and crafts.

Linville

Grandfather Mountain, off US 221 and the Blue Ridge Pkwy, tel: (704) 733-4337 or (800) 468-7325. Native animal habitat, Nature Center, and a mile-high swinging bridge, plus the annual Grandfather Games, make this a popular attraction.

Maggie Valley

Ghost Town in the Sky, US 19, tel: (704) 926-1140. Open May through October, this western theme park offers gun fights, live shows, and thrilling rides. A chairlift and an incline railway carry passengers over 3,000 ft (900 meters) up the mountain from the parking lot.

Cataloochee Ski Area, Route 1, Box 502, 28751, tel: (704) 926-0285 or (800) 768-0285. Adjacent to a dude ranch by the same name, this ski resort offers nine slopes and overnight lodging.

Manteo

Fort Raleigh National Historic Site, Roanoke Island, tel: (919) 473-5772. About 3 miles (5 km) north of Manteo, this is the site of "The Lost Colony," the first English settlement in America which was established in 1587 and vanished three years later. The story is the subject of the summer outdoor drama that is presented at Waterside Theatre, also here.

Mount Gilead

Town Creek Indian Mound State Historic Site, between Routes 731 and 73, tel: (910) 439-6802. This state historic site brings to life the Creek Indian culture of 300 years ago via interpretive exhibits and a program.

New Bern

Tryon Palace Restorations and Gardens Complex, George and Pollock Sts, tel: (919) 638-1560. The elaborate palace and gardens of Royal Governor William Tryon, who lived in the 1770s, have been constructed on the original site. Also here are the 1828 Dixon-Stevenson House, the 1783 John Wright Stanly House, and the 1809 New Bern Academy Museum.

Raleigh

Executive Mansion, 200 North Blount St, tel: (919) 733-3456. Built in 1891, the Queen Anne-style Victorian mansion is the official residence of the Governor. It is open for tours.

Mordecei Historic Park, 1 Mimosa St, tel: (919) 834-4844. Once an antebellum plantation, the park includes the Greek-Revival Mordecei House and the cabin where President Andrew Johnson was born.

North Carolina Museum of Art, 2110 Blue Ridge Rd, tel: (919) 833-1935 or (919) 839-NCMA. Collections represent 5,000 years of artistic achievement from ancient Egypt to the present.

North Carolina Museum of History, 1 East Edenton St, tel: (919) 733-3894. Opened in 1994, this museum portrays the state's history through innovative exhibits.

North Carolina State Capitol, Capitol Square, tel: (919) 733-4994. Built between 1833 and 1840, this National Historic Landmark is a fine example of Greek Revival architecture.

North Carolina State Legislative Building, Jones and Salisbury Sts, tel: (919) 733-7928. Home of the North Carolina General Assembly, the building is open for tours.

Smithfield

Ava Gardner Museum, 205 South Third St, tel: (919) 934-5830. Photos, costumes, posters, and personal belongings tell the story of this famous Hollywood actress.

Valle Crucis

Mast General Store, tel: (704) 963-6511. On the National Register of Historic Places, this country store has been serving the community since 1883.

Waynesville

North Carolina International Folk Festival – Folkmoot USA, tel: (704) 648-2730. An annual festival, held in late July and early August, features singers and dancers from around the globe, as well as local cloggers and musicians.

Wilmington

Bellamy Mansion Museum of History and Design Arts, 503 Market St, tel: (910) 251-3700. Guided tours and exhibits on history, restoration, architecture, and regional art are the focus of this 1859 restored mansion.

Brunswick Town State Historic Site, NC 133, tel: (910) 371-6613. Museum and excavated remains of a colonial town.

Cape Fear Museum, 814 Market St, tel: (910) 341-7413. Interprets southeastern North Carolina history and natural history.

Henrietta II, Cape Fear Riverboats, Inc., Wilmington Waterfront, tel: (919) 343-1611 or (800) 676-0162. Sightseeing, dinner, moonlight, and sunset cruises are offered aboard this paddlewheeler.

St John's Museum of Art, 114 Orange St, tel: (910) 763-0281. Permanent collections highlight three centuries of North Carolina works, plus an American Collection, including color prints by artist Mary Cassatt.

***USS North Carolina* Battleship Memorial**, Wilmington Harbor, tel: (919) 251-5797. A World War II battleship that's now a memorial.

Winston-Salem

The Delta Arts Center, Winston-Salem State University, 1511 East Third St, tel: (910) 722-2625. Offers classes, workshops, lectures, exhibitions, and performances with a focus on African-American artists and performers.

Museum of Early Decorative Arts, 924 South Main St, tel: (910) 721-7360. Period rooms and galleries showcase regional furniture and decorative arts of the early South.

Old Salem, off I-40, tel: (910) 721-7300. Buildings and shops in the restored Moravian village dating to the mid-1700s. Guided tours available.

Reynolda House Museum of American Art, Reynolda Rd, tel: (910) 725-5325. Formerly a private home, the mansion houses an outstanding collection of American art, as well as costumes and toys belonging to the R. J. Reynolds family.

Southeastern Center for Contemporary Art, 750 Marguerite Dr., tel: (910) 725-1904. Southern painting, sculpture, and printmaking are displayed at this museum.

Tanglewood Park, Hwy 158, off I-40 West at Clemmons, tel: (910) 766-0591. The former private estate of William and Kate Reynolds is now a public park, and their home is open to overnight guests.

Civil War Sites

Historic Places

Atlantic Beach

Fort Macon State Park, Route 1190, tel: (919) 726-3775. This five-sided brick fort was engineered by Robert E. Lee and was garrisoned from 1834 until 1903. Museum, tours, picnicking, hiking, swimming.

Durham

Bennett Place State Historic Site, 4409 Bennett Memorial Rd, tel: (919) 383-4345. Confederate and Union generals worked out the terms of surrender here.

New Bern

The New Bern Civil War Museum, 301 Metcalf St, tel: (919) 633-2818. An extensive collection of Civil War memorabilia includes General Ulysses S. Grant's folding chair.

Newton Grove

Bentonville Battleground State Historic Site, NC 1008 East (I-95, Exit 90) tel: (919) 594-0789. The Confederates, 30,000 strong under the command of General Joseph E. Johnston, launched their last offensive against Union General William T. Sherman and his 60,000 troops here.

Raleigh

Pettigrew Hospital, US 64. Served as a Confederate hospital, US army barracks, and later on as a Confederate soldier's home.

National Cemetery, southeast corner of East Davie St and Rock Quarry Rd. Has the graves of over 1,000 soldiers who died during the War.

Washington

Fowle House, 203 West Main St. This was the home of the Confederate officer Gov. Daniel G. Fowle. There is a plaque at the site.

Williamston

Fort Branch, State 125, 11½ miles (18 km) northwest of Williamston. Situated at Rainbow Banks, this fort was built by the Confederates to guard the railroads and the upper part of the Roanoke River valley.

Wilmington

Fort Fisher State Historic Site, US 421, Kure Beach. Earthwork fortifications and a museum feature Civil War artifacts. The North Carolina Aquarium is also here.

SOUTH CAROLINA

Getting Acquainted

The Place

Known as: The Palmetto State for the strength of the palmetto log walls of Fort Moultrie that withstood British cannon fire and protected Charleston Harbor during the years of American Revolution.

Origin of Name: The name Carolina was given to a vast colonial territory by Sir Robert Heath in honor of King Charles I. When the area was carved into states, what remained of Carolina was divided into two states: North and South Carolina.

Motto: "*Animis Opibusque Parati*" – Prepared in Mind and Resources.

Entered Union: The 8th state entered the Union on May 23, 1788.

Population: 3½ million.

Population Density: Approximately 45.9 percent of the population lives in rural areas, and 54.1 percent lives in urban areas.

Area: 1,113 sq. miles (2,882 sq. km), including 186 miles (300 km) of coastline.

Time Zone: Eastern Time Zone (GMT minus five hours).

Highest Point: Sassafras Mountain, 3,560 ft (1,085 meters).

Climate: Mild. Temperatures usually range from 28°F (-2°C) to 91°F (33°C) with a summertime rainy season producing up to 20 inches (50 cm) of precipitation in coastal areas. Annual precipitation is 45 inches (115 cm). Humid year round.

Economy: The main industries are tobacco, beef cattle, broiler chicken, soy beans, dairy products, eggs, hogs, and corn. Tourism is becoming the number one industry in many of the areas.

Local Government: Made up of 46 counties, the state provides two senators and six representatives to US Congress.

Annual Visitors: 27 million.

Capital: Columbia.

Local Dialing Codes: 803 in the mid and lower part of the state and 864 in the upper part.

Famous Figures: Author Pat Conroy of *Prince of Tides* fame and Jim Rice of the Boston Red Sox.

Useful Addresses

State Office

South Carolina Division of Tourism, 1205 Pendleton St, Suite 104, Columbia, SC 29201. Tel: (803) 734-0129 (International), (803) 734-0122 (US), (800) 346-3634.

Local Offices

CHARLESTON

Charleston Trident Convention & Visitors Bureau, tel: (803) 853-8000, fax: (803) 723-4853.

COLUMBIA

Columbia Metropolitan Convention & Visitors Bureau, tel: (803) 254-0479 or (800) 264-4884, fax: (803) 799-6529.

HILTON HEAD ISLAND

Hilton Head Island Visitor & Convention Bureau, tel: (803) 785-3673, fax: (803) 785-7110.

MYRTLE BEACH

Myrtle Beach Area Convention Bureau, tel: (803) 448-1629 or (800) 488-8998, fax: (803) 448-3010.

Where to Stay

Accommodation

Abbeville

Abbewood, 509 North Main St, tel: (864) 459-5822. B&B. This *circa* 1860s restored home features a leaded glass entrance and wraparound veranda. $

The Belmont Inn, 106 Court Square, tel: (864) 459-9625. This historic inn features 24 guest rooms. $$

The Vintage Inn, 909 North Main St, tel: (864) 459-4784. An elegantly restored 1870s Victorian home, the Vintage sports wicker furniture on a wraparound porch. $–$$

Aiken

Annie's Inn, US 78 East, tel: (803) 649-6836. Escape to this 150-year-old farmhouse, and enjoy a stroll through its 200-year-old cemetery and expansive pecan grove. $

New Berry Inn, 240 Newberry St SW, tel: (803) 649-2935. Start the day with a full breakfast at this two-story Dutch Colonial home. $

Beaufort

Bay Street Inn, 601 Bay St, tel: (803) 522-0050. A filming site for the movie *The Prince of Tides*, this restored *circa* 1852 antebellum home fronts directly on the intracoastal waterway. $–$$

The Rhett House Inn, 1009 Craven St, tel: (803) 524-9030. Located in Beaufort's Historic District, this restored antebellum home features a full breakfast and afternoon tea and hors d' oeuvres. $$–$$$$

TwoSuns Inn, 1705 Bay St, tel: (803) 522-1122. With a sunrise view of the bay, this 1917 home prides itself on antiques and collectibles. $$

Camden

Candlelight Inn, 1904 Broad St, tel: (803) 424-1057. B&B. Situated in Camden's Historic District and shaded by a canopy of live oaks, the Candlelight Inn displays a variety of needlework, quilts, and antiques. $

Greenleaf Inn, 1308/10 North Broad St, tel: (800) 437-5874. Comprised of the Reynold's House (c. 1805) and the McLean House (c. 1890), this bed and breakfast has been carefully restored to retain its traditional flavor. $

Charleston

Ansonborough Inn, 21 Hassell St, tel: (800) 522-2073. Once a stationer's warehouse, this all-suite, *circa* 1900 inn features heart-pine beams, locally fired bricks, and an impressive atrium lobby. $$

Battery Carriage House, 20 South Battery, tel: (800) 775-5575. Named one of the most romantic of Charleston's inns by *Los Angeles Times* magazine, this inn overlooks White Point Gardens and Charleston Harbor. $$$

Capers Motte House, 69 Church St, tel: (803) 722-2263. Located in one of Charleston's prime residential areas, this four-story Georgian mansion boasts original moldings and outbuildings, Delft tile fireplaces, Adam mantels, and Waterford chandeliers. $–$$

Kings Courthouse Inn, 198 King St, tel: (803) 723-7000 or (800) 845-6119. This Greek-Revival style inn has unusual Egyptian detail. One of Historic King Street's largest and oldest structures. $$–$$$

The Mills House Hotel, 115 Meeting St, tel: (800) 874-9600. In 1861, Gen. Robert E. Lee stayed at this antebellum hotel located in Charleston's historic district. $$$$

Two Meeting Street Inn, 2 Meeting St, tel: (803) 723-7322. This Victorian home stands at a prominent point on the tip of the peninsula. Its Queen Ann-style veranda, graced by ornate arches, offers a stunning view of the Battery. $$–$$$$

Clemson

Nord-Lac, PO Box 1111, tel: (803) 639-2939. This 1826 log cabin features 17th-, 18th-, and 19th-century antiques, a billiard room, tennis court, and an electro-mechanical museum on the premises. $

Columbia

Claussen's Inn, 2003 Green St, tel: (803) 765-0440. With 29 king-size guest rooms, this historic inn is situated in the Claussen bakery building and features a three-story atrium. $$

Richland Street, 1425 Richland St, tel: (800) 779-7011. B&B. Each room exhibits its own personality and period antiques at this property located in the heart of Columbia's Historic District. $–$$

Edisto Island

Cassina Point Plantation, off Clark Rd, tel: (803) 869-2535. Situated 100 ft (30 meters) from a quiet tidal creek and pristine salt marsh, this *circa* 1847 bed and breakfast is the perfect spot to bird watch, fish, crab, or just set a while. $–$$

Georgetown

DuPre House, 921 Prince St, tel: (800) 921-3877. One of the oldest homes in Georgetown, the *circa* 1750 Du Pre House features four fireplaces, two verandas, and three sitting rooms. $

1790 House, 630 Highmarket St, tel: (800) 890-7432. B&B. Situated in Georgetown's Historic District, this historic inn is known for its hospitality. $–$$

Shaw House, 613 Cypress Ct., tel: (803) 546-9663. B&B. Overlooking miles of marsh land, the Colonial-style

Shaw House offers spacious rooms and numerous activities including bird watching and biking. $

Greenville

Pettigru Place, 302 Pettigru St, tel: (864) 242-4529. B&B. This restored 1920s home offers a tranquil rest on the quiet, historic street of Pettigru in downtown Greenville. $–$$

Hilton Head Island

Hilton Head Beach and Tennis Resort, Folly Field, tel: (803) 842-4402 or (800) 777-1700. This 200-villa, oceanfront resort features 10 tennis courts, two pools, and a restaurant. $$$–$$$$

Sea Pines Resort, Sea Pines and Shipyard plantations, tel: (800) 845-6131. This resort offers more than 500 oceanfront, marshside, and wooded accommodations. It also features the island's popular Harbour Town shopping village, yacht basin, and golf links. $$$–$$$$

Westin Resort, Port Royal Plantation, tel: (800) 933-3102. Considered the most luxurious of the island resort hotels, Westin Resort boasts a touted Sunday Brunch and a five-diamond AAA rating. $$$–$$$$

Isle of Palms

Wild Dunes Resort, 5757 Palm Blvd, tel: (800) 845-8880. Located on the northern tip of Isle of Palms, Wild Dunes is ranked a Top 50 tennis resort. It offers 2½ miles (4 km) of beach, two nationally acclaimed golf courses, and numerous vacation homes, villas and cottages. $$–$$$

Kiawah Island

Kiawah Island Inn and Villas, 12 Kiawah Beach Dr., tel: (800) 654-2924. In addition to its many famed golf courses, Kiawah Island Resort ranks among the Top 50 in tennis. And its Night Heron Park is home to the resort's highly acclaimed recreation program. $$$–$$$$

McClellanville

Laurel Hill Plantation, 8913 North, Hwy 17, tel: (803) 887-3708. The wrap-around porches of this plantation overlook Cape Romain Wildlife Refuge's expansive salt marshes. $

Mt Pleasant

Sunny Meadows, 1459 Venning Rd, tel: (803) 884-7062. A two-story, Southern Colonial home situated on 3 acres (1 hectare) of lush, Low Country landscape, Sunny Meadows is just 15 minutes from downtown Charleston. $

Myrtle Beach

Brustman House, 400 25th Ave South, tel: (803) 448-7699. Set against a wooded backdrop, this bed and breakfast is only 300 yards (275 meters) from the beach and offers its 10-grain buttermilk pancakes as a house breakfast specialty. $

Serendipity Inn, 407-71 Ave North, tel: (803) 449-5268. This award-winning, Spanish mission-style inn offers a heated pool, shuffleboard, and beach access 300 yards (275 meters) away. $–$$

Pawley's Island

Litchfield Plantation-A Country Inn, River Rd, tel: (800) 869-1410. Escape to this *circa* 1750 plantation house once situated on a sweeping rice plantation. $$–$$$

Sea View Inn, 414 Myrtle Ave, tel: (803) 237-4253. This quiet, oceanfront inn contains 14 rooms and three meals a day included. $$–$$$

Pendleton

Liberty Hall Inn, 621 South Mechanic St, tel: (864) 646-7500. Housed in the restored *circa* 1840 Piedmont Plantation House, this inn is located on 4 acres (2 hectares) near the town square and only five minutes from Clemson University. $

Seabrook Island

Seabrook Island Resort, 1002 Landfall Way, tel: (800) 845-2475. Just 20 miles (32 km) south of Charleston, this private beach resort features 36 holes of championship golf, 13 Har-Tru tennis courts, and an equestrian center with trail and beach rides. $$–$$$

Spartanburg

Nicholls Crook Plantation House, 120 Plantation Dr., tel: (864) 476-8820. This *circa* 1790, Georgian-style plantation house includes a parlor, tavern room, and period gardens. $

St Helena Island

The Royal Frogmore Inn, Hwy 21 East, tel: (803) 838-5400. Located in downtown Frogmore, this 50-room hotel lies no more than 10 minutes from Hunting Island. $

Walterboro

Mt Carmel Farm, Route 2, tel: (803) 538-5770. B&B. Take a break in one of the two rooms of this 75-year-old farm house that visitors say feels just like Grandma's house. Located 10 minutes from downtown. $

Eating Out

Where to Eat

Abbeville

The Village Grill, 114 Trinity St, tel: (864) 459-2500. Located right off the town square, this casual restaurant has something for everyone with a host of chicken, steak, and seafood dishes. $–$$

Aiken

No. 10 Downing Street, 241 Laurens St SW, tel: (803) 642-9062. For a special lunch or a memorable dinner, visit one of No. 10 Downing Street's four dining rooms, complete with fire places and a bakery. $–$$

Whiskey Road Bar-B-Que, 4248 Whiskey Rd, tel: (803) 649-4260. Sample South Carolina Bar-B-Que at its best. $

Beaufort

Plum's, 904½ Bay St, tel: (803) 525-1946. A front-porch eatery on Waterfront Park, Plum's satisfies locals and visitors with hot Reubens and evening blues. $–$$

Sgt White's Diner, 1908 Boundary St, tel: (803) 522-2029. This diner is locally heralded for its Southern cooking and down-home atmosphere. $

The Anchorage, 1103 Bay St, tel: (803) 524-9392. This quiet, elegant local haunt is located in an 18th-century mansion overlooking the Beaufort River. $$–$$$

Camden

The Tavern, 1308/10 North Broad St, tel: (800) 437-5874. Located beside the Greenleaf Inn, The Tavern serves up European-style cuisine prepared by an Austrian chef. $–$$

Charleston

Aaron's Deli, 215 Meeting St, tel: (803) 723-0233. Situated a block from the historic market, this deli is the perfect breakfast and lunch spot with bagels and chicory coffee. $

A.W. Shuck's Seafood Restaurant, 35 Market St, tel: (803) 723-1151. Fresh seafood in a lively atmosphere draws hungry visitors to this restaurant located in the heart of the historic market. $–$$

Blossom Cafe, 171 East Bay St, tel: (803) 722-9200. Blossom features light, innovative Italian fare served beneath a glass atrium and in an outdoor, walled garden. $–$$

Carolina's, 10 Exchange St, tel: (803) 724-3800. Recommended by Charlestonians, this American bistro is set against a backdrop of historic architecture and serves regional cuisine. $$

82 Queen, 82 Queen St, tel: (803) 723-7591. This 18th-century landmark features Low Country favorites and encompasses three buildings which are situated around a garden courtyard. $–$$$

Hyman's Seafood Co., 215 Meeting St, tel: (803) 723-6000. Adjoining Aaron's Deli, this seafood restaurant and popular raw bar draws a lively crowd. $–$$$

Le Midi, 337 King St, tel: (803) 557-5571. This restaurant features French country cooking in an elegant setting. Try the shrimp provencal. $–$$

Louis's Charleston Grill, 224 King St, tel: (803) 577-4522. Located at Charleston Place, Louis's boasts the regional cuisine of chef Louis Osteen, named "one of the most gifted chefs in America" by Town *and Country*. $$$

Magnolia's, 185 East Bay St, tel: (803) Located at the site of the original Customs House (c. 1739), Magnolia's slogan is "Award-winning uptown American cuisine with a down South flavor." $–$$

McCrady's, 2 Unity Alley, tel: (803) 853-8484. Located in the oldest tavern in the United States, McCrady's maintains a historic flavor peppered with contemporary cuisine. $–$$

Restaurant Million, 2 Unity Alley, tel: (803) 577-7472. Charleston's only member of the prestigious Relais & Chateaux chain, Restaurant Million serves up a delicious array of haute cuisine. $$$

Saracen, 141 East Bay St, tel: (803) 723-6242. This elegant restaurant situated in a Moorish-style building a few blocks from historic Rainbow Row features contemporary international fare. $$–$$$

Clemson

Nick's Tavern & Deli, 107-2 Sloan St, no telephone listing. Downtown Clemson's oldest tavern and deli offers an extensive appetizer, deli, and beer menu amidst a milieu of memorabilia. $–$$

Uniquely Clemson, Clemson University Campus, tel: (803) 656-3242. Located in Newman Hall, this quick stop sells Clemson's very famous ice cream and blue cheese, along with other dairy products. $

Columbia

Maurice's Piggy Park, 1600 Charleston Hwy, tel: (803) 791-5887. With nine locations throughout the area, Piggy Park is a midland South Carolina tradition you won't want to miss. $

Villa Tronco, 1213 Blanding St, tel: (803) 256-7677. Columbia's oldest Italian restaurant has been serving residents and visitors alike for over 50 years with fabulous food and old-world charm. $–$$

Edisto Island

Old Post Office Restaurant, 1442 Hwy 174, tel: (803) 869-2339. Specializing in fresh local seafood, this popular restaurant really is located in an old post office. $–$$

Georgetown

The Rice Paddy, 408 Duke St, tel: (803) 546-2021. This fine restaurant takes its name from the rice plantations plentiful in the 1700s and 1800s. $$

The River Room, 801 Front St, tel: (803) 527-4110. Located in an 1800s dry goods port, this casual restaurant specializes in grilled fish and features original brick and wood work. $–$$

Greenville

Annie's Natural Cafe, 121 South Main St, tel: (864) 271-4872. The award-winning staff of Greenville's unique vegetarian restaurant adds atmosphere with European-style courtyard dining. $–$$

Nippon Center Yagoto, 500 Congaree Rd, tel: (864) 288-8471. This Japanese restaurant and cultural center features 16th-, 17th-, and 18th-century cuisine with an emphasis on the artistry of presentation. $$–$$$

Hilton Head Island

Crazy Crab, Harbour Town, tel: (803) 363-CRAB. Steamed, fried, baked or broiled, Crazy Crab's seafood hits the spot in a family atmosphere. $–$$

The Quarterdeck, Harbour Town, tel: (803) 671-2222. Overlooking Calibogue Sound and the 18th hole of Harbour Town Golf Links, The Quarterdeck offers fine dining and a popular happy hour. $–$$

Isle of Palms

Sea Biscuit Cafe, 21 J.C. Long Blvd, tel: (803) 886-4079. Locals come from all around to relax at this favorite breakfast spot. $–$$

Johns Island

St Johns Island Cafe, 3140 Maybank Hwy, tel: (803) 559-9090. This casual roadside restaurant serves up iced tea and sandwiches on the weekdays with a Sunday brunch featuring beef tenderloin and eggs. $

Kiawah Island

Jasmine Porch, 12 Kiawah Beach Dr., tel: (800) 654-2924. Overlooking the Atlantic Ocean and adjacent to the Kiawah Island Inn, this restaurant specializes in contemporary Low Country seafood, with the rosemary- and garlic-roasted pork tenderloin a chef favorite. $$–$$$

Lady's Island

The Steamer, Hwy 21, tel: (803) 522-0210. From shrimp to oysters to flounder to shark, this local seafood restaurant always attracts a crowd with its plentiful menu. $$$

The Upper Crust, Hwy 21, tel: (803) 521-1999. Crab, lobster, and shrimp take the place of the traditional pepperoni pizza topping at this restaurant. $–$$

Whitehall Plantation Inn, Hwy 21 over the Woods Bridge, tel: (803) 521-1700. Enjoy a dinner of veal, lamb, or duckling against a backdrop of sunset and oak. $$

McClellanville

The Crab Pot Restaurant, Hwy 17, tel: (803) 887-3156. This casual roadside restaurant draws a crowd hungry for owner Laura McClellan's crab cakes. $–$$

Mt Pleasant

RB's Seafood Restaurant and Bar, 97 Church St, tel: (803) 881-0466. Overlooking Shem Creek, this casual family restaurant serves a wide range of seafood. $–$$

Shem Creek Bar and Grill, 508 Mill St, tel: (803) 884-8102. This dockside restaurant is popular for its raw bar and views of shrimp trawlers and sail boats lining Shem Creek. $–$$

Murrells Inlet

The Seafarer Restaurant, Hwy 17 and Hwy 707, tel: (803) 651-7666. This local restaurant's seafood buffet includes oyster, shrimp, crab legs, and clams. $–$$

Myrtle Beach

Bennett's Calabash Seafood, 9701 Hwy 17 North Kings Hwy, tel: (803) 449-7865. Originating in Calabash, North Carolina, Calabash-style seafood has been popular in the area since the 1940s when local fishermen first lightly battered and deep fried their catch. $–$$

Dixie Stampede, North Junction of Hwy 17 and 17 By-pass, tel: (803) 497-9700. Enjoy an Old South, nonalcoholic family dinner theater experience featuring a four-course feast of meat and potatoes. $$

Pawley's Island

The Carriage House, River Rd, tel: (803) 237-9322. Located at the *circa* 1750 Litchfield Plantation, this fine dining establishment serves fish, steak, pork, and pasta and requires reservations. $$

Tyler's Cove, Hwy 17 North, tel: (803) 237-4848. Experience the relaxed atmosphere indicative of Pawley's Island over a seafood, pasta, or steak dinner on the outdoor deck at this restaurant located at The Hammock Shops. $$

Pendleton

Lazy Islander, 134 Exchange St, tel: (864) 646-6337. Located on the square in historic downtown, this restaurant serves breakfast, lunch, and dinner and specializes in fresh seafood and daily raw bar specials. $–$$

Seabrook Island

The Island House, 1002 Landfall Way, tel: (803) 768-2571. The only restaurant on Seabrook, The Island House, like the island itself, is private. Only those staying on the island may enjoy this fine establishment. $$

Spartanburg

Simple Simon, Pine St, tel: (864) 582-9169. This 1950s diner is a popular spot for local students and old timers. Don't bother calling for an address. They'll just tell you to head down Pine almost to Main. $

The Beacon, 255 Ridgeville Rd, tel: (864) 585-9387. It's best to know which Bar-B-Que plate you wish to order before stepping up to the Beacon's ominous counter and answering to an impatient waiter. The stress is part of the charm. $

St Helena Island

The Gullah House Restaurant, Hwy 21, tel: (803) 838-2402. Located in Frogmore, The Gullah House serves up area favorites including crab cakes, Low Country boil, country fried steaks, and bean stew. $

The Shrimp Shack, on the way to Hunting Island, tel: (803) 838-2962. Try the shrimp burger at this casual roadside stop. $

Sullivan's Island

Sullivan's Restaurant, 2019 Middle St, tel: (803) 883-3222. Hearty portions of Southern cooking and seafood specials make this local dinner spot enjoyable. $–$$

Sully's, 2213-B Middle St, tel: (803) 883-9777. Enjoy raw oysters, steamed crab legs, shrimp and scallops in a casual beach atmosphere. $$

Walterboro

Duke's Bar-B-Que, Robertson Blvd, tel: (803) 549-1446. Open Thursday through Saturday, Duke's satisfies the soul with all-you-can-eat all the time and bread straight out of bags placed on every table. $

Drinking Laws

South Carolina is one of the few states that adheres to old laws regulating the distribution of alcohol. Whereas most drinking establishments in the US follow the free-pour method – that is, mixing drinks from full-sized liquor bottles – Palmetto State legislators say that using one mini bottle per drink allows for more efficient taxation and better accountability.

According to some, the antiquated laws deny bar patrons the generosity of free-wheeling, free-pouring bar tenders. On the other hand, police say the amount of alcohol contained in a mini bottle exceeds the amount of alcohol they'd like to see customers imbibe per drink. They feel bar owners would encourage under-pouring under the free-pour system.

In any event, those bars licensed to sell mini bottle drinks can now sell beer on Sunday in some cities – as can many restaurants and grocers stocking alcoholic beverages. In response to citizen pressure and the demands of the restaurant industry in particular, Charleston, Columbia, Edisto Beach, Hilton Head, the Myrtle Beach area, and Santee are among those to embrace this law.

Most of the state, though, cannot serve alcoholic beverages after midnight Saturday and all day Sunday. And package store sales of alcoholic beverages are permitted only between 9am and 7pm Monday through Saturday.

Anyone appearing with an open container of beer or the like – especially in a moving vehicle or on South Carolina highways – faces a very hefty penalty.

Attractions

Places of Interest

Abbeville

Abbeville Opera House, The Town Square, tel: (864) 459-2157. Fanny Brice, Jimmy Durante, and Groucho Marx have all graced this stage.

Poliakoff Collection of Western Art, 203 South Main St, tel: (864) 459-4009. Located in the Abbeville County Library, this is one of the best collections of contemporary Native American art outside the Southwest.

Aiken

Aiken County Historical Museum, 433 Newberry St, SW, tel: (803) 642-2015. Indian and early settlement artifacts are displayed in a former winter colony mansion.

Thoroughbred Hall of Fame, Whiskey Rd and Dupree Pl., tel: (803) 642-7630. Open fall through spring, this collection of racing memorabilia commemorates winning locally bred and trained horses.

Beaufort

Henry C. Chambers Waterfront Park, Bay St. This public park designed by landscape architect Robert Marvin offers lovely views of the bay, a covered pavilion, swings, picnic areas, and many area events.

Fort Frederick, SC 280. Fort built by the British in 1732 for protection from the Spanish, French and Indians.

Camden

Carolina Cup and Colonial Cup, tel: (803) 432-6513. A popular place for equestrian pursuits, Camden's two steeplechases held at the Springdale Race Course the first in March and the second in November draw many a tailgater.

Historic Camden Revolutionary War Site, tel: (803) 432-9841. This 92-acre (38-hectare) site includes the Georgian-Colonial mansion, the Kershaw-Cornwallis House, powder magazine, log cabins, nature trails, and more.

Charleston

Avery Research Center for African-American History and Culture, 125 Bull St, tel: (803) 727-2009. This restored 1865 facility documents, preserves, and promotes Low Country African-American culture and history.

Charlestowne Landing, Hwy 171, tel: (803) 852-4200. Situated on 80 acres (32 hectares) of landscaped gardens, this April 1670 Charleston settlement site features an indigenous animal forest and full-scale replica of a 17th-century trading vessel.

Edmondston-Alston House, 21 East Battery, tel: (803) 722-7171. Prosperous merchant and wharf owner Charles Edmondston built this historic home, which was bought in 1838 by rice planter Colonel Charles Alston.

French Protestant (Huguenot) Church, 136 Church St, tel: (803) 722-4385. Designed by Edward B. White and built in 1844–45, this is the fourth church to be sited here. French Huguenots seeking religious freedom first worshipped at this site in 1687.

Heyward-Washington House, 87 Church St, tel: (803) 722-0354. This is the *circa* 1772 home of wealthy rice planter Daniel Heyward and his son, Thomas, who was a signer of the Declaration of Independence. George Washington was a guest here in 1791.

Joseph Manigault House, 350 Meeting St, tel: (803) 723-2926. This *circa* 1803, Adam-style home with its cantilevered staircase was designed by Charleston architect Gabriel Manigault for his brother Joseph.

Middleton Place, Ashley River Rd, tel: (800) 782-3608. Laid out by Henry Middleton in 1741, this is America's oldest landscaped gardens. The plantation house and stableyards of this National Historic Landmark offer a glimpse into plantation life.

Nathaniel Russell House, 51 Meeting St, tel: (803) 724-8481. Built before 1809 by Nathaniel Russell, son of a Chief Justice of Rhode Island, this Adam-style home features a flying staircase, music room, and a south wing tier of elliptical rooms.

Spoleto Festival U.S.A., tel: (800) 255-4659. Happening late May through mid-June, this city-wide festival created by maestro Jean Carlo Menotti offers opera, dance, theater, jazz, chamber music, and more.

The Dock Street Theater, 135 Church St, tel: (803) 723-5648. A combination of reconstructions of an early Georgian playhouse and Planters Hotel formed this theater, on the site of one of America's first playhouses.

The Circular Congregational Church, 150 Meeting St, tel: (803) 577-6400. The church's present design was created by Robert Mills in 1806 – only to have the fire of 1861 destroy the building. It was rebuilt on the site in 1891.

The Citadel, 171 Moultrie St, tel: (803) 792-5006. Author and Citadel graduate Pat Conroy based his novel, *Lords of Discipline*, on life at this military college with a history that dates back to the Civil War.

The City Market, Market St. In operation as a public market since the Revolutionary War, this facility was never used to auction slaves, as many people believe.

The College of Charleston, St Phillip and George Sts, tel: (803) 792-5507. Founded in 1770, this was the first municipal college in America.

The Gibbes Museum of Art, 135 Meeting St, tel: (803) 722-2706. This museum houses a collection of American art with a focus on South Carolina.

The Preservation Society of Charleston, 147 King St, tel: (803) 722-4630. Founded in 1920, the Preservation Society of Charleston is the nation's oldest community-based preservation organization. It also sponsors house and garden tours September through October.

Clemson

Clemson University, tel: (803) 656-4789. This agricultural college is best known in these parts for its football team the Tigers, and its fierce rivalry with the University of South Carolina's Gamecocks.

Fort Hill, Clemson University Campus, tel: (803) 656-2475. This is the antebellum home of John C. Calhoun, noted statesman and vice president under Andrew Jackson and John Quincey Adams.

Hanover House, Clemson University Campus, tel: (803) 656-4789. This *circa* 1716 plantation house was built by a Huguenot family on what is now the site of the Santee-Cooper project.

South Carolina State Botanical Garden, Clemson University Campus, tel: (803) 656-2458. Some 2,200 varieties of ornamental plants are raised in this 256-acre (104-hectare) consolidation of five smaller gardens.

Columbia

Columbia Museum of Art and Gibbes Planetarium, Senate and Bull Sts, tel: (803) 254-7827. Contemporary, Baroque, and Renaissance art, as well as weekend planetarium programs.

Memorial Park, Hampton and Gadsden Streets. Commemorating 980 South Carolinians who died in Vietnam, this park houses the largest monument of its type outside of Washington, DC.

Riverbanks Zoo and Garden, off I-26, tel: (803) 779-8717. Ranked among the top zoos in the nation, Riverbanks features 2,000 animals, a microscopic rain forest, desert, undersea kingdom, and Southern farm. Visit its 70-acre (28-hectare) botanical garden across the Saluda River.

South Carolina State Museum, 301 Gervais St, tel: (803) 737-4921. Displays covering four floors of this renovated textile mill touch on everything from art, to history, to natural history, to science technology.

The Fort Jackson Museum, Jackson Blvd, tel: (803) 751-7419. Memorabilia and displays celebrate the life and times of President Andrew Jackson, for whom the fort was named.

Woodrow Wilson's Boyhood Home, 1705 Hamton St, tel: (803) 252-1770. Woodrow Wilson spent his teenage years here while his father taught at Columbia Theological Seminary.

Edisto Island

Edisto Beach State Park, SC 174, tel: (803) 869-2156. Stay in a marshside cabin or oceanfront campsite along nearly 3 miles (5 km) of South Carolina beaches.

Edisto Island Presbyterian and Legare Mausoleum, SC 174, tel: (803) 869-2326. Although the church is usually locked, the cemetery holds ornate tombstones marking the graves of sea island planters, and the mausoleum holds a story of its own.

Edisto River Canoe and Kayak Trail, off I-95 on US 15. Travel the state's official, 56-mile (90-km) blackwater river kayak and canoe trail.

Windsor Plantation, SC 174. This privately owned, *circa* 1857 home is typical of sea island homes built up on piers to catch the breeze and skirt stormy seas.

Georgetown

Georgetown County Courthouse, Screven and Price Sts. This circa 1824 building was designed by heralded American architect Robert Mills.

Hampton Plantation State Park, off US 17, tel: (803) 546-9361. The *circa* 1750 plantation house and outbuildings of South Carolina's poet laureate Archibald Rutledge are a National Historic Landmark.

Hopsewee Plantation, US 17, tel: (803) 546-7891. This plantation is the 1740 home of Continental Congressman Thomas Lynch and his son Thomas Jr, who signed the Declaration of Independence.

Waterman-Kaminski House, 1003 Front St, tel: (803) 546-7706. This late 18th-century town home displays a fine collection of antiques and furnishings.

Greenville

Gallery of Sacred Art and Bible Lands Museum and Planetarium, Bob Jones University, tel: (864) 242-5100. This museum houses one of the world's most extraordinary collections of religious art and Biblical antiquities.

Greenville County Museum of Art, 420 College St, tel: (864) 271-7570. Included in a large collection of Southern art are works by Georgia O'Keeffe and Jasper Johns.

Paris Mountain State Park, State Park Rd, tel: (864) 244-5565. Rising 1,000 ft (300 meters) above Greenville, this park has been protected since 1890.

Roper Mountain Science Center, Roper Mtn Rd, tel: (864) 281-1188. This educational center includes an observatory, planetarium, nature trail, Discovery Room, Sea Life Room, and more.

Table Rock State Park, SC 11, tel: (864) 878-9813. One of the state's oldest and most popular parks, Table Rock is easily recognizable by the rounded dome of its crest.

Hilton Head Island

Harbour Town, Sea Pines Plantation, tel: (800) 845-6131. This shopping area centered around Harbour Town Yacht Basin and Marina features numerous shops and restaurants clustered around a lighthouse.

Museum of Hilton Head, US 278, tel: (803) 689-6767. This small natural history museum above the welcome center details the area's wildlife.

New Hall Audubon Preserve, Palmetto Bay Rd. This is the perfect place to see the nearly 200 species of birds that flock to the island each year.

Pinkney Island National Wildlife Refuge, US 278. Over 4,000 acres (1,600 hectares) of salt marsh and secluded islands offer 14 miles (23 km) of nature trails.

Sea Pines Forest Preserve, Sea Pines Plantation, tel: (800) 845-6131. This 400-acre (160-hectare) preserve offers walking trails and picnic areas, along with its famed Indian Shell Ring.

Mt Pleasant

Boone Hall Plantation, Hwy 17, tel: (803) 884-4371. Originally a 17,000-acre (7,000-hectare) cotton plantation, Boone Hall is most noted for its nine original slave cabins and its avenue of oaks that inspired *Gone With The Wind*.

Palmetto Islands County Park, near Boone Hall, tel: (803) 884-0832. Marsh boardwalks, a 2-acre (1-hectare) pond, mile-long canoe trail, playground, and water slide are a few of the activities this park has to offer.

Patriot's Point Naval and Maritime Museum, US 17 North, tel: (803) 884-2727. Just across the Cooper River from Charleston, Patriot's Point boasts the aircraft carrier *Yorktown*, the second of its name, replacing the *Fighting Lady* of WWII.

Murrells Inlet

Brookgreen Gardens, US 17, tel: (800) 849-1931. Developed by Archer and Anna Hyatt Huntington in the 1930s, this landscaped sculpture garden features more than 500 of America's finest 19th- and 20th-century sculptures.

Huntington Beach State Park, US 17 South, tel: (803) 237-4440. Camping, picnicking, and hiking highlight the winter home and studio of famed sculptor Anna Hyatt Huntington.

Myrtle Beach

Carolina Opry, junction of US 17 and 17 Bypass, tel: (803) 238-8888. See a variety of music and comedy featuring everything from country, to bluegrass, to 1940s medleys.

Motion Master Moving Theater, 917 North Ocean Blvd, tel: (803) 626-0069. Buckle your seatbelts. This theater's seats allow you to move with the action on the screen.

Myrtle Beach National Wax Museum, 1000 North Ocean Blvd, tel: (803) 448-9921. See a host of historical figures presented in period costume.

Myrtle Beach Pavilion and Amusement Park, 9th Ave North and Ocean Blvd. Experience the antique Herschel-Spillman merry-go-round, the 1900 German pipe organ, and the many rides at this popular amusement park.

Ripley's Believe It Or Not Museum, 901 North Ocean Blvd, tel: (803) 448-2331. Enjoy a self-guided tour of over

500 exhibits profiling the mysteries Robert Ripley encountered in his travels to 198 countries.

South Carolina Hall of Fame, 21st Ave North and Oak St, tel: (803) 448-4021. Interactive video displays pay tribute to famous South Carolinians.

Pendleton

Woodburn, SC 88 East and US 76 West, tel: (864) 646-3782. This Upcountry plantation serves as a prime example of mansions built by wealthy Low Country planters to escape the malarial coast of the early 1800s.

Hunters Store, the Square, tel: (864) 646-3782. Now the home of the Pendleton District Historical, Recreational, and Tourism Commission, this structure was the heart of commerce for the area in 1850.

Pendleton District Agriculture Museum, US 76 West, tel: (864) 646-3782. This by-appointment-only museum houses antique farm tools and equipment, including a cotton gin that pre-dates Eli Whitney's.

Pendleton Farmers Society Hall, the Square, tel: (864) 646-3782. Constructed in 1826 as the local county court house, this structure once housed the nation's third oldest agrarian association.

Spartanburg

Croft State Park, off SC 56, tel: (864) 585-1283. An old WWII training ground, this park features a large swimming pool, equestrian facilities, a 160-acre (65-hectare) fishing lake, and more.

Kings Mountain National Military Park, between SC 161 and I-85 northwest of York. The 3,590-acre (1,450-hectare) park marks the site of one of the most important battles of the American Revolution's Southern theater.

The Price House, off I-26 on US 221, tel: (864) 596-3501. This *circa* 1795 house of Flemish bond features indoor chimneys and a Dutch Gambrel roof.

Walnut Grove Plantation. Located in the countryside near Spartanburg, this *circa* 1765 plantation includes a doctor's office, school, smokehouse, gristmill, and family burial ground on its premises.

St Helena Island

Fort Fremont, Lands End Rd. Built during the Spanish-American War to guard the entrance to Port Royal Sound, this fort is rumored to house the ghost of a soldier who lost his head in battle.

Penn Center Historic District, Mt Luther King Dr., tel: (803) 838-2432. On this site was established the Penn School, the first school for freed slaves in the South. It is a good place to discover more about the gullan dialects.

York W. Bailey Museum, Mt Luther King Dr., tel: (803) 838-2432. This museum contains exhibits on the history of African-American Sea Island residents.

Sullivan's Island

Officer's Row, I'on Ave. This block of 10 beautiful homes along I'on Avenue was originally constructed to house Fort Moultrie field officers and their families.

Wadmalaw Island

The Charleston Tea Plantation, 6617 Maybank Hwy, tel: (803) 559-0383. The only tea plantation in the US, this plantation grows American Classic Tea, which is served at the White House.

Walterboro

South Carolina Artisans Center, 334 Wichman St, tel: (803) 549-0011. Support South Carolina artists and craftsmen while watching them create hand crafted jewelry, baskets, pottery, and more.

The Colleton Museum, corner of Jeffries Blvd and Benson St, tel: (803) 549-2303. Colleton County's history as a major center of rice production is maintained in this restored 1855 jail.

Walterboro Library Society Building, tel: (803) 549-9595. This small-frame, Federalist-style building defined the city's boundaries when it was incorporated in 1826.

Civil War Sites

Historic Places

Most towns in South Carolina have Civil War Sites and stories. Here are some of the most interesting:

Abbeville

Burt-Stark House, 306 North Main St, tel: (864) 459-4297. Confederate President Jefferson Davis held his last war cabinet meeting here.

Perrin House, across from Burt-Stark House. This is the former home of Thomas Chiles, the first to sign the Ordinance of Secession. Members of the Confederate cabinet stayed at the Perrin House when President Davis visited the Burt-Stark House.

Upper Long Cane Cemetery, SC 20. Thomas Chiles Perrin and David Lewis Wardlaw, delegates to the secession convention of 1860 are buried in this cemetry. Wardlaw's brother, Chancellor Francis Hugh Wardlaw, prepared the original draft of the secession ordinance.

Beaufort

Beaufort Museum, 713 Craven St, tel: (803) 525-7077. Nature, war, and early industry relics are housed in this 1798 arsenal.

National Cemetery, US 21. Created in 1863 by Abraham Lincoln for victims of war in the South, this cemetery is home to 12,000 Union soldiers and a group of Confederate soldiers.

Secession House, 1113 Craven St. South Carolina's Ordinance of Secession was first drafted at this *circa* 1813 home. Union soldiers' graffiti can still be seen on the basement walls.

Camden

Battle of Boykin's Mill, SC 261 at Boykin's Mill. On April 8, 1865, 2,700 Union troops marched from Georgetown to destroy the railroad between Sumter and Camden. At Boykin's Mill on April 19, a small force of Confederates delayed their action for a day in one of the last engagements of the war.

Confederate Generals Monument, Chestnut and Lyttleton Sts. This six-columned fountain in Rectory Square commemorates six of the area's Confederate generals.

Greenleaf Villa, 1307 Broad St, tel: (800) 437-5874. This was the home of Gen. Robert E. Lee's cousin, Dr Lee, who used the residence as a Confederate hospital. The house was saved by Mrs Lee and her bucket brigade when Federal troops tried to burn it.

Mulberry Plantation, 3 miles (5 km) south of Camden. This is the boyhood home of Confederate statesman and general James Chestnut Jr.

Charleston

American Military Museum, 40 Pinckney St, tel: (803) 723-9620. This off-the-beaten-track museum houses hundreds of uniforms and artifacts from all branches of the military covering the Vietnam, Korean, World, Spanish American, Indian, and Civil wars.

Confederate Museum, 188 Meeting St, tel: (803) 723-1541. This museum is housed in the *circa* 1841 Market Hall at the head of The City Market and is operated by the Daughters of the Confederacy.

Drayton Hall, 3380 Ashley River Rd, tel: (803) 766-0188. This *circa* 1738 Georgian Palladian-style home of the Drayton family survived the Civil War with the help of a family member who fibbed a small pox epidemic inside to Union troops at the doorstep.

Fort Johnson, James Island. On April 12, 1861, Confederate troops at Fort Johnson fired the first shots of the Civil War on a Union-occupied Fort Sumter in Charleston Harbor.

Fort Sumter National Monument,tel: (803) 883-3123, Charleston Harbor. On December 26, 1860, Federal forces under Major Robert Anderson occupied this fort. Not four months later, Confederate forces at Fort Johnson fired on the fort, marking the beginning of the long Civil War. Boat tours leave from Charleston marina.

Magnolia Cemetery, 70 Cunnington Ave, tel: (803) 722-8638. Founded in 1849 on the banks of the Cooper River, this cemetery is home to numerous Southern leaders and is on the National Register of Historic Places.

Magnolia Plantation and Gardens, Hwy 61, tel: (803) 571-1266. America's oldest garden boasts one of the largest collections of azaleas and camellias in America. The summer home of the Drayton family, the plantation house holds Civil War memorabilia.

Pringle House, 27 King St. Also known as the Miles Brewton House, this *circa* 1765 home served as headquarters for Federal troops in 1865. Two Pringle sons were killed in Confederate service – one died on the front steps after being carried home from battle.

The Charleston Museum, 360 Meeting St, tel: (803) 722-2996. This first and oldest museum in the United States houses a full-scale replica of the Confederate States' submarine *Hunley*.

Columbia

Confederate Relic Room and Museum, Sumter and Pendleton Sts, tel: (803) 734-9813. From the American Revolution and beyond, this museum located in the War Memorial Building includes weapons, clothing, flags, money, and more.

Duncan Home Site, 1615 Gervais St. On this location, Gen. Sherman used Col Blanton Duncan's home as his Southern headquarters.

First Baptist Church, 1306 Hampton St, tel: (803) 256-4251. This church features the pulpit, slave gallery, and brick-pillard portico in existence in 1860 when the first Secession Convention in the South was held here.

Governor's Mansion and Green, 800 block of Richland St, tel: (603) 737-1710. Built in 1855 to house Columbia Academy officers training for The Citadel, the mansion was the only building left standing after Union troops burned the arsenal.

Guignard House, 1527 Senate St. Rumor has it that this house was saved from Sherman's fires by Dilcie the slave cook who confronted the general, offering him and his men the best cooking in Columbia.

Hampton-Preston Mansion, 1615 Blanding St, tel: (803) 252-1770. The city home of Confederate leader and popular South Carolina Governor Gen. Wade Hampton, this antebellum mansion was occupied by Union forces in 1865.

Mann-Simons Cottage: Museum of African-American Culture, 1403 Richland St, tel: (803) 252-1770. This white-frame cottage is the former home of Celia Mann, who bought her freedom from slavery in Charleston and walked to Columbia to start anew.

Monument to the Confederate Dead, north of the State House. This impressive sculpture was carved by Italian sculptor Nicoli.

Monument to the Women of the Confederacy, State House Grounds. Sculptor F.W. Ruckstuhl represents Columbia women, led by Isabella Martin, who established the first Wayside Hospital for soldiers in 1861.

State Archives, 1430 Senate St, tel: (803) 734-8577. This building contains the official state and county records dating back to colonial times, including the Ordinance of Secession.

The State House, Main and Gervais Sts. Impressions made by Sherman's cannons still pock the west and south walls of this *circa* 1855 building, and Confederate statues dot the grounds.

Trinity Episcopal Church, 1100 Sumter St, tel: (803) 771-7300. Six governors are buried in the cemetery of this cathedral situated near the Capitol building. Lead finials from the church's roof were used to make bullets during the Civil War.

Georgetown

Belle Isle Plantation and Battery White, Belle Isle Rd, tel: (803) 546-8491. This boyhood home of South Carolina Revolutionary War hero Francis Marion is also the site of Battery White, a Civil War battery protecting a Confederate fort captured by the Federal navy in 1865.

Town Clock/Old Market, Front and Screven Sts, tel: (803) 546-7423. Now a museum, this *circa* 1835 building is the site of an old slave market and the place where Union troops who attempted to take over the town came ashore. The building now houses The Rice Museum.

Prince George-Winyah Episcopal Church, 301 Broad St, tel: (803) 546-4358. The Church of England established this church in 1721 for local colonists, and Confederate soldiers are buried in its cemetery.

Spartanburg

Cowpens National Battlefield, tel: (864) 594-5000. Eighteen miles (29 km) northeast of Spartanburg, this 893-acre (360-hectare) battle site saw a decisive Confederate victory in January 1781.

Art/Photo Credits

All contemporary photography by LYLE LAWSON except for:

Jan Arnow 78/79, 80, 81, 82, 84, 85
C. M. Glover 54, 67L, 76, 102/103, 104/105, 108, 125, 135, 151, 152L, 152R, 153, 155, 164, 165, 166, 167, 265, 267, 302, 307
Grand Ole Opry 98
Bob Krist 62/63, 118, 119, 276, 280, 281, 282, 284, 285R, 287, 288, 289, 290, 291, 292, 293, 310, 312
Bill Lea 169, 240
Robert Llewellyn 126, 134, 136, 137, 141, 142, 143, 144, 145, 146, 147, 148, 154, 160, 161, 168
Laura A. McElroy 89, 100, 101, 223, 228
North Carolina Travel and Tourism Division 257
The Peabody Hotel 225L
Carl Purcell 309
William Schemmel 163, 221, 233, 297, 304
W. Lynn Seldon Jr 138, 264, 268, 269, 270, 306
Rebecca Troutbeck 226, 227
Larry Ulrich 230
Jonathan Wallen Cover, 124, 232, 238, 239, 248, 255, 266, 271, 272 273, 274/275
E.C. Withers/courtesy Steve La Vere 99
Martha Ellen Zenfell 156

Maps Berndtson & Berndtson

Visual Consultant V. Barl

Index

A

B

C

M

T

U–V

W–Z